ARCTIC SECURITY IN AN AGE OF CLIMATE CHANGE

This is the first book to examine Arctic defense policy and military security from the perspective of all eight Arctic states. In light of climate change and melting ice in the Arctic Ocean, Canada, Russia, Denmark (Greenland), Norway, and the United States, as well as Iceland, Sweden, and Finland, are grappling with an emerging Arctic security paradigm. This volume brings together the world's most seasoned Arctic political-military experts from Europe and North America to analyze how Arctic nations are adapting their security postures to accommodate increased shipping, expanding naval presence, and energy and mineral development in the polar region. The book analyzes the ascent of Russia as the first "Arctic superpower," the growing importance of polar security for NATO and the Nordic states, and the increasing role of Canada and the United States in the region.

Dr. James Kraska serves as the Howard S. Levie Chair of Operational Law at the U.S. Naval War College, where he also teaches on the faculty of the International Law Department. Kraska is a commander and judge advocate in the U.S. Navy. He has served as legal adviser to joint and naval task force commanders in the Asia-Pacific and has completed four Pentagon major staff assignments. He was the principal military contributor to the president's U.S. Arctic Region Policy, and he coordinated Arctic issues and law of the sea for the armed forces at the National Security Council and International Maritime Organization. Author of *Maritime Power and the Law of the Sea* (2011), Kraska also holds appointments as Senior Fellow at the Foreign Policy Research Institute in Philadelphia and as Guest Investigator at the Marine Policy Center, Woods Hole Oceanographic Institution in Woods Hole, Massachusetts. In 2010, he was selected for the Alfred Thayer Mahan Award for Literary Achievement by the Navy League of the United States.

Arctic Security in an Age of Climate Change

Edited by

JAMES KRASKA

U.S. Naval War College
and
Foreign Policy Research Institute

CAMBRIDGE UNIVERSITY PRESS
Cambridge, New York, Melbourne, Madrid, Cape Town,
Singapore, São Paulo, Delhi, Tokyo, Mexico City

Cambridge University Press
32 Avenue of the Americas, New York, NY 10013-2473, USA

www.cambridge.org
Information on this title: www.cambridge.org/9781107006607

First published 2011

Printed in the United States of America

A catalog record for this publication is available from the British Library.

Library of Congress Cataloging in Publication data

Arctic security in an age of climate change / [edited by] James Kraska.
    p.   cm.
Includes bibliographical references and index.
ISBN 978-1-107-00660-7 (hardback)
1. Arctic regions – Military policy.   2. Security, International – Arctic regions.
3. Arctic regions – Strategic aspects.   I. Kraska, James.
UA880.A76   2011
355′.0335113–dc22   2011001952

ISBN 978-1-107-00660-7 Hardback

*The views presented are those of the contributors and do not reflect the official policy
or position of their institutions or governments.*

For Kim, Olivia, and Caroline

Contents

Figures and Tables

Contributor Biographies

Caitlyn L. Antrim
Rule of Law Committee for the Oceans

Caitlyn L. Antrim is the executive director of the Rule of Law Committee for the Oceans (http://www.oceanlaw.org) and author of the widely distributed newsletter *Ocean Law Daily*, which reaches more than three hundred people each day. Antrim is a leading expert on the U.S. experience with the UN Convention on the Law of the Sea, having served as a deputy U.S. representative to the third UN Conference on the Law of the Sea, a consultant on law-of-the-sea matters to the United Nations and the International Seabed Authority, and a member of the board of directors of the Council on Ocean Law. She has worked for U.S. acceptance of the treaty for nearly three decades and has a particular interest in the deep-seabed mining regime and Arctic policy. She holds the professional degree of environmental engineer and an S.B. in mechanical engineering, both from Massachusetts Institute of Technology. Following her undergraduate studies she was designated a Distinguished Naval Graduate and commissioned in the U.S. Navy. Her articles have appeared in *World Politics Review*, *Naval War College Review*, *New York Times*, and other publications. An earlier version of her chapter appeared as the lead article for *Naval War College Review* (Summer 2010) under the title "The Next Geographical Pivot: The Russian Arctic in the Twenty-First Century."

Lawson W. Brigham
University of Alaska Fairbanks

Dr. Lawson W. Brigham is distinguished professor of geography and Arctic policy at the University of Alaska Fairbanks and a senior Fellow at the Institute of the North in Anchorage. During 2005–09 he was chair of the Arctic Council's Arctic Marine Shipping Assessment and vice chair of the Council's working group on Protection of the Arctic Marine Environment (PAME). Brigham was also a contributing author to the Council's Arctic Climate Impact Assessment. A career U.S. Coast Guard officer (1970–95), he was commanding officer of four ships including the polar icebreaker *Polar Sea* on voyages to the Arctic and Antarctic, and also chief of the Coast Guard's Strategic Planning Staff in Washington, D.C. Brigham has been a marine policy Fellow at Woods Hole Oceanographic Institution, a faculty member of the U.S. Coast Guard Academy and Naval Postgraduate School, and deputy director of the U.S. Arctic Research Commission. He received his Ph.D. from Cambridge University, and his research interests for more than three decades have included the Russian maritime Arctic, ice navigation, remote sensing of sea ice, and polar geopolitics. Captain Brigham is a 2008 signer of the American Geographical Society's Fliers and Explorers Globe, which has been signed by 75 prominent explorers. This was in recognition of the 1994 voyages of *Polar Sea*, when it became the first ship in history to reach the ends of the global ocean.

Geir Flikke
Norwegian Institute of International Affairs and High North Center, Bodø, Norway

Dr. Geir Flikke is a senior research Fellow at the Norwegian Institute of International Affairs (NUPI), where he has been affiliated with the Center for Russian Studies and currently with the Department of International Politics. He attained his doctoral degree in 2006 at the University of Oslo, with his dissertation "The Failure of a Movement: The Rise and Fall of Democratic Russia (1989–92)," on the conflict between social mobilization and organization in the Russian democracy movement. From 2006 to 2010, he was assistant director at NUPI and, since 2009, Professor II at the High North Center in Bodø. He was also a Fellow with the U.S. National Security Institute at the University of Delaware in 2010. Flikke speaks Russian fluently and has taught Russian history at the University of Oslo and courses in transitions to democratic rule from post-Soviet rule at the Kyiv Mohyla Academy. Among recent publications are *Balancing Acts: Russian-Chinese Relations and Developments in the SCO and CSTO* (NUPI 2009) and "Pacts, Parties and Elite Struggle: Ukraine's Troubled Post-Orange Transition" (*Europe Asia Studies*, 2008). His academic publication lists include case studies of voting patterns in the Russian Duma, transition politics in Russia and Ukraine, and Russian foreign and security policies in the Commonwealth of Independent States. Flikke worked as a political adviser to the Conservative Party (Høyre) in parliament and is currently a member of the Sjur Lindebrække Democracy Award Committee with the Conservative Party.

Franklyn Griffiths
University of Toronto, Canada

Senior Fellow at Massey College, University of Toronto, Franklyn Griffiths is professor emeritus of political science and George Ignatieff Chair Emeritus of peace and conflict studies at the University of Toronto. His research and policy interests center on the Arctic, Russia, and international security affairs. Among his authored and edited publications are *A Northern Foreign Policy* (1979), *Politics of the Northwest Passage* (1987), *Arctic Alternatives: Civility or Militarism in the Circumpolar North* (1992), *Strong and Free: Canada and the New Sovereignty* (1997), and "Built to Last: Conditionality and What It Can Do for the Disposition of Russian Weapon-Grade Plutonium" (Department of Foreign Affairs and International Trade, 2002). His most recent work is "Towards a Canadian Arctic Strategy," which was published by the Canadian International Council in June 2009. At various times he served as director of the Centre for Russian and East European Studies at the University of Toronto, as senior policy adviser in the Office of the Secretary of State for External Affairs, as visiting professor at Stanford University, and as visiting scholar at the University of Cambridge (Scott Polar Research Institute). He retired in 2001 and, in addition to Arctic issues, is writing a book on the incivilities of Western civilization.

Joshua H. Ho
Singapore Navy and Rajaratnam School of International Studies, Singapore

Lieutenant Colonel Joshua H. Ho is a senior Fellow at the S. Rajaratnam School of International Studies, Singapore, and works in the Maritime Security Programme. He earned an M.A. from Cambridge University on an SAF (Overseas) Scholarship and also holds a M.Sc. (management, with distinctions) from the Naval Postgraduate School, California, where he was awarded the Graduate School of Business and Public Policy Faculty Award for Excellence in Management. He is also a Fellow of the Cambridge Commonwealth Society, an associate member of the U.S. Naval Institute, and a member of the International Institute for Strategic Studies. Lieutenant Colonel Ho is a serving naval officer with twenty-three years of service. He has served in various shipboard and staff appointments, including the command of a missile gun boat and stints in the Naval Operations, Plans, and Personnel Departments and the Future Systems Directorate, MINDEF. He has also held concurrent appointments of honorary aide-de-camp to the president, secretary to the Naval Staff Meeting, and secretary to the Policy and Strategy Meeting, MINDEF. He has edited or coedited five volumes: *Best of Times, Worst of Times: Maritime Security in the Asia-Pacific*, *The Evolving Maritime Balance of Power in the Asia-Pacific: Maritime Doctrines and Nuclear Weapons at Sea*, *Globalisation and Defence in the Asia-Pacific: Arms Across Asia*, *Realising Safe and Secure Seas for All*, and *Southeast Asia and the Rise of Chinese and Indian Naval Power: Between Rising Naval Powers*. He has also published in local and overseas journals, including *Asian Survey*, *Australian Army Journal*, *Contemporary Southeast Asia*, *Defence Studies*, *Journal of the Australian Naval Institute*, *Maritime Affairs*, *Korean Journal of Defense Analyses*, *Maritime Studies*, *Marine Policy*, *Military Technology*, *Ocean Development and International Law*, *Pointer*, and *Security Challenges*, and he has contributed to numerous books. He has also taught professional courses at the Home Team Academy and at the Singapore Armed Forces Military Institute.

Rob Huebert
Department of Political Science, University of Calgary, Canada

Dr. Rob Huebert is an associate professor in the Department of Political Science at the University of Calgary. He is also the associate director of the Centre for Military and Strategic Studies. He is currently a senior research Fellow of the Canadian International Council and a Fellow with Canadian Defence and Foreign Affairs Institute. Huebert has also taught at Memorial University, Dalhousie University, and the University of Manitoba. His areas of research interest include international relations, strategic studies, law of the sea, maritime affairs, Canadian foreign and defense policy, and circumpolar relations. He publishes on the issues of Canadian Arctic security, maritime security, and Canadian defense. His work has appeared in *International Journal, Canadian Foreign Policy, Isuma: Canadian Journal of Policy Research*, and *Canadian Military Journal*. He is coauthor of *Report to Secure a Nation: Canadian Defence and Security into the 21st Century* and coeditor of *Commercial Satellite Imagery and United Nations Peacekeeping* and *Breaking Ice: Canadian Integrated Ocean Management in the Canadian North*. He also comments on Canadian security and Arctic issues in both the Canadian and international media. In 2009, he released a study of U.S. Arctic policy, *The Reluctant Arctic Power*, as a monograph of the School of Public Policy, University of Calgary.

Valur Ingimundarson
Historical Institute, University of Iceland, Reykjavik, Iceland

Valur Ingimundarson is professor of contemporary history and chair of the Historical Institute at the University of Iceland. He is also associate Fellow at the London-based Royal United Services Institute and chair of the board of EDDA – Center of Excellence in Critical Contemporary Research at the University of Iceland. He received his Ph.D. from Columbia University. He is the author of several monographs and has written extensively on the Cold War, U.S.-European relations, Icelandic foreign and security policy, the Arctic, and postconflict politics in the Balkans. Among recent publications are "The Geopolitics of Arctic Natural Resources" (a report prepared for the European Parliament, 2010); "A Crisis of Affluence: The Politics of an Economic Breakdown in Iceland," *Irish Studies in International Affairs* (2010); "War Crimes and Anti-Communist Resistance in World War II: (Re)interpreting Individual Guilt and National Pasts through a (Post–)Cold War Lens," in *European Cold War Cultures* (Bern Stoever et al., eds., 2010); "Iceland's Post-American Security Policy, Russian Geopolitics, and the Arctic Question," *RUSI Journal* (2009); *A Risk Assessment for Iceland: Global, Societal, and Military Factors: Findings of an Interdisciplinary Commission* (2009); *Ideological Shifts: The Reconfiguration of Icelandic Foreign and Security Policy 1991–2007* (ed., 2008); "Iceland's Security Policy and Geopolitics in the North," in *Emerging from the Frost: Security in the 21st Century Arctic* (Kjetil Skogrand, ed., 2008); and "The Politics of Memory and the Reconstruction of Albanian National Identity in Post-War Kosovo," *History and Memory* (2007).

Pauli Järvenpää
Finnish Ambassador to Afghanistan

Dr. Pauli Järvenpää is director general, Department of Defense Policy, at the Ministry of Defense in Helsinki, Finland. He is responsible for both national and international defense policy, including EU security and defense policy issues, NATO cooperation, Russia, the United States, Nordic cooperation, Baltic security issues, arms control questions, and Arctic security. He assumed this position in March 2002. Järvenpää has academic degrees from Harvard College and Cornell University. He was a research associate at the International Institute for Strategic Studies in London, 1979–80; minister-counsellor at the Embassy of Finland in Washington, D.C., 1991–94; and defense counsellor at the Mission of Finland to NATO, 1999–2002. Järvenpää has been Finland's ambassador to Afghanistan since September 2010.

James Kraska
Judge Advocate General's Corps, U.S. Navy, and
U.S. Naval War College

James Kraska serves as an active duty commander in the U.S. Navy Judge Advocate General's Corps and was appointed by the provost as Howard S. Levie Chair of Operational Law at the U.S. Naval War College in Newport, Rhode Island. A member of the faculty of the International Law Department and a senior associate in the Center for Irregular Warfare and Armed Groups at the Naval War College, he also holds appointments as a senior Fellow at the Foreign Policy Research Institute and as a guest investigator at the Marine Policy Center, Woods Hole Oceanographic Institution in Woods Hole, Massachusetts. He has completed two operational law assignments with joint and naval task forces; two tours in Japan; and four Pentagon major staff assignments, including as chief of the International Negotiations Division on the Joint Staff. In his last Pentagon assignment, he served as the principal military drafter of the U.S. Arctic Region Policy, signed by the president in 2009. His books include *Maritime Power and the Law of the Sea* (Oxford University Press 2011) and *Contemporary Maritime Piracy: International Law, Strategy and Diplomacy at Sea* (Praeger Security International). He earned a research doctorate in law (J.S.D.) and a master's degree in law (LL.M.) from the University of Virginia School of Law; a professional doctorate in law (J.D.) from Indiana University Maurer School of Law, Bloomington; and a master of arts degree in defense policy from Claremont.

P. Whitney Lackenbauer
Department of History, St. Jerome's University (University of Waterloo),
Waterloo, Canada

Dr. P. Whitney Lackenbauer is associate professor and chair of the department of history at St. Jerome's University (University of Waterloo), Waterloo, Ontario, Canada. He is also a Fellow with the Canadian Defense and Foreign Affairs Institute, the Arctic Institute of North America, and the Wilfrid Laurier Centre for Military and Strategic Disarmament Studies. His recent books include *Canada and Arctic*

Sovereignty and Security: Historical Perspectives (2011); *The Canadian Forces and Arctic Sovereignty: Debating Roles, Interests, and Requirements, 1968–1974* (2010); *A Commemorative History of Aboriginal People in the Canadian Military* (2010); *Arctic Front: Defending Canada in the Far North* (with Ken Coates, Bill Morrison, and Greg Poelzer, 2008, winner of the 2009 Donner Prize for the best book on Canadian public policy); and *Battle Grounds: The Canadian Military and Aboriginal Lands* (2007). As a Canadian International Council research Fellow in 2008–09, he completed a major report titled *From Polar Race to Polar Saga: An Integrated Strategy for Canada and the Circumpolar World*. He has also served as a consultant to federal departments and is an adviser to the Gwich'in Council International. Lackenbauer's current research includes histories of the Canadian Rangers, the Distant Early Warning Line, Arctic sovereignty and security since the Second World War, and community-based histories of Cambridge Bay in partnership with the Kitikmeot Heritage Society.

Nikolaj Petersen
Department of Political Science, Aarhus University, Denmark

Nikolaj Petersen is emeritus professor of international relations, Department of Political Science, Aarhus University. His research focus has been on foreign policy theory, Danish foreign policy, the European Union and NATO, Cold War politics, and Arctic security and politics. He was editor of *Cooperation and Conflict* from 1976 to 1979; *Dansk Udenrigspolitisk Årbog* (Danish Foreign Policy Yearbook) from 1988 to 1994; and *Dansk Udenrigspolitiks Historie* (History of Danish Foreign Policy), 6 vols., from 2001 to 2004. Recent publications include *Europæisk og globalt engagement 1973–2006* [European and global engagement, 1973–2006], vol. 6, 2nd ed. (2006); "The Iceman That Never Came: 'Project Iceworm,' the Search for a NATO Deterrent, and Denmark 1960–62," *Scandinavian Journal of History* (2008); "Globalisation Strategies: The Diplomacy of the Danish Cartoon Crisis 2005–06," in *Diplomacy in Theory and Practice* (K. Aggestam and M. Jerneck, eds., 2008); "The Arctic as a New Arena for Danish Foreign Policy: The Ilulissat Initiative and Its Implications," *Danish Foreign Policy Yearbook* (2009); "Kampen om den Kolde Krig i dansk politik og forskning" [The Cold War battle in Danish politics and research], *Historisk Tidsskrift* (2009); and "SAC at Thule: Greenland in the Global Strategy," *Journal of Cold War Studies* (2010).

Tomas Ries
Swedish National Defence College, Stockholm, Sweden

Dr. Tomas Ries is senior lecturer at the Swedish National Defence College in Stockholm, focusing on issues of globalization and security. From 2005 to 2010, Ries was director of the Swedish Institute of International Affairs. From 1997 to 2004, he was senior researcher at the Finnish National Defence College in Helsinki, focusing on globalization and security, Finland's security policy, EU and NATO affairs, and security issues in the High North. From 1992 to 1997, he was director of the International Training Course in Geneva, Switzerland, and deputy director of the Geneva Centre for Security Policy. From 1986 to 1992, he worked at the Institute for Defence Studies in Oslo, focusing on Soviet military strategy and forces in the High North. Ries holds a B.Sc. (economics) from the London School of Economics and Political Science and a Ph.D. from the Graduate Institute of International Studies at the Geneva University.

Courtney C. St. John
U.S. Navy

Courtney C. St. John is the climate change affairs officer for the U.S. Navy's Task Force Climate Change. Prior to holding her current position, she was John A. Knauss Marine Policy Fellow in the office of the oceanographer of the U.S. Navy. St. John holds a master's degree in environmental planning and policy from Clemson University, where her research focused on shoreline change policy in the coastal United States; she holds an undergraduate degree from Mary Washington College.

Rolf Tamnes
Norwegian Institute for Defence Studies, Oslo, Norway

Dr. Rolf Tamnes is director of the Norwegian Institute for Defence Studies in Oslo and member of the Leadership Group at the Norwegian Defence University College. He is leading the international research program Geopolitics in the High North. Tamnes has been adjunct professor at the University of Oslo for many years. He was a member of the Government Defence Review Committee in 1999–2000 and of the Parliament Oversight Committee on Intelligence and Security in 2001–03. He was a public policy scholar at the Woodrow Wilson Center in 2005–06 and a visiting Fellow at the Center for Strategic and International Studies in 2006. Among his publications are *Et større Norge*, in *Vendepunkter i norsk utenrikspolitikk. Nye internasjonale vilkår etter den kalde krigen* [An expanding small power], in *Turning-Points in Norwegian Foreign Policy* (Even Lange, Helge Pharo, and Øyvind Østerud, eds., 2009); with Jacob Børresen and Gullow Gjeseth, *Norsk forsvarshistorie, bd. 5, Allianseforsvar i endring, 1970–2000* [The history of Norwegian defense], vol. 5 (2004); with Kjetil Skogrand, *Fryktens likevekt. Atombomben, Norge og verden 1945–1970* [Equilibrium of fear: The atom bomb, Norway, and the world, 1945–1970] (2001); *Norsk Utenrikspolitikks Historie, bind 6, Oljealder 1965–1995* [The history of Norwegian foreign policy, vol. 6, Oil age, 1965–1995] (1997); *The United States and the Cold War in the High North* (1991).

David W. Titley
U.S. Navy

A native of Schenectady, New York, Rear Admiral David W. Titley, U.S. Navy, was commissioned through the Naval Reserve Officers Training Commissioning program in 1980. He has served for more than ten years at sea on six ships. He has commanded the Fleet Numerical Meteorology and Oceanography Command in Monterey, California, and the Naval Oceanography Operations Command based at Stennis Space Center, Mississippi. Shore tours include serving on the staff of the U.S. Commission on Ocean Policy and as the senior military assistant to the director of net assessment in the Office of the Secretary of Defense. During his first flag tour he served as commander, Naval Meteorology and Oceanography Command. His education includes a B.S. in meteorology from the Pennsylvania State University and a Ph.D. in meteorology from the Naval Postgraduate School. He was elected a Fellow of the American Meteorological Society in 2009. Rear Admiral Titley currently serves as oceanographer and navigator of the U.S. Navy, and as director of the U.S. Navy's Task Force on Climate Change.

Lee Willett
Royal United Services Institute for Defence and Security Studies

Dr. Lee Willett is head of the Maritime Studies Programme, in the Military Sciences Department at the Royal United Services Institute (RUSI) for Defence and Security Studies. He also is a Fellow of the Royal Society of Naval Sciences, Sweden, and a visiting lecturer at the University of Greenwich. He has published and lectured widely on maritime security issues. His most recent publications include the following RUSI articles and papers: "Mind the Gap: Strategic Risk in the UK's Anti-Submarine Warfare Capability," "An Awakening at Sea? NATO and Maritime Strategy," "The Navy in Russia's Resurgence," and "British Defence and Security Policy: The Maritime Contribution." He also authored "Old Roles and New Capabilities for Maritime Coalitions in the New World Order," in *Sea Power: Challenges Old and New* (Forbes, A. ed., 2007, Sea Power Centre – Australia: Proceedings of Royal Australian Navy Pacific Seapower 2006 Conference. Sydney: Halstead Press) and "Maritime Security: A Choice or Obligation – and the Implications for the European Union," in *The Question Marks over Europe's Maritime Security* (Security and Defence Agenda Discussion Paper, 2007, Brussels: SDA).

Adam Worm
Greenland Representation, Copenhagen, Denmark

Adam Worm earned a master of law degree from the University of Copenhagen in 1980 and served as head of section in several ministry posts from 1980 to 1985. From 1985 to 1989, he served as head of section and head of department, Agency for Salaries, Civil Servants Greenland. From 1989 to 2007, he served as senior adviser and head of department, Greenland Representation in Copenhagen. Since 2007, he has served as senior adviser and deputy, Greenland Representation in Copenhagen. Worm's career has dealt mostly with issues related to Greenland, including participation in negotiations for salaries for civil servants in Greenland; preparation of legislation; law of the sea; issues related to the U.S. base in Thule, Greenland; and work with international affairs and the internal administration of Greenland and representation of Greenland in Copenhagen, Denmark.

Oran R. Young
Institutional and International Governance, Environmental Institutions

Oran R. Young is a renowned Arctic expert and a world leader in the fields of international governance and environmental institutions. Professor Young has served as vice-president of the International Arctic Science Committee and was the founding chair of the Board of Governors of the University of the Arctic. He was the first chair of the Committee on the Human Dimensions of Global Change within the National Academy of Sciences in the United States and has chaired the Scientific Committee of the International Human Dimensions Programme on Global Environmental Change and the Steering Committee of the Arctic Governance Project. Among the more than 20 books he has authored are *The Institutional Dimensions of Environmental Change* and *Governance in World Affairs*. His most recent book is *Institutional Dynamics: Emergent Patterns in International Environmental Governance*.

Katarzyna Zysk
Department of International Security Policy, Norwegian Institute for Defence Studies, Oslo, Norway

Dr. Katarzyna Zysk is a senior Fellow in the Department of International Security Policy at the Norwegian Institute for Defence Studies. She is a participant in the international research program Geopolitics in the High North, sponsored by the Norwegian Research Council and chaired by the Norwegian Institute for Defence Studies. Within the program, Zysk is working on a postdoctoral research project on security and military developments in the Arctic, with special focus on Russia's policies. Zysk earned her Ph.D. from the Institute for International Relations (2006) and her M.A. (2002, with distinctions) in history and international relations from Nicolaus Copernicus University in Torun, Poland. She served as a visiting research scholar at the Center for Naval Warfare Studies, Strategic Research Department, at the U.S. Naval War College in 2010. She was assistant lecturer in international relations and security policy at the Institute for International Relations in Torun (2005–06) and visiting researcher at the University of Oslo (2001, 2003–04). Proficient in Russian, Norwegian, English, Polish, and French, Zysk has conducted extensive research and published a monograph; a number of book chapters; and articles in academic journals and the media on a variety of subjects, including transformations in the Arctic security environment, Russia's policies in the polar regions, security in Central Europe and transatlantic relations, NATO enlargement, foreign and security policies of Norway and Poland, and diplomatic history. Her current research interests include strategic studies; contemporary international security affairs, in particular Russian security and defense policy; Russia-China relations; the Russian navy; and circumpolar relations.

Foreword

ARCTIC FUTURES: THE POLITICS OF TRANSFORMATION

Oran R. Young

It is beyond doubt that the Arctic is experiencing transformative change. Driven by the interacting forces of climate change and globalization, this transformation has turned the spotlight of public attention to a region previously known to the outside world largely as a homeland for indigenous peoples and a playing field for intrepid adventurers. Rapid melting of sea ice has given rise to visions of an ice-free Arctic Ocean during the foreseeable future. While uncertainty makes projections hazardous in this realm, it is reasonable to expect that the Arctic basin will be ice-free during parts of the year by 2050, and perhaps during much of the year by 2100.[1] Equally important from the perspective of commercial shipping and natural resource extraction, much of the remaining ice will be first-year ice in contrast to thicker and tougher multiyear ice. Combined with projections indicating that a sizable fraction of the world's remaining undiscovered reserves of oil and gas are located in the circumpolar Arctic, this development has sparked a surge of interest in the region among multinational corporations desiring to exploit Arctic hydrocarbons and minerals, shipping companies attracted by the prospect of using Arctic sea lanes for intercontinental as well as coastal commerce, and environmental organizations concerned about the ecological consequences of a rapid growth of economic activities in the region. It is no exaggeration to say that the Arctic has crossed a threshold leading to what systems analysts refer to as a state change. Like state changes occurring in other complex systems, the transformation now occurring in the Arctic is altering the landscape dramatically, proceeding at a rapid pace, and producing results that are almost certain to be irreversible.

---

1 The actual decline in Arctic sea ice has been more rapid than climate models have anticipated. It is possible but by no means certain that this will lead to an ice-free Arctic basin sooner than current projections anticipate. See H. Koc et al. eds., *Melting Snow and Ice: A Call for Action.* (Tromsø: Norwegian Polar Institute, 2009).

Many observers have sought both to document and to understand the causes of the biogeochemical elements of this transformation. Others have taken up the challenge of assessing the economic calculations underlying the attractions of oil and gas production, commercial shipping, industrial fishing, and even adventure tourism likely to occur in the region in the decades to come. But what are the political implications of this suite of developments? How will the transformation of the Arctic affect the interests and capabilities of both Arctic and non-Arctic states? What will be the consequences for interested nonstate actors, including indigenous peoples' organizations as well as multinational corporations and environmental NGOs? Will we see fundamental shifts in the Arctic policy agenda? Will existing governance arrangements like the Arctic Council be up to the task of promoting cooperation and avoiding conflict in this setting? *Arctic Security in an Age of Climate Change* provides the first book-length effort to wrestle with these questions in a sustained and rigorous fashion. While it does not provide all the answers, it does give us a lot to think about as we seek to come to terms with these issues.

ARCTIC STATE CHANGES

From a political perspective, the essential feature of the transformation now occurring in the Arctic is a tightening of the links between global forces and regional processes. During the Cold War, the Arctic was divided into two armed camps with the Soviet Union on one side and the United States and four of its NATO allies – Canada, Denmark, Iceland, and Norway – on the other. The region loomed large in strategic calculations, not because of its intrinsic value but because it provided an attractive theater of operations for strategic weapons systems and especially nuclear-powered submarines equipped with submarine-launched ballistic missiles. However, the sensitivity of the Arctic in military terms had the side effect of inhibiting other activities in the region. In the aftermath of the Cold War, the Arctic emerged as a low-tension area of limited importance in global terms. Starting with Mikhail Gorbachev's "Arctic zone of peace" speech in October 1987, the region became a target of opportunity for those interested in promoting various forms of international and transnational cooperation. A flurry of regional initiatives ensued, culminating in the establishment of the Arctic Council in 1996 and in the development of the council into an increasingly prominent vehicle for addressing Arctic issues and promoting international cooperation in the intervening years.

The state change occurring now involves a dramatic shift in the role of the Arctic in the global system. Climate change, whose effects are being felt in the Arctic both sooner and more dramatically than in other areas, is a consequence of anthropogenic forces originating far beyond the bounds of the region. For better or worse, the Arctic has emerged as the leading edge with regard to the impacts of climate change. Ironically, the rapid growth of interest in exploiting the Arctic's natural resources and taking advantage of new opportunities for commercial shipping reflects the needs of those responsible for the biogeochemical forces that have given rise to the transformation in the region. The Arctic is thus on the receiving end of a combination of forces whose origins lie far beyond the boundaries of the region itself. It may be going too far to describe these developments as the start of a new chapter in core-periphery relations; however, the asymmetry is striking. Global forces largely beyond the control of Arctic stakeholders and rights holders have triggered a cascade of changes that have brought the region to the attention of powerful political and economic leaders who showed little or no interest in the Arctic in earlier times and who are not particularly sensitive to the fate of the Arctic and its permanent inhabitants today.

What can we say about the political consequences of this new relationship between the Arctic and the outside world? In this commentary, I draw attention to three prominent features of the politics of transformation: one involving the interests of the "ice states" in contrast to the Arctic states, a second involving the interests of non-Arctic states as distinct from the Arctic states, and a third reflecting the growing importance of nonstate actors in world affairs.

ARCTIC STATES/ICE STATES – TENSIONS WITHIN THE FAMILY

Since the late 1980s, eight states (Canada, Russia, the United States, and the five Nordic states) have taken the lead in launching cooperative measures in the Arctic first in the form of the Arctic Environmental Protection Strategy adopted in 1991 and then in the form of the Arctic Council established in 1996. The acceptance of the Arctic Eight as the appropriate grouping of actors to take these steps was not a foregone conclusion. Some key actors fought hard at the time to limit these initiatives to the Arctic Five or, in other words, Canada, Denmark, Norway, Russia, and the United States. Nonetheless, with the initiation by Finland of the Rovaniemi Process in 1989, the Arctic Eight became the accepted cast of characters for purposes of addressing Arctic issues at the international level. For all practical purposes, the question of membership was laid to rest.

The current transformation has triggered renewed interest in this question. Because both the biogeochemical and the socioeconomic forces at work in the Arctic today focus largely on the Arctic Ocean and adjacent coastal areas, the five ice states have taken steps to enhance their ability to dominate Arctic policy, without engaging Finland, Iceland, and Sweden and without showing much concern for the views of the indigenous peoples' organizations that have the status of Permanent Participants in the Arctic Council. To be sure, the Arctic Five have made a point of stressing their adherence to applicable international agreements (e.g., the UN Convention on the Law of the Sea [UNCLOS]) and their commitment to managing Arctic affairs in a law-abiding manner. In the 2008 Ilulissat Declaration, for instance, they made much of the proposition that they are in a unique position to address the consequences of biogeochemical and socioeconomic changes in the

Arctic in a responsible manner. However, while the ice states proclaim their loyalty to existing governance systems and especially the arrangements established under UNCLOS, there is no getting around the gap that has opened between the Arctic Five and the Arctic Eight in political terms. The significance of this gap lies not only in its implications for relations among those concerned with Arctic issues by virtue of their geographical locations. As we shall see, it makes a difference also when it comes to engaging non-Arctic states and nonstate actors in the handling of Arctic affairs.

ARCTIC STATES/NON-ARCTIC STATES: THE ARCTIC IN WORLD AFFAIRS

A major impetus behind the effort of the Arctic Five to assert effective control over what happens in the Arctic basin lies in the growing interest in Arctic issues on the part of non-Arctic states (e.g., China, Japan, Korea, and even India and Singapore) and associations of states (e.g., the European Union). It is no accident that these non-Arctic players are expressing a growing interest in Arctic affairs through initiatives ranging from high-profile research programs to the development of explicit Arctic policies. Naturally, these initiatives are couched in diplomatic language emphasizing the importance of sustainable development, the welfare of the Arctic's indigenous peoples, and, more generally, the pursuit of good governance in the Arctic. However, this cannot conceal the fact that the non-Arctic states are motivated to a considerable degree by the attractions of exploiting the Arctic's natural resources and of taking advantage of opportunities for commercial shipping in the region.

Three things make it impossible to ignore this growth of interest on the part of key non-Arctic states in the politics of the region. Under the terms of UNCLOS, non-Arctic states have a right to engage in a range of activities in parts of the Arctic basin, including commercial shipping and industrial fishing. Equally important are the incentives that some of the Arctic states have to enter into cooperative agreements with non-Arctic states regarding the exploitation of the region's natural resources. Russia, for instance, is already cultivating relationships with several members of the EU, China, and even India, focusing on collaborative efforts to develop oil and gas reserves located in its portion of the Arctic. Underpinning these practical concerns are the shifts now taking place in the broader landscape of world politics. The United States is no longer the undisputed hegemon in world affairs. Increasingly, other powers like China and India are forces to be reckoned with at the global level. This does not mean that the Arctic Eight or even the Arctic Five have no special role to play in the management of Arctic affairs. But it is unrealistic to suppose that powerful actors like China and the European Union will be content for long with (permanent) observer status in the Arctic Council. When it comes to promoting their growing interests in the Arctic, they will demand some status that gives them a seat at the table in making decisions about Arctic issues.

BEYOND THE NATION-STATE: GLOBAL SOCIETY IN THE ARCTIC

Many have noted that the traditional conception of international society as a society of states no longer provides an adequate framework for organizing our thinking about world affairs. A sizable number of multinational corporations have economies that rival those of all but the largest states. Subnational units of government (e.g., states, provinces, oblasts, and even cities) have begun to play autonomous roles at the international level. Global civil society has become a force to be reckoned with in addressing a range of prominent issues. Nowhere is this phenomenon more in evidence than in the Arctic. Multinational corporations, like BP and ExxonMobil as well as major shipping companies, have emerged as major players in the landscape of what some are calling the "new" Arctic. The Northern Forum, an association of subnational units of government, has become a significant player in Arctic politics. Indigenous peoples' organizations, like the Inuit Circumpolar Council and the Saami Council, have acquired Permanent Participant status in the Arctic Council and achieved a prominent role in efforts to secure indigenous rights at the global level through the adoption of measures like the UN Declaration on the Rights of Indigenous Peoples.

The Arctic Eight and especially the Arctic Five have exhibited a pronounced preference for dealing with Arctic affairs through the traditional channels of international diplomacy. To them, Arctic issues are matters to be handled by governments and, first and foremost, by representatives of ministries of foreign affairs. Whatever its merits in substantive terms, for example, the 2008 Ilulissat Declaration was crafted by foreign ministries intent on asserting their primacy in the realm of Arctic politics. This approach, however, cannot prevail for long in the global society that is becoming a major feature of the landscape in the world today. This is not only a matter of recognizing indigenous peoples' organizations as legitimate players on the stage of Arctic politics; it is also a matter of acknowledging that foreign ministries must be responsive to the concerns of a range of nonstate actors in coming to terms with the challenges of governance in a rapidly changing Arctic. It is not necessary to embrace the recent call of the Aspen Institute for the adoption of a "global civil society model" in efforts to address issues of governance in the Arctic during the coming years. But the politics of the new Arctic are producing conditions in which it is illusory to suppose that we can deal with policy concerns arising in the region today without finding effective ways to take into account the interests of key nonstate actors as well as the interests of influential non-Arctic states.

THE POWER OF FRAMING: ARCTIC SECURITY VS. ARCTIC STEWARDSHIP

As we seek to navigate the politics of the new Arctic in the coming years, much will depend on how we frame the issues that find their way onto the agenda in various policy forums. Given the title of this book, it may seem natural to address the policy agenda of the Arctic in terms of the familiar discourse of security. But there are several reasons to adopt a skeptical attitude toward this presumption. Securitizing Arctic politics draws attention to the potential for conflict in the Far North in contrast to opportunities for promoting cooperation in meeting emerging needs for governance in an era of transformation. By focusing on military activities in the region, for instance, this way of thinking treats as emerging threats activities that are most likely routine operations (e.g., the flights of Russian bombers over the Arctic basin). The lens of security has a tendency as well to direct attention to matters of interaction between or among human groups. It highlights issues such as jurisdictional conflicts regarding the control of shipping lanes or the delimitation of the boundaries of coastal state authority over prolongations of the seabed beyond the outer limits of the exclusive economic zones. But, above all, the discourse of security is in danger of losing analytic traction in an era in which we speak casually of economic security, social security, food security, environmental security, and even human security, as well as national security. Do these concerns have something in common that justifies treating them all as matters of security? Are there important propositions of a general nature about security that can help us to comprehend this wide range of issues and to identify appropriate ways of dealing with them as matters of policy? Or has the expanding scope of this discourse drained its content and diluted its usefulness as a way of thinking about Arctic politics?

We are not without options when it comes to framing questions of policy arising in a rapidly changing Arctic. As Franklyn Griffiths observes in the opening chapter of this book, for instance, it may make sense to approach the politics of transformation in the Arctic in terms of a discourse of stewardship in contrast to the discourse of security. Such an alternative would draw attention to the fact that it is important to think about matters of human-environment interactions in framing issues of Arctic policy, to recognize the value of traditional or indigenous ecological knowledge in thinking about the merits of alternative responses to these issues, and, perhaps most importantly, to acknowledge the importance of sustainability in contrast to some vision of national security in defining the goals we pursue in the realm of Arctic politics. If we fail to achieve a measure of sustainability in the Arctic, the pursuit of national security in this realm may become increasingly irrelevant.

Is the frame of stewardship preferable to the frame of security as we seek to navigate the politics of transformation in the new Arctic? My personal answer to this question is "yes." As we move deeper into an era of human-dominated ecosystems or what even the *New York Times* now refers to as the Anthropocene, the importance of developing new ways of thinking about human-environment interactions is rising steadily. Nowhere is this more apparent than in the Arctic, where the effects of anthropogenic forces are both undeniable and dramatic. But this is not the central message of this short commentary. Rather, I want to direct attention to the importance of framing as a determinant of the politics of a rapidly changing region like the Arctic. How we choose to frame the issues will have a profound effect on how we define the range of policy options available for consideration and how we weigh the pros and cons of individual options. One of the appealing features of this book is that, taken together, the insights of the contributors draw our attention to a number of discourses that are available to those seeking to understand the politics of transformation in the Arctic. The book is not an ideological project dedicated to the promotion of a preferred way to think about the future of the Arctic. Rather, it is a thoughtful exploration of the implications of alternative futures for the Arctic. As such, it makes a significant contribution to our understanding of the politics of transformation, a major concern in the Arctic today that is likely to become relevant to other regions during the foreseeable future.

PART I

Introduction: Circumpolar Perspectives

Arctic Security

The Indirect Approach

Franklyn Griffiths

Invited to sum up at the end of a distinguished international conference on Arctic policy, law, and security in an era of climate change, I chose not to listen primarily for commonalities and differences in the national perspectives of the eight Arctic countries. Instead, it seemed more promising to ask, "Where do we go from here?" and to begin by considering "Where is here?" in the first place. Now, in early 2011, I write with the same questions in mind, but with the intention to elaborate. I start with impressions of the meeting and then open a discussion of tendencies in domestic and international interaction among the Arctic states. Lacking the knowledge required to consider the tendencies of all eight, I confine myself to the Canadian case, which I know best, and to Russia, which holds the future of Arctic international relations very largely in its hands. I end with thoughts on answers to the question of where next in light of recent developments, principally the appearance of the U.S. Navy's "Arctic Roadmap."[1]

POINTS OF DEPARTURE

The conference that gave rise to this book was conducted by Commander Kraska, the volume editor, and held at the U.S. Naval War College in September, 2009. Discussions at the conference were marked by consensus on some matters, ambiguity on others, and silence on still others. As to consensus, it seemed generally to be agreed that prevailing commentary on the Arctic is too much given to drama and exaggeration when it comes to the potential for international competition and conflict. At issue here are frequent references to an Arctic meltdown, to the perfect storm that's just ahead as states clash in pursuit of resources and are ensured access to them, to the Arctic as location for the start of World War III, and so on. Prompted by certain expert analysts (purveyors of polar peril, I call them) and amplified by

---

[1] Chapter 15 of this volume contains an analysis of the U.S. Navy's "Arctic Roadmap."

news editors and journalists in search of a story, the outcome is ill-judged reportage that captures public attention by overstating the likelihood of armed conflict and the need to be on guard. As I interpret the thoughts of my colleagues, there is a tacit transnational agreement among informed Arctic observers that this kind of talk is not to be trusted.

Consistent with a readiness to resist overblown reports of danger, the conference also seemed well disposed to Arctic international cooperation. Although all present would doubtless have supported the defense of the national interest by military means when unavoidable, in the different reports on national thinking there was no sign of Arctic gung-ho; of eagerness to prevail in incidents at sea or in the air; in heightened international tension, arms races, or armed clashes in the region. On the contrary, I thought it broadly agreed that the ice states ought to get together in joint action on a wide range of nonmilitary or civil issues related to resource development, to ensured access and transit, and to climate change itself. Furthermore, they were to find ways of managing their differences when these could not be resolved. For such things to be achieved there is in turn no substitute for reliable knowledge, scientific knowledge, in the first place and, I infer, no place for groundless fear and not a lot to be gained from unilateralism in relations among interdependent actors.

As to ambiguity, it was evident primarily in the context of remarks on dissention between the Arctic Five and the Arctic Three concerning Arctic governance. The reference in this case is to differences between the five regional states with frontage on the Arctic Ocean (Canada, Denmark and Greenland, Norway, Russia, and the United States) and the three that are without it (Finland, Iceland, and Sweden) but are joined with the Arctic Five in the region's central governance institution, the Arctic Council. In May 2008, the Arctic Five chose to meet outside the Arctic Council, which is to say without the Arctic Three, at Ilulissat in Greenland, where they produced a declaration of their own on Arctic affairs. At Newport we heard criticism of the Arctic Five for their exclusiveness, this from among speakers reporting on views of the Arctic Three. When it came to the Arctic Five, however, there was neither insistence on their primacy nor an indication of readiness to include the Arctic Three, even though the Ilulissat Declaration had taken care to commend the Arctic Council. In summary, important questions of regional governance were left hanging, which happens to be the way it is in the world out there. The underlying issues deserve further discussion.

Good government is at once a precondition and a consequence of security, the prime concern of this conference and this book. To the extent that security is lacking, self-help is likely to prevail over cooperation. In contrast, the more extensive and consensual the governance, the more secure everyone will feel and be, especially in a dynamic frontier region marked by large uncertainties. Further, the greater the international collaboration on civil issues, the greater will be the security in thickening webs of common interest, in reduced potential for fundamental disagreement, and in diminished prospects for the use of armed force. Current Arctic realities, however, are such that regional governance is not a high priority for the eight Arctic Council members as a whole. Of course, they vary in their approaches to cooperation. But taken together they remain reluctant either to view the region as greatly more than a set of subregions or to accept agreed-on regionwide constraints on national freedom of action, this despite physical and political interdependencies that are increasingly evident. Just who is to participate in what Arctic self-management and regulatory arrangements are matters of uncertainty and irresolution that persist. They will persist until new leadership is forthcoming from within the Arctic Five and until there is greater understanding of Arctic interconnectedness.

In regard to silence, I thought it remarkable that nothing was said about arms control and next to nothing about confidence building. Arms control means military cooperation among actual and potential adversaries to reduce the likelihood of war, its destructiveness if it occurs, and the costs of being prepared for it. Complete silence on arms control strongly implies no expectation of war in the Arctic. If this were indeed the unspoken consensus, it would follow that the region is at present secure against the use of armed force and likely to remain so for the foreseeable future. There may well be some truth to such a view, but the cumulative effects of a self-imposed vow of silence must also be taken into account. Originating in the experience of the Cold War, persisting in the mandate of the Arctic Council, and continuing to meet with ready acceptance by others of the eight members, this is a vow that stems from a U.S. injunction not to consider military matters in Arctic forums. Weapons, their characteristics, levels, and possible uses are instead to be discussed elsewhere and preferably by the possessors alone. So, which is it: no real security problem, or no real justification for the discussion of military security in an Arctic context? Or both at once? On balance, I say silence on Arctic arms control owes more to convention than to conviction. Again, there's a need for discussion.

The Arctic is quite pacific now, but might it be time to revisit the ban on Arctic-specific arms control with an eye to the constraining of conflict down the road? Should the Arctic Eight or subsets of the Arctic Eight free themselves to address the regional implications of new developments in military technology, for instance in missile defense and the weaponization of space? Might they consider making the Arctic into a nuclear weapons–free zone, as the Canadian Pugwash Group proposes? Or ought the discussion to begin with better prospects of success, for example with a demilitarization of the ice and surface waters seaward of the exclusive economic zone in the Arctic Ocean?[2] Alternatively, and as distinct from arms control, might Arctic-specific confidence building provide the optimum point of departure, again

[2] Several decades ago I made such a proposal to no avail. Franklyn Griffiths, "A Northern Foreign Policy," *Wellesley Papers*, No. 7 (Toronto: Canadian Institute of International Affairs, 1979), pp. 60–62. To check on whether anything might have changed in the interim, I raised the idea at a track-two, or unofficial, NATO Arctic workshop at the University of Cambridge in October 2010. It was right away shot down as unrealistic and as undesirable in proposing to alter the high-seas regime in international law, this by leading participants from Norway, Russia, and the United States. There was no support.

by subsets of or by all of the Arctic Eight as required by the issue? There would
be a choice here between military and civil confidence-building measures (CBMs),
the former, for example, concerning strategic bomber exercises and the latter in
collective action that's at once directly beneficial on the merits of issues such as oil-
spill cleanup and indirectly so in building shared interests and the habit of working
together. In fact, joint use of military capabilities in Arctic search and rescue and in
emergency response provides a ready means of engaging separate national defense
establishments in joint support of civil cooperation and confidence building. This
is surely a good place to begin channeling the political development of the region
to the benefit of cooperation and stability.

   Overall, then, what are we to make of the current situation and outlook for security
in this part of the world? Rolf Tamnes gave us the essentials of the answer. As I heard
him, he was speaking primarily about Norwegian-Russian security relations. Taking
the liberty of generalizing from his remarks, I would state the bigger picture as
follows. First, the use of force in the Arctic is unlikely today unless linked to an
external conflict. If there's to be serious trouble, it will probably come from the
global surround and not from within the region itself. Second, the Arctic is not a
whole region for purposes of hard security. On the contrary, it is a set of subregions.
As such, it lends itself to the handling of local security issues as they arise, and not to
regionwide collective measures to constrain the acquisition, deployment, and use of
armed force. Third, whereas an Arctic-specific hard security agenda is very hard, if
not impossible, to enact on a regional basis, climate change does serve to render the
region rather more of an entirety for purposes of soft security and, as I have termed
it thus far, civil cooperation. Factor in a shared commitment to the rule of law by all
of the Arctic Eight, especially by the Arctic Five at Ilulissat, and the road ahead for
common security in the Arctic does not point directly to regional action on matters
of hard security. These can be managed for now by national means, and possibly by
subregional CBMs of a military nature as required. Instead, the road ahead is one of
indirection. It lies with soft security and civil cooperation both in building mutually
advantageous regional interdependence and in hardening the region as best we can
against destabilizing conflict from the world outside.

ARCTIC TENDENCIES

Despite the constraints on war and collaboration alike in the Arctic today, the region
is coming alive politically under the effects of climate change, resource scarcity, and
geostrategic competition. Separately and together, the Arctic Eight are being faced
with increasingly consequential choices both in defining the national purpose and
in charting a future for the region or subregion that best meets the national interest.
Although the discourse on Arctic issues is varied and unevenly developed from one
country to the next, persistent patterns of interaction are starting to emerge. Let us
call them tendencies. They are to be found in national policy debates and in the

international interplay between otherwise separate debates. Given an understanding of Arctic tendencies, even a partial and impressionistic understanding to begin, we may gain an ability to determine what to encourage and what to suppress in channeling Arctic regional development toward collaboration and stability. But what exactly do we want to encourage? I suggest it is not security, hard or soft. Nor is it civil cooperation. Rather, we should be aiming for stewardship.

Stewardship in an Arctic setting means locally informed governance that not only polices but also shows respect and care for the natural environment and living things in it. The reference to the local is to the singular need for cooperation and input from Arctic indigenous peoples if national and international action is to be not only well adapted to on-site realities but also ethical in recognizing the rights and needs of those most directly exposed to the consequences of central determination and central inaction. As to viewing stewardship in terms of national and international policing, the reference is to the greater fitness of constabulary rather than combat forces in the management of Arctic spaces and processes. To some, stewardship will signify little more than environmental protection and pollution prevention. But there is much more to it. At the heart of Arctic stewardship lies the governance of a region in which interaction between states and their physical milieu, and between the states themselves, cannot be left to evolve at will without avoidable deprivation to milieu and human alike. This is governance that generates common security through the provision of mutual reassurance from joint action to ensure the well-being of people and their surround. Although, as I have noted, the Arctic Eight are not well disposed to regionwide governance, there are tendencies among them that, if amplified, could improve the prospects for cooperative stewardship.

The tendencies of Arctic states can be captured in terms of goals and attitudes. Whereas goals relate to general objectives, attitudes are to be regarded as predispositions to act in given circumstances.

Writing about state behavior in *Discord and Collaboration* back in 1962, Arnold Wolfers made a distinction between possession and milieu goals. Possession goals are keyed to values that a state has or wants for itself, for example, a particular territory or a seat on the UN Security Council. In an Arctic setting, possession goals relate primarily to lands, waters, and the resources they contain, all of which may be vulnerable to encroachment or invasion by others, or legitimately contested, as is the case with the outer continental shelf under the Arctic Ocean. Readily and persuasively framed in terms of national security, the case for possession becomes still more compelling when stated in the language of sovereignty. This is a language that proceeds from the perspective of the autonomous actor who would and should remain free of foreign entanglement. It is a language that favors self-reliance and, with the exception of point sources of danger and external objects of possessiveness, one that mutes the significance of what's going on beyond the limits of national jurisdiction and control. Wrapped in talk of sovereignty and security, Arctic possession goals have the advantage of being readily understood.

Milieu goals, in contrast, are less familiar and less commanding. They draw attention to the international environment in which states operate and from which unwanted effects short of outright challenges to possession may be delivered to the national domain. In pursuit of milieu goals, states seek to shape the international military, legal, economic, and numerous other dimensions of their external environment. In the Arctic, milieu goals are focused on the law of the sea, on transboundary natural processes, and on the politics of interdependence among states that cannot make the most of exclusive jurisdiction without international collaboration. A random selection from among the issues considered by the Arctic Council is perhaps the best way to gain a sense of what's meant here: assessment of and response to climate change, curtailment of short-lived forcers of Arctic climate change in particular, regulation of marine shipping and ecotourism, protection of the marine environment from the consequences of land-based activity, furtherance of human development, creation and implementation of offshore oil and gas guidelines, emergency prevention and response, protection of biodiversity, hazardous waste management, spread of best practice in ocean-based ecosystem management, and so on.

As to attitudes as they figure in policy debate and the articulation of tendencies in Arctic practice, they predispose us to one line of action and not another. They may draw people from outside the Arctic – "southerners" – to the region. They also make for avoidance. Attitudes come in two varieties, material and ideational. They are interconnected.

Materially, some of us are attracted to the region as a source of huge wealth, of power and national greatness. The extraordinary beauty of Arctic places, their pristine quality, appeals as well. We may therefore be stirred to powerful care for the natural environment and its preservation in the Arctic as symbolic of overarching human need in an era of climate change. And yet we are also held back. The southerner who has learned of the climate and the experiences of Arctic adventurers is easily arrested by the prospect of a harsh and dismal setting, one in which disaster threatens and human existence is reduced to exile. Combine varied attitudes such as these, and we emerge all too readily with an idea of Arctic spaces that are to be conquered, possessed, and then left, or best viewed from the safety of a cruise ship or coffee-table book. Material attitudes tend to reinforce possession goals and a southern desire for remote control.

Ideational attitudes, for their part, may be reduced to those that bear on the national identity of southern populations. Few among the southern majorities of the Arctic Eight identify strongly with the Arctic. If anything, we prefer the national North and its subregional surround, as in Canada's Northern Strategy, Norway's High Northern Strategy, and the deep-seated Russian attachment to the северо-запад or *sever*, which is Russia's Northwest.[3] Nevertheless, as the Arctic is transformed, new

---

[3] The Russian Northwest is distinct from Siberia, which runs east from the Ural Mountains.

feelings as well as new reflections about the national purpose, the nation's destiny, its security and sovereignty, may be evoked. There is an obvious connection with material attitudes and possession goals here, but ideational attitudes are something else. They focus not on what the Arctic itself is and what it has to offer, but on who we southerners imagine ourselves to be and on how the Arctic and the North add to our collective sense of self. When this is our perspective, the making of Arctic policy is liable to be shaped by identity politics. This is a politics in which decision makers, political entrepreneurs, civil-society activists, or only some of the above, seek advantage over their opponents by using Arctic references to bolster themselves as champions of the national identity. How this is accomplished will soon be made clear. Suffice it to note for now that identity politics play strongly to possession goals and to the potential for material loss and material gain. An alternative response, one that presents Arctic stewardship as an expression of the national identity, is intimated in the official activity and public opinion of the Arctic Eight but has yet to gain prominence.

Rather than respond to climate change in like manner, the Arctic countries blend goals and attitudes to suit themselves in assessing the situation and in deciding on action. As the pace of Arctic international activity and comment accelerates, they are brought to modify established national policy debates and in some cases to start new ones. Overall, Arctic national policy processes show signs of differentiation between hawk and dove positions, and between those of more finely feathered "dawks" and "hoves" at the middle of the policy spectrum. For brevity's sake, the domestic politics of Arctic and High Northern affairs will be framed here as an interplay simply between isolationist and internationalist tendencies. To begin to see what can be done with a tendency analysis, let us first consider the politics of Canadian Arctic policy.

The Canadian variant of Arctic isolationism is dominated by possession goals expressed in terms of sovereignty and by ideational attitudes keyed to the national identity, including the future wealth of the nation. In assessments that are often highly exaggerated, sovereignty is seen to be under threat from the United States in the Northwest Passage and the Beaufort Sea, from Denmark in regard to tiny Hans Island and the offshore boundary in the Lincoln Sea, and from Russia in the delimitation of the outer continental shelf. Even Sweden's ability to defend itself in the North may be cause for concern in a mind-set that sees Canada as isolated and resolute against all comers in defense of the True North Strong and Free and all those resources up there. Serving to restrain Canadian involvement in the affairs of the Arctic as a region, isolationist thinking varies in vehemence and detail among political leaders, the media, private analysts, and the general public. In common with Canadian nationalism in general, it tends to be laid back in the absence of a clear and present danger, for example an unauthorized transit of the Northwest Passage by a U.S. vessel. Nevertheless, isolationist sentiment is a political resource that can be aroused and turned to advantage by the skilled practitioner. Understanding a bit of this to begin with, the present Conservative government of Canada has gone on to perform an all but elegant exercise in identity politics.

Recent success in the promotion of Arctic isolationism with identity politics in mind began with the need of would-be Prime Minister Stephen Harper to distance himself from the United States in the eyes of the electorate during the federal campaign of December 2005 and January 2006.[4] The result was the delivery of a speech that made clear the determination of a Conservative government to deny all unauthorized use of the Northwest Passage by foreign submarines, including those of the United States, which was mentioned repeatedly as a reported or potential offender. Accordingly, a submarine sensor system was to be emplaced, a trio of heavy naval icebreakers procured and deployed, an army training facility established on the passage, and a deepwater Arctic seaport built. Armed force was thus the hallmark of a stance that would defend Arctic sovereignty against the United States, and in so doing provide Canadians with new reasons to vote Conservative.

The outcome, as of early 2011, is a Conservative minority government that holds the high ground in defense of Canada's identity and future as a great northern nation; that adds domestic Arctic resonance to heightened reliance on military means in foreign affairs; that helps bias the national political agenda toward minimal government in which the military, correctional services, and border control are the prime areas of personnel growth; that disables political opposition to the extent that Arctic sovereignty is made a continuing public concern; and, to cap it all, that meets with the approval of the United States, given by President George W. Bush in August 2007, as a contribution to continental defense, in effect to homeland security.[5] Appealing simultaneously to anti-American sentiment in Canada and to the towering American concern for the homeland, government-sponsored Arctic isolationism is quite a trick. It works. It is unlikely to be set aside by the prime minister and may instead be modified by moving Russia closer to the forefront of rhetoric about Canada's Arctic adversaries. All along, however, Canada's approach to the Arctic has also been shaped by another tendency.

Whereas isolationist practice reduces the Arctic to the Canadian Arctic, assigns top priority to ensured possession, and treats the North as integral to the identity of the southern majority, Canadian Arctic internationalism also stands for sovereignty but is not greatly taken either by identity politics or by possession anxiety. Instead, the approach is one of confidence and readiness to deal with the realities of the Arctic as they exist not only in Canada but also in the region beyond. This is basically the knowledgeable operator's perspective. Its sources are to be found in the federal

[4] See the discussion of identity politics in Tom Flanagan, *Harper's Team: Behind the Scenes in the Conservative Rise to Power* (Montreal: McGill-Queen's University Press, 2007), chap. 8 and esp. pp. 245–46.
[5] See Richard Foot and Norma Greenaway, "Bush Praises Mission," *National Post*, August 22, 2007; Alan Freeman, "Troops Doing Fabulous Job, Bush Says," *Globe and Mail*, August 22, 2007.

civil service – specifically in the Department of Foreign Affairs and International Trade, the Canadian Coast Guard, Transport Canada, the Canadian Ice Service, and the Department of National Defence – and in Inuit and other national aboriginal organizations, to say nothing of a small community of private analysts. Over the years, it is the Legal Bureau of the Department of Foreign Affairs and International Trade that has made the greatest contribution to Canadian Arctic internationalist practice. In the past year or so, it must be added that, Canada's foreign minister has shown a personal interest in Arctic international cooperation, even as he and other ministers continue to single out Russia for its belligerence in the region.

Although internationalist officials are in no position to resist isolationist views directly and publicly, they are relied on by ministers and do provide a steadying hand in the conduct of Canada's Arctic foreign relations. In Canada's participation in the Arctic Council and its working groups, for example, officialdom acts on a wide range of milieu goals in seeking to govern the region's natural and political interdependencies to Canadian advantage. The milieu goal that is most pronounced, however, is the rule of law as encoded in the UN Convention on the Law of the Sea. As a party to the convention, Canada is part of an international order that, in internationalist thinking, provides stability as well as a framework for problem solving in the Arctic. From an internationalist point of view, Canada has good reason to move out confidently from behind its straight baselines and to engage actively in the quickening pace of regional affairs. Conversely, confidence is not to be subverted by "use it or lose it" talk of the Northwest Passage that tells Canadians the passage can be lost, when, in truth, it is irrevocably theirs.

In evaluating the relative strength of isolationism and internationalism in Canada's Arctic performance, we need to distinguish the domestic from the foreign. Much of the verbiage and internal military emphasis of isolationist practice can be written off as domestic politics and not foreign policy. And although not a lot is heard on behalf of Arctic internationalism, it is alive in the humdrum of Canadian participation in regional affairs. Strategically, internationalist confidence in the legal order also strengthens a Canadian sense of common cause among the Arctic Five, the drumbeat of polar peril notwithstanding. Thereby it adds to the thought of forward movement in relations among all of the Arctic Eight. And yet Canadian Arctic internationalism is constrained. It is barred from hot pursuit of cooperative stewardship or anything like it. It will remain so until domestic or international events bring on the exploration of a strategy for the region in its entirety. That said, and before we turn to Russia in the Arctic, there is one last observation to be made on the Canadian case. It applies to all the Arctic countries.

Homeland security and stewardship are complementary objectives. Both require policing of the national domain and its approaches. Policing is better done with constabulary than with war-fighting forces, the former being more effective and cheaper, especially so in a novel frontier region that is just opening. Despite all the huffing and puffing about sovereignty, despite the assertions that U.S. nuclear submarines will not go through without authorization, that we will not be bullied by Russia in the Arctic, Canada has contented itself with a series of mild-mannered, Clark Kentish commitments centered on the acquisition of lightly armed and minimally ice-capable offshore patrol vessels (under development but dependent on creation of the requisite shipbuilding capacity). The outcome here is inadvertent, but ultimately it is sensible. It represents a moderate response to a modest threat in an unfamiliar part of the world. There is nothing here for Russians and others to ooh and ah about, any more than Canada should be alarmed by Denmark's defense policy consensus and intention to deploy special forces to Greenland or by the prospect of Russian special forces parachuting onto the ice at the North Pole. With one exception, all the Arctic states are moving ahead in appropriate constabulary mode when it comes to acquiring and deploying new Arctic-specific military capabilities and to learning how to use them under extraordinary physical conditions. The exception, which also happens to prove the rule, is Norway's acquisition of new naval and air war-fighting capabilities, less for combat than for purposes of diplomacy and deterrence in its dealings with a perennially overbearing, possessive, and yet cooperative Russia.

With nearly 180 degrees of exposure, by far the most heavily industrialized and populated territory, and thus the greatest occupancy in the region, the Russian Federation is the commanding presence in the Arctic. Nothing of great significance can be done without its participation. Russia, however, is far from welcoming the participation of others in affairs of its own that may be of concern to them. As opposed to cooperative stewardship, it wants the freedom to act on its rights in a vast and growing zone that extends far onto the outer continental shelf. Possession goals loom large here, as do material attitudes with regard to the vast wealth and power potential of Arctic hydrocarbon and hard mineral resources.

As well, the Russian identity, and the pride and military and economic confidence that ought to accompany it, are still suffering from the near-death experience of Soviet collapse. This point was rightly emphasized by Fyodor Lyukanov, editor of the journal "Russia in Global Affairs," at the conference at the U.S. Naval War College in September, 2009. As in Canada but far more so, there is fertile ground here for identity politics that appeals to nationalist sentiment, for example, simply in the planting of a flag on the sea bottom at the North Pole. Given the perceived humiliations subsequently experienced on the west and south of their former frontiers at the hands of the United States and NATO, and given also the opening of the Arctic zone and its assets to foreign intrusion as a consequence of climate change, post-Soviet Russians are more likely than not to identify more strongly with their part of the Arctic and to do so in fear and with support for deterrent action that is hard to distinguish from belligerence. Hence the unusual hostility and apprehension of published Russian discourse on the intentions and activities of others in the Arctic. Hence the nasty runs of Russian strategic bombers at Norway and around Iceland, as well as the comparatively restrained but still persistent flights against Canada and the United States.

All this duly noted, Russia nevertheless holds to the rule of international law in the Arctic. It is a proponent of Arctic international cooperation for emergency response and for search and rescue. And, as is noted by Katarzyna Zysk in her chapter of this volume, Russia shows signs of interest in asymmetrical and soft-security issues such as smuggling, terrorism, and illegal migration, and in international negotiation on adaptation to climate change and economic development effects in the region. Milieu goals, readiness for regional cooperation, and a potential for cooperative stewardship are all in evidence here. Just as isolationist sentiment would use Russia's position in the Arctic to recover some of its capacity to dominate in world politics, the internationalist impulse in the region can be seen as reflecting a larger commitment to shared gain in Russia's approach to the wider world. Either way, the Arctic is not so much a place unto itself but a point of departure in Russia's world policy.

Russia's approach to the Arctic is obviously conflicted. In its fundamentals, the conflict between variants of isolationism and internationalism is not unlike that of the Soviet era.[6] The question for the Westerner is not which tendency prevails or is about to prevail. Both will endure. The issue is the correlation among them. In the Canadian case, the U.S. government overlooks and presumably downplays the significance of domestic practices in which the ruling party makes political use of anti-Americanism on Arctic issues. Although elections do not count for much in Russia, I propose we do something similar by devaluing the bellicose alarmism of isolationist discourse, however, without by any means writing it off.[7] To take away from the force of isolationism is to suggest there is more to Arctic internationalism than meets the eye. I believe there is. The internationalist affirmation of the law of the sea can mean only one thing: the navy is part of the supporting coalition. If this is indeed the case, the Russian navy is a potential ally in the generation of a regionwide effort on behalf of cooperative stewardship. How to make good on the potential brings us to the question of where we go from here.

[6] For the Soviet years, see Franklyn Griffiths, "The Sources of American Conduct: Soviet Perspectives and Their Policy Implications," *International Security* 9, no. 10 (Fall 1984), pp. 3–50. Of course the ideology is gone and the situation transformed, but the underlying approaches to foreign relations persist.

[7] A testament to the force of isolationist preferences is to be found in the recent Russian proposal for a European security treaty, which is caught in a time warp with the Kellogg-Briand Pact of 1928 and the Litvinov Pact of the following year. Despite the fact that Europe proper has since evolved into a security community, those in Moscow who remain isolated from it continue to view it as a space in which armed attack is possible and the sole concern of contemporary security policy. The proposed treaty reaches well beyond Europe proper to include everything west and east from Vancouver to Vladivostok, south to former states of the Soviet Union, and north to take in the Arctic region. For the Arctic, the Russian isolationist evidently envisages security as hardest of hard, and little else. President of Russia, "European Security Treaty," *Office Web Portal*, November 29, 2009, accessed October 4, 2010, at http://www.globalsecurity.org/wmd/library/news/russia/2009/russia-091130-kremlin01.htm.

WHERE NEXT?

Given the strife and the human and environmental degradation that could come in an Arctic left to look after itself, I take it that we intend to achieve greater cooperation. Ultimately, it can be had in two ways. It can be done step by step, working skillfully with existing materials as circumstance allows. Or it can come from a calculated effort to create enabling circumstances. On balance, I am for the latter course. When all is said and done, present circumstance makes Russia the main challenge to regionwide collaboration. Many other efforts will make a difference, but if the Arctic is to hold against competition and enmity, internationalism must be strengthened in Russia's policy process. Clearly, there are large limits on the ability of other states to shape the debate in Russia. Still, they are not without opportunity to influence Russian choices and thereby Russian foreign conduct. This includes conduct in the Arctic, which again is largely a derivative of Russia's world policy. A concerted approach is best, but if one state is essential to success in global and Arctic dealings with the Russian Federation, it is the United States.

In an interview late in 2009 interview, Secretary of State Hillary Clinton described the Arctic as "an area that we're beginning to pay attention to" and "an area we have to pay real attention to."[8] Given the powerful internationalist preferences of the administration, this was good news for the region. Still, things have not been going all that well for President Barack Obama in the United States as of winter 2011, this despite a rebound following the 2010 mid-term elections. In the field of foreign affairs isolationist opinion inside the United States has never been stronger. Calls have been heard for a bloc to counterbalance what's taken to be Russia's Arctic rise. The administration experiences continuing difficulty with Congress, although less so now on strategic nuclear arms control with Russia. And if the Tea Party tendency continues to grow in the political life of the fortress-America preferences could gain as an outcome of the presidential election of 2012. Not only Russian internationalism but also its U.S. counterpart may need strengthening if Arctic cooperation is to move ahead in the next few years.

In a world of linked national policy debates, isolationists support one another far more readily than do internationalists. They do so with threatening signals and acts that serve to legitimate what their counterparts already want to do.[9] Parallel unilateral acts of restraint can be of mutual assistance to internationalists, but really there is no substitute for agreements. A case in point is the Ilulissat Declaration,

---

[8] Interview with Secretary of State Hillary Clinton, *Newsweek*, December 22, 2009.

[9] To offer a current example, Canada's decision to buy sixty-five F-35 fighter jets at a cost of $16 billion has been justified by the need to defend against a Russian strategic bomber threat as represented by sorties of elderly aircraft that do approach Canadian airspace (four flights in 2007; five in 2008; three in 2009; and three in 2010). John Ivison, "Sabre-Rattling Not Doing Us Any Favours," *National Post*, August 26, 2010; David Puglise, "Threat of Russian Planes Overplayed, Statistics Show," *National Post*, September 4, 2010.

which enables Russian internationalists to tell their fellow isolationists that the United States and others have agreed that the Arctic is to be ruled by international law and is not to become a free-for-all. Accordingly, the declaration ought to be universally endorsed and, if there is also to be criticism, it should be confined to issues of exclusion.[10] Further, to reinforce Russian Arctic internationalism, the United States could consider enlarging the declaration into an "Arctic Basic Principles Agreement," sponsored jointly with Russia and patterned on the Soviet-American Basic Principles Agreement of 1972.[11] Fanciful perhaps, but the "U.S. Navy Arctic Roadmap" suggests that the Arctic is to become a region in which the United States not only "pays attention" but also takes the initiative for international cooperation.[12]

An elaborate statement that is to be updated in the light of events and continuing work until fiscal year 2013–14 and then revisited at regular intervals, the Roadmap is not easily summarized. In my view it is best read on two levels, operational-technical and strategic. Both represent the navy's response to climate change and to the anticipated actions of states, resource developers, shipping firms, and others in an increasingly accessible region. On one level, we have the navy's thinking on what is required to do its job pursuant to national policy guidance and, on another level, we have the U.S. government's view of desired outcomes in the region. At the end of the road lies a competent and capable navy in full readiness. Taken as strategy, however, the Roadmap seems intent on shaping not only the guidance the navy receives but also the region in which the navy is to operate.

Governed by the formula "look forward and think backward," the Roadmap is strategic in its concern for what it takes to achieve the outcome of a "safe, secure, and stable" Arctic. With safe, secure, and stable as desired end state, we are clearly in the realm of milieu goals. Decidedly regional and not subregional in outlook,

[10] In my view, Secretary Clinton was justified in reproaching Canada for not inviting the three nonlittoral Arctic states and the indigenous participants in the Arctic Council to an Ilulissat follow-on meeting held at Chelsea, Quebec, in March 2010. "News: Clinton's Criticisms Not a Snub, Cannon Says," *Toronto Star*, April 5, 2010. As already stated, indigenous participation is essential if Arctic stewardship is to be not merely locally informed but also practically and ethically sound. The notion of stewardship as locally informed has an additional advantage. It justifies not the exclusion but the relegation of non-Arctic states and intergovernmental entities to a secondary role in regional governance arrangements. Incidentally, if Greenlanders were soon to strike oil or natural gas in quantity, they would almost certainly seek and obtain independence from Denmark. Displacing Denmark in the Arctic Council, a sovereign Greenland would surely make for change, indeed favorable change, in Arctic regional policy discourse. As to Denmark, it would cease to be an Arctic state and instead join the ranks of non-Arctic observers at the Arctic Council if it so wished.

[11] An Arctic basic principles agreement and other approaches in encouraging Russian cooperation in the region are discussed in Franklyn Griffiths, "Towards a Canadian Arctic Strategy" (Toronto: Canadian International Council, June 2009), accessed October 4, 2010, at http://www.onlinecic.org/research/research_areas/arctic.

[12] U.S. Navy, Task Force Climate Change/Oceanographer of the Navy, "U.S. Navy Arctic Roadmap," October 2009, accessed October 4, 2010, at http://www.wired.com/images_blogs/dangerroom/2009/11/us-navy-arctic-roadmap-nov-2009.pdf.

the Roadmap also cites but is not dominated by the requirements of hard security (strategic deterrence, undersea and other forms of warfare, missile defense, strategic sealift, homeland security in depth). Seemingly informed by the view that the Arctic will not gain new life as an arena for strategic military interaction any time soon, the navy's statement conveys a strong commitment to cooperation with foreign militaries on nonmilitary matters, such as search and rescue, maritime domain awareness, and humanitarian assistance and disaster relief (HA/DR). Passing references are also made to stewardship under the heading of environmental protection and to consultation with Arctic indigenous peoples in the state of Alaska. The question is whether and how U.S. actions might contribute to the strengthening of Russian internationalism, without which a safer, more secure, and stable Arctic cannot be attained.

In my view, the Russian state, the navy included, has to oppose an Arctic outcome in which the region becomes a bear pit, in which critical possessions in the country's northernmost zone are destabilized and in which naval operations in the region become increasingly demanding and costly when a chief aim of the state is reliable egress to and return from the world ocean. Russian isolationists may well consider war and its precursors inevitable, as they did under Stalin. But isolationism and the sense of inevitability do not govern Russia's Arctic practice today. Nor, it seems, does the expectation of a stable rather than a fractious Arctic region. Actually, a stable Arctic by mutual agreement is a choice that has never been put to Russia. In offering the possibility of joint action for regional stability, the Roadmap signals readiness for a new departure in bilateral relations and regional affairs alike. In proposing to channel the region's future toward safety, security, and stability, the Roadmap holds forth the promise of consensual, step-by-step improvement in the surety of Russia's possessions and, thereby, in the strength of incentives for internationalism in the Russian policy process.

Whether or not the Roadmap goes on to a more elaborate specification of stewardship in achieving the desired U.S. outcome, the stability that comes with locally informed governance ought generally to be recognized as a source of security and safety in the region. Cooperative stewardship optimizes naval operations by stabilizing the milieu for naval mobility both in military mode and in support of safety at sea. As I have emphasized, it also builds security in deepening the habit of cooperation and in thickening webs of practical interdependence among potential adversaries as well as allies and friends. Regional governance arrangements can be pursued within the framework provided by the UN Convention on the Law of the Sea, all the more so if and when the United States ratifies, as the Roadmap urges. But the Arctic Council provides a further forum for the coordination of multilateral cooperation in the region, be it by subsets of the Arctic Eight, with or without the participation of non-Arctic states and international organizations, or by all of the Arctic Eight according to the nature of the task. Reasoning backward from greater safety, security, and stability as desired outcome for the region, the United States and Canada in particular ought now to be planning for new cooperative stewardship activity in an invigorated Arctic Council.

The United States is to take the chair of the council for a two-year period beginning in the spring of 2015. Before that, Canada is to hold the chair in 2013–15. Canada and the United States are thus slated to lead the principal forum for Arctic collaboration from 2013 to 2017. There is a great opportunity here for the two governments to develop and seek the assent of Russia and others of the Arctic Eight on an integrated approach to the region. They should take the opportunity. They should aim for an initial joint action plan in the early part of 2012, which is before the next U.S. presidential election, around the time the first iteration of the Roadmap is to be completed, and in time for Canada to begin the pre-negotiation of key items with other members of the council before its term as chair formally begins. Although there is not a lot of time, the prospects of Arctic internationalism are on the upswing for the moment.

Laying decades of uncertainty and tension to rest, Norway and the Russian Federation have defused the Arctic offshore boundary dispute with the greatest potential for escalation into violence. This they did in signing a treaty on delimitation and cooperation in the Barents Sea and Arctic Ocean in September 2010.[13] Shortly thereafter, Prime Minister Vladimir Putin delivered an address in which, for the first time since a speech on the region by Mikhail Gorbachev in 1987, a Russian leader called for international dialogue to make the Arctic a zone of cooperation and peace.[14] Validated by the Barents treaty and by Russia's joint leadership, with the United States, of the Arctic Council's task force on search and rescue, Prime Minister Putin's remarks signaled a tendency shift or change in the correlation of isolationism and internationalism, to the benefit of the latter, in Russian Arctic behavior.[15] A shift toward internationalism was also evident in the publication, in August 2010, of a Canadian statement on Arctic foreign policy.[16] Said to have been approved by the prime minister personally, the statement described the United States as "premier

[13] "Treaty between the Kingdom of Norway and the Russian Federation concerning Maritime Delimitation and Cooperation in the Barents Sea and the Arctic Ocean," signed September 15, 2010, accessed October 4, 2010, at http://www.regjeringen.no/upload/SMK/Vedlegg/2010/avtale_engelsk.pdf. Given the extensive dispute-resolution provisions of the treaty, the negotiators evidently expected some difficulty with implementation. Soon after the signing, the Norwegian and Russian foreign ministers called for others to follow their lead. Sergei Lavrov and Jonas Gahr Støre, "Canada, Take Note: Here's How to Solve Maritime Boundary Disputes," *Globe and Mail*, September 21, 2010.

[14] Prime Minister of the Russian Federation, "Prime Minister Vladimir Putin Addresses the International Forum 'The Arctic: Territory of Dialogue,'" September 23, 2010, accessed October 4, 2010, at http://www.premier.gov.ru/eng/events/news/12304/print/.

[15] Authorized by the Arctic Council in 2009, the search-and-rescue task force aims to generate the council's first treaty, for signature by all eight members at a ministerial meeting scheduled for May 2011. Work is said to be going well on the coordination of existing assets, as distinct from the acquisition of new capabilities, which is evidently not on the agenda.

[16] "Statement on Canada's Arctic Foreign Policy," released August 20, 2010, accessed October 4, 2010, at http://www.international.gc.ca/polar-polaire/assets/pdfs/CAFP/_booklet-PECA_livret.eng.pdf.

partner" in the Arctic and pledged an attempt to resolve offshore boundary disagreements with neighbors. It also committed Canada to stewardship in building a region responsive to Canadian interests, among which, however, sovereignty continued to come first.[17] Meanwhile, the Canadian and U.S. defense departments had already embarked on a series of binational Arctic planning ventures; Canadian and Danish armed forces had conducted a joint search and rescue exercise; U.S. and Canadian icebreakers had jointly surveyed the outer continental shelf north of Alaska and Yukon; U.S. and Canadian officials had met to consider a resolution of the Beaufort dispute, as had Canadian and Danish counterparts over the Hans Island issue; and Canadian, Danish, Russian, and U.S. experts were preparing for a fourth annual meeting to consider scientific data relevant to the delimitation of respective national claims to the outer continental shelf. All the while, the U.S. Navy's Arctic Roadmap was being elaborated. More could be said, but the trend is clear: as of early 2011, Arctic internationalism and the outlook for a safe, secure, and stable region are on the rise. The Arctic Eight should take the tide while it lasts. Indeed, they should do what they can to prolong the tide, which in this case is shorthand for a favorable milieu. This brings me to last thoughts, on indirection as such.

Those who favor a realpolitik understanding of security are likely to resist the discussion of milieu, indirection, and stewardship that has been broached here. I will be seen to have slighted the potential for misperception and enmity in foreign affairs, the primacy of opposed forces in strategic practice, and the pervasiveness of zero-sum thinking in which shared gains yield to self-help. As well, I have given only the scantiest of attention to hardware. The Bulava missile is not even mentioned. And to the extent that weaponry is considered at all, the discussion is heavily biased toward constabulary as distinct from combat capabilities. All of which might be apposite except for a few things.

Arctic realities do not now support the primacy of a hard-security agenda, much less a *parabellum* perspective in which preparation for war is the best defense of peace. Local sentiment and historical memories aside, I say that enmity has yet to become a coherent force in the region on issues specific to it. To emphasize it today is to bring it on. As regards opposed-forces thinking, it is increasingly offset by notions of common security and by mounting awareness of physical and political interdependence, indeed by elite awareness of the Arctic Eight having the future of the region very largely in their hands. And where zero-sum calculation is concerned, the Barents treaty is testimony to a gradually widening appreciation of the potential to achieve Arctic arrangements that make for security and shared advantage alike.

---

[17] Prime Minister Harper seemed not entirely pleased with the statement. As he put it, "I want to be absolutely clear about this: while we are giving more detail in the paper than we have in the past and we will continue to make announcements in a wide range of areas, all of these things serve our No. 1 and, quite frankly, non-negotiable priority in northern sovereignty, and that is the protection and the promotion of Canada's sovereignty over what is our North." Mark Kennedy, "Ottawa Unveils Sovereignty Blueprint," *National Post*, August 21, 2010.

Nevertheless, not all is well. Isolationist argumentation demands increased reliance on armed force. It does so in varying degree throughout the region, feeds on perceived military threats, and cannot be ignored. Accordingly, and by way of small comfort to the prophet of adversarial relations, it may be said that a struggle is indeed taking shape in the region. Although armed force and the potential for combat are certainly implicated, the struggle is political and not military in nature.

The struggle counterposes those throughout the Arctic Eight who incline to trust and to get along with one another, and those who tend to pessimism, prefer self-reliance, and resist more than minimal international engagement. The challenge of Arctic security policy is not to channel the region's military affairs directly toward comity. Nor, especially in an era of adaptation to climate change, is it to bring on a milieu favorable to multiple isolated sovereignties. The challenge is to create, primarily through cooperative stewardship, an increasingly safe and stable Arctic environment. This is an environment in which trust grows together with shared norms; in which militaries maintain an active role even as Arctic-specific combat forces decline in salience; and in which all, made more secure, are able to hold together in the face of the enormities that lie ahead. The way to security in the Arctic is an indirect one. Taking it, we may come to understand that stewardship is not only a means to security but also an end in its own right.

2

The Challenges and Security Issues of Arctic Marine Transport

Lawson W. Brigham

INTRODUCTION

Early in the twenty-first century, a nexus of globalization, climate change, and geopolitics is shaping the future of the maritime Arctic. The implications of these forces have never been more compelling for Arctic marine transport. Exploration and development of the Arctic's vast natural resources, such as oil, gas, and hard minerals (e.g., nickel, copper, zinc), have been driven by high commodity prices and worldwide demand, and the result is that the Arctic is becoming much more integrated with the global economy. Importantly, most of these activities rely on marine transport systems. At the same time, the Arctic's sea ice cover is undergoing a historic transformation – thinning, extent reduction in all seasons, and reduction in the area of multiyear ice in the central Arctic Ocean. These changes allow for increases in marine access throughout the Arctic Ocean and for potential longer seasons of navigation and possibly transarctic voyages in the summer. Surface ships in recent years have also reached previously difficult coastal areas and remote regions of the central Arctic Ocean. In addition, the ongoing process for delimitation of the outer continental shelf in the Arctic Ocean under article 76 of the UN Convention on the Law of the Sea (UNCLOS) presents unique marine challenges for gathering data and adds to the already complex geopolitics influencing the future of the maritime Arctic. Taken together, these changes present very real challenges to the existing legal and regulatory structures governing marine safety and environmental protection, and to the general lack of adequate marine infrastructure in most of the Arctic. However, the evolving process of moving to an integrated system of rules and regulations for Arctic navigation will have to be sensitive to the basic principles of freedom of navigation and the overall security concerns of the Arctic states.

THE ARCTIC MARINE SHIPPING ASSESSMENT

No discussion of Arctic marine transport can be made without at least a cursory review of the Arctic Council's *Arctic Marine Shipping Assessment [AMSA] 2009*

Report.[1] On 29 April 2009 at the council's ministerial meeting in Tromsø, Norway, the Arctic ministers approved the AMSA report, a key study for the future of the maritime Arctic. The study is the culmination of work by nearly two hundred experts under the council's working group Protection of the Arctic Marine Environment (PAME). Led by Canada, Finland, and the United States during 2005–09, the study is a follow-on effort to the council's Arctic Climate Impact Assessment and Arctic Marine Strategic Plan, both released in 2004 and each indicating future increases in Arctic marine operations. The AMSA is an assessment of current and future Arctic marine activity with a focus on Arctic marine safety and environmental protection; these key themes are consistent with the Arctic Council's mandates of environmental protection and sustainable development. Although naval-military security issues are not addressed directly, the assessment has security implications with regard to marine navigation rights and infrastructure issues. Overall, AMSA is a message from the Arctic states to the world that contains an environmental security framework and strategy to address the many complex challenges of protecting Arctic people and the environment in an era of expanding use in the Arctic Ocean. In addition, AMSA can be viewed in three ways:

- As a baseline assessment of Arctic marine activity using the AMSA 2004 database as an historic snapshot of Arctic marine use.
- As a strategic guide for use by a host of Arctic and non-Arctic actors and stakeholders.
- As a policy document of the Arctic Council, because the *AMSA 2009 Report* was negotiated and consensus for its approval was reached by the eight Arctic states in the council.

The *AMSA 2009 Report* is a key Arctic Council study and policy document, not a scientific assessment, although some of the elements of the report are based on the most recent scientific research, especially those related to climate change and environmental impacts. The report is appropriately much broader than science and includes such topics as geography, law of the sea, scenarios of the future, marine infrastructure, globalization of the Arctic, indigenous viewpoints, resource development, and other practical issues of Arctic marine navigation; ninety-six findings are outlined in the assessment.[2]

It probably comes as no surprise that AMSA found that Parts I-VII of UNC-LOS provide the fundamental legal framework for governance of Arctic marine navigation and overall marine use. During the conduct of AMSA, this theme was echoed by the five Arctic states bordering on the Arctic Ocean when they met in Ilulissat, Greenland, for what was billed as an Arctic Ocean conference. Key in

[1] Arctic Council, *Arctic Marine Shipping Assessment 2009 Report*, April 2009.
[2] The *AMSA 2009 Report* and AMSA background research documents (research papers that were not approved or negotiated by the Arctic Council but are valuable studies important to AMSA's results) can be found on the PAME website (http://www.pame.is).

both the Ilulissat Declaration[3] and the findings of AMSA is that a majority of the
Arctic – the maritime Arctic – is to be governed by international law that has
already been established. The top of the world is not a lawless region undergoing
near anarchy, as has been promoted by some. The AMSA report reminds us that
UNCLOS sets out the legal framework for the regulation of shipping, globally and in
the Arctic Ocean, according to maritime zones of jurisdiction. Significantly for the
Arctic Ocean, UNCLOS also allows the coastal states the right to adopt and enforce
nondiscriminatory laws and regulations for the prevention, reduction, and control
of marine pollution in ice-covered waters (article 234). The AMSA report indicates
that the International Maritime Organization (IMO) is the principal and competent
UN agency for issues related to international shipping, including maritime safety,
security, and environmental protection. The IMO acts as a secretariat for most international maritime conventions and facilitates their global implementation through
adoption of codes and regulations that become international rules and standards.
All eight Arctic states are active and influential IMO members. Working in consort
at IMO with the global maritime community, the states can attain acceptance of
Arctic-specific rules and regulations for improved marine safety and environmental
protection in polar waters. This long-term process is ongoing at IMO.

The seventeen recommendations of AMSA are presented under three, interrelated themes: (A) Enhancing Arctic Marine Safety, (B) Protecting Arctic People and
the Environment, and (C) Building the Arctic Marine Infrastructure.[4] The recommendations in these themes are fundamental to responding to increased marine use
and to future investment required to achieve enhanced marine safety and protection
throughout the Arctic Ocean. The AMSA report acknowledges that the recommendations will require extensive international cooperation and that implementation
could come from the Arctic states, industry, and/or public-private partnerships.

Selected AMSA recommendations that could have security implications include
the following:

- Development of a comprehensive, multination Arctic search-and-rescue (SAR)
  agreement. (This is currently being conducted by an Arctic Council task force
  led by the United States and Russia, with a potentially binding agreement ready
  for signature by 2011.)
- Mandatory application of relevant parts of the IMO's current and voluntary
  Guidelines for Ships Operating in Arctic Ice-Covered Waters. (A plan of action
  at IMO is under way.)
- Augmentation of global IMO ship safety and pollution prevention conventions with specific mandatory Arctic requirements or other provisions for ship
  construction, design, equipment, crewing, training, and operations.

[3] In the Ilulissat Declaration, the five Arctic Ocean border states noted that they "were committed to
this legal framework [UNCLOS]" and "see no need to develop a new comprehensive international
legal regime to govern the Arctic Ocean."
[4] *AMSA 2009 Report*, pp. 6–7.

- Exploration of the possible harmonization of Arctic marine shipping regulatory regimes (in coastal Arctic seas), including measures to protect the central Arctic Ocean (high-seas area), consistent with UNCLOS. (Such actions could plausibly reduce tension among the Arctic states and provide uniform rules and regulations to the global maritime industry.)
- Identification of (coastal) areas of heightened ecological and cultural significance and encouragement of protection measures in coordination with all stakeholders and consistent with international law. (New protection measures in coastal waters could possibly limit navigation.)
- Exploring the potential need for internationally designated areas for environmental protection in the Arctic Ocean; tools include use of "special areas" or a "particularly sensitive sea area" (PSSA) designation by the IMO. (The potential exists for new protection measures in international waters.)
- Continued development of a comprehensive Arctic marine-traffic awareness system to improve monitoring and tracking of marine activity; also enhancement of data sharing in near real time and augmenting of vessel management services to reduce the risk of incidents, facilitate response to accidents, and provide awareness of potential user conflict. (Commercial and indigenous users may overlap in areas of high Arctic marine traffic necessitating greater monitoring and tracking.)
- Further assessment (by relevant international organizations such as the IMO and the International Whaling Commission) of the effects on marine mammals of ship noise, disturbance, and ship strikes in Arctic waters. (Actions would result in future rules and regulations.)
- Increased cooperation in oil-spill prevention and continued development of circumpolar pollution response capacities. (This is a possible subject for an Arctic state agreement in light of the BP Deepwater Horizon spill in the Gulf of Mexico during 2010.)
- Investment in hydrographic, meteorological, and oceanographic data in support of safe navigation and voyaging in Arctic waters. (An Arctic observing network called for during the International Polar Year 2007–08 would be important for scientific research and marine operations.)

ARCTIC MARINE OPERATIONS

A vast majority of today's Arctic voyages are "destinational," where a ship sails into the Arctic, performs an activity, and then sails south. Most of these voyages are also conducted in the coastal seas off the Arctic states, usually in their exclusive economic zones (EEZs). The major Arctic marine routes, including the multiple voyage options of Russia's Northern Sea Route and the Northwest Passage, are identified in Figure 2.1. Also indicated in Figure 2.1 is a plausible transarctic route across the central Arctic Ocean, although no commercial cargo ship has yet sailed those waters. The near maximum and minimum sea-ice extents for 2007 also provide

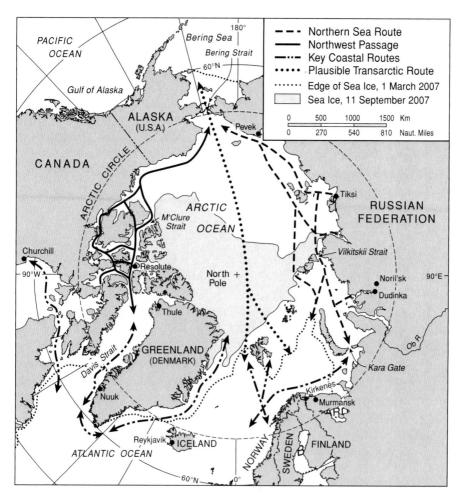

FIGURE 2.1. Marine Routes in the Arctic Ocean and Arctic Region. *Note:* Included in the map are the eight Arctic states, selected ports, and near maximum and minimum of sea-ice extent for 2007. The Northern Sea Route in Russian law is located between Bering Strait and Kara Gate. The Northwest Passage is defined as the set of routes between Baffin Bay in the east and Bering Strait in the west. A plausible transarctic route is indicated across the central Arctic Ocean from the Bering Strait to possible exit points to the east and west of Svalbard.

a visual perspective of the winter and summer covers. Notably, there have been only seven transarctic voyages by icebreakers (across the Arctic Ocean through the North Pole), all in summer and completed for research and tourism during the period 1991–2005.[5] There were eighty icebreaker voyages to the North Pole during 1977–2009, twenty in support of research (aboard icebreakers of six nations) and sixty for marine

---

[5] *AMSA 2009 Report*, p. 74.

tourism aboard Russian icebreakers.[6] Although the total number of such voyages is low, this does indicate the presence of surface ship operations in the central Arctic Ocean in summer, including several voyages to the remotest reaches of the ocean. This number will surely grow as increasing numbers of polar icebreakers conduct scientific research and survey the Arctic Ocean's seabed in support of UNCLOS article 76 claims by the coastal states.

Arctic natural resource development is driving the need for marine transport systems in the Barents, Kara, Norwegian, and Chukchi seas, and most recently off Greenland's west coast. From a security perspective, each of these systems is highly regulated and, in some sense, tightly controlled by the Arctic coastal states involved. Year-round navigation has been maintained since 1979 to the port of Dudinka, which services the industrial mining complex at Noril'sk (see Figure 2.1), the world's largest producer of nickel and palladium. An advanced fleet of ice-breaking carriers links the Yenisey River port in western Siberia to Murmansk on the Kola Peninsula. A second year-round operation is a tanker shuttle system – three ice-breaking tankers operated by the shipping company Sovcomflot – from the offshore Varandey terminal in the Pechora Sea (at the southeastern corner of the Barents Sea) to Murmansk. Both of these Russian ventures rely on modern ice-breaking carriers that are designed to operate independently, without the need for icebreaker escort. In Norway's Arctic offshore, subsea gas is produced at the Snøhvit complex and piped to a liquefied natural gas (LNG) plant near the port of Hammerfest. The LNG tankers initially sailed from this operation to global markets in Spain and the U.S. east coast in 2007 and 2008. In northwest Alaska, the largest zinc mine in the world, Red Dog, is serviced by foreign-flag (non-U.S.) large bulk carriers during a short summer season in ice-free conditions; longer navigation seasons may be possible given the recent retreat of Arctic sea ice in the Chukchi Sea. Finally, Cairn Energy, a U.K. firm, has begun to drill for oil 175 kilometers off Disko Island on the west coast of Greenland. Two drilling rigs and a small fleet of support ships and icebreakers (to contend with drifting icebergs) commenced operations in June 2010.[7]

The AMSA survey of Arctic marine activity showed an estimated six thousand individual ships operated in or near the Arctic during calendar year 2004.[8] Slightly less than 50 percent of the total were identified as fishing vessels and 20 percent as bulk carriers.[9] High regional concentrations of commercial ships were found off coastal Norway and northwestern Russia, around Iceland, off Greenland's west coast (increasing cruise ship traffic and supply ships), and along the Aleutian Islands in southwestern Alaska (ships sailing along the North Pacific Great Circle Route). A summer sealift to Arctic communities in the Canadian Arctic in recent years has

---

[6] L. Brigham, "The Fast-Changing Maritime Arctic," *U.S. Naval Institute Proceedings* 136, no. 5 (2010): pp. 58–59.
[7] "Cairn Energy Begins Greenland Oil Exploration," BBC News, 1 July 2010.
[8] The total included ships along the North Pacific Great Circle Route around the Aleutians.
[9] AMSA 2009 *Report*, p. 72.

averaged one hundred voyages by commercial ships; an undetermined number of
ships have also supported communities by summer sealift in the Russian Arctic. This
cursory look confirms that most Arctic marine operations today are conducted in
coastal waters, with the exceptions being icebreaker voyages into the central Arctic
Ocean for research and tourism.

UNCERTAINTIES AND SECURITY FACTORS

A key challenge for the Arctic states and the global maritime community is the range
of uncertainties that can shape the future of Arctic marine use. A scenarios creation
effort as part of the AMSA study identified nearly 120 factors and uncertainties that
could be influential in determining the future of the maritime Arctic. Key among
them are the stability of the legal or governance framework in the Arctic Ocean;
global trade dynamics and world trade patterns; the severity of climate change (and
the resulting influence on changes in the Arctic sea-ice cover) and the socioeconomic
impacts of global weather changes; global oil prices; a global shift to nuclear power
(reducing the need for Arctic hydrocarbon developments); limited "windows of
operation" for Arctic shipping in summer (the economics of seasonal versus year-
round Arctic marine operations); the role of transit fees in coastal Arctic routes; the
engagement and roles of the maritime insurance industry in Arctic navigation; the
timing and breadth of global (IMO) agreements on construction rules and standards;
and the emergence of new marine operators in the Arctic Ocean from non-Arctic
states such as China, Japan, and Korea.[10] A significant influence on future Arctic
shipping, and a potential game changer, would be a major shipping disaster such
as a fire or loss of a cruise ship or commercial ship in Arctic waters. Also, any new
resource discovery, either offshore or onshore oil and gas or hard mineral discovery,
would require new marine transport systems to bring the resource to global markets.

Although Arctic and global security issues are not discussed at the Arctic Council,
several have relevance to Arctic marine transport. The safety and security of global
maritime trade routes are of interest in future discussions particularly in light of
piracy off Somalia and incidents in choke points such as the Straits of Hormuz. The
security (and potential catastrophic loss) of the Suez or Panama canals could also
have ramifications for future maritime operations in Arctic waters. These potential
disruptions of global maritime routes would not necessarily stimulate increases in
transarctic navigation but could change, for example, maritime trading and carriage
of oil and gas, plausibly from Arctic sources. In the Arctic, the escalation of Arctic
boundary disputes and conflicts among indigenous and commercial users could
surely influence the viability of Arctic marine operations.

This cursory review of critical factors and uncertainties illustrates the complexity
and range of global and regional connections surrounding future Arctic marine use.
Globalization, climate change, governance, and security issues are all at play in
influencing the region's future.

---

[10] *AMSA 2009 Report*, table 6.1, p. 93.

INFRASTRUCTURE CONCERNS

One of the major concerns and challenges expressed by the Arctic states in the AMSA report is the general lack of marine infrastructure in the Arctic, except for the Norwegian coast and select coastal regions of northwestern Russia. Missing or lacking infrastructure in most Arctic areas include hydrographic data and marine charts, complete and adequate coverage of communications, environmental monitoring (for weather, sea ice, and icebergs), SAR capability, environmental response capacity, ship monitoring and tracking, aids to navigation, and more. For much of the Arctic, the lack of deepwater ports, places of refuge, salvage and towing services, and port reception facilities – all normally available to the global maritime industry – is of serious concern. The AMSA report concludes that the vastness and harshness of the Arctic environment make conduct of marine emergency response more difficult throughout the region. The Arctic Ocean's hydrographic database for charting is not adequate in most areas to support current and future levels of Arctic marine operations. In addition, the monitoring network of meteorological and oceanographic observations critical to safe navigation is extremely sparse and not adequate to support increases in Arctic marine transport.[11] What is relevant to this volume on security is that the infrastructure that is missing in the Arctic Ocean for the commercial maritime world is likewise absent for naval and military operations. The lack of ice information, charts, communications, and emergency response, as key examples, is no less critical to the safe operation of security forces as it is to commercial Arctic marine transport. This places importance on having civil and military organizations in the Arctic working together on infrastructure issues and developing mechanisms specifically for emergency response well in advance of a maritime incident or crisis situation.

PLAUSIBLE ARCTIC MARINE INCIDENTS

The challenges and ramifications of plausible Arctic marine incidents were studied in a scenarios-based workshop held as part of the AMSA study in March 2008. Fifty maritime experts from six Arctic state governments, industry, indigenous groups, research universities, and nongovernmental organizations met at the Coastal Response Research Center of the University of New Hampshire in the United States. Five relevant and plausible incidents were reviewed: (1) a grounded tug and barge (with hazardous materials onboard) on St. Lawrence Island in the Bering Sea in early spring, (2) a cruise ship grounding in mid-September and subsequent abandoning of the ship (1,400 passengers and additional crew) off the west coast of Greenland, (3) an oil tanker and fishing vessel collision with an oil spill near the (formerly) disputed boundary between Norway and Russia in the Barents Sea, (4) an ore carrier

---

[11] *AMSA 2009 Report*, pp. 154–81; on the infrastructure findings, see pp. 186–87.

trapped in the ice and sinking near the North Pole in international waters during a late-September crossing, and (5) a fire and collision in offshore drilling operations (between an icebreaker and drill ship) in late winter in the Beaufort Sea near the disputed boundary between the United States and Canada.[12] The selected incidents were chosen to highlight issues related to spill response, salvage, search and rescue, communications, and governance and jurisdiction.

Each of the marine incidents exposed a host of challenges for the Arctic states and the maritime industry. Inadequacies related to marine infrastructure were readily apparent. For example, timely and available salvage services were lacking in each of the scenarios as the incident evolved. Ports of refuge in the Arctic were not readily identified and guidelines for their use not available. The lack of mandatory Arctic ship-safety guidelines was a significant issue for the trapped ore carrier in the central Arctic Ocean and the cruise ship incident off western Greenland. Effective responses to the scenario incidents were hampered by the lack of detailed information regarding existing SAR agreements and regional pollution contingency plans. Thus, there were calls for an international Arctic SAR agreement (that might facilitate the pooling of resources), expanded regional environmental response networks in Arctic coastal seas, and the establishment of an international Arctic response fund. The workshop participants also suggested the development of forward-operating response bases with enhanced assets and equipment which could be formed with international contributions.

Improved communications (satellite and shore-based very high frequency [VHF] and high frequency [HF]), expanded environmental monitoring, requirements for effective Arctic vessel tracking, and a need for enhanced logistical support to responders in the Arctic were consistent practical outcomes from the five scenarios. A need to consider alternative countermeasures for oil-spill cleanup and continued research funding to improve responses to oil spills in ice were key recommendations. It was clear from this workshop that the most urgent needs were for the Arctic states to foster their cooperation in SAR and environmental response, and together develop more effective preparedness measures throughout the Arctic. Expanded information sharing and more coordinated surveillance and monitoring of Arctic marine traffic will require enhanced cooperation and minimal discord within the Arctic community to achieve increased levels of marine safety and environmental protection.

TRANSARCTIC NAVIGATION

The presence or absence of sea ice along Arctic navigation routes has serious economic, operational, and regulatory implications for the global shipping industry. One key issue is whether polar-class ships will be required most of the year in the

[12] Coastal Response Research Center, *Opening the Arctic Seas: Envisioning Disasters and Framing Solutions* (University of New Hampshire, Durham, NH, 2009), available at http://www.crrc.unh.edu.

Arctic Ocean or whether non-ice-capable ships will be used during long periods of ice-free conditions. There is little debate that marine access throughout the Arctic Ocean is increasing as a result of the relentless, observed decrease in Arctic sea-ice thickness and extent. However, most of the Arctic Ocean remains fully or partially covered in ice for all but a short period in summer. Although several climate model simulations show an ice-free Arctic Ocean for a brief period as early as summer 2030, it is noteworthy that they also indicate significant sea ice present in winter, spring, and autumn through the twenty-first century and beyond. It is also important that no climate model simulations show the Arctic Ocean to be ice-free throughout the year. Reports in recent years that the Northwest Passage and the Northern Sea Route were open or ice-free are accurate, but the periods that they were observed open (throughout their length) were from a few days to several weeks in autumn, near the minimum extent of Arctic sea ice. As a practical matter, the more sea ice present along an Arctic waterway, the slower is the ship's speed (even for polar-class ships). The lower speeds can negate the shorter distances gained by transarctic routes compared with open-water transits at lower latitudes and higher speeds. Transarctic navigation is likely today to be technically feasible in summer, but the shipping economics of such voyages (especially where just-in-time cargoes are at stake) have yet to be fully assessed.

The AMSA report outlines a number of challenges and key questions regarding transarctic navigation.[13] New polar ships built to mandatory IMO rules will be the norm in a few years – how will those rules influence the economics of transarctic shipping? How will shippers respond to seasonal operations if year-round navigation is not available? Can seasonal transits be viable and what cargoes can be most viable? How will the insurance industry respond to Arctic shipping if the operators sail longer in ice, and if the ships are navigating independently without icebreaker escort? One of the most pressing issues is whether long voyages across the Arctic Ocean can be conducted safely and reliably, given most global operations' need for schedule reliability. More shipping economic analyses are required to determine what type of cargoes and ships can profitably sail various routes, even during a short summer season (bulk carriers or ships with specialized cargoes).

Recent operations along the Northern Sea Route and the Northeast Passage have captured international media attention to the possibilities for transarctic voyages. During August and September 2009, two German heavy-lift ships, *Beluga Fraternity* and *Beluga Foresight*, sailed across the top of Eurasia.[14]

Figure 2.2 shows the routes of the two ice-strengthened ships; forty-four heavy plant modules were delivered from Korea to barges in the Ob Gulf in western Siberia. Additional cargo was carried from Archangel on the White Sea to Nigeria,

[13] *AMSA 2009 Report*, pp. 162–64.
[14] "A Shortcut through the Arctic Ocean," *Blue Line Magazine* (Beluga Shipping, Bremen, Germany), February 2010, pp. 10–12.

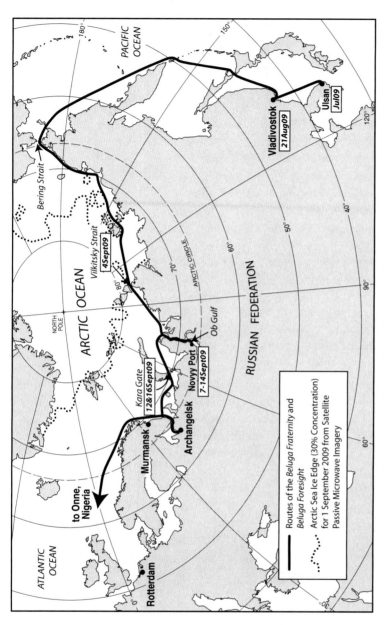

FIGURE 2.2. Summer 2009 Commercial Voyages along the Northeast Passage. *Note:* Indicated are the routes of two German heavy-lift ships, *Beluga Fraternity* and *Beluga Foresight*, from Korea to western Siberia (discharging cargo in the Ob Gulf) and then to Archangelsk and subsequently to Nigeria. The two commercial ships were escorted along sections of the Northern Sea Route by Russian nuclear icebreakers. Also indicated on the map are the generally light ice conditions on 1 September 2009 across the Russian maritime Arctic.

thus completing a full transit of the Northeast Passage. Although ice conditions were relatively light (see the Arctic sea-ice edge for 1 September 2009 in Figure 2.2), icebreaker escort was provided by Russian nuclear icebreakers. The voyages represent a new maritime linkage of Asian manufacturers to the Russian Arctic and expanded links of Siberia to the global economy. Significantly, it was widely reported that the voyages were successful financially for Beluga Shipping, yet the overall economics and cost accounting are unclear, as the details of the fees paid for icebreaker escort services and Russian ice pilots while on the Northern Sea Route are not available. The fact that icebreaker escort was mandatory even though the ice conditions were very light is notable. Fee structures and sailing requirements will have to be made more transparent and available in a timely fashion if regular use of the Northern Sea Route by the international maritime community is to become a reality.

KEY ARCTIC POLICY ISSUES AHEAD

A post-AMSA policy workshop was held in October 2009 at the University of Alaska Fairbanks as part of a series of workshops under the University of the Arctic's Institute for Applied Circumpolar Policy. A number of key policy issues for the Arctic were identified, as well as road maps and key issues highlighted for each of the AMSA's recommendations by the expert working groups.[15] The highest priority issue consistently identified by most experts and stakeholders is the urgent need for a mandatory IMO polar code. Agreements on SAR (ongoing) and potentially on circumpolar response capacity (e.g., the pooling of resources to enhance regional capacity in response to a spill or other marine incident) are key policy challenges for the Arctic states. The AMSA report also identified as a significant requirement the undertaking of surveys of indigenous use in Arctic seas. Conducted on regional and local scales, the results of such surveys will be critical to developing multiuse strategies in all Arctic waterways.

The policy issues associated with the tracking and monitoring of Arctic commercial ships (using Automated Identification System, or AIS) will likely follow progress of IMO's efforts for the global oceans. Perhaps more critical will be the policy and funding challenges confronting the Arctic states in providing sufficient resources for increased hydrography and surveying of Arctic waters. Improved marine navigation charts are essential for all future uses of the Arctic Ocean and the development of a unified strategy and list of high-priority regions for attention are critical needs to be addressed by the Arctic states and commercial interests. The implementation of an Arctic Observing Network – a system of observations to enhance knowledge

---

[15] L. Brigham and M. Sfraga, 2010, *Considering a Roadmap Forward: The Arctic Marine Shipping Assessment*, workshop report, University of Alaska Fairbanks and the University of the Arctic Institute for Applied Circumpolar Policy, 22–24 October 2009.

of the Arctic environment – is also a key element of marine infrastructure when considering the importance of ice and weather information to Arctic marine operations. This effort will require the merging of many policies and interests of the Arctic states and important non-Arctic states who are key contributors to Arctic research. Finally, a comprehensive study is required to identify future Arctic marine protected areas and the regions that could be recommended for IMO designation as particularly sensitive sea areas (PSSAs). The results of such a study will have broad Arctic policy implications including security concerns related to marine access.

FINAL THOUGHTS – ARCTIC MARINE TRANSPORT AND SECURITY ISSUES

It is plausible that future Arctic marine transport will not be the root cause for increased discord and potential conflict in the Arctic. Addressing the myriad issues of Arctic marine use may in fact drive enhanced Arctic cooperation and, in some cases, international collaboration at IMO and other bodies. The AMSA is one example of the close cooperation and consensus in the Arctic Council necessary to develop a lasting strategy for protecting Arctic people and the marine environment in an era of increasing marine use. The ongoing Arctic Council task force developing a potentially binding Arctic SAR agreement is another example of improving cooperation; enhancing the Arctic's environmental response capabilities may yet be another critical need where the Arctic states can collaborate and reach new, effective regional response agreements. Addressing the Arctic maritime infrastructure deficit – for surveillance and monitoring, charting and hydrography, data sharing in near real time, vessel traffic systems, environmental observing systems, and more – will also require close (and lasting) Arctic state and public-private partnerships. The acceptance by IMO of a mandatory code for ships operating in the polar regions will be a seminal achievement that can provide impetus for having a future set of uniform coastal state rules and regulations that could further strengthen Arctic state maritime ties. The Arctic states as well as many domestic and international stakeholders are very keen to foster and maintain regional stability so that Arctic natural resources can be fully developed and reach future global markets. Focusing on the overall environmental security challenges of Arctic marine transport may be a successful strategy for fostering unprecedented international cooperation and dialogue in the Arctic.

3

The Arctic Meltdown and Its Implication
for Ports and Shipping in Asia

Joshua H. Ho

INTRODUCTION

Long neglected and dismissed as scientifically unfounded, global warming has been accepted as a new reality that will have a direct impact on the safety, security, and environment of human habitats. The effects of climate change due to global warming include the increase in frequency and intensity of adverse weather events; water shortages; sea-level rise and, as a consequence, flooding and subsequent destruction of coastlines; a decrease in crop yields as a result of increasing temperatures and a reduction in water supply; and an increase in climate-sensitive illnesses and deaths.[1] Traditional industries such as agriculture, fisheries, and tourism might be reduced or even disappear altogether in regions that are heavily affected by climate change. Port cities located in the deltaic regions, mostly in Asia, with its vast coastline and dense population, will have to endure detrimental effects from climate-linked storm surges and rises in sea level. Hundreds of millions of people living near low-lying coasts will be displaced. Asia may soon be faced with disappearing states and loss of livelihood as a result of inundation. If societies are not able to adapt to climate change, great human suffering will occur.

If global warming due to greenhouse-gas accumulations is expected to be severe worldwide, it is enhanced in the Arctic regions. Climate-model studies of increasing atmospheric greenhouse-gas scenarios confirm that anthropogenic global warming will be more severe in the high northern latitudes because of complex feedback mechanisms in the atmosphere-ocean-ice system.[2] The coupled climate models used by the Intergovernmental Panel on Climate Change (IPCC) in 2007 predicted

[1] Simon Tay, Phir Pangmalit, and Elaine Teng, "Special Report on Climate Change Challenges in Southeast Asia," *Report of Shell – SIIA Expert Roundtable on Climate Change Challenges in Southeast Asia* (Singapore: Singapore Institute of International Affairs, 2008).
[2] Intergovernmental Panel on Climate Change, *Climate Change 2007: Synthesis Report* (Geneva: World Meteorological Organization, 2008).

that the warming in the Arctic over the next fifty years is in the range of three to four degrees Celsius, more than twice the global average. However, the models also indicate a large spread in the results, suggesting that the Arctic may be where the most rapid and dramatic changes will occur during the twenty-first century.[3]

LATEST FINDINGS ON THE RATE OF CLIMATE CHANGE

Recently, the Tyndall Center for Climate Change Research at the University of Oxford and the Hadley Center at the U.K. Met Office jointly sponsored the international climate conference "4 Degrees and Beyond" in Oxford, United Kingdom, from 28–30 September 2009. The key message at that conference was that global warming of up to four degrees Celsius average was likely. A four-degree increase translates to a two-degree increase in some places, and an increase of twelve degrees or more in others, which makes these places uninhabitable for plants, animals, and humans. Relying on the Hadley Center's HadCM3 model, which is an amalgamation of climate models, Dr. Richard Betts, head of climate impacts at the Hadley Center, mentioned that current emissions are already at the upper end of the IPCC models and that we are faced with the prospect of dealing with the worst-case scenarios developed by the IPCC. The models are based on human emissions alone and exclude heat-amplifying feedbacks from melting ice or changes in carbon sinks. When those are factored in, the timeline will move forward. As Betts puts it, "Reaching four degrees by 2060 is a plausible, worst-case scenario," with the median year being 2070. By 2100, an average global temperature rise of five and a half degrees is possible.[4]

Hence, the previous notion of limiting emissions so that global warming does not increase globally beyond an average of two degrees Celsius is increasingly indefensible given the limited reductions on the part of all stakeholders to date. If emissions reductions are not implemented soon, there is also the possibility of a limited runaway greenhouse effect and the more unlikely Venus effect, a situation in which the Earth would heat up uncontrollably, which would eventually make it uninhabitable, like the planet Venus.[5] Basically, once global warming reaches a certain threshold, which is estimated to be at the average of three degrees Celsius in the global rise in temperature, natural warming feedback cycles will take over and accelerate

---

[3] Intergovernmental Panel on Climate Change, *Climate Change 2007: The Physical Science Basis: Contribution of Working Group I to the Fourth Assessment Report* (Cambridge: Cambridge University Press, 2007).

[4] Richard Betts, Michael Sanderson, Deborah Hemming, Mark New, Jason Lowe, and Chris Jones, "4 Degrees Celsius of Global Warming: Regional Patterns and Timing," presentation at the International Climate Conference, Oxford, 28–30 September 2009, available at http://www.eci.ox.ac.uk/4degrees/ppt/1–2betts.pdf.

[5] H. J. Schellnhuber, "Terra Quasi-Incognita: Beyond the 2 Degree Line," presentation at the International Climate Conference, Oxford, 28–30 September 2009, available at http://www.eci.ox.ac.uk/4degrees/ppt/1–1schellnhuber.pdf.

the warming process. The natural positive feedback mechanism includes the reduction in oceanic carbon dioxide uptake, the release of methane from thawing permafrost and peatland, the release of methane from oceanic methane hydrates, and the albedo effect, the reduction in the reflectivity of sunlight from the surface of the earth with the consequent greater absorption of heat, arising from Greenland and Antarctic ice melting. These positive feedbacks will increase average global temperatures quickly to about eight degrees Celsius. Hence, the longer emissions reductions are postponed, the harder it is to even defend this four-degree limit.

As far as the Arctic is concerned, the thawing of permafrost and peatland is a critical positive feedback that will increase the rate of warming. Scientists have discovered that even a modest thaw of the perennially frozen soil that lies under the lakes surrounding the Arctic and on the caps on the dry land around them could trigger a vicious warming cycle, as the methane gas released will trap twenty-five times more of the sun's heat than carbon dioxide does.[6] A complete thaw would discharge ten times the current amount of methane already in the atmosphere. Simply put, thawed permafrost releases methane and carbon dioxide, and when those gases reach the atmosphere, they help heat the Earth via the greenhouse effect. The trapped heat thaws more permafrost, thus exacerbating the entire warming cycle. Over the past hundred years, the air temperature in the Arctic has increased at double the rate of the global average, with the total ice extent decreasing at a rate of 3–5 percent per decade, the older multiyear ice decreasing twice as fast, river discharge from Russia increasing, the tundra permafrost thawing, and snow cover on land decreasing.[7] These observations and analysis of current warming trends indicate that global warming is happening at a quicker rate and that the Arctic sea ice is melting at a faster rate than the median case.

THE IMPACT OF CLIMATE CHANGE ON PORTS IN ASIA

According to the latest World Wide Fund for Nature (WWF) report on the impacts of climate change on megacities, released in November 2009, Asia is arguably the continent that is most vulnerable. The report focused on the climate variability and adaptive capacity of eleven key Asian cities: Dhaka, Jakarta, Manila, Calcutta, Phnom Penh, Ho Chi Minh, Shanghai, Bangkok, Hong Kong, Kuala Lumpur, and Singapore. There is widespread evidence of climate change in Asia that includes overall temperature increases from one to three degrees Celsius over the past hundred years, changing precipitation patterns, an increasing number of extreme weather events, and rising sea levels. Many of the largest cities in Asia are extremely susceptible to the impacts of climate change, as they are located along the coast and in major

[6] Sarah Simpson, "The Arctic Thaw Could Make Global Warming Worse," *Scientific American*, 29 June 2009, available at http://www.scientificamerican.com/article.cfm?id=the-peril-below-the-ice.
[7] Leonid P. Bobylev, Kirill Ya. Kondratyev, and Ola M. Johannessen, *Arctic Environment Variability in the Context of Global Change* (New York: Springer-Praxis, 2004), p. 470.

river deltas. Excessive carbon dioxide in the atmosphere also contributes to the acid-ification of the oceans, the shifting in climate zones, and the reduction of water availability. The acidification of the oceans endangers calcifying organisms such as corals, which are the cradle for sea life. In addition, deoxygenation due to excessive carbon dioxide absorption by the ocean causes reduction in fisheries habitats. As a result, those who depend on fish and seafood as a source of food and livelihood in South and Southeast Asia, especially traditional fishers, will be threatened with food shortages and declines in fish populations. A shift in climate zones in the tropics and semiarid regions will affect agricultural and crop yields, and ultimately livestock production and food security at the national level. The Himalayan glaciers that feed the great rivers of Asia and supply millions of people with drinking water are also at risk of drying up, and to a certain extent, they are drying up already.[8]

The key finding in the report was that the vulnerability of Asia to climate change is relatively high, as millions of lives will be affected and countries' natural assets and gross domestic product (GDP) will be reduced. The overall vulnerability score is calculated by taking the average of three categories: a country's exposure, sensitivity, and adaptive capacity. For example, the cities in less developed countries, like Dhaka (Bangladesh), Jakarta (Indonesia), and Manila (Philippines), rank high on the most vulnerable list because they are susceptible to extreme weather events such as tropical cyclones, flooding, and drought. Compounded by the size of the cities and low adaptive capacity, the WWF urges the government, businesses, and influential scientists to implement immediate adaptation and mitigation strategies and policies.[9]

Importantly, many of the coastal cities in Asia will be affected by sea-level rise, which is projected by the 2007 IPCC AR4 (Fourth Assessment Report) reports to increase from 0.17 meters in the twentieth century to between 0.18 to 0.59 meters by the end of the twenty-first century. However, this projection excludes the uncertain-ties in climate–carbon cycle feedback and the full effects of changes in Greenland and Antarctic ice-sheet flow as a result of the paucity of published literature.[10] Already, scientists gathering at a climate-change summit in Copenhagen in Decem-ber 2009 warned that global sea levels will rise by an amount that is more than that previously projected by the IPCC AR4 models. Even if the world manages to cut the emission of greenhouse gases, the best estimate of possible sea-level rise was about 1 meter, or in the range of 0.75 to 1.90 meters, by 2100, as noted Professor Stefan Rahmstorf of the Potsdam Institute for Climate Impact Research in Germany.[11] The latest Potsdam Institute report, titled the "Copenhagen Diagnosis," was compiled

[8] World Wide Fund for Nature, _Mega-Stress for Mega-Cities: A Climate Vulnerability Ranking of Major Coastal Cities in Asia_, 2009, available at http://assets.panda.org/downloads/mega_cities_report.pdf.

[9] Ibid.

[10] Intergovernmental Panel on Climate Change, _Climate Change 2007_.

[11] Stefan Rahmstorf, "A Semi-Empirical Approach to Projecting Future Sea-Level Rise," _Science_, 19 Jan-uary 2007, available at http://www.pik-potsdam.de/~stefan/Publications/Nature/rahmstorf_science_2007.pdf.

by twenty-six researchers, most of whom were also authors of the IPCC report, estimated that the global sea-level rise could exceed one meter by the year 2100, with the upper limit estimated at two meters. This is at least twice as much as that projected by Working Group 1 of the IPCC's AR4.[12]

Asia is a region that will be seriously affected by this rise in sea level, as large numbers of people will be displaced. An analysis conducted by the Tyndall Center for Climate Change Research at the University of Oxford calculated that, by the end of this century, a one-meter increase in sea level will displace more than 100 million people and inundate close to nine hundred thousand square kilometers of land in Asia.[13] Similarly, the Organisation for Economic Co-operation and Development (OECD) has estimated that fifteen of the top twenty port cities that will be affected by coastal flooding by 2070 will be in Asia. The fifteen cities are projected to have a combined flood-exposed population of nearly 95 million; the cities include those in India (Kolkata and Mumbai), Bangladesh (Dhaka, Khulna, and Chittagong), Vietnam (Ho Chih Minh and Hai Phong), Thailand (Bangkok), Myanmar (Yangon), Indonesia (Jakarta), Japan (Tokyo), and China (Guangzhou, Shanghai, Tianjin, and Ningbo).[14]

According to the *Stern Review*, the expected costs for stabilization at 500–550 parts per million of CO2e is likely to average around 1 percent of annual global GDP, with a range between –2 percent and 5 percent by 2050, with the variability of estimates diverging strongly thereafter and especially by 2100. Through cost-benefit analysis, the review also concluded that the benefits of strong early action will outweigh the costs, as tackling climate change was the pro-economic growth strategy, and ignoring climate change will eventually damage economic growth.[15]

THE IMPACT OF CLIMATE CHANGE ON SEA LANES – THE OPENING OF THE NORTHERN SEA ROUTE

Besides sea-level rise affecting port cities in Asia, the maritime industry in Asia could also be affected by climate change, particularly when the Northern Sea Route (NSR)

[12] I. Allison, N. L. Bindoff, R. A. Bindschadler, P. M. Cox, N. de Noblet, M. H. England, J. E. Francis, N. Gruber, A. M. Haywood, D. J. Karoly et al., *The Copenhagen Diagnosis: Updating the World on the Latest Climate Science* (Sydney: University of New South Wales Climate Change Research Center, 2009), available at http://www.ccrc.unsw.edu.au/Copenhagen/Copenhagen_Diagnosis_HIGH.pdf.

[13] David Anthoff, Robert J. Nicholls, Richard S. J. Tol, and Athanasios T. Vafeidis, "Global and Regional Exposure to Large Rises in Sea-Level: A Sensitivity Analysis," Tyndall Center for Climate Change Research Working Paper No. 96, October 2006, available at http://www.tyndall.ac.uk/sites/default/files/wp96_0.pdf.

[14] R. J. Nicholls, S. Hanson, C. Herweijer, N. Patmore, S. Hallegatte, J. Corfee-Morlot, J. Chateau, and R. Muir-Wood, "Ranking Port Cities with High Exposure and Vulnerability to Climate Extremes: Exposure Estimates," Organisation for Economic Co-operation and Development Environment Working Paper No. 1, 19 November 2008, available at http://www.oils.oecd.org/olis/2007/doc.nsf/LinkTo/NT0000588E/$FILE/JT03255617.PDF.

[15] Nicholas Stern, *The Economics of Climate Change: The Stern Review* (Cambridge: Cambridge University Press, 2007), pp. 168, 239, available at http://www.hm-treasury.gov.uk/stern_review_report.htm.

opens up for ship transportation in the Arctic as a result of declining sea-ice levels from global warming. During the past seventy-five years, the Soviet Union and then Russian Federation have operated in the NSR. Maritime transport has been extensive and reached its peak of 6.6 million tons in 1987, mainly in the form of the regional export of natural resources and, to a lesser extent, cargo to communities along the Siberian coast.[16] After the collapse of the Soviet Union, there was much optimism in the 1990s with respect to the increased use of the Northern Sea Route for maritime transport between Europe and Asia. This optimism has yet to become a reality, mainly because the Northern Sea Route has never been ice-free, even during the summer months, to allow for significant maritime transportation between Europe and Asia. The current volume of shipping appears to be 2.13 million tons in 2007, and the transportation of hydrocarbons within the Barents and White seas reached 8.5 million tons in 2006.[17]

The *Arctic Council's Arctic Marine Shipping Assessment* (AMSA) *2009 Report* has determined that shipping in the coming decades will remain dominated by an increase in regional transportation in waters close to Norwegian interests, namely in the Barents, Pechora, and Kara seas.[18] Coastal and port access in all these areas will experience immediate seasonal improvements due to the reduced appearance of sea ice. From around 2025, AMSA expects that transit traffic in the Northern Sea Route may be more regular. Even though the sea routes along the Siberian coast may open up earlier, the depth of water along the coast may limit the size and freight capacity of ships that can transit the route. The AMSA estimates that regular transpolar summer transport (four months) may not occur until toward the middle of this century, from 2040 onward.

However, the AMSA assessment is likely to be conservative, given the current rates of global warming. Consistent with the increasing rate of global warming, the observed maritime activities along the Northern Sea Route have also changed over the past five years. Previously, no non-Russian ships traversed the Northern Sea Route along the Siberian coast, but merchant, research, and expedition vessels have journeyed through the Northern Sea Route during the summer seasons since 2004, and that volume is set to increase. For example, the predicted volume of transport in the Northern Sea Route, primarily transport of natural resources, gas, and oil, may increase by up to 5.5 million tons in 2010 and by up to 12.8 million tons by 2020.[19]

There have also been other maritime activities that indicate that transarctic passage may open up much earlier than expected. For example, in 2008, the Arctic Ocean experienced for the first time an ice-free and navigable Northern Sea Route along the

[16] I. E. Frolov and B. A. Krutskih, eds., *Hydrometeorological Supplying of Arctic Navigation in XX and Beginning of XXI Centuries: Federal Survey on Hydrometeorology and Environmental Monitoring* (St. Petersburg: Arctic and Antarctic Research Institute, 2008).

[17] Ibid.

[18] Arctic Council, *Arctic Marine Shipping Assessment 2009 Report*, April 2009.

[19] Frolov and Krutskih, *Hydrometeorological Supplying of Arctic Navigation.*

Siberian coast.[20] This occurred during a summer melt season after a winter during which the maximum ice extent was greater than had been observed in the previous five years, which suggests that seasonal temperature fluctuations have increased and that future ice-free passages during the summer months along the Siberian coast are highly likely. On 9 September 2009, it was reported that two German merchant vessels were the first to make it through the formerly impenetrable Northeast Passage, or the Northern Sea Route, departing from Ulsan in South Korea to Novy Port in Russia.[21] The ice-class ships were to eventually sail around the Yamal Peninsula, cross the Barents Sea to Murmansk, and head on to Rotterdam. Sea-ice maps from the Advance Microwave Scanning Radiometer – Earth Observing System (AMSR-E) also highlight the possibility of a clear passage through the Northern Sea Route. For example, since 2008, a clear passage of the NSR along the Siberian coast has opened up. Although the sea-ice coverage in 2010 has not declined as rapidly as in the previous two years, it is still at the third lowest point since data was first collected.

FUTURE SHIPPING IN THE ARCTIC

The Center for High North Logistics in Norway, a private-sector funded center, has undertaken studies, due to be completed in June 2009, on the business case for transarctic container shipping. The viability of deploying ships of various sizes by 2015 is being examined and include hundred-thousand-metric ton LNG carriers and up to five thousand twenty-foot-equivalent container ships.[22] There is also the possibility that the city of Adak, located in the Aleutian Islands of Alaska, in the United States, could serve as a possible international hub for Arctic shipping.[23] Both these developments seem to indicate an earlier ice-free passage via the Northern Sea Route. The U.S. National Intelligence Council, in its study *Global Trends 2025*, has suggested that the date for a seasonally ice-free Arctic could even be as soon as 2013.[24]

[20] Ola M. Johannessen and Lasse H. Pettersson, "Arctic Climate and Shipping," in *High North, High Stakes: Security, Energy, Transport, Environment*, eds. Rose Gottemoeller and Rolf Tamnes (Oslo: Fagbokforlaget, 2008), pp. 95–114.

[21] "First through Northeast Passage," *Barents Observer*, 9 September 2009, available at http://www.barentsobserver.com/first-through-northeast-passage.4629485–116320.html.

[22] Felix H. Tschudi, "Norwegian Commercial Perspective," presentation at the Conference on Energy Security in Asia, organized by the Norwegian Institute for Defence Studies and the China Foundation for International and Strategic Studies, Beijing, 21–22 May 2009, available at http://www.mil.no/multimedia/archive/00123/Tschudi_Energy_Secu_123699a.pdf.

[23] Hiromitsu Kitagawa, "Japanese Perspective," presentation at the Conference on Energy Security in Asia, organized by the Norwegian Institute for Defence Studies and the China Foundation for International and Strategic Studies, Beijing, 21–22 May 2009, available at http://www.mil.no/multimedia/archive/00123/Kitagawa_Beijing_Co_123695a.pdf.

[24] National Intelligence Council, *Global Trends 2025: A Transformed World* (Washington, D.C.: U.S. Government Printing Office, 2008), p. 53, available at http://www.dni.gov/nic/PDF_2025/2025_Global_Trends_Final_Report.pdf.

When the Northern Sea Route opens up, transiting through the NSR above Russia between the North Atlantic and the North Pacific would trim about five thousand nautical miles and a week's sailing time from the use of the Suez Canal and the Malacca Straits. This may have an adverse impact on existing regional container hubs like Singapore, which sits astride the main east-west transportation thoroughfare and is a major regional transshipment port. When container ships use the Northern Sea Route, it would make more economic sense for them to stop at new or existing ports in Northeast Asia and to use these ports instead of Singapore as transshipment centers to Southeast Asia. Possible ports that could be used in Northeast Asia include Hong Kong, Shanghai, and Tokyo. If this shift were to occur, the container volumes handled by the port of Singapore may decrease for four months of the year.

Despite the fact that a "blue" Arctic Ocean is predicted (four months) to occur during summertime from the middle of this century, current rates of warming indicate that this may occur much earlier. However, even before transpolar navigation is realized, routes along the coast of Siberia will be navigable much earlier. The opening up of the Northern Sea Route will have an adverse impact on the operations of current regional hub ports. It will also have an impact on the profitability of the current liners operating between Europe and Asia. Both liner and terminal operators, including those in Southeast Asia, will have to factor the early opening of the Northern Sea Route into their plans so that they are not to be caught off guard.[25]

IMPROVEMENTS NEEDED BEFORE SHIPPING IN THE ARCTIC BECOMES A REALITY

Before the Northern Sea Route can reliably be used as a transit route between Europe and Asia, several issues will need to be resolved. For example, for vessels operating in the Arctic, it is crucial for navigation to have access to synoptic environmental observations of the weather, sea-ice and ocean conditions, and their forecasts. Such information will be essential in both strategic and tactical navigation support and will help to ensure safe and efficient operation in ice-covered waters. In particular, though, six issues will need to be resolved. First, environmental monitoring and forecasting services providing meteorological, oceanographic, and sea-ice information to support shipping year-round will need to be significantly enhanced. Second, search and rescue as well as icebreaker support services, with increased seasonal and regional access, will need to be provided in a comprehensive manner. Third, experienced mariners who are trained for Arctic operations are needed to operate the ships. Fourth, new ship technology is required for independent ship operations in ice-covered waters, which will remain present for most of the year. Fifth, when

[25] Joshua Ho, "Arctic Meltdown Could Hurt Singapore," *Straits Times (Singapore)*, 6 July 2009, available at http://straitstimesasia1.com.sg.

traffic gets heavier, it may be necessary to implement vessel traffic systems (VTS) along narrow straits, which may end up as choke points, like the Barents Strait. Last, an integrated governance and regulatory framework based on the UN Convention on the Law of the Sea (UNCLOS) is needed.

When it comes to governance, there may be a need to adopt a more inclusive approach for the management of the Arctic routes. Currently, the Arctic Council is the forum for promoting cooperation, coordination, and interaction among the Arctic states, with the involvement of the Arctic indigenous communities and other inhabitants in common Arctic issues, in particular sustainable development and environmental protection in the Arctic. The council is a nontreaty, intergovernmental ministerial-level forum established by the Ottawa Declaration of 1996.[26] Members of the Arctic Council include Canada, Denmark, Finland, Iceland, Norway, Russia, Sweden, and the United States, five of which have Arctic Ocean basin coastlines and three of which have no coastlines in the central Arctic Ocean. As issues regarding the Arctic, especially shipping issues, may affect other stakeholders that are not members of the Arctic Council, a more inclusive approach may be required. Models exist in which stakeholders are included in discussions of the management of a critical waterway used for international navigation. For example, the Malacca Straits Cooperative Mechanism was established in 2007 under the principles of article 43 of UNCLOS to deal primarily with the safety and environmental protection issues along the Malacca Straits.[27] Maritime security issues may be addressed within the context of the cooperative mechanism, but they are secondary. The cooperative mechanism is led by the littoral states of Indonesia, Malaysia, and Singapore, but it includes other stakeholders, such as the International Maritime Organization, the Nippon Foundation, members of the shipping industry (e.g., Intertanko, Intercargo, BIMCO, International Chamber of Shipping), and other interested nonlittoral states in its Forum for Cooperation discussions.

CONCLUSION

Global warming and the resultant climate change are occurring at a rate that is much quicker than the median projections of previous IPCC models, and current global emissions of global greenhouse gases are already at the upper end of the IPCC model projections. The likelihood of global warming occurring beyond current

[26] Arctic Council Secretariat, "About the Arctic Council," 22 October 2007, available at http://arctic-council.org/article/about. See also "Declaration on the Establishment of the Arctic Council," available at http://arctic-council.org/filearchive/Declaration%20on%20the%20Establishment%20of%20the%20Arctic%20Council-1.pdf.
[27] Joshua H. Ho, "Enhancing Safety, Security and Environmental Protection of the Straits of Malacca and Singapore: The Cooperative Mechanism," *Ocean Development and International Law* 40, no. 2 (2009): pp. 233–47.

expectations is high if nothing is done to curb greenhouse-gas emissions. If indeed the warming trend does not abate, there will be severe consequences, including loss of habitat and arable land as a result of sea-level rise, which will reduce crop yields. Fish stocks are also expected to diminish as a result of ocean acidification and the degradation of coral reefs. Water resources are expected to diminish as a result of saltwater contamination from the rising sea level, reduced precipitation, and the drying up of the Himalayan glaciers which supply water to many Asian countries. Warm-weather afflictions, like malaria, and deaths are also expected to occur more frequently, and the extent of damage to physical infrastructure is expected to be larger given the increasing frequency and intensity of extreme weather events. As a secondary consequence, climate change is expected to exacerbate local conflicts, especially in regions where the governance structure is weak and thus unable to effectively redistribute scarce food and water resources equitably or quickly enough, thus resulting in a rush on those resources for survival.

In the area of shipping, many hub ports will have to either readjust their operational activities or to upgrade existing infrastructure to accommodate sea-level rise, which is expected to affect cities like Shanghai, Ningbo, Tokyo, and Singapore. The Arctic will be where warming will be the greatest, which will result in the opening up of new sea lanes, like the Northern Sea Route. The new sea lanes will enable shorter transit times between Europe and Northeast Asia, which will reduce sailing times by about a week, thus resulting in substantial cost savings for ship operators. However, although climate change may result in some benefits, in this case, the opening of new sea lanes, there will also be negative impacts. For example, with the opening up of the Northern Sea Route, current hub ports that lie along the east-west transportation thoroughfare, like Singapore, might be adversely affected as ship operators decide to use the ports in Northeast Asia as transshipment centers instead.

Despite the fact that there will be regional variation in the costs and benefits resulting from climate change, if nothing is done to reduce global greenhouse-gas emissions, the subsequent net global effect will be negative. Hence, tackling the effects of climate change is a true transnational issue and a global commons problem that requires substantial leadership commitment at the global level before it can be resolved. The *Stern Review* mentioned that there was no distinction in terms of impacts between developed and less developed countries – everyone will be affected, and hence everyone will have to contribute to limiting greenhouse-gas emissions to an acceptable rate.

Governments will have to overcome their deeply embedded shorter-term planning cycles and start embracing a longer time horizon, as some of the negative effects will be felt much sooner than expected, even if the full negative consequences will be felt in forty to fifty years' time. There is an urgency to substantially reduce carbon emissions – the longer the delay, the more difficult it is to reduce emissions, either because the reduction target may become too high and costly to implement or because it may be technologically impossible to remove such large amounts of carbon dioxide and its equivalents from the atmosphere. If we fail to act decisively soon, it will be doubtful whether we can avert this disaster on a global scale, and when that happens, we would have committed acts against humanity, essentially global genocide on our children and grandchildren, who are not represented at the elite levels or in government.

PART II

European Security Interests in the Arctic

4

Arctic Security and Norway

Rolf Tamnes

INTRODUCTION

Global warming is one of the most serious threats facing mankind. Many regions and countries will be affected, and there will be many losers. The earliest and most intense climatic changes are being experienced in the Arctic region. Arctic average temperature has risen at twice the rate of the global average in the past half century. These changes provide an early indication for the world of the environmental and societal significance of global warming. For that reason, the Arctic presents itself as an important scientific laboratory for improving our understanding of the causes and patterns of climate changes.

The rapidly rising temperature threatens the Arctic ecosystem, but the human consequences seem to be far less dramatic there than in many other places in the world. According to the U.S. National Intelligence Council, Russia has the potential to gain the most from increasingly temperate weather, because its petroleum reserves become more accessible and because the opening of an Arctic waterway could provide economic and commercial advantages.[1] Norway might also be fortunate. Some years ago, the *Financial Times* asked: "What should Norway do about the fact that global warming will make their climate more hospitable and enhance their financial situation, even as it inflicts damage on other parts of the world?"[2]

In many regions of the world, climate change might become a new source of conflict. According to some scholars and observers, confrontations will occur over rights to resources and boundaries in the Arctic as well. The overall picture in the north is one of cooperation, however, not conflict, and the region will probably remain one of the least troubled parts of the world. That being said, there are challenges, which are outlined in this chapter.

---

[1] National Intelligence Council, *Global Trends 2025: A Transformed World* (Washington, D.C.: National Intelligence Council, November 2008), p. 52.
[2] "There Is No New Chill in the Arctic," *Financial Times*, August 21, 2007.

This chapter focuses on the European Arctic, or the High North, in particular. Although the High North is an elastic concept and open to wide interpretation, here it means the northern parts of the Nordic countries and Russia, and the oceans and islands from Novaya Zemlya to Iceland.[3] The High North is Norway's main area of interest in the north. To some extent, it is also a distinct functional area, characterized by high activity and extensive cooperation in a number of fields. Although the High North will remain Norway's core area of interest in the north, Norwegian policy is about to take on a broader Arctic perspective because of the changes in the region. At the same time, one should bear in mind that neither the Arctic nor the High North can be seen in isolation from the rest of the world. Norwegian interests in the High North can be undermined by regional disputes or accidents, but of equal importance, events in other parts of the world may have repercussions for the north and put Norwegian interests to the test: security is indivisible.

To set the scene, first, I outline the connections between regional and global security. Second, I discuss the Arctic and High North security environment of today and tomorrow, both in terms of hard and soft security. Third, I address the main features of Norwegian policy in the north. Last, I wind up with some reflections over the conflict potential in the Arctic region in general and in the High North in particular.

INDIVISIBLE SECURITY

The advent of the nuclear age and revolutionary missile technology made it abundantly clear that security had become indivisible. Today, after a surge in globalization over the past two decades, "indivisible security" is more meaningful than ever before.

The security of the Arctic should be seen in such a perspective, because of the obvious connections between regional and global security. During the Cold War, the northern region played an important role in the nuclear and maritime contest between the two major blocs and superpowers. Some even argued that the region would become a strategic front in the case of a new world war. The reason for this assertion was the position of the Arctic in the so-called central balance between the superpowers. The far north was along the direct flight path of strategic missiles and bombers to and from the Soviet Union and United States. Furthermore, the buildup of the Kola bases from the 1960s made the region the centerpiece of Soviet maritime and sea-based strategic forces, which in turn contributed to a stronger U.S. and NATO involvement in the High North. Norway's role in this strategic environment was, first, to form a reasonable defense in strategically important parts of the country while awaiting the arrival of external reinforcements. A great number

---

[3] See, e.g., "Where Is the 'High North?'" GeoPolitics in the High North, http://www.geopoliticsnorth .org/index.php?option=com_content&;view=article&id=1:an-international-research-project&catid=1: latest-news, accessed February 1, 2011.

of preparations were made in peacetime to make early and effective Allied support a credible option. Second, large arrays of intelligence and early warning stations and facilities in Norway were a significant contribution to watching Soviet strategic forces and activities.[4]

Although the end of the Cold War saw the High North quickly lose its geopolitical significance, and as NATO resources allotted to the defense of Norway were reduced, there was still an obvious connection between regional Arctic and global security. The Kola Peninsula was one of the regions in Russia with the highest concentration of surplus and deteriorating nuclear material. With the deep crisis in President Boris Yeltsin's Russia as a backdrop, the extensive Cold War legacy and severe safety and security shortcomings presented substantial global threats. A nuclear accident in Russia could have had far-reaching implications, and dangerous material could have come into the hands of terrorists or states aspiring for a place in the club of the nuclear powers. Many nations and institutions have been involved in trying to manage the problem. Norway, for example, has spent about US $240 million under the framework of its Action Plan for Nuclear Safety to eliminate tactical submarines, spent nuclear fuel, and radioactive waste.[5] The United States has been involved in a number of nonproliferation programs as well, including the important contribution of the Nunn-Lugar Cooperative Threat Reduction (CTR) Program, the aim of which is to secure and reduce strategic nuclear weapons in the former Soviet Union (FSU) area. Under this program, more than thirty strategic submarines and hundreds of launchers and missiles have been dismantled and destroyed. Since 2002, these efforts are included in the G8 Global Partnership against the Spread of Weapons and Materials of Mass Destruction, which is the G8's principal response to the attacks of September 11, 2001, and global proliferation concerns. Important work remains to be done, but the challenges we face today are modest compared to those of the early 1990s.

In the future, a number of both traditional and new factors will sustain the linkage between regional and global security. The High North will remain important in Russia's maritime and nuclear strategy. High North security will be influenced by melting ice and intensified exploration of the Arctic for transportation and energy purposes, and both questions are closely linked to developments in global markets and politics. Secure and stable access to energy is vital to any state. The resources in the north could enhance energy security by reducing the estimated gaps between demand and supply, although the value of the High North in terms of diversification of supply is debatable, as most of the petroleum potential is found in the Russian

---

[4] Rolf Tamnes, "The Strategic Importance of the High North during the Cold War," in *A History of NATO: The First Fifty Years*, vol. 3, ed. Gustav Schmidt (Basingstoke, UK: Palgrave, 2001).

[5] Norwegian Ministry of Foreign Affairs, "Cooperation with Russia on Nuclear Safety and Environmental Protection in the High North," Government White Paper No. 11 (2009–10), April 23, 2010, http://www.regjeringen.no/nb/dep/ud/dok/regpubl/stmeld/2009–2010/Meld-St-11–2009-2010.html?id=601598.

sector. Norway could add value to energy security because it is a stable supplier, but Norway's resources in the north are quite small compared to those of Russia. In a long-term perspective, with the rise of Asia on the international arena, major Asian powers are likely to look to the north as well. Will that make the Arctic and the High North less peaceful? That will depend first of all on developments outside the region. In a world of multipolarity, the security of the north will be heavily influenced by the overall relationship between the major powers. Conflicts or events in other parts of the world could have severe repercussions in the north and put Norwegian interests to the test. Security is indivisible. That makes the security environment of the north very unpredictable.

THE RUSSIA FACTOR, HARD AND SOFT SECURITY

Because of Russia's size and stature, it has the potential to play a prominent role in shaping the security environment of the Arctic. Russia has enormous petroleum resources and important deposits of other mineral and biological resources in the north, and its shoreline covers around 50 percent of the latitude circle. Although that makes Russia vulnerable to new threats and risks associated with melting ice, it also gives it a unique chance to influence many of the activities in the Arctic in the future. Moscow is a determined player in the north and it has high ambitions in the region. Will the Russians succeed in fulfilling their ambitions? How cooperative can we expect them to be? We don't know the answers to these questions. Russia's social, economic, and political structures are fragile, and that makes it particularly hard to predict the future of the country.

Hard-core realism is an important feature of Russia's strategic culture. Key factors in its conception of international relations are the primacy of military power and natural resources, competition among great powers, spheres of interests, and zero-sum games. Since the turn of the century, the Russian discourse has given more prominence to reversing the "retreats" of the 1990s.[6] At the same time, Russian foreign policy has been characterized by turmoil and change. Yeltsin's Russia was pragmatic but chaotic and impotent. During the presidency of Vladimir Putin, a period that coincided with high oil and gas prices, Russian policy was overly self-confident and nationalistic. Under Dmitry Medvedev, the world has since 2008 seen a more cooperative and conciliatory Russia. That might be the beginning of a new era, or yet another swing of the pendulum.

These patterns are also mirrored in the north. After the collapse of the Soviet empire and the perceived humiliations on other fronts, the north stands out as an intriguing arena for Russia eager to sustain its status as a great power. Its Arctic policy contains elements of isolationism and exclusiveness, illustrated by its opposition to NATO's involvement and to non-Arctic nations as partners in the region. At the same

[6] Pavel K. Baev, "Troublemaking and Risk-Taking: The North in Russian Military Activities," in *Russia and the North*, ed. Elana Wilson Rowe (Ottawa: University of Ottawa Press, 2009), p. 17.

time, its foreign policy in the north has become more conspicuously cooperative in recent years. The dialogue among the northern nations about Arctic affairs has created a spirit of confidence, and the economic downturn has made the Russians realize how much they need partners to handle future challenges and benefit from the new opportunities. It is also in Russia's interest to maintain peace and stability, and working together is instrumental in its attempt to avert a joint NATO front in the Arctic. There is therefore reason to assume that Russia will play an important and constructive role in the years to come in coping with the many Arctic challenges that lay ahead of us, including the new security challenges created by the receding ice cap and increased activity in the north.

At the same time, there are limits to cooperation. Traditional hard-core security is a particular obstacle. The north remains a crucial factor in Russia's geostrategy. The High North region is an important test bed for new weapons and has a prominent place in Russia's nuclear strategy. Strong nuclear forces are essential for Russia to uphold its great power status, even more so because its weakness in conventional forces has led it to emphasize the role of nuclear deterrent in military strategy. For those reasons, maintaining and upgrading Russia's nuclear force has the highest priority. Since 2006, following a long period of economic hardship and decay, we have seen a major increase in Russian military activity in the north, both in the air and maritime domains.

Russia's strategic nuclear submarines are an essential part of the triad of deterrence, and the protection of the nuclear ballistic-missile submarine force (or SSBNs) is one of the most important missions of the Russian navy in general. According to some sources, the navy attracts more than 40 percent of the defense budget, and half of that money is spent on the strategic submarine force. It consists of ten fully operational submarines – six *Delta IV*s in the Northern Fleet and four *Delta III*s in the Pacific Fleet. In addition, one *Typhoon* is used as a test platform for new missiles. Russia is facing formidable problems modernizing its SSBN fleet, especially in building the new *Borey* or *Dolgoruky* class and even more so in developing Bulava, the new generation missile.[7] The Russians will probably succeed in the end, but the size of the force will shrink before it can possibly grow again, and in the short term, the number of submarines will be far lower than estimated in Russian plans. In 2015, for example, the Russians plan to have about fourteen submarines. Up to ten submarines is a more realistic figure, including *Delta IV*–class and *Dolgoruky*-class submarines.[8]

The submarine nuclear force is one factor shaping the strategic environment of the High North, because the submarines are located in the Kola Peninsula and because they operate near or under the ice cap, known as the bastion. The bastion

7 Pavel Felgenhauer, "The Bulava SLBM and the US-Russian Arms Talks," *Eurasia Daily Monitor*, December 17, 2009.
8 The *Typhoon*-class submarines were an important part of the SSBN force during the last part of the Cold War, but none of them has operative missiles today. Two of them will most likely be retrofitted to carry a new generation of sea-based cruise missiles.

concept was abandoned in the late 1980s, but deployments were resumed some years ago. Furthermore, the Northern Fleet's general-purpose forces operate in a wide area in the vicinity of Norway, including the Norwegian Sea, to prevent Western air and naval forces from threatening Russian interest in general and the SSBN fleet in particular.

Russia's airborne nuclear capability is another important element of the strategic environment of the north. The strategic bombers of Russia's Long Range Aviation (LRA) represent the core of that capability. In 2007, Russia resumed regular strategic flights over the Arctic and started to make more extensive use of bases in the north. The main mission of the flights is basically the same as during the Cold War, as demonstrated by training sorties with Tu-95MS Bear H and Tu-160 Blackjack flown toward North America along the western, northern, and eastern routes. The aircraft operate from the main air bases at Engels and Ukrainka and are normally supported by aircraft operating out of the forward air bases at Olenegorsk, Vorkuta, Tiksi, and Anadyr. Strategic sorties along the western route are usually combined with operations into the High North and the North Atlantic with medium and light bombers such as Tu-22M Backfire C and Su-24 Fencer. Furthermore, Russia has carried out separate training operations toward strategically important areas in northern Norway, especially Bodø and Lofoten, traditionally a key area in Norwegian and NATO defense efforts. In line with recent years' heightened activity in Russian military forces, there have been more flights with strategic bombers per year than in the entire period from 1991 to 2006. At the same time, we must keep in mind that activity levels are far lower than during an average year during the Cold War.

Russia also keeps a variety of nonstrategic combat-ready forces from all services in the northern area of the Leningrad Military District, and they include a significant number of tactical nuclear weapons of all kinds. The Northern Fleet's "blue water" assets are key among the nonstrategic forces. In addition are the local forces, whose main task is to protect Russia's sovereignty and interests in general and the maritime and strategic forces in particular against perceived threats from NATO and the United States. The Russians are also preparing themselves to send reinforcements to the High North. The pattern of operations is similar to what occurred during the Cold War, although the scale is more modest.

These are the present military postures. Some of them will change in the future. First, new threats and risks might lead Russia to broaden the target lists of the strategic nuclear forces to cover other major powers and objects along its southern perimeter to a greater extent than today. To the LRA in particular, the northern forward bases and flight paths may become less important in relative terms than they are today. Second, in the long term, there is every reason to ask whether Russia will have the economic muscle to uphold a fully fledged nuclear triad. One hypothetical scenario sees Russia, for economic or technological reasons, failing to develop or make use of the next generations of strategic submarines and missiles. The problem could be further aggravated should the Arctic Ocean become ice-free for the warmer part of the year, thus preventing strategic submarines from taking shelter near or under the ice cap. Should this happen, Russia might abandon the sea leg of its triad. Such a step would remove a major rationale for the Northern Fleet and indeed reduce significantly the geostrategic importance of the High North.[9] Such a chain of events cannot be ruled out.

However, in the foreseeable future, traditional hard security will continue to play an important role in Russia's strategy for the High North and influence its relationship with Norway. Russia will uphold major military bases close to Norway, and the forces will operate in the vicinity of Norway for both defensive and offensive purposes. From a Russian perspective, Norway will be seen not only as a good neighbor but also as a member of NATO – and through the prism of the power ministries.

In recent years, much attention has been paid to the soft security challenges that will come with the rapidly diminishing Arctic ice cover and the subsequent surge in activity. Many tend to overdramatize the speed and scale at which the ice is melting. Although we should expect major changes, there is every reason to warn against those who hold that the Arctic is about to become ice-free and navigable for most of the year.[10] Ice conditions vary from one part of the Arctic to another. Most of the European Arctic is accessible most of the year already, and of the main transpolar routes, the Northern Sea Route (NSR) along the Russian coast most probably will be the first route to be developed, not only to ship more natural resources out and supplies in but also to enable intercontinental transit.[11] The economic potential of the NSR to Russia is very great indeed, and from a military viewpoint, the sea route is important in binding Russia's Northern and Pacific fleets together. The most difficult aspects of international transit passage are the ice conditions, and also Russian national interests, red tape and high fees, and indeed Russia's traditional attitude of exclusiveness. The overall economic viability of transpolar voyages remains unclear. Should the NSR be opened up for extensive passage by foreign vessels, the international community, including Norway, would have to bear some of the responsibility for tackling the soft security challenges that come with it.

[9] Rolf Tamnes: "Et større Norge," in *Vendepunkter i norsk utenrikspolitikk. Nye internasjonale vilkår etter den kalde krigen* [An Expanding Small State: Turning Points in Norwegian Foreign Policy], eds. Even Lange, Helge Pharo, and Øyvind Østerud (Oslo: Unipub, 2009), pp. 306–21.

[10] Arctic Council, *Arctic Marine Shipping Assessment 2009 Report*, approved at the 2009 Arctic Council Ministerial meeting in Tromsø in April 2009.

[11] Russia claims the straits along the route as part of its internal waters. On the basis of the UN Convention on the Law of the Sea (UNCLOS), Russia also claims formal jurisdiction in its exclusive economic zone to unilaterally adopt and enforce nondiscriminatory laws and environmental regulations where ice coverage and severe climate conditions cause exceptional hazards to navigation and where pollution could cause major harm to the ecological balance. The United States in particular maintains that the NSR should be considered international straits, and thus open to transit passage. See Claes Lykke Ragner, *The Northern Sea Route*, Fridtjof Nansen Institute, http://www.fni.no/publ/marine.html#nsr_norden.

In addition to transportation, energy exploitation represents the most dynamic activity in the Arctic. According to a study published by the U.S. Geological Survey (USGS) in 2008, 13 percent of the world's undiscovered oil resources and 30 percent of the natural gas resources are located north of the Arctic Circle; 70 percent of natural gas resources are in the Russia sector.[12] On the basis of these assessments, the Arctic stands out as one of the most promising new energy frontiers in the world. However, there are many pitfalls along the road. First, the USGS figures involve a high degree of uncertainty. Second, in a global perspective, the size of Arctic resources is less impressive if we also include the significant discovered resources. Of the world's remaining recoverable petroleum resources – discovered and undiscovered – between 10 percent and 15 percent is estimated to be in the Arctic. Third, the technological, logistical, and environmental challenges are tremendous, and the Arctic will remain a high cost region for extraction. Fourth, exploitation of Russian offshore resources could be severely hampered by the many dysfunctional features of the political and economic systems of the country. Fifth, exploitation of unconventional gas resources, notably shale gas production in North America, is gathering momentum as successful development and deployment of new technologies enable such resources to be produced at costs similar to those of conventional gas. Russia's resources in the north could therefore become less attractive in a market perspective. Some would emphasize the political merits of the matter, that unconventional gas may prove pivotal in curbing Russia's ability to use its natural gas as an energy weapon.[13] In any case, the pace at which Russia's natural gas in the Arctic is exploited will be much slower than was anticipated only a few years ago. This is the broad Arctic picture.

Extraction of most of the Arctic petroleum has no bearing on the High North, neither the considerable onshore and offshore resources in Alaska and Canada nor most of the significant Russia petroleum resources in the Arctic that will be piped overland to markets in Europe and Asia. However, petroleum activity will also grow in the High North. First, production within the High North region will increase, both in the energy-rich Russian sector and in the Norwegian sector. Second, petroleum in general and liquefied natural gas (LNG) in particular from Russian fields farther to the east, such as the Yamal Peninsula and the Kara Sea, might be shipped at some future time to international markets via the High North.

The opening of the Arctic and increased activity create a number of soft security challenges, such as oil spills, sabotage, smuggling, illegal migration, and cruise ship

[12] U.S. Geological Survey, *Circum-Arctic Resource Appraisal: Estimates of Undiscovered Oil and Gas North of the Arctic Circle* (Washington, D.C.: U.S. Geological Survey, 2008), http://energy.usgs.gov/arctic/.

[13] International Energy Agency, *World Energy Outlook* (Paris: Organization for Economic Cooperation and Development and International Energy Agency, 2009), pp. 397–413; Amy Myers Jaffe, "Russia and the Caspian States in the Global Energy Balance," working paper, James A. Baker III Institute for Public Policy, Rice University, May 6, 2009.

accidents. One of the nightmare scenarios would be a cruise ship catastrophe. In June 1989, the Russian cruise liner *Maxim Gorkiy* hit old, solid ice near Svalbard and started taking in water. Fortunately for the more than one thousand passengers and crew, the weather was good and a Norwegian Coast Guard vessel near the ship. The outcome could have been far more dramatic had the accident taken place in a more remote place and in worse weather.

Enhanced governance is essential to meet the soft security challenges in the Arctic. The U.S. Deputy Secretary of State James Steinberg argued in April 2010 that the Arctic stands out as a test case of the ability of the international community to deal with the great transnational issues of the twenty-first century.[14] The cooperative spirit in the north is basically good, but it will take a far broader multistakeholder approach to succeed. The UN Convention on the Law of the Sea (UNCLOS) is the overall legal framework and basic tool for managing the Arctic Ocean and its resources, including soft security challenges. An UNCLOS-based governance system could enhance security and stability, and ensure strict environmental management and sustainable use of resources. A binding and more comprehensive polar code under the framework of the International Maritime Organization could also make a significant difference.[15] The Arctic Council, which has strengthened its reputation in recent years, plays a constructive role in designing cooperative frameworks in many fields, including in search and rescue.

To meet the soft security challenges, the five littoral states will have to take on a special responsibility to procure new capabilities, to develop more adequate emergency response facilities, and to pool resources to achieve maximum effect, but they will have to act in concert with a great number of countries and institutions. Contributions from non-Arctic stakeholders are of particular interest, such as shipping and oil companies and other nations that will have strong footprints in the north in the future.

Some argue for an extended role for NATO in the north. The central purpose of the NATO alliance, embodied in article 5 of the North Atlantic Treaty, is to safeguard the security of its member nations. The new soft security challenges are primarily in the maritime domain and at the margins of the core obligation, but the alliance has transformed and contributes already to the broader security of the Euro-Atlantic region. The capabilities of NATO could contribute significantly to enhancing situational awareness while adding value to protecting maritime trade, lines of communication, and critical infrastructure. However, such participation is controversial because the Russians insist on keeping the alliance at arm's length in the north. Their opposition carries a great deal of weight, even more so because

[14] U.S. Strategic Interests in the Arctic, Center for Strategic and International Studies conference, April 8, 2010, http://csis.org/event/us-strategic-interests-high-north-0.

[15] Joe Borg, "Opportunities and Responsibilities in the Arctic Region: The European Union's Perspective," *Zeitschrift für ausländisches öffentliches Recht und Völkerrecht* Vol. 69, No. 3 (2009): pp. 517–22.

cooperation in tackling soft security challenges represents a unique opportunity to build mutually beneficial relations with the Russians. Russia and NATO might eventually come to terms, but in the near future, drawing on NATO will have to be balanced against the need for engaging Russia.

ARCTIC STRATEGIES – THE CASE OF NORWAY

Over the past few years, many countries and international bodies have taken a stronger interest in Arctic matters, and many of them will play an important role in shaping the Arctic's future. However, the key responsibility will rest with the five nations bordering the Arctic Ocean.

All littoral states have launched broad strategies or authoritative statements that deal not only with traditional security but also with the new great opportunities and the challenges that come with the opening up of the region. They all address – to various degrees – the need to strengthen efforts in exercising sovereignty, in protecting the environment, in promoting economic and social development, and in improving northern governance.[16] Traditional security is more prominent in Russian and Norwegian plans than in those of the United States, Canada, and Denmark. To the latter states, soft security or homeland security is the overarching concern in the Arctic, although the rhetoric emanating from them might sometimes create a different impression. As General Walter J. Natyncyk, chief of the defense staff, Canada, pointed out in November 2009, "There is no conventional military threat to the Arctic. If someone were to invade the Canadian Arctic my first task would be to rescue them."[17]

Russia and Norway are unique among the Arctic states in their long-lasting and wide-ranging engagement in the north, both economically and militarily, and in both cases there is a high degree of continuity in their policies. The Arctic features prominently in Russia's many documents on policy and strategy. Although Russia has high ambitions in the north, the challenges are at the same time daunting. Russia plans to re-create a powerful navy in the next ten years, develop a number of third-generation nuclear-powered icebreakers, and reinforce the FSB-controlled border groups by establishing a coast guard service to patrol Russia's Arctic borders. It is hard to believe that Russia has the capacity to meet such high ambitions. The gaps between plans, budgetary means, and administrative efficiency are overwhelming.

Norway's High North policy has traditionally paid special attention to three main issues. The first has been to manage the often-demanding relationship with the Soviet Union and then Russia. The second has been to uphold sovereignty and

---

[16] Rob Huebert, *The Newly Emerging Arctic Security Environment*, Canadian Defence and Foreign Affairs Institute, March 2010, http://www.geopoliticsnorth.org/index.php?option=com_content&view=article&id=84&Itemid=69.

[17] Halifax International Security Forum, "Panel IV: Arctic Security: The New Great Game?," November 21, 2009, http://www.gmfus.org/halifax/transcripts.html.

exercise authority over the Svalbard archipelago in accordance with the Svalbard Treaty of 1920. The treaty recognizes Norway's full and absolute sovereignty over the archipelago but forbids the use of Svalbard for warlike purposes and requires the nationals of the signatory powers to be treated equally with respect to certain activities specified in the treaty. Svalbard has been one of the most difficult issues in Norwegian foreign policy, especially because the Russians have tried to make it a bilateral relationship and acquire special rights for Russia. To maintain a foothold there is vital to the Kremlin to secure a Russian presence in the western Atlantic.[18] Since the 1970s, Norway has invested significantly in modernizing what had traditionally been a primitive coal mining community. The Russians tend to see the rules and regulations that come with modernization – including a strict environmental policy – as a deliberate effort to oust them from the archipelago.

The third issue has been to take care of Norway's economic interests, first and foremost the harvesting of marine resources. This interest portfolio has become broader in recent years.[19] The revolution in the law of the sea in the 1960s and 1970s, which led Norway to proclaim sovereign rights over its continental shelf as well as two-hundred-mile zones, laid the foundation for prosperous economic activities at sea. The Barents Sea has long been appreciated for its rich stocks of fish, which are managed jointly and successfully by Norway and Russia.[20] However, the law-of-the-sea revolution also created a number of foreign policy challenges vis-à-vis other countries, and new platforms were needed to manage and control the fisheries.

The king of the Norwegian economy, however, is the petroleum sector. Although total production is modest on a global scale, the production makes a difference in world markets because most of it is sent abroad. Whereas oil production is falling, gas production is going up, and Norway is today the second-largest natural gas exporter in the world. Gas from Norway represents 30 percent of what Germany and France consume. Until recently, Norwegian production was concentrated in the North Sea and the Norwegian Sea, but Norway is about to enter the Barents Sea as well. The Snow White gas field, the world's northernmost LNG facility, came on stream in 2007. About 17 percent of the total petroleum resources – and 30 percent of the undiscovered resources – on the Norwegian continental shelf are probably in the Barents Sea.[21] Although that number is a significant volume for a small country, Norway's share of the undiscovered Arctic resources is quite small, some 3.3 percent of the estimated total. Oil and gas production in the north will present Norway, like the other Arctic states, with a number of challenges – including protection of the

[18] "Spitsbergen Secures Russian Presence in Western Arctic," *Barents Observer*, October 19, 2007.

[19] Rolf Tamnes, *Norsk Utenrikspolitikks Historie*, vol. 6, *Oljealder 1965–1995* [The History of Norwegian Foreign Policy, vol. 6, Oil Age, 1965–1995] (Oslo: Universitetsforlaget, 1997), pp. 257–73.

[20] Øystein Jensen and Svein Vigeland Rottem, "The Politics of Security and International Law in Norway's Arctic Waters," *Polar Record* 46, no. 236 (2010): p. 78.

[21] Ministry of Petroleum and Energy and Norwegian Petroleum Directorate, *Facts: The Norwegian Petroleum Sector 2009*, 2009, pp. 30, 82, http://www.npd.no/en/Publications/Facts/Facts-2009/ June 9, 2009.

fragile Arctic environment, preservation and conservation of the valuable renewable fish resources, and the security of the petroleum infrastructure.

The awareness of major climate change and of the great petroleum potential in the Arctic gained momentum in Norway shortly after the turn of the century, nourished by the reports from the U.S. Geological Survey in 2000 and the Arctic Climate Impact Assessment four years later. In the fall of 2005, the new center-left government declared the High North Norway's most important strategic priority in the years ahead. In addition to the perception of fundamental change in the Arctic, domestic politics also played a role when the government launched a more ambitious High North policy. The north was seen as a winning card in the general election that year. In Norway, as in Canada and Russia, the north is an important component of the national identity. Indeed, since 2005, it has been politically incorrect to criticize active involvement in the north. Critics of the government's policy have argued that the ambitions are not bold enough.

The government identified in 2005 a number of challenges in the north but also new and great opportunities. Authorities in Oslo were euphoric about the prospects of working with Russia on petroleum matters across a wide front, and they envisaged benefits accruing to Norway from exploitation in Russia, especially the huge Shtokman gas and condensate field in the Barents Sea, which is estimated to contain 3.8 trillion cubic meters of gas. The scale of this optimism faded after a while, however, both because the Putin regime proved far less interested in foreign involvement than expected and because many obstacles to exploitation of Russian oil and natural gas remained. Today, the government sees developments in the north in a generational perspective.[22] That perspective does not prevent it from designating the north Norway's most important strategic priority area.

Norway's High North policy has a number of dimensions. I deal with three of them here: foreign policy, defense policy, and development policy.

The main objective of the overarching foreign policy is to protect national sovereignty and sovereign rights. To that end, high priority is given to promoting stability, predictability, and low tension ("High North – low tension"), and to ensuring sustainable management of the rich fisheries and energy resources in the region. Enhanced cooperation with Russia and other partners is a key foreign policy objective. Cooperation with Russia is based on the idea of two neighbors sharing a common destiny. Since the end of the Cold War, bridges have been built in a great number of fields. Today, the bilateral cooperation flourishes, and the political dialogue is better than ever before. However, the bilateral relationship is also characterized by asymmetry: a small state on the one hand and an unpredictable great power on the other hand. Engaging with Russia is therefore balanced by a

---

[22] Jonas Gahr Støre (foreign minister), "Perspectives on Current and Future Challenges in the High North," in *High North: High Stakes – Security, Energy, Transport, Environment*, eds. Rose Gottemoeller and Rolf Tamnes (Bergen: Fagbokforlaget, 2008), pp. 11–21.

policy of reassurance to create a multilateral cooperative environment involving Western countries and institutions. One visible expression of this policy since 2005 is Norway's invitation to a number of Western countries and the European Union to participate in so-called High North dialogues, another is the Norwegian government's "core function initiative" of 2008, which highlights the importance of the concept of collective self-defense in NATO's article 5 and the need for more tangible Alliance footprints "in area."[23] Now, NATO is about respond to such expectations and will in the years to come do more to reaffirm its readiness in practice.

That brings me to the second dimension of Norway's High North policy. In its defense policy, the government has been anxious not only to revitalize the NATO guarantee but also to maintain a visible national military presence in the north. This ambition was strengthened after the change of government in 2005. Since 1990, a major portion of the Norwegian Armed Forces' material investments has been allocated to platforms and weapons whose main theater of operations is the maritime domain and the north. Among these investments are a coast guard icebreaker, five frigates, six missile torpedo boats, and fourteen helicopters for frigates and coast guard ships. The priority of the north is even more striking if we also include the relocation since 2008 of the national joint headquarters, the coast guard headquarters, and the army inspector general from the south to the north.

Although hard security continues to explain the government's prioritizing of the north, in recent years, soft security considerations have gained momentum. They include the need to control fishing boats, protect oil and gas infrastructure, and handle oil spills and shipping accidents. International coordination of search-and-rescue and emergency capabilities and joint exercises is an area where the activity has increased. One example is the biannual Barents Rescue exercises, which involve the Nordic countries and Russia. The first exercise took place in 2001, the fourth in September 2009. Another example is the joint Russian-Norwegian naval exercise Pomor 2010, the first bilateral military exercise in sixteen years and the most extensive bilateral exercise ever. The forces trained a great number of missions, stretching from firings at aerial and sea surface targets and antipiracy operations to rescue of sailors in distress.

The third dimension, what we could call development policy, has been a key component of the government's High North agenda since 2005. Its main features were presented in the government's "Strategy for the High North" in December 2006 and elaborated further in March 2009 in the document "New Building Blocks in the North: The Next Step in the Government's High North Strategy."[24] The

---

[23] Cf. Espen Barth Eide (state secretary of defense), "Collective Defence in Today's Security Environment," presentation at the Strategic Concept Seminar, Luxembourg, October 16, 2009, http://www.regjeringen.no/nb/dep/fd/aktuelt/taler_artikler/politisk_ledelse/statssekretaer_espen_barth_eide/2009/collective-defence-in-todays-security-en.html?id=582015.

[24] "The Norwegian Government's Strategy for the High North," December 1, 2006, http://www.regjeringen.no/en/dep/ud/Documents/Reports-programmes-of-action-and-plans/Action-plans-and-

policy is guided by three principles: presence, activity, and knowledge. Of several development initiatives one should mention the plans to establish an international center of climate and environmental research in Tromsø in northern Norway; to develop an integrated monitoring and notification system; to commission a new ice-class research vessel; to improve maritime safety, emergency systems, and oil-spill response; to stimulate marine bioprospecting; and to map the diversity of the seabed. The objective of the development policy is to facilitate the efforts to meet the many challenges and lay the foundations of economic and social development in the north. In addition, the many concrete measures could also serve wider foreign policy aims, such as securing a strong Norwegian footprint in the north, engaging with Russia, and involving Western countries and institutions.

Norway's combined military and nonmilitary measures in the north in recent years are significant compared with those of the other Arctic states. These activities can be explained by what is at stake and Norway's strong economic muscle.

THE CONFLICT POTENTIAL

Many see a potential for conflict over establishing boundaries and rights to resources in the Arctic. In October 2008, the European Parliament expressed concern about "the ongoing race for natural resources in the Arctic, which may lead to security threats for the EU and overall international instability."[25] There are numerous references to "the scramble for the Arctic," reminiscent of "the scramble for Africa" in the age of imperialism more than a century ago. "The great game in a cold climate" is another catch phrase, and we are led to think of the rivalry between the Russian and British empires in Central Asia in the nineteenth century. These metaphors create a highly misleading image of the situation in the Arctic. As Brooke Smith-Windsor has rightly pointed out, it is time to stop "sexing up" Arctic security issues.[26]

We should bear in mind the long history of successful regional cooperation on resources management by the states in the region and that the most promising petroleum reserves are probably in areas of undisputed national jurisdiction. The Arctic states have common interests in securing peace and stability in the region to lay the ground for economic activity, and all Arctic states have consistently reiterated their commitment to solving overlapping claims under established treaties, notably

programmes/2006/strategy-for-the-high-north.html?id=448697; "New Building Blocks in the North: The Next Step in the Government's High North Strategy," March 12, 2009, http://www.regjeringen.no/upload/UD/Vedlegg/Nordområdene/new_building_blocks_in_the_north.pdf.

[25] European Parliament resolution on Arctic Governance, October 9, 2008, http://www.europarl.europa.eu/sides/getDoc.do?type=TA&language=EN&reference=P6-TA-2008--0474.

[26] Brooke Smith-Windsor, "Time to Stop 'Sexing Up' Arctic Security Issues," *Jane's Defence Weekly*, August 19, 2009, p. 21.

UNCLOS, and customary international law. Four of the five littoral Arctic states are NATO allies, and the likelihood of their not being able to solve disputes amicably is extremely remote. We might face diplomatic crises and incidents involving military forces, but all-out military conflict over resources and boundaries is unlikely.[27]

Norway has for all practical purposes settled all its maritime boundary delimitation issues in the north. The ultimate issue was resolved in September 2010, when Norway and Russia signed an agreement on maritime delimitation in the Barents Sea and the Arctic Ocean. The agreement divides the formerly disputed area of about 175,000 square kilometers between the Norwegian median line position and the Russian sector line position into two parts of approximately the same size. The question had been a bone of contention for forty years, and compromise was complicated by Russia's Northern Fleet operating in those waters and the considerable petroleum reserves.[28] Norway had been willing to accept a deal along the lines of the agreement since the 1970s, so it was a change on the Russian side that catalyzed the breakthrough. The agreement underlines the primacy of peaceful negotiations based on international law and matches Russia's new tendency to adopt a mellower tone in the conduct of its foreign policy.[29] The agreement will be politically beneficial to both countries. It offers new opportunities for Norwegian companies who are hungry for new pastures to replace the dwindling North Sea resources. To the Russians, the resources in the area may stand out as an attractive alternative to exploitation farther north, and, in the longer run, as a possible springboard for production deep inside the Arctic.

One major legal question remains to be settled in the High North, however. As mentioned earlier, Svalbard has been a difficult issue in Norwegian foreign policy. Norwegian legislation and enforcement in the archipelago have been and remain a source of friction with Russia in particular. Furthermore, the legal status of the waters and the continental shelf around Svalbard is disputed. Under the Norwegian position, the 1920 treaty provisions, including the principle of equal rights, do not apply beyond the territories of the archipelago and their territorial waters, and Norway therefore has full jurisdiction in maritime areas beyond the

27 Cf. Alf Håkon Hoel, "The High North Legal-Political Regime," in *Security Prospects in the High North: Geostrategic Thaw or Freeze?*, eds. Sven G. Holtsmark and Brooke A. Smith-Windsor, NATO Defense College (NDC) Forum Paper No. 7 (Rome: NATO Defense College, 2009), pp. 81–101.

28 Some argue that the reserves of the entire area surpass those of the Shtokman field, but the estimates are uncertain because no drilling has taken place. "Rosneft wants opening of Russian-Norwegian disputed waters," *Barents Observer* October 15, 2009; Llion Wyn Pritchard, "The Norwegian Barents Sea: Historical Overview and Future Perspectives," Information Handling Services (IHS), http://energy.ihs.com/News/published-articles/articles/norwegian-barents-sea-historical-overview-future-perspectives.htm.

29 "Thaw in the Arctic," *Financial Times* April 29, 2010; Norwegian Ministry of Foreign Affairs, "Treaty on Maritime Delimitation and Cooperation in the Barents Sea and the Arctic Ocean Signed Today," September 15, 2010, http://www.regjeringen.no/en/dep/ud/aktuelt/nyheter/2010/avtale_undertegnet.html?id=614295.

territorial waters.[30] This view is contested by Russia, Britain, Iceland, and a number of other countries. The Svalbard issues could ignite disputes but hardly a major conflict unless linked to broader conflict patterns or major changes in Russian politics.

What is the conflict potential in the Arctic and the High North in the longer-term perspective? Prediction is hard, even more so because the flapping of a butterfly's wing might change the course of history. However, one factor deserves to be mentioned in particular. The rise of Asia will reshape the power dynamics in the world, and should the Arctic ice cover continue to diminish, countries like China, Japan, and South Korea will probably become major actors in the north. They may find the Arctic petroleum resources attractive, make significant footprints in commercial shipping, and possibly establish a visible military presence in the Arctic. Could such involvement lead to more conflicts in the Arctic? Much will depend on the character of the future multipolar system. Tensions and conflicts between the great powers also probably will affect security in the north. Should a concert of great powers emerge, however, similar to the concert of Europe by the victorious powers of the Napoleonic wars, conflicts might be solved through consultation. If anything, these reflections illustrate the indivisibility of security.

CONCLUSION

In the foreseeable future, the High North will most likely remain one of the most untroubled parts of the world. That being said, traditional hard security will continue to play an important role in the High North, especially because Russia will keep strategic forces and continue operate in the area. Some regional issues also have the potential of igniting disputes that can threaten or undermine Norwegian interests and security.

Of equal importance, the rapidly melting ice and the surge in activity will introduce a number of demanding soft security challenges. It will take a multistakeholder approach to succeed. Russia is a key player in the north and must be part of any solution. The new challenges represent a unique opportunity to build mutually beneficial relations with the Russians.

How will the strategic environment of the north look like in a long-term perspective? Will the Arctic ice cover continue to diminish at a fast pace? How attractive will the Arctic resources be thirty years from now? Where will the fragile Russia go from here? Major Asian powers might become important actors in the north. Will that make the High North less peaceful or not? We don't know.

---

[30] Rolf Einar Fife (director general, Legal Affairs Department, Royal Ministry of Foreign Affairs), "Svalbard and the Surrounding Maritime Areas: Background and Legal Issues – Frequently Asked Questions," http://www.regjeringen.no/en/dep/ud/selected-topics/civil–rights/spesiell-folkerett/folkerettslige-sporsmal-i-tilknytning-ti.html?id=537481.

We do know that neither the Arctic nor the High North can be seen in isolation. Multipolarity, globalization, and deeper interdependence connect the High North to broader patterns and outside events and make the security environment of the region unpredictable. Conflicts or events in other parts of the world might have repercussions in the north and put Norwegian interests to the test. Security is indivisible.

5

Norway and the Arctic

Between Multilateral Governance and Geopolitics

Geir Flikke

INTRODUCTION

The Arctic region has risen to significance at the crossroads of climate change, new and more accessible oil deposits, and the littoral states' claims to maritime domains within the procedures stipulated by the UN Convention on the Law of the Sea (UNCLOS). Its significance is thus deeply ambivalent. On the one hand, the vulnerabilities of Arctic ecology and the legal issues allude to global interdependence. With this change come certain codes of conduct embedded in multilateral institutions and arrangements. These norms and practices could have a continued impact on interaction among states bordering on the region, as they have had in the past. On the other hand, the rise of the Arctic on the international agenda is caused by changes throughout the international system. These processes, vaguely termed *globalization*, potentially make the Arctic an object of "politics," and possibly less "governance." As Alyson Bailes suggests, "If the region is being invaded by global processes, at least this current set of issues is arising at a time when globalization is a recognized, much analyzed, and (to a limited but increasing extent) a directed phenomenon."[1] It is under the pressure of this directed phenomenon that future state interaction in the region is – under the emerging paradigm of energy shortages and a subsequent "crude rush" to Arctic waters – fraught with new uncertainties. As states position themselves for the ensuing dash to the north, expectations of gains may come to dominate over the expectations shaped by the knowledge-based institutions and legal regimes of the Arctic. More so, as the Arctic has been termed a region with a limited potential for civilian multilateral cooperation,[2] the prospects that states may "securitize" Arctic policies may further preclude constructive interaction.[3]

---

[1] Bailes, Alyson J. K. (2009), "Options for Closer Cooperation in the High North: What Is Needed?" in Holtsmark and Smith-Windsor, *Security Prospects in the High North*, pp. 30–31.

[2] Griffiths, Franklyn (ed.) (1992), "Arctic Alternatives: Civility or Militarism in the Circumpolar North," p. 3.

[3] The term *securitization* is defined by Buzan, Waever, and de Wilde (1998), *Security*, p. 23. Security is not a static concern but rather a rhetorical move (by means of action or speech) that "takes politics

Definitely a small state in Arctic military affairs, Norway professes to have a long tradition as a stakeholder in Arctic legal regimes and scientific circumpolar cooperation. In this context, the policies of reassurance and normalization are still key.[4] Norway depends on predictable legal regimes and holds that traditional alliance affiliation will suffice in security calculations. Yet the attention given to the Arctic has also confronted Norway with a new set of uncertainties. Since 2003, Norwegian High North policies have been framed as a strategic interest area in a period of rapid globalization, including the prospect that a new Arctic great game is emerging.[5] This alert has affected Norwegian policies in two distinct ways. First, the region-building agenda of the High North and the low politics of the border areas in the north have meshed with expectations of orderliness in Arctic governance. This process is in one sense the politics of "normalization" projected onto Arctic affairs. Second – and in contrast to the first – Norway's visions of continuity in Arctic governance are under duress. The orderliness of "low" politics does not apply to Arctic governance, given the very scope of challenges in the region. Low politics also seem poorly in style with the attention that the Arctic is receiving globally. In summary, the multifaceted challenges in the Arctic question whether old institutional arrangements are sufficient and whether new ones are needed. Policies of continuity are challenged by the very dynamic in Arctic and global affairs as caused by globalization, but also by the incremental development of the institutions and regimes designed to respond to new challenges.

This chapter argues that Norway's High North policies are a function of liberal expectations and the continuity of legal regimes. It discusses the institutional baseline for the notions of cooperative security in the High North and moves on to map how this notion has become relevant for the Norwegian perspective on the High North – and more broadly – Arctic challenges. For purposes of analysis, the article employs a definition of multilateral institutions and the institutions of multilateralism, discerning between the formal organizational rules of multilateral

---

beyond the established rules of the game and frames the issue either as a special kind of politics or as above politics." *Securitization* means, in this context, moves that are designed to create an impression that certain rules are no longer valid in the sense that they are of massive "national" importance. These may again be directed by notions of globalization, competition, and national survival.

4 During the Cold War, Norway's High North policies were explicitly framed as "normalcy." This framing was partially conditioned by the fact that the northern flank of NATO was inscribed in the strategic balance between the United States and the Soviet Union and that the Arctic region itself was considered a remote and inaccessible region. Norway's contribution to stability was thus reassurance and normalization in the border regions. In later conceptualizations of post–Cold War policies of the High North, the dominant frame has remained that of normalization, but with specific reference to a new security situation in the north. See Holst, Johan J., Kenneth Hunt, and Anders Sjaastad (eds.) (1985), *Deterrence and Defense in the North.*

5 *Globalization* has, in domestic parlance, come to signify processes through which faraway influences are brought to relevance for national interests, and when common interests formerly associated with the effect of low politics have become dependent on global processes. See "Towards the North" (2003).

organizations, and the expectations that states shape in their appeals to certain codified habits in international affairs. This is an important distinction, in the sense that
Arctic multilateralism is not solidly codified but rather a system for appeals (claims)
and discrete codes of conduct (procedures). Background documents include those
of the High North strategies adopted in the period from 2003 to 2009, as well as
speeches and policy documents issued by government officials on the issue. These
strategies and policy documents may be seen in conjunction with what is understood as a line of continuity in Norwegian foreign policies – to stress multilateral
cooperation above that of self-help in international politics.

The contrasting element in this chapter is the discontinuous aspects of the legal
regimes and the rising and competing frames of Arctic security. Facing these,
Norway reacts more like a hedgehog, taking a position as a traditional littoral
maritime state defying institutional "innovation" and defending the status quo in
circumpolar cooperation. This spinal reflex places Norway between multilateral
interaction and self-help, especially under conditions in which speech acts of securitization dominate. This phenomenon has been especially visible since 2007, when
the prime driver of securitization, Russia, emerged as a state emphasizing traditional
state-centered security by playing a central role in bringing the Arctic out from the
"low politics" of the 1990s and on to a geostrategic agenda. In the light of this, the
chapter discusses whether Norway's focus on the importance of the High North is
sufficiently backed by an understanding of the strategic aspects involved or simply
too reliant on liberal expectations.

SECURITY: CONCEPT, REGIMES, AND INSTITUTIONS

Concepts and perceptions of security have changed substantially since the Cold
War. Responding to the challenges evoked by the collapse of the Soviet Union,
security in Europe has become tightly associated with a liberal order encompassing
former Warsaw Pact countries and reaching into wider Europe. This unique institutional context has made arguments of liberal norms and multilateral cooperation
prevalent. In Europe, the web of institutions has not only removed conflict. It has
also come to actively promote a set of practices (governance) among states, as well
as integration (European Union) and arrangements for cooperative security (Organization for Security and Cooperation in Europe). The essence of this approach
is multilateralism, and multilateral governance is derived from the acceptance of
certain legal principles that secure continuity of practices. Moreover, the effect is
twofold – multilateralism codifies norms and shapes expectations. In the definition
of Stephen Krasner, norms are based on "implicit or explicit principles, norms, rules,
and decision-making procedures around which actors' expectations converge in a
given area of international relations."[6] These expectations often reach further than

[6] Keohane, Robert O. (1995), "The Analysis of International Regimes: Towards a European-American
Research Programme," in Rittberger, *Regime Theory and International Relations*, pp. 23–45, at
p. 27.

what the organizations mirror in their structure or charter. Hence, the distinction between multilateral institutions and the institutions of multilateralism in liberal theories, where the former signifies the "organizational elements of international life" and the latter is "grounded in appeals to the less formal, less codified habits, practices, ideas and norms of international society." Multilateralism is thus a way in which states conduct policies. In summary, "bilateralism, imperial hierarchy, and multilateralism are alternative conceptions of how the world might be organized; they are not just different types of concrete organization."[7]

Since the 1990s, this model partially also applies to security cooperation, where the web of institutions has come to matter more than in the past. In the realm of security practices, the embedded liberal order of wider Europe has proved able to shape expectations beyond the security communities of Europe and the transatlantic NATO alliance. This process is conditioned on the continuity of security communities. In terms of governance, the process has given impetus to the wider definition of security – that is, there is not one single security complex that can be seen as separate from different sets of security challenges. In other words, the spectrum of security challenges suggests interdependence rather than sectorwise compartmentalization. Distinctions between the military and civilian realms disappear. Security challenges are seen as on a continuum, encompassing incidents related to safety of transport, environmental damage, and implications for human security; incidents at sea; and complex securitized events involving conflicting perceptions, interests, and intents. This perspective is prevalent in the European Union, which is conceived of as a new actor in foreign and security politics. The European Union is, as a union of nations, a "civilian" actor, combining incentives for integration and economic trade with norm-based discrete conditionality. But also NATO has adopted many functions in the realm of civilian security and has extended those through cooperative arrangements.

The changing perception of security notwithstanding, two misinterpretations often blur security analysis. First, the rise of the new concept of security has often been misinterpreted to imply that security regimes should encompass all spheres of security. This is especially pertinent under the pressures of globalization. But as stated by Müller, security regimes are not global, "just as there is no regime for the global economy, but instead regimes in trade, finance[,] etc."[8] European and transatlantic security regimes are a case in point. Although much of what is considered security is associated with the expansion of NATO and the European Union, security regimes are more than the political dimensions and outreach of those organizations. Multilateral security in Europe has been facilitated by numerous comprehensive security regimes facilitating arms reductions. The continuity of these regimes is important.

---

7 Caporaso, James A. (1993), "International Relations Theory and Multilateralism: The Search for Foundations," in Ruggie, *Multilateralism Matters*, pp. 51–90, at p. 54.

8 Müller, Harald (1995), "The Internalization of Principles, Norms and Rules by Governments: The Case of Security Regimes," in Rittberger, *Regime Theory and International Relations*, pp. 361–90, at p. 361.

Second, security studies have devoted less attention to the effect of changes in the security regimes and seem to couple security tightly with prospects for a liberal economic order. Be it so that the territorial outstretch of NATO and the European Union – coupled with the modus operandi of the states inscribed in it – form a coherent and seamless liberal order. Under conditions in which the Arctic regions defreeze and draw global attention, this order might find itself under siege. As Margaret Blunden states: "focusing on security [in the Arctic] is bound to increase because of the economic stakes."9 The reasons are obvious: the low politics of regional integration and the gradual reconfiguration of European security are receiving signals from the high politics of maritime navigation between Europe and Asia, global warming, and the new quest for nonrenewable resources. As a relative terra incognita – a term that Norway's government does not approve of – the Arctic may ignite discourses that make resource development and governance a matter of national interests and not global governance and cooperative security.

Regime change and disruption are important factors in understanding the framework of international relations, also in the Arctic. Among the four security regimes identified by Müller in 1995, some have been changed, adapted, or frozen.10 The Anti-Ballistic Missile Treaty was abolished unilaterally in 2001, and the Strategic Arms Reduction Treaty (START) was replaced by a bilateral strategic reduction treaty between the United States and Russia in 2002 (Moscow Treaty). With the new START agreement between Obama and Medvedev in April 2010 on strategic arms reductions within a START framework, continuity is secured. Still, the treaty on conventional arms reductions in Europe (Adapted Conventional Armed Forces in Europe Treaty) remains effectively suspended by the Russian Federation since 2007. Rather than reflecting fatal regime flaws or the prevalence of self-help priorities over cooperative security, it could be argued that these changes reflect in one way lacking coordination between the United States and the European Union. The net result is still increased uncertainty over the continuity of security regimes.11 This is further aggravated by disruptions. The institution of multilateralism consists – as mentioned earlier – of appeals to the discrete norms and habits of international conduct. Moscow has as a declared policy the insertion of elements of "multipolarity" in

---

9 Blunden, Margaret (2010), "The New Problem of Arctic Stability," pp. 121–42, at p. 132.
10 Müller (1995), in "Internalization of Principles, Norms and Rules by Governments," operates with four distinct security regimes: the strategic nuclear weapons regime (Strategic Arms Limitation Talks I and II, Anti-Ballistic Missile Treaty, Intermediate-Range Nuclear Forces Treaty and Outer Space, and Strategic Arms Reduction Treaty); European security regimes (INF Treaty, Stockholm and Paris agreements on confidence-building measures, the Treaty on Conventional Armed Forces in Europe, and military visitors' programs); the nuclear war prevention regime; and the Non-Proliferation Treaty. Since 1995, these regimes have undergone changes.
11 For regimes to be effective, compliance is a key point. As Müller (1995), "The Internalization of Principles, Norms and Rules by Governments" (p. 362) observes, "States' compliance with regime requirements is one important aspect of regime effectiveness."

European and transatlantic security discourse, but also through the argument that a new treaty on European security is needed.

The distinct message in this campaign is to render NATO irrelevant and the European Union dependent on Russia economically and for its energy security. Such strategies move security away from regimes and into the arena of politics, downplaying regime discontinuity and selectively sculpting bilateral relations in Europe in accordance with likes and dislikes. It also mirrors the inherent dislikes of Russia to all binding multilateral commitments and organizations – at least those that do not give Russia a special place in them.[12] Obviously, the sense of disruption and discontinuity can also be induced in other ways. One example is the linking of rhetorical demarches with territorial claims, in the manner recently done by the Russian Federation in the allegedly scientific pursuit of the North Pole and the resumption of flights in the North Atlantic in 2007. The changes in the security regimes may be deep harbingers of a more competitive international order in and of itself. In summary, the development of these security regimes may play an indirect role in Arctic affairs, as the region is sensitive to shifts in U.S.-Russian relations.

Even if competition resumes, the "return of geopolitics" is not a very precise label for what is happening in the Arctic region. Unlike former times of geopolitical contestation, the one rising in the Arctic is about subsea territory, economic zones, and transport. Moreover, the very nature of Arctic challenges does not evoke self-help policies. Climate change and ice melting offer opportunities, but derived from this regional and global scale, challenges may follow.[13] Ice melting creates further complex challenges for tourism and transport at sea. With chunks of ice floating freely in northern waters, navigation becomes difficult, and emergency situations may occur that demand multinational responses. Finally, hydrocarbon resources in Arctic regions, roughly estimated at about 25 percent of the world's undiscovered resources, can be used only if states agree on the letter of international law and if complex technology is developed to make these resources available in environmentally safe ways. Transport and navigation in these areas will demand joint navigation surveillance and measures for assistance at sea. Clearly, none of these challenges belongs to any sharply defined "compartment," and they may even seem intrinsically interconnected.

Paradoxically, then, the very conditions prompting resource availability are at the same time those that call for immediate global concern and attention. Arctic security is thus reliant on international developments, and on the realities – or illusions – of interdependence. The strategic space of the Arctic as a transport route and a potential energy hub invites the actors to adopt new policies. This may entail new

[12] This point is briefly discussed and made relevant to Russia's Arctic policies in Haftendorn, Helga (2010), "Soft Solutions for Hard Problems," p. 817.

[13] For the past thirty years, annual average sea-ice extent has decreased by about 8 percent, which comprises an area larger than that of Scandinavia taken together (Hassol, Susan Joy [2004], "Impacts of a Warming Arctic).

rounds of securitization through speech acts, and actions that define the area as more than simply important. There is a contest of strategic definitions rising. Is the Arctic about resource availability or climate challenges? Does it offer trade opportunities or environmental security risks? Is it a global resource hub or an area for geopolitical enclosure and competition? Responses to these questions could run either in line with or against the legal framework and the patterns developed through circumpolar cooperation. The answer to any of these questions is instrumental in shaping not only perceptions of Arctic challenges but also responses to those questions. And responses may either enhance or lower prospects for cooperative security. Norway is in all aspects inscribed in this contest.

NORWAY'S HIGH NORTH POLICY: THE DILEMMAS OF LOW AND HIGH POLITICS

As a nonmember of the European Union and a NATO member, Norway is dependent on security regime continuity in Europe, and Oslo has been an ardent advocate for the imperative of circumpolar cooperation in the Arctic. Regarding the former, Norway is still "inextricably linked to the broad pattern of East-West relations," and it is also conducting a policy that is somewhere between adjustments and influence.[14] The adjustment sought by Norway since the 1990s relates to issues of governance and civic security, whereas influence is partially sought in highlighting the immense economic prospects in the north. But the policies of adjustment and influence also relate to the gap between the ideal and reality in dealing with Russia. Until April 2010, unresolved bilateral maritime border issues with Russia dominated, as did Norway's policy of transforming the patterns of political normalization sought during the Cold War into a tool for effective cooperation in Europe. Even with the agreement of intention between Norway and the Russian Federation signed on April 28, 2010 and subsequent ratification, it is not granted that this compromise will fuel effective cooperation with or in Europe, let alone open up a new oil era in the North. There are several factors that are still nested into the larger issues of Arctic governance, and the policies of adjustment and influence will be at variance with these.

Norwegian policies will not cross the lines defined by the institutions of multilateralism, however, but will repeatedly appeal to norms, legal regimes, and codes of conduct. This holds true even if the policies of adjustment and influence play out in bilateral and multilateral contexts. Since the early 1990s, Norway's policies have gradually been moving from bilateral issues to more complex multilateralism in some spheres, seeking always to focus on the "doable" issues in dealing with Russia. The larger context is that of European policies. Norway's response to the demise of the Cold War was to embrace new opportunities to deal with the residual challenges in the north. With the creation of the Barents Euro-Arctic Region (BEAR)

[14] Holst, Hunt, and Sjaastad (1985), *Deterrence and Defense in the North*, p. 93.

in Kirkenes, in 1992, the strategic significance of the north as a NATO flank was replaced by models and policies of interstate cooperation and regionalization. By initiating a region-to-region cooperation, Norway also found a way out of the more delicate situation created by the proposal offered by then Prime Minister Vladimir Ryzhkov in 1989 to create a bilateral economic zone of cooperation in the High North. Rather than embarking on bilateral arrangements with a post–Cold War Soviet Russia, Norway preferred to frame northern cooperation in the context of wider Europe, and a Europe of regions, a priority that persists to this day.

Although the Kirkenes declaration initiated people-to-people contacts within the framework of the Barents Sea Region Council, its outlook was larger than this. The declaration referred to regional cooperation as a contribution to international peace and security, and it made references to international charters, such as the European Energy Charter. New initiatives were also taken, among them a bilateral assistance program in radiation safety. The action plan for nuclear safety was adopted in 1995, and by 1998 Norway and Russia had established a bilateral nuclear safety commission. In the period from 1995 to 2009, Norway spent NOK 1.5 billion ($2.6 billion) on nuclear safety projects relating both to storage and site cleanup. According to Hønneland, the bilateral design also was a platform for bringing global attention to the residual nuclear challenges in the region.[15] The long-term aim was to boost multilateralism. As the G8 pledged $20 billion to fight proliferation in 2002, the Multilateral Nuclear Environmental Program (MNEPR) was set up with Russia in 2003. The MNEPR is supported by a separate "nuclear window" within the Northern Dimension Environmental Partnership (NDEP), and in June 2008, the European Bank for Reconstruction and Development (EBRD) signed four projects with Rosatom, involving costs of around €74 million.[16] The NDEP has thus gained in significance for Norway as a multilateral context through which former bilateral initiatives are being conducted.

The paradox of this design is, as suggested by Lindeman, that "Norway's bilateral and regional policy orientations, and Russia's global ambitions and intentions regarding the North, cause differences in policy that create challenges of their own."[17] The combination of people-to-people cooperation and the several dialogues on energy and infrastructure developments has coexisted with a focus on bilateral radiation safety issues. For Norway – unlike for Russia – multilateralism has been the lead star, in conjunction with "normalization" and the civic dimensions of security associated with the European Union. Illustratively, the larger Northern Dimension framework of the European Union in the north includes more than environmental programs and continues the tradition of Norway's bilateral policy, that is, to "transform

[15] Hønneland, Geir (2009), "Cross-Border Cooperation in the North: The Case of Northwest Russia," in Rowe (2009), *Russia and the North*, pp. 35–52, at pp. 43–44.
[16] Smith, Hanna et al. (2009), *The New Northern Dimension of the European Neighborhood*, pp. 29–31.
[17] Lindeman, Ole A. (2009), "Norwegian Foreign Policy in the High North," p. 119.

grand designs into more pragmatic considerations."[18] To be sure, the European north differs from other regions of the European Union, and the European Union has more than one policy on its perimeter. Yet the specific regional approach in the High North, with project management and EBRD conditionality, has effectively lifted dialogues and initiatives that have emerged in the region-building context of the 1990s onto an agenda of European integration that encompasses the Nordic countries and pools their resources together.

As for the paradox, Russia's propensity to define Arctic interests as "security" remains. Russia has – illustratively – cut back on multilateral nuclear safety coop-eration related to military sites. The Arctic Military Environmental Cooperation (AMEC) – initiated in 1996 as a multilateral framework for the United States, United Kingdom, Russia, and Norway to facilitate the decommissioning of nuclear submarines at Kola naval bases – was rendered irrelevant as Norwegian officials linked to the program were denied entrance permit in routine visits. The shift of rhetoric from Russia was made even more explicit as the Russians resumed strategic flights in the North Atlantic in the latter part of 2007, combining this with an urge to define the Arctic as geostrategically important. Although this partly tallies with Rus-sia's definition of certain "economic" sectors as strategic state resources, it certainly also lends itself to a more visible grand strategy of Russia to enhance the significance of the European Union at the cost of NATO, thus moving several agenda questions over to a civilian realm in the European Union while securitizing the significance of state-governed and closed sectors within Russia itself.[19]

The rise of the Arctic as a geostrategic arena has created a notable shift in Norway's rhetorical framing of the High North, and in the political practices of drawing more attention to this region. While preoccupied with Arctic circumpolar multilateralism, Norway's attempt to bring attention to Northern issues has since 2003 materialized in a set of bilateral dialogues with central European partners. These dialogues have been designed to promote Norwegian interests, but the effect has often been the opposite. According to Pedersen, Norwegian diplomacy has often preceded reservations expressed by European states as to Norwegian claims.[20] Since 2008 the Barents Council has become the international Barents Council; this does not necessarily alleviate the relative isolation of the High North from European affairs, and there is no coherent EU policy that could back Norwegian policies had it come down to realpolitik. Certainly, inter-Nordic cooperation has become more active through the Stoltenberg initiative on common maritime surveillance and monitoring system and adjacent initiatives within Nordic defense cooperation. These are arrangements for practical cooperation that cross over the various NATO and EU affiliations of the Nordic countries. All the more, these arrangements contrast

---

[18] Smith, Hanna et al. (2009), *The New Northern Dimension of the European Neighborhood*, p. 3.

[19] For more on this, see Rowe (2009), *Russia and the North*, and Smith et al. (2009), *The New Northern Dimension*.

[20] Pedersen, Torbjørn (2009), "Endringer i internasjonal Svalbard-politikk," pp. 31–44.

with the fact that the Norwegian government has beefed up the strategic importance of the Arctic in the perspective of an exclusively national interest. The High North policy document defines the region as a "strategic area," a "national undertaking," and a "foreign policy initiative."[21] Minister of Foreign Affairs Jonas Gahr Støre went even farther, describing the Arctic not as a "backwater" but as a "strategic balcony" for Norwegian interests.[22] In other contexts, Norway is considered gatekeeper, a dialogue partner, and a stakeholder. The overarching paradigm is globalization – processes that erase the traditional differences between close-to-home interests and global issues. These processes have made the political expression of Norway's interests even more acute. In the preface to the governmental strategy on the High North, Prime Minister Jens Stoltenberg thus claims:

> This is more than just a foreign policy, and more than just a domestic policy. It is a question of our ability to continue our tradition of responsible management of resources, predictable exercise of sovereignty, and close cooperation with our neighbors, partners and allies. . . . We are not talking about a project for the High North alone, but a project for the whole country and for the whole of Northern Europe, with consequences for the whole continent.[23]

The statement announces a diffuse change in the perception of what is foreign and what is domestic policy – that is, anything far away becomes close. Although the inverse statement hopefully is not true, the Arctic holds a dual challenge that may evoke such notions: it is a region that mirrors challenges stemming from globalization and a region that will be embedded in global politics. What Norway believes to be the case regionally cannot be applied as a rule for what the Arctic will look like, however. Moreover, the traditional noninterest policy will also be challenged by developments in the Arctic. Traditionally, there has been a distinct division between Norwegian Arctic policies and the policies of the High North. Partially, this is linked to the understanding of traditional security policies and the adjacent conceptualization of interests versus that of Norwegian global policies, that is, the suggestion that Norway holds a unique position internationally, as it in most conflict settings is perceived as not being a stakeholder. In the Arctic setting, the nonstakeholder policies of Norway have been conceived of as linked to research and the formation of sustainable circumpolar epistemic communities. To this end, even the Norwegian white paper on the High North, "Towards the North" (2003), was conceived of as a paper compiled by researchers and feeding into the national process of adopting comprehensive research agendas for Norway's new High North policies.

[21] "Towards the North" (2003).
[22] Støre, Jonas Gahr (2009a), "Etter Stortingsvalget: Om utenrikspolitiske hovedprioriteringer og 14 hovedområder," speech at the International Forum, Labor Party, accessed 3 December 2009, http://www.regjeringen.no/nb/dep/ud/aktuelt/taler_artikler/utenriksministeren/2009/hovedomraader .html?id=587212.
[23] Lindeman (2009), "Norwegian Foreign Policy in the High North," p. 7.

In contrast, the white paper made clear that Norway is a stakeholder in the High North. It made a sharp distinction between national and global interests, suggesting that there was a clear geographical factor governing Norwegian policies – namely that "the major part of Norway's Economic Zone and one-third of the coastline of the mainland is north of the Polar circle, and including Spitsbergen, Norwegian areas reach deep into the Arctic Ocean. These interests border on those of many others." Hence, the white paper concluded: "Norway should have a powerful Northern policy in an unpredictable world."[24]

In summary, government policies have encountered both a geographic and a more policy-related dilemma. First, although the distinction between the High North and the Arctic is blurred in most policy speeches, these are separate challenges that need separate strategies. At the conceptual level, this implies that the distinction between state policies of national interests in the High North has been juxtaposed with that of idealistic expectations in the Arctic. Second, the government's policies seem confined to research and innovation, and to national mobilization.[25] Although this is a preparation to the expected "knowledge-based economy" in the north, the Arctic poses challenges that may reach beyond such expectations. The policies of adjustment and influence may be justified, given the context, but they articulate deeper dilemmas. *Security* in Norwegian parlance means simply the continuity of legal regimes in the Arctic and predictable exercises of sovereignty. What is absent is – in other words – a strategic assessment of security in the High North. To be sure, the legal framework of the Arctic rests on the assumption that the multilateralism of institutions will prevail, and this is the context in which *security* is read. Also this legal framework has loopholes, however, and may depend on external factors.

LEGAL REGIMES: CONTINUITY OR CHANGE?

A primary condition for cooperative security is the continuity of regimes and practices that enhance compliance. But how continuous are the legal regimes? How predictable are developments in the Arctic? Traditionally, the UN Convention on the Law of the Sea stands out as a classic example of the significance of multilateral frameworks and legal regimes.[26] The law was made in response to emerging conflicts over sea territories, and it has successfully set precedence for the two-hundred-mile economic zone.[27] The legal regime of UNCLOS is thus an illustrative case study of a multilateralism that matters, and that works. The discrete procedures of announcing

---

[24] "Towards the North" (2003).
[25] This was done in 2009, when the government presented a new strategy "New Building Blocks in the North" emphasizing the need for new insfrastructure projects and trade.
[26] Krasner, Stephen (ed.) (1983), *International Regimes* (Ithaca, NY: Cornell University Press).
[27] Zacher, Mark W. (1993), "Multilateral Organizations and the Institutions of Multilateralism: The Development of Regimes for Nonterrestial Spaces," in Ruggie, *Multilateralism Matters* (1993), pp. 399–439.

claims while expecting other stakeholders to respond and act in accordance with similar procedures meet the criteria of converging expectations, as well as the practices of appeals to a recognized legal order and set of procedures. This said, the process leading up to the adoption of UNCLOS was colored by great-power politics and the decision of the United States to invest in multilateralism. Starting from the Truman proclamation of September 28, 1945, through the second conference on the law of the seas (1960), it took a total of twelve years to resume negotiations and nine years of negotiations to end with UNCLOS in 1982.[28] Furthermore, UNCLOS's framing of procedures is instrumental in raising the international focus on the Arctic. Article 76 of UNCLOS on the definitions and reach of the littoral states' continental shelves also contains a clause that littoral states shall submit their claims within ten years of ratification of UNCLOS. For the littoral states, this implies that claims have to be fronted in the time span from 2004 to 2014, and, as observed by Øystein Jensen at the Fridtjof Nansen Institute, "time passes quickly, at least when time is limited."[29]

The legal regime is partially inscribed in a larger future security complex characterized by Blunden as an "archetype of the complex, multi-dimensional global problems of the twenty-first century. Military security, environmental security and economic security interact."[30] To be sure, there is also a continuity of epistemic communities in the Arctic, as well as a circumpolar cooperative arrangement that boosts the institutions of multilateralism. Norway supports the Arctic Council, again making interdependence and multilateralism the frame of reference for Norwegian policies. As Gahr Støre stated at the Trilateral Commission summit in Oslo in October 2009: "Tonight, my perspective on security and interdependence will be the High North," and he continued by referring to the Arctic Council not as a "decision-making body" but as a "decision-shaping body."[31] This was also emphasized earlier by the minister, in April 2009, at the opening of the ministerial meeting of the Arctic Council. Gahr Støre stated then: "The Arctic Council is emerging as the key decision-shaping body on Arctic affairs."[32] In such settings, continuity means cooperation and predictability: "The Arctic is a region characterized by close cooperation and the absence of conflict, an area of peace and stability. Our primary responsibility is to maintain this favorable situation in the interests of all mankind."[33]

---

28 Østreng, Willy, and Yngvild Prydz (2007), "Delelinjen i Barentshavet: Planlagt samarbeid versus uforutsett konflikt?" [The Maritime Border in the Barents Sea: Planned Cooperation versus Unexpected Conflict?]. Oslo: Stortingets utredningsseksjon, *Perspektiv*, no. 4.

29 Jensen, Øystein (2008), "Kontinentalsokkelens avgrensing utenfor 200 nautiske mil: Norske og russiske perspektiver i de nordlige havområder" [The Delimitation of the Continental Shelf Outside the 200-Mile Zone: Norwegian and Russian Perspectives]. *Internasjonal Politikk* 66, no. 4, pp. 563–90, at p. 570.

30 Blunden (2010), "The New Problem of Arctic Stability," p. 137.

31 Støre, Jonas Gahr (2009d), "The Trilateral Commission," speech in Oslo, October 17, http://www.regjeringen.no/nb/dep/ud/aktuelt/taler_artikler/utenriksministeren/2009/trilateral_commission.html?id=582686.

32 Støre, Jonas Gahr (2009c), "Opening Speech at the 6th Ministerial Meeting of the Arctic Council."

33 Ibid.

Whether the Arctic Council will suffice as a multilateral framework for cooperative interaction in the Arctic remains uncertain. In the framework of governance, the Norwegian government welcomes new observers to the Arctic Council but seeks to avoid any fundamental revision of the existing legal regime, let alone any separate Arctic treaty. Pursuant to the policies of normalization, the Norwegian government does not see alternatives to the current legal regime, nor does it want to see alternatives to it. As Gahr Støre pointed out to his Labor Party, "We have, in reality, 'discovered' a new ocean. Where there used to be ice, there is now only water. And then some say: 'this is new – we have to create a new legal regime for this ocean.' And here Norway says: 'no – we have the law of the seas'"[34] Addressing the Trilateral Commission, he reiterated this:

[A] few words on the legal situation in the region. The outstanding questions of jurisdiction in the Arctic area all concern either the extent of the continental shelf. . . . All the necessary legal instruments and provisions for settling these questions in an orderly way are in place, and all states concerned comply with these one hundred per cent. The United Nations Convention on the Law of the Sea is fundamental in this respect.[35]

The Ilulissat Declaration of 2008 stands out as a milestone for Norway's High North policy, bolstering the continuity of UNCLOS and an agreement between the littoral states that no other framework shall regulate interstate affairs in the Arctic. The declaration also effectively stopped a freeze in territorial claims, like the Antarctic Treaty.[36] Though challenged for being too strict as to defining exclusive coastal states' claim to stewardship in protecting the ecosystems,[37] and for the discrete linkage made to the ongoing UNCLOS process, the declaration fortifies a long-wanted multilateral bulwark against a renegotiation of the legal regimes on the Arctic. Again, quoting Gahr Støre:

It is important not to forget one simple fact: whereas the Antarctic is an uninhabited continent surrounded by oceans, the Arctic is an ocean plus the surrounding territories, which are both inhabited and integrated parts of sovereign, long-established states. This is the simple reason why there is no room for a separate Arctic treaty. Loose ideas about the need for such a treaty are all based on the misunderstanding that in the Arctic, there is some kind of "no man's land."[38]

The essence of the government's position is understandable: there is not necessarily a contradiction between a functional system of states and multilateral interaction.

---

[34] Støre, Jonas Gahr (2009a), "Etter Stortingsvalget."
[35] Støre, Jonas Gahr (2009d), "The Trilateral Commission."
[36] Haftendorn (2010), "Soft Solutions for Hard Problems."
[37] Blunden (2010), "The New Problem of Arctic Stability," p. 124, observes that the declaration was interpreted as an embrace of a legal regime that preserved status quo rather than widening the scope for interaction.
[38] Støre, Jonas Gahr (2009d), "The Trilateral Commission."

Continuity in Norway's foreign policy parlance is often viewed precisely in the context of multilateral mediation. Still, the epistemic communities so widely cultivated by the government have found that there are elements in the legal regime that add to the uncertainties of governability in the High North. Jensen draws attention to cases regarding the meeting of the commission's deadlines.[39] Where certifying claims to the continental shelf beyond the two-hundred-mile zone are concerned, he concludes that "procedure" and "time frame" are essential in clarifying a coastal state's sovereignty claim. Moreover, in case of insufficient information to certify the claim, the commission may – as in the case of the Russian Federation's claims submitted to the Commission on the Limits of the Continental Shelf (CLCS) in 2001 – ask to resubmit claims that are inadequately founded. Finally, the commission offers "recommendations" on the basis of information provided by the littoral states. The validity of claims is thus pending on legal processes within or among them.

The case of Norway and Russia over the delimitation issue in the Barents Sea is illustrative. An intentional agreement has been made that may have come about as a result of Norway's strategy to strengthen the validity of legal regimes and to appeal to institutions of multilateralism. This has been an incremental process. When the government adopted its High North strategy in 2006, careful diplomacy was initiated. Norway and Denmark agreed on the midline principle in delineating border between Greenland and Spitsbergen in 2006, thus strengthening this argument in the negotiations with Russia.[40] This solved a dispute over 150,000 square kilometers. In that same year, agreement was also reached among Iceland, the Faeroe Islands, and Norway on the intersection between the outer limits of the national economic zones (NEZs) of the three. This added 56,000 square kilometers to Norway's seabed jurisdiction and was the first time in history that states reached an agreement on the seas outside of the NEZ.[41] That same year, Norway presented new claims to the CLCS in the areas north of Spitsbergen called the Loophole, a total of 250,000 square kilometers. In 2009, UNCLOS accepted Norway's claim (235,000 square kilometers).[42] In the upshot, the discussions between Norway and Russia over the delimitation in the Barents Sea were reportedly entering into a new and improved phase leading up to the presidential visit in April 2010. Even after ratification, further opportunities still hinge on the degree of Russia's domestic transformation. In summary, although claims of legal continuity and circumpolar cooperation based on the evaluations of epistemic communities are central in Norway's Arctic policies, uncertainties remain. What is certain, however, is that the region will remain important. Again, the minister of foreign affairs,

[39] Jensen (2008), "Kontinentalsokkelens avgrensing utenfor 200 nautiske mil."

[40] Dragnes, Kjell (2006a), "Delimitation around Greenland: Norwegian-Danish Agreement on Mid-Line Principle," *Aftenposten*, 20 February.

[41] Dragnes, Kjell (2006b), "Major Agreement on Continental Shelf Reached," *Aftenposten*, 21 September.

[42] "Limits of Norway's Arctic Seabed Agreed," *Barents Observer*, 16 April 2009, http://www.barent sobserver.com/limits-of-norways-arctic-seabed-agreed.4580729-16149.html.

having supervised a study on the big oil bonanza in the High North, stressed the following:

> The Barents Sea will also become an important source of energy supply to Europe and North America. Perhaps as much as a quarter of the world's undiscovered petroleum reserves may be located in the Arctic. Politically this is a stable region. In the years to come, Britain, continental Europe and the United States may well be looking to the High North for additional supplies of oil and gas.[43]

This not only has drawn the attention of future stakeholders to the High North but also has raised the stakes. Russian interpretations and readings of the High North are adding suspense to this, not least because Russia reads the Arctic in a specifically strategic context that indicates increased geopolitical competition.

RUSSIA AND THE ARCTIC

Although the Arctic was not a preoccupation for Russia in the 1990s, now it is seen as somewhat of a new frontier for national security in a globalized system of international relations. In the 2009 *National Security Doctrine towards 2020*, the Barents Sea and the Arctic are considered an area of geopolitical strategic interest and future competition in line with that of the Caspian Basin, the Middle East, and Central Asia. This is more than simply a policy statement; it's a policy perspective. The *Security Doctrine* has been made subject also to a long process of adoption, starting from discussions at the level of Russia's macro-regions and ending in the final adoption by the Security Council. Thus, it unites the various administrative units of Russia behind a common strategic outlook, which is presidential policy. The doctrine is – in other words – security writ large in the Russian political system, testifying also to the Russian compartmentalization of world regions in a seamless web of challenges surrounding the Russian heartland.

The broad anchoring of the doctrine in the Russian political system indicates that there are few domestic political constraints that the president has to overcome. Former presidencies, such as Yeltsin's, were embroiled in domestic constraints that made it virtually impossible to form a coherent foreign and security policy. The Putin presidency either removed them or consolidated the political elite to such an extent that institutional obstacles were replaced by effective managerial handling of policies.[44] This had an effect also on foreign and security policies, as it reduced uncertainties and institutional constraints. In the current political system in Russia, there are still challenges to presidential legitimacy, however. President Medvedev

[43] Støre, Jonas Gahr (2005), "Norwegian Foreign Policy Priorities," speech at the LSE, 26 October, available at http://www.regjeringen.no/nb/dep/ud/aktuelt/taler_artikler/utenriksministeren/2005/norwegian-foreign-policy-priorities.html?id=420708.
[44] For an encompassing discussion of presidential policies and constraints, see Breslauer, George W. (2002), *Gorbachev and Yeltsin as Leaders* (Cambridge: Cambridge University Press).

has clearly invested substantial presidential legitimacy in an active Arctic policy, and economic modernization. He has proclaimed that the north is the future source of Russia's economic revival, and the country's own estimates seem to suggest that there is a "whole world" up there waiting to be exploited (*osvaivat'*). With 8 percent of the total population, the north is considered to deliver about 20 percent of Russia's gross domestic product and 22 percent of its total exports.[45] According to other estimates, the "north" or "Arctic," as defined by Russia, holds 90 percent of the country's available unexploited gas resources, more than 60 percent of oil resources, more than 90 percent of nickel resources, 60 percent of copper, and 98 percent of platinum metals. Most of the hydrocarbons are to be found offshore. Conservative estimates by Norwegian scholars suggest that about 4 million square kilometers of the continental shelf (6.2 million square kilometers) hold deposits.[46]

There is a notable convergence between the identification of available resources in the Russian Arctic and the development of an offshore strategy toward 2020. This process started in October 2003, initiated by the ministry of natural resources. The state companies Rosneft and Gazprom are situated at the center point of future projects.[47] The state is to play the central role in the development of infrastructure, resource extraction, and future fields. Philip Hanson claims that, although the share of state-controlled companies in 2003 was about 24 percent, it was close to 40 percent in 2007.[48] Jeffrey Mankoff estimates the total share of state-controlled oil output as having risen from 6 percent in 2000 to 44 percent in 2008, with Rosneft alone holding 21.5 percent of the total oil production in Russia.[49] Furthermore, there is substantial evidence that Russia's offshore strategy, developed as it was in the urge for state control over strategic sectors starting in 2004, and ending with the law on strategic sectors adopted in 2008, is indeed a state-favored strategic area. As observed by Rowe and Moe, Russia does not have the technology to go offshore unless international companies invest, but at the same time "offshore oil and gas are clearly defined as strategic natural resource assets and, consequently, fall under the evolving legislation and policy on strategic resources that explicitly limit such non-Russian involvement."[50] In other words, the development of companies, the urge for technology, and the securitization of Arctic affairs are much interrelated.

---

45 Citing Medvedev when launching the Russian Arctic strategy, *Osnovy* (2008). The latter does probably also encompass oil and gas reserves, which have suffered from a lack of reinvestments from 2003. Kryukov, Valery, and Arild Moe (2007), "Russia's Oil Industry: Risk Aversion in a Risk-Prone Environment," pp. 341–57.

46 Rowe (2009), *Russia and the North.*

47 Rowe (2009), *Russia and the North*, p. 112.

48 Hanson (2009), "The Resistible Rise of State Control in the Russian Oil Industry," p.21.

49 Mankoff (2009a), "Eurasian Energy Security," Council of Foreign Relations Report No. 43.

50 Rowe (2009), *Russia and the North*, p. 107. According to Rowe, this works two ways: either there will be more bureaucratic red tape or a liberal-minded government can use executive authority to rubber-stamp favored projects. She contends that the latter seems less likely (p. 110).

Equally important for the Russian state, at least in terms of addressing these issues as pertinent challenges for the state to handle, are issues of demography and migration. In fact, the dire demographic status of Russia has made the north, as well as Russia proper, a withering frontier. From 1989 to 2006, the net outflow of migrants from northern regions amounted to 17 percent of the total population, with Chukotka and Magadan as the extreme cases.[51] Adding this to the demographic decline of Russia, with death rates exceeding birthrates by 70 percent and a population dwindling by 0.7 percent annually, Russia stands a continuous challenge in conquering its own territories.[52] That said, Russia has defined the development of hydrocarbon resources as a key to national revival as provided by the state. Having moved that strategic sector over to the state, starting in 2003, Russia has elevated energy relations as a strategic ingredient in its foreign and security calculations in the international system. The 2008 agreement with China to collaborate on an oil pipeline through Siberia to the Chinese-Russian border (East Siberia–Pacific Ocean oil pipeline) was struck to balance EU energy initiatives in Central Asia. It partially also serves as a long-term and very much needed investment in infrastructure in Siberia. Russian officials found in this setting that Russia was engaged in "economically viable geopolitics."[53]

Whether Russia will see the Arctic in any other perspective than that of increased competition for access to resources is hence doubtful. True, the Arctic strategy signed by President Medvedev on September 18, 2008, sees the region both as a strategic resource pool for Russia's revival and as a "zone for peace and cooperation."[54] Still, in ratifying UNCLOS in 1997, Russia stated that it did not accept procedures regulating border disputes, military activities, and law enforcement.[55] Adding to this, the growing Russian perception of international affairs as a system that is dominated not only by the West but also by Western institutions has led to a distinct transition in Russian foreign policy away from a status quo position in international affairs. Also in northern affairs, outside of the Northern Dimension and a consultative mechanism with NATO, Russia judges its policy by its effect, and it does not hide the fact that it will continue to play on differences within the Nordic-Baltic context, the European Union, and even NATO. As observed in a recent article in *Russia in Global Affairs*:

> Russia remains a non-regional actor with regard to Northern Europe and the Baltic region due to its weak interaction with the European Union and NATO. . . . The position of a non-regional actor offers some advantages, the main ones are that

[51] Rowe (2009), *Russia and the North*.

[52] The latest and perhaps still the best analysis of Russian population decline is in Herspring, Dale (ed.) (2005), *Putin's Russia: Past Imperfect, Future Uncertain*.

[53] See Flikke, Geir (2009), "Balancing Acts: Russian-Chinese Relations and Developments in the SCO and the CSTO."

[54] Osnovy gosudarstvennoy politiki Rossiyskoy Federatsii v Arktike na period do 2020 goda i dal'neyshuyu perspektivu (2008), 18 September, available at: http://www.scrf.gov.ru/documents/98.html.

[55] Haftendorn (2010), "Soft Solutions for Hard Problems," p. 817.

Russia's hands are not tied and it can conduct a flexible multi-vector policy and form alliances with other interested parties.[56]

Clearly, this is the core of strategic bilateralism, and also an outlook that reads international relations as a zero-sum game and an interaction of states in pursuit of relative gains. Rather than conduct appeals to the institutions of multilateralism, this approach sees the world through the lenses of competition, state interests, and relative gains. In contrast, the indicated "low level of interaction" between NATO and the European Union and Russia offers a continuous question as to the effectiveness of the institutions of multilateralism. However, strategic bilateralism has its costs. Russia's own inherent ambivalence between what is "legal" in terms of international law and what is "national security" in terms of sovereign rights is poorly designed to deal with the challenges posed by globalization, and indeed by the domestic dimension, the dire need for modernization included. Hence, although there are few doubts as to geopolitics being the prevalent perception in Russia's Arctic outlook, this partially reinforces the significance of effective multilateralism.

CONCLUSION

A core argument of this chapter is that Arctic governance is best secured through the institutions of multilateralism for it to remain a matter of appeals to legal regimes, which again deal with disputes in a coordinated and open fashion. Arctic security also reaches further, however, and depends on broad and effective cooperative security regimes. The continuity of these regimes is important, not least because disruption can involve direct relative gains in international relations, even if these are not representative for the general distribution of power in the international system. Adding to this, Arctic security regimes are underdeveloped in the face of new challenges, thus making great power politics more likely to occur.

This dilemma is reflected in Norway's policies. Norway's Arctic policy on the one hand has been colored by liberal expectations and on the other hand has been in favor of a status quo approach to the existing multilateral frameworks for the Arctic. Clearly, seeing the NATO–Russia Council (NRC) as an "all weather forum to be used also when times are difficult"[57] tallies with the dominant liberal expectation created by European and transatlantic security organizations, and also with those that Norway holds as valid for the Arctic. Moreover, underlining the significance of epistemic communities and UNCLOS, Norway upholds the institutions of multilateralism. The Arctic is certainly a region where policies must be "tempered by an awareness of interdependence,"[58] which implies that, even if the multilateral

[56] Alexandrov, Oleg (2009), "Labyrinths of the Arctic Policy," pp. 110–19.
[57] Støre (2009c), "Opening Speech at the 6th Ministerial Meeting of the Arctic Council."
[58] Griffiths (1992), *Arctic Alternatives*, p. 281.

institutions themselves may not be encompassing, they at least contribute to raising the awareness that self-help offers no solution. Norwegian High North policy is interpreted exactly in this light and emphasizes the multilateral dimension of these policies, even if Norway has also contributed to introducing a high politics agenda in Arctic issues by framing it as "strategic" and putting a massive emphasis on the possible "oil bonanza" in the North.[59]

This continuity aside, the High North is also sensitive to shifts in the rhetorical display of states, and is not "frozen" as in former times. As high politics enters into the domain of what has continuously been low politics, new dilemmas may arise, and these also represent distinct continuities in Norway's political discourse. In the strategic theater of the Cold War, emphasis was on the fact that the High North and the North Atlantic were indeed also part and parcel of the transatlantic core of NATO.[60] These considerations should balance what is now a status quo in circumpolar Arctic governance – that domestic mobilization to bring Arctic issues onto an international awareness agenda suffices in securing sound Arctic governance.

Currently, the former strategic dimension has faded into the background, for obvious reasons. Yet in a globalized world, disruptions, discontinuities, and abrupt shifts may occur. In spite of the suspension and changes in security regimes from the mid-1990s, the Norwegian government seems to understand collective security as "multilateral, transatlantic and all-European"[61] at the same time, and yet without any visible sense of priority. Again, this rhetorical shift appears to be less in line with the fact that the Arctic is a region in which security regimes are made reliant on global politics. Changes in the security regimes briefly mentioned herein could have immediate repercussions for the Arctic. The most obvious reason for this would not be that European and transatlantic security is not comprehensive, inclusive, or capable of addressing a wide range of civic issues. The main reason for this would be the erosion of security regimes and games of suspension and noncompliance in response to the influence of these communities.

FURTHER READING

Alexandrov, Oleg (2009). "Labyrinths of the Arctic Policy." *Russia in Global Affairs* 7(3): 110–19.

Bailes, Alyson J. K. (2009). "Options for Closer Cooperation in the High North: What Is Needed?" In Holtsmark and Smith-Windsor, *Security Prospects in the High North*: 28–57.

[59] Jonas Gahr Støre led the institute that compiled a study on the High North. The study involved researchers from several institutes and is called *Big Oil Playground, Russian Bear Preserve or European Periphery?* (Brunstad et al [2004]). Designed as a study in scenarios, the scenarios might not be mutually exclusive.

[60] Holst, Hunt, and Sjaastad (1985), *Deterrence and Defense in the North.*

[61] Støre, Jonas Gahr (2009d), "The Trilateral Commission."

Blunden, Margaret (2010). "The New Problem of Arctic Stability." *Survival* 51 (5): 121–142.

Breslauer, George W. (2002). *Gorbachev and Yeltsin as Leaders*. Cambridge: Cambridge University Press.

Brunstad, Bjørn, et al. (2004). *Big Oil Playground, Russian Bear Preserve or European Periphery? The Russian Barents Sea towards 2015*. Delft: Eburon Publishers.

Buzan, Barry, Ole Waever, and Jaap de Wilde (1998). *Security: A New Framework for Analysis*. London: Lynne Rienner Publishers.

Caporaso, James A. (1993). "International Relations Theory and Multilateralism: The Search for Foundations." In Ruggie, *Multilateralism Matters*, pp. 51–90.

Dragnes, Kjell (2006a). "Delimitation around Greenland: Norwegian-Danish Agreement on Mid-Line Principle." *Aftenposten*, 20 February.

Dragnes, Kjell (2006b). "Major Agreement on Continental Shelf Reached." *Aftenposten*, 21 September.

Flikke, Geir (2009). "Balancing Acts: Russian-Chinese Relations and Developments in the SCO and the CSTO." Oslo: Norwegian Institute of International Affairs Report.

Griffiths, Franklyn, ed. (1992). *Arctic Alternatives: Civility or Militarism in the Circumpolar North*. Toronto: Canadian Papers in Peace Studies No. 3.

Haftendorn, Helga (2010). "Soft Solutions for Hard Problems." *International Journal* 65: 4, 809–24.

Hanson, Philip (2009). "The Resistible Rise of State Control in the Russian Oil Industry." *Eurasian Geography and Economics* 50 (1): 14–27.

Hassol, Susan Joy (2004). "Impacts of a Warming Arctic: Arctic Climate Impact Assessment." Cambridge: Cambridge University Press.

Herspring, Dale, ed. (2005). *Putin's Russia: Past Imperfect, Future Uncertain*. Lanham & Plymouth: Rowman and Littlefield.

Holst, Johan J., Kenneth Hunt, and Anders Sjaastad, eds. (1985). *Deterrence and Defense in the North*. Oslo: Norwegian University Press.

Holtsmark, Sven G., and Brooke A. Smith-Windsor, eds. (2009). *Security Prospects in the High North: Geostrategic Thaw or Freeze?* Rome: NATO Defense College.

Hønneland, Geir (2009). "Cross-Border Cooperation in the North: The Case of Northwest Russia." In Rowe, *Russia and the North*, pp. 35–52.

Jensen, Øystein (2008). "Kontinentalsokkelens avgrensing utenfor 200 nautiske mil: Norske og russiske perspektiver i de nordlige havområder" [The Delimitation of the Continental Shelf Outside the 200-Mile Zone: Norwegian and Russian Perspectives]. *Internasjonal Politikk* 66(4): 563–90.

Keohane, Robert O. (1995). "The Analysis of International Regimes: Towards a European-American Research Programme." In Rittberger, *Regime Theory and International Relations*, pp. 23–45.

Krasner, Stephen D., ed. (1983). *International Regimes*. Ithaca, NY: Cornell University Press.

Kryukov, Valery, and Arild Moe (2007). "Russia's Oil Industry: Risk Aversion in a Risk-Prone Environment." *Eurasian Geography and Economics* 48(3): 341–57.

Lindeman, Ole A. (2009), "Norwegian Foreign Policy in the High North." *Oslo Files*, no. 1. Oslo: Institute for Defense Studies.

Mankoff, Jeffrey (2009a). "Eurasian Energy Security." *Council of Foreign Relations Report No. 43*. NY: Council of Foreign Relations.

Mankoff, Jeffrey (2009b). *Russian Foreign Policy: The Return of Great Power Politics*. Lanham & Plymouth: Rowman and Littlefield.

Müller, Harald (1995). "The Internalization of Principles, Norms and Rules by Governments: The Case of Security Regimes." In Rittberger, *Regime Theory and International Relations*, pp. 361–90.

Osnovy gosudarstvennoy politiki Rossiyskoy Federatsii v Arktike na period do 2020 goda i dal'neyshuyu perspektivu (2008), 18 September, available at: http://www.scrf.gov.ru/documents/98.html.

Pedersen, Torbjørn (2009). "Endringer i internasjonal Svalbard-politikk" [Changes in International Policies on Spitsbergen]. *Internasjonal Politikk* 67(1): 31–44.

Rittberger, Volker, ed. (1995). *Regime Theory and International Relations*. Oxford: Oxford University Press.

Rowe, Elana Wilson, ed. (2009). *Russia and the North*. Ottawa: University of Ottawa Press.

Ruggie, John Gerhard, ed. (1993). *Multilateralism Matters: The Theory and Praxis of an Institutional Form*. New York: Columbia University Press.

Smith, Hanna, Pami Aalto, and Helge Blakkisrud, eds. (2009). *The New Northern Dimension of the European Neighborhood*. Brussels: Centre for European Policy Studies.

Støre, Jonas Gahr (2005). "Norwegian Foreign Policy Priorities." Speech at the London School of Economics, 26 October, available at the Ministry of Foreign Affairs web page, http://www.regjeringen.no/nb/dep/ud/aktuelt/taler_artikler/utenriksministeren/2005/norwegian-foreign-policy-priorities.html?id=420708.

Støre, Jonas Gahr (2009a). "Etter Stortingsvalget: Om utenrikspolitiske hovedprioriteringer og 14 hovedområder," speech International Forum, Labor Party, available at Ministry of Foreign Affairs web page, http://www.regjeringen.no/nb/dep/ud/aktuelt/taler_artikler/utenriksministeren/2009/hovedomraader.html?id=587212.

Støre, Jonas Gahr (2009b). "The NATO–Russia Council NRC," speech to the council, 27 June, available at Ministry of Foreign Affairs web page, http://www.regjeringen.no/nb/dep/ud/aktuelt/taler_artikler/utenriksministeren/2009/ncr.html?id=572334.

Støre, Jonas Gahr (2009c). "Opening Speech at the 6th Ministerial Meeting of the Arctic Council," Tromsø, 29 April, available at http://www.regjeringen.no/nb/dep/ud/aktuelt/taler_artikler/utenriksministeren/2009/arktisk_velkommen.html?id=557916.

Støre, Jonas Gahr (2009d). "The Trilateral Commission," speech in Oslo, 17 October, available at Ministry of Foreign Affairs web page, http://www.regjeringen.no/nb/dep/ud/aktuelt/taler_artikler/utenriksministeren/2009/trilateral_commission.html?id=582686.

"Towards the North: Challenges and Possibilities in the High North" (2003). Norges Offentlige Utredninger No. 32. Oslo: Statens Forvaltningstjeneste.

Zacher, Mark W. (1993). "Multilateral Organizations and the Institutions of Multilateralism: The Development of Regimes for Nonterrestrial Spaces." In Ruggie, *Multilateralism Matters*, pp. 399–439.

Østreng, Willy, and Yngvild Prydz (2007). "Delelinjen i Barentshavet: Planlagt samarbeid versus uforutsett konflikt?" [The Maritime Border in the Barents Sea: Planned Cooperation versus Unexpected Conflict?]. Oslo: Stortingets utredningsseksjon, *Perspektiv*, no. 4: 1–31.

6

Military Aspects of Russia's Arctic Policy

Hard Power and Natural Resources

Katarzyna Zysk

INTRODUCTION

Russia's Arctic policies have a strong bearing on the regional strategic environment for a number of factors.[1] One obvious reason is the geography and the fact that Russia's Arctic shoreline covers nearly half of the latitudinal circle, which gives the country a unique potential to influence future Arctic activities. Second, despite radical changes in the regional security environment after the end of the Cold War, the Arctic and the High North (the European Arctic), in particular has maintained its central role in Russian strategic thinking and defense policy. Russia still has a strong military presence in the region, with a variety of activities and interests, despite weaknesses and problems facing the Russian armed forces. Third, and finally, Russia has enormous petroleum and other natural riches in the Arctic, and the leadership is laying on ambitious plans for development of commercial activities in the region. Understanding Russia's approaches to security is thus clearly important to surrounding Arctic nations and other stakeholders.

Russian military activity in the Arctic has tangibly increased in recent years, adding perhaps the most controversial topic in debates on the region's future security. Combined with political assertiveness and rhetorical hostility toward the West, which was a particular feature of Vladimir Putin's second presidential term (2004–2008), the intensified presence of the Russian naval and air forces operating in the region

---

[1] The term *Arctic* pertains in this chapter to all areas to the north of the Arctic Circle. The Russian authorities define the Arctic as the northern part of Earth, including the deep Arctic basin and shallow adjacent seas, with the islands and bordering parts of Europe, Asia, and North America. According to this definition, within the Arctic borders are situated parts of five polar states that have exclusive economic zones and continental shelves in the Arctic Ocean: Russia, Canada, the United States, Norway, and Denmark (Greenland); Security Council of the Russian Federation (SCRF), *Osnovy gosudarstvennoi politiki Rossiiskoi Federatsii v Arktike na period do 2020 goda i dal'neishuyu perspektivu*, 18 September 2008, http://www.scrf.gov.ru.

has drawn much of the international attention and contributed to the image of Russia as the wild card in the Arctic strategic equation.

Undoubtedly, one of the Russian policy goals was to reassert its national interests and the country's key position in the region, partly as a reaction to increased interest of other state and nonstate actors for the Arctic. However, the intensified military activities, often presented by outside observers as one single policy, have been composed of several different layers taken from the country's broader defense and foreign policy strategies, often not directed at the Arctic explicitly. Perceived in combination with a self-assured foreign policy, Russian military activity in the Arctic has contributed to a distorted picture of the regional security dynamics that overstated the probability for an armed conflict and created misconceptions about the underlying motives in Russian Arctic policies, viewed as an expression of the country's allegedly aggressive plans in the region.

This chapter analyzes the various elements that constitute Russia's defense policy in the Arctic. First, it gives a broad overview of the armed forces' role in the Russian foreign policy and the uses of the military as a tool in recovery of the state's international status. Further, it explores the role of the Arctic in Russia's nuclear deterrence and military mission requirements related to the region's economic significance. It also examines the impact of the opening Arctic Ocean on Russia's symmetrical and nontraditional threat perceptions. Finally, this chapter draws conclusions from the Russian policies and explores their consequences for the regional security environment.

THE MILITARY AND RUSSIA'S FOREIGN POLICY STRATEGY

Over the past few years, Russian activity in the Arctic has clearly increased compared to the period following the demise of the Soviet Union in 1991. Resumption of the activity of nuclear- and general-purpose forces in the High North air and maritime domains has been followed by the Russian leaderships' statements that attracted a fair degree of international and domestic attention. The renewed activity has included regular aircraft surveillance patrols by Russia's long-range-aviation (LRA) and support aircrafts to the Atlantic, across the Arctic and into the Pacific Ocean, a practice resumed in August 2007 after fifteen years long pause. The increase in their activity was indeed remarkable: while fourteen Russian strategic bombers were identified flying along the Norwegian coast in 2006, in the following year, the number was higher than all flights conducted in the ten preceding years, reaching eighty-eight. The number further increased to ninety-seven in 2008, and then was slightly reduced in 2009 to seventy-five sorties (see Figures 6.1–6.3).[2]

The activity of the Russian navy has also been on the rise, in particular since the end of 2007. In line with missions defined in the *Concept for Use of the Russian Navy in Peacetime for the Period up to 2020*, which was endorsed by the Ministry

---

[2] Pål Guttormsen, "Møter færre russerfly," *Finnmarken*, 3 August 2010.

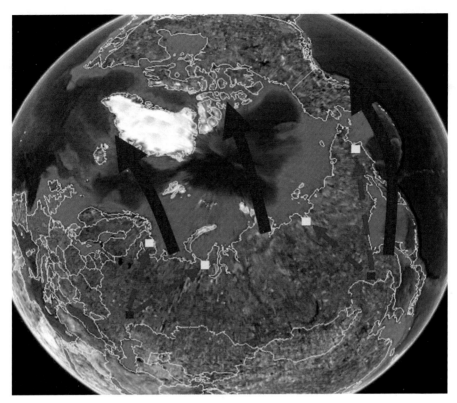

FIGURE 6.1. Russian Long-Range-Aviation Basing for the Arctic – Primary Bases and Forward Operating Locations

of Defense (MoD) in January 2007, Russia has stepped up its naval presence in "operatively important regions" in different parts of the world.[3] As Russian long-range deployments and high-profile exercises have shown, the regions that are deemed "operationally important" have been rather broadly defined and include the North Atlantic, Mediterranean Sea, the Caribbean Sea, the Sea of Japan, and the Indian Ocean. The Arctic has also been included among the regions defined as strategic. In June 2008, the Russian MoD announced resumption of the Northern Fleet's routine and active presence in the Arctic.[4]

[3] The document has not been published but is referred to in various sources; e.g., Rear Admiral A. Yakovlev, "Kto vladaet Arktikoi, tot upravlaet mirom," *Morskoi sbornik*, September 2008; Admiral Mikhail Abramov, Deputy Commander in Chief of the Russian navy, address at a conference organized by the Russian Government's Maritime Board, Moscow, 13 June 2007, http://www.morskayakollegiya. ru. See also statement by Navy Commander Vladimir Vysotskii, "Korabli Severnogo Flota vernulis' v Severomorsk," February 4, 2008, http://murman.ru.

[4] "Russia Prepares for Future Combat in the Arctic," *RIA novosti*, 24 June 2008; "Russian Navy Resumes Military Presence Near Svalbard," *RIA novosti*, 14 July 2008; "VS RF obespechat interesy Rossii v

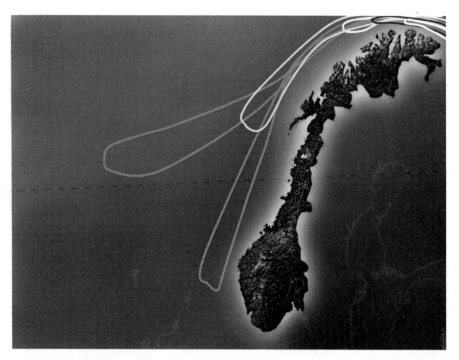

FIGURE 6.2. Graphic representation of Russian Long-Range-Aviation Flights along the Norwegian Coast in 2006

Russia's increased focus on military activity has coincided with an adoption of a more self-assured anti-Western rhetoric by the leadership, at times bordering on belligerence. One of the best-known examples of the newfound assertiveness is found in a famous speech by then president Putin at the 2007 Security Conference in Munich.[5] The address, which many observers felt as a reminiscence of the Cold War, spurred a wave of bewilderment across the diplomatic world. It has contributed to the perception of Russia as a resurgent power with an approach to international relations rooted deeply in classical realpolitik and an inherently conflictual zero-sum game. The Russian perceptions of external threat, combined with nationalism and resentment about the "humiliating" loss of great-power status in the 1990s, together with the quest for international prestige and influence through reliance on shows of strength, have been central elements of the strategic culture under Putin.[6] The belief that the military is an important element of the process of reconstituting the

Arktike – Minoborony," *RIA novosti*, 10 June 2008; Aleksandr Shaverdov, "Arktika: Lëd i plamen'," *Voennyi diplomat*, no. 2, 30 June 2008, 110–119.

[5] The speech was delivered on 10 February 2007 and is available at the conference's website, http://www.securityconference.de.

[6] See a report by Fritz W. Ermarth, "Russia's Strategic Culture: Past, Present, and . . . in Transition?", prepared for Defense Threat Reduction Agency, Advanced Systems and Concepts Office, (Science Applications International Corporation, October 2006).

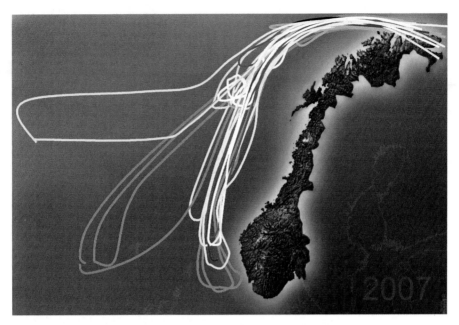

FIGURE 6.3. Graphic representation Russian Long-Range-Aviation Flights along the Norwegian Coast in 2007

country's international standing has resulted in increased attention and funding for the military, and in a greater use of the armed forces.[7]

The Russian navy has been seen as a particularly well-suited tool to enhance the county's international visibility, demonstrate its power, and highlight global ambitions.[8] As a fundamental underpinning of Russia's maritime defense, the Northern Fleet, based on the Kola Peninsula in the western Arctic, has played a central role in the Russian "come-back" strategy.[9] The naval activity has included long-range surface operations, in which capital ships from the Northern Fleet, as well as from the Pacific and the Black Sea, increasingly have been engaged in intertheater

---

[7] For example, Russian naval exercises with Venezuela in December 2008 in the midst of diplomatic tension with the United States and NATO signaled displeasure over plans to deploy missile-defense systems in Central Europe and Western admonishment of Moscow over the Russo-Georgian War.

[8] The Russian Government's Maritime Board, "Tseli i zadachi primeneniia VMF, sostoianie i rezultaty ego deiatelnosti v 2007 godu,"; M. Abramov, address at conference organized by the Maritime Board, Moscow, 13 June 2007, http://www.morskayakollegiya.ru; interview with Commander in Chief of the Navy Admiral Vladimir Vysotskii, back then Commander of the Northern Fleet, "My obespechivaem bezopasnost' Rossii na vazhneishem strategicheskom napravlenii," *Orientir*, no. 6, June 2007, 15–20.

[9] In Russian sources, the term *western Arctic* is often referred to as the European North (Evropeiskii Sever, Sever Evropy), or in a broader sense the western (European) Arctic as opposed to the eastern (Asian) Arctic; A. Smolovskii, "Voenno-strategicheskaya obstanovka v Arktike. Istochniki ugroz interesam Rossii v Arktike i osnovnye napravleniya prilozheniya usidlii v etom regione dla VMF i drugikh vidov VS RF," *Morskoi sbornik*, no. 12 (December 2006), 55.

warship exercises, aimed at rapid redeployment of vessels from one remote naval theater of operations to another. These maneuvers were rehearsed among others during large scale military drills "Stability-2008," "West-2009," and "East-2010."[10]

The increased visibility of the Russian armed forces would not be possible without the improved performance of the national economy, fueled by high energy prices, which peaked in July 2008.[11] The surplus from Russia's energy sales has been directed to desperately needed military modernization and training. The defense budgets have systematically augmented, in particular since 2005. A further 60 percent increase from the current levels is planned for the period 2011–2012.[12] The Russian MoD, under the lead of unprecedented in that position civilian "outsider" Anatolii Serdyukov, has taken steps to restore control over military finances, widespread corruption, and low morale in the deteriorated armed forces.[13] The structural modernization program includes important milestones, such as replacing the Soviet model of a mass-mobilization army with smaller, highly maneuverable permanent readiness brigades, aimed at dominating local and regional wars and addressing insurgency and terrorism – the forms of conflict considered among the most likely in the future.[14]

The increased military activity and assertive rhetoric have been accompanied by a deterioration in the relations between the United States/NATO and Russia. Disagreements on a number of issues, including plans for deployment of the missile-defense system in Central Europe, the war in Georgia, and NATO enlargement, to name just a few, have had ripple effects on perceptions of the state of security also in the Arctic. The striking contrast between the renewed visibility of the Russian armed forces and their long stagnation and decay during the 1990s, has attracted a strong international attention toward the hard security sphere in the region and has contributed to overstatements of the scale and significance of Russian military activity.

---

[10] The rehearsals were broadly covered in the international and Russian media. See, e.g., *RIA novosti*,; http://www.rian.ru/defense_safety/20080922/151469840.html; http://www.rian.ru/analytics/20090908/184193961.html; http://www.rian.ru/defense_safety/20100721/256846411.html.

[11] The price then reached $147 per barrel, compared to $17 in January 1997.

[12] "Russia to Boost Defense Budget with 60 percent," *Barents Observer*, 30 July 2010.

[13] Serdukov came to the MoD from the Tax Service.

[14] For a broader discussion of the developments in the Russian armed forces after 1991, see Carolina Vendil Pallin, *Russian Military Reform: A Failed Exercise in Defense Decision Making* (London: Routledge, 2009); Dale R. Herspring, *The Kremlin and the High Command: Presidential Impact on the Russian Military from Gorbachev to Putin* (Lawrence: University Press of Kansas, 2006); Steven E. Miller and Dmitri Trenin, eds., *The Russian Military: Power and Policy* (Cambridge: Massachusetts Institute of Technology Press, 2004); Zoltan Barany, *Democratic Breakdown and the Decline of the Russian Military* (Princeton, NJ: Princeton University Press, 2007). A recent analysis of the progress in military modernization has been conducted by Dale R. Herspring, Roger McDermott, "Serdyukov Promotes Systematic Russian Military Reform," *Orbis: Journal of World Affairs* 54, no. 2 (Spring 2010), 284–301; Iva Savic, "The Russian Soldier Today," *Journal of International Affairs* 63, no. 2 (Spring 2010), 219–230.

In recent years, the Russian Arctic policy has relied on two basic elements – deterrence and engagement. Ostensibly, these two approaches appear contradictory and thus sometimes confusing to outside observers. The harsh rhetoric at times has intertwined with more conciliatory signals and pragmatic bilateral and multilateral regional collaboration. Both components though are integral parts of the Russian policy, aimed at promoting national interests under a variety of circumstances with diplomatic, political, economic, and military means. However, the fact that each of the elements may be on display simultaneously has been at times confusing and challenging for Russia's partners.

Since 2009, however, the conciliatory and accommodative tendencies in Russian foreign policy have become more tangible. The Kremlin leadership has avoided rhetorical confrontation and focused on presenting Russia as a responsible stakeholder open to cooperation and Western countries as key partners rather than as rivals. These adjustments have been prompted by a number of domestic and external factors. Among the major incentives for the change in approach was the downturn in the Russian economy, impelled by the 2008 global recession and the fall in energy prices that sharply reduced state revenue. Russia also nurtures an interest in receiving transfers of Western technology and investments to accelerate modernization of the economy, and there is hope that the country can leverage the "reset" in U.S.-Russian relations. The adjustments in Russian foreign policy strategy, however, have taken place in a relatively short period of time. It remains to be seen if they indeed reflect a revised vision of Russia's place in the world or rather are merely tactical in nature – temporary maneuvers aimed at achieving old and new goals with different tools.

THE ARCTIC IN THE NUCLEAR DETERRENCE

Russian military activity in the Arctic has been connected most closely to the region's central role in the country's nuclear deterrence strategy. The Arctic constitutes a transit channel for long-range aviation and is a central basing and operational area for the sea-based nuclear forces, deployed mostly with the Northern Fleet. The importance of the northern theater of naval operations has been strengthened by reduction of Russia's access to the Baltic and Black seas after the breakdown of the Soviet Union.[15] Russia's direct and easy access to the world's oceans is through its vast window on the Arctic Ocean and the northern seas.[16] In addition, the Arctic hosts an array of important components of Russian defense industry and industrial infrastructure, including shipyards and intelligence installations of all branches of

[15] Vice Admiral Yurii Kviatkovskii, "The Future of the Russian Fleets," in *The Russian Navy Facing the 21st Century*, ed. Ingmar Oldberg (Stockholm: Defense Research Establishment, 2007), 39; S. Kozmenko and M. Orlov, "Energeticheskii faktor morskoi strategii Rossii," *Morskoi sbornik*, no. 9 (September 2007), 57.
[16] S. Kozmenko and M. Orlov, op. cit.; V. Vysotskii, "My obespechivaem bezopasnost' Rossii," 15

TABLE 6.1. *The Russian Ballistic-Missile Submarine Fleet*

Today	2020?
1 *Typhoon* – (Northern Fleet)	1 *Typhoon* – 20 SS-NX-30?
6 *Delta IV* – 16 SS-N-23 (Northern Fleet)	4 *Delta IV* – 16 SS-N-23
4 *Delta III* – 16 SS-N-18 (Pacific Fleet)	4 *Borei* (*Yurii Dolgorukii*) – 16 SS-NX-30?

the Russian armed forces.[17] The role of the northern regions has been further strengthened by an intensification of activities at the launch site in Plesetsk, south from Arkhangelsk, used for placing military satellites into orbit and for test launching intercontinental ballistic missiles.

The prominent role of nuclear weapons in Russian post–Cold War defense policy has been magnified further by the deficiencies in Russian conventional forces, as well as by the ongoing military reforms.[18] Among others, Russia holds out the possibility to threaten first use of nuclear weapons in case of a large-scale war and aggression from an overwhelming conventional power.[19] Given the continued central role of nuclear forces in the country's defense posture, the Arctic is likely to remain of high strategic importance to Russia in the foreseeable future.

After the demise of the Soviet Union, however, Russia's nuclear containment capacity has rapidly deteriorated. The number of operative submarines of the Northern Fleet declined from 153, including 37 strategic submarines in 1991, to 41, including six *Delta IV*–class nuclear ballistic-missile submarines (SSBNs) in 2010.[20] Four older *Delta III*–class SSBNs are deployed with the Pacific Fleet, but these platforms are quickly approaching end of service and are expected to be decommissioned within the next few years.

Hence, maintaining and modernizing the nuclear component has been given the highest priority in the state armament programs for the period 2007–2015 and 2011–2020.[21] The overhaul of the *Delta IV*s has been completed, and the refurbishments

[17] A. Smolovskii, "Voenno-strategicheskaya obstanovka v Arktike"; Lada Karitskaya, "V zashchitu national'nykh interesov," *Na strazhe zapolariya*, 24 March 2007; V. Selin, I. Kozinskii, and E. Tereshchenko, "Ekonomicheskoe soderzhanie morskoi politiki v Rossiiskoi Arktike," *Morskoi sbornik*, 8 August 2007.

[18] *Voennaya doktrina Rossiiskoi Federatsii*, 5 February 2010; *Strategiya natsional'noi bezopasnosti Rossiiskoi Federatsii na period do 2020 goda*. The documents are available at the website of the SCRF, http://www.scrf.gov.ru/documents/18/33.html.

[19] Interview with Vitaly Shlykov, head of the Security Policy Commission of the MoD's Public Council, *RIA novosti*, 14 September 2009.

[20] The *Typhoon*-class used is as a platform for test launches of the Bulava missile.

[21] The documents have not been published but are referred to in various sources; see, e.g., M. Abramov, address at conference organized by the Maritime Board, Moscow, 13 June 2007, http://www.morskayakollegiya.ru ; A. Gavrilenko, "Morskie prioritety Rossii," *Krasnaya zvezda*, 10 February 2007; "L'vinaya dolya byudzheta MO idёt VMF, v osnovnom yadernym silam – Ivanov,"

are expected to extend their service lives until 2015–2020.[22] Construction of fourth-generation SSBNs of the *Borei* class,[23] the future backbone of Russia's strategic naval deterrent, has been at the top of the defense acquisition list. Together with development of the armament for the submarines, the *Bulava* sea-launched ballistic missile (SLBM), and the *Borei*-class boats has consumed a large share of the navy's budget.[24] As a result of repeated problems with the *Bulava* missile, which failed in more than 50 percent flight tests since 2005, the program faces significant delays.[25] Nevertheless, the political and military leadership is determined to continue work on the project, as there is no alternative.[26] *Bulava* is the only missile that can be launched from the *Borei* SSBNs. Refitting the submarines with another missile (e.g., the older Sineva) is viewed as both too expensive and questionable from the perspective of technological progress.[27]

The increased political attention and funding has resulted in more SSBN patrols and efforts to restore navigation capability in the Arctic necessary for missile launches in circumpolar conditions.[28] The polar ice still plays a central role in securing Russia's second strike capability. As before, the SSBNs operate under the Arctic Ocean in bastions behind layers of combined air, surface, and undersea defenses. The area surrounding the North Pole is perceived as particularly suitable for SLBM launches because the submarines can loiter undetected under the ice and wait in readiness to strike back.[29]

In the 1990s and early 2000s, Russia had a limited capability to deploy SSBNs in the bastions. A resumption of underwater missile launches in Arctic conditions was thus given top priority and eventually resumed in 2006, after eleven years of

RIA novosti, 3 June 2009; "Gosudarstvo potratit bole 13 trln rublei na programme vooruzhenii s 2011 po 2020 god," *Rossiiskaya gazeta*, 12 August 2010; "Russia to boost defense budget with 60 percent," *Barents Observer*, 30 July 2010.

[22] The last one, *Novomoskovsk*, joined the Northern Fleet in December 2010.

[23] Also called the *Yurii Dolgorukii* class, after the flagship that entered the service in 2010. Two others, *Alexander Nevskii* and *Vladimir Monomakh*, are to be completed by 2010 and 2011, respectively. Launch of the fourth submarine, *Sviatitel Nikolai*, has been postponed; "Russia to Conduct Five Tests of Bulava Missile in 2009," *RIA novosti*, 28 April 2009; Lev Sidorenko, "Russian Navy Future Developments," *Military Parade*, no. 3 (2008), 61–62; Interview with V. Vysotskii, *RIA novosti*, 26 July 2009; "Prestige submarines will not sail for Northern Fleet," *Barents Observer*, 11 July 2007.

[24] "L'vinaya dolya byudzheta"; "Gosudarstvo potratit bole 13 trln rublei."

[25] Eight out of fourteen flight tests conducted since 2005 failed. For an overview, see the Russian Strategic Nuclear Forces website, at http://russianforces.org.

[26] Interview with, V. Vysotskii, "The Navy Should Reflect the National Interests and Economic Potential of Our Country," *Moscow Defense Brief* 2010/1.

[27] Ibid.

[28] A. Shemetov, "O shturmanskoi sluzhbe Voenno-Morskogo Flota," *Morskoi sbornik*, January 2007; Nikita Petrov, "Russia's Navy Gets Ambitious," *RIA novosti*, 31 July 2007.

[29] Interview with the former Commander in Chief of the Russian navy, Admiral Vladimir Masorin, in Andrei Gavrilenko, "Rossiiskii flot vernulsya v Arktiku," *Krasnaya zvezda*, 26 September 2006; "Russia Proves Effectiveness of Its Naval Nuclear Force – Navy," *RIA novosti*, 15 July 2009.

suspension. The successful launch of a Sineva SLMB from a *Delta IV* was assessed by the military leadership as the navy's biggest success of the year.[30] Missile launch exercises have been conducted regularly since, mostly from the *Delta IVs*, although Russia has also demonstrated the combat readiness of the older *Delta III* delivery platforms.

Open-source discourse in Russia has not addressed the implications of thinning and contracting ice cover for the nation's nuclear deterrence strategy. It seems conceivable, however, that as the ice diminishes, the operating areas shrink, potentially increasing the vulnerability of the SSBNs, which are virtually undetectable under the ice. The changing acoustic environment may also require adjustments. Nevertheless, their basing and operational areas still represent a particular challenge for potential adversaries. Even in an ice-diminished Arctic, the oceanic geography in the north affords Russia an advantage sufficient to maintain a credible deterrence capability.

NATURAL RESOURCES AND MILITARY MISSION REQUIREMENTS

After the turn of the century and Putin's access to power, the Russian navy's missions have expanded in the sphere of protection of the country's maritime activities and resources in the ocean, as defined in *Foundations of Russia's Policy within the Naval Activity for the Period up to 2010*[31] and the *2001 Maritime Doctrine.*[32] In the Arctic and northern regions, Russia's maritime economic interests are primarily connected to a number of large oil and gas deposits on the continental shelf, strategically important seabed metals and minerals, and fisheries and maritime shipping.[33]

The Northern Fleet's tasks embrace, among others, protection of maritime shipping on the Northern Sea Route (NSR) along the Siberian coast, including tankers carrying hydrocarbons and other important trade commodities on their way to world markets; providing search-and-rescue (SAR) support; preventing and responding to terrorist attacks on gas pipelines and other important transportation infrastructure, including platforms, roadsteads, terminals, filling stations, harbors, and railways. The armed forces also protect of facilities involved in the processing and

---

[30] A. Gavrilenko, "Rossiiskii flot vernulsya v Arktiku"; V. Vysotskii, "My obespechivaem bezopasnost' Rossii"; see also *Russian Strategic Nuclear Forces.*

[31] *Osnovy politiki Rossiyskoi Federatsii v oblasti voienno-morskoi deyatel'nosti na period do 2010 goda,* available at http://www.morskayakollegiya.ru.

[32] *Morskaya doktrina RF na period do 2020 goda,* 27 July 2001, available at http://www.morskayakollegiya .ru.

[33] For example, nickel and cobalt (90 percent of the Russian extraction), apatite, barite and diamonds (100 percent), copper (60 percent), platinum (96 percent), and gold (40 percent); *Osnovy gosudarstvennoi politiki Rossiiskoi Federatsii v Arktike,* The Government of the Russian Federation, Moscow, 14 June 2001, Protocol no. 24, Chapter III, www.sci.aha.ru/econ/A11c.htm; Dimitrii Dimitrienko, "Arktika – Persidskii zaliv XXI veka," *Gazeta.ru,* 15 September 2010; press release from a meeting of the SCRF on 12 September 2008, available at http://www.scrf.gov.ru.

production of nuclear weapons and nuclear fuel.[34] The Northern Fleet has participated in ocean exploration programs aimed at determining the maritime borders of
the Russian continental shelf in the Arctic and marine surveys of ocean areas adjacent to the Russian territory.[35] The increasing economic significance of the Arctic
to Russia and prospects for development of commercial activities are likely to create
additional mission requirements for naval forces and other branches of the armed
services stationed in the region.

In 2008, Russia defined the Arctic as a region of permanent strategic importance for maintaining the country's national interests.[36] The development of the
Arctic is considered directly related to meeting long-term political, economic,
defense, and social needs of the country, and to ensuring Russian competitiveness in the global markets.[37] Although merely 2 percent of the Russian population
lives in the Arctic, the region generates 14 percent of the country's gross domestic product (GDP).[38] Twenty-five percent of the nation's total exports come from
the region.[39] By 2020, the Russian government aims to further increase that share
by transforming the Arctic into the country's foremost base for natural resource
development.[40]

The economic importance of the Arctic has been highlighted in an array of key
policy documents recently adopted or being drafted by Russia including in the energy
strategy up to 2030,[41] as well as a similar document for the development of national
transportation,[42] a concept for Russia's long-term socioeconomic development up to

[34] M. Abramov, address at conference organized by the Maritime Board, Moscow, 13 June 2007, http://www.morskayakollegiya.ru; V. Vysotskii, "My obespechivaem bezopasnost' Rossii"; A. Smolovskii, "Voenno-strategicheskaya obstanovka v Arktike"; L. Karitskaya, "V zashchitu national'nykh interesov"; *Voprosy obespecheniya natsional'noi bezopasnosti*; *Morskaya doktrina RF*, "Concept for Use of the Russian Navy in Peacetime"; "Voprosy obespecheniya natsionalnoi bezopasnosti v raion-akh Severa. Rabochaya Gruppa Gosudarstvennogo Soveta Rossiiskoi Federatsii po voprosam politiki v otnoshenii severnykh territorii Rossiiskoi Federatsii, 2004," *Arktika Segodnya*, http://arctictoday.ru/russ/facts/200000439.

[35] Interview with Deputy Chief of the Navy's Main Staff, Vice Admiral Oleg Burtsev, "Submarines of the Northern Fleet Will Take Part in Exploration and Guarding of Arctic Seabed," *RIA novosti*, 23 March 2009.

[36] According to Deputy Prime Minister Sergei Ivanov, quoted in Alexander Balyberdin, "Arctic in the System of Priorities for Maritime Activities," *Military Parade*, no. 4 (2009), 48.

[37] Ibid.

[38] Ministry for Regional Development of the Russian Federation, "Arkticheskii Murmanskii mezhdunar-odnyi forum," 1 October 2010, available at http://www.minregion.ru. Depending on which regions are included, the numbers may vary; for example, according to Nikolai Patrushev, the Arctic accounts for 11 percent of national income and 22 percent of total Russian exports. Press release, Security Council of the Russian Federation, 13 September 2008.

[39] Ibid.

[40] *Osnovy gosudarstvennoi politiki Rossiiskoi Federatsii v Arktike na period do 2020 goda,*.

[41] *Energeticheskaya strategiya Rossii na period do 2030 goda*, 13 November 2009, available at http://www.energystrategy.ru.

[42] Ministry of Transport of the Russian Federation, *Transportnaya strategiya Rossiiskoi Federatsii na period do 2030 goda*, 22 November 2008, http://www.mintrans.ru.

2020,[43] and a project of strategy for examination and development of energy on the extended continental shelf.[44] According to official announcements, the Arctic also is a central element in defining the Russian maritime activity to 2020.[45]

In particular, the development of Arctic hydrocarbon resources has been perceived as directly connected to several dimensions of national security. The security strategy of 2009 associates Russia's international position and influence in world affairs with control of energy reserves.[46] According to official estimates, up to 90 percent of hydrocarbon reserves found on the entire Russian continental shelf are located in the Arctic, 66.5 percent of which are in the western part – in the areas of the Barents Sea and Kara Sea.[47]

The anticipated increase in demand for energy worldwide, together with diminishing production in existing Russian fields expected between 2015 and 2030, turns the attention of the Russian leadership northward. One of the main goals of Russian Arctic policy is to increase extraction of natural resources in the region.[48] Until today, Russian petroleum production has been developed only in the Timan-Pechora oil field in the south Pechora Sea and on the Yamal Peninsula. Russia has started development of the biggest gas and oil deposits in the region discovered at the end of 1980s, the Shtokman condensate gas field, north of the Kola Peninsula in the eastern Barents Sea and the oil field Prirazlomnoe in the Pechora Sea, south of the island Novaya Zemlya.

Russia has also ambitions to develop the NSR as a major link in maritime transportation between Europe and Asia. Production of energy resources in the region and other economic activities in the Arctic are expected to increase the level of shipping through the NSR from the Barents and Kara Seas westward, as well as eastward toward Asia. In the future, Russia aims at increasing the share of Asian markets in export revenues to keep the state's incomes.[49] As a corollary, the NSR may constitute an important element the country's energy security in the future.

A few Russian and international shipping companies have shown an increasing interest in testing this maritime channel. The passageway from Saint Petersburg to Vladivostok through the Arctic is fourteen thousand kilometers long, whereas the same trip via the Suez Canal and the Cape of Good Hope are twenty-three

---

[43] Ministry for Economic Development (currently Ministry for Economic Development and Trade), *Kontseptsiya dolgostrochnogo sotsial'no-ekonomicheskogo razvitiya Rossiiskoi Federatsii na period do 2020 goda*, 17 November 2008, http://www.government.ru.

[44] Ministry of Natural Resources of the Russian Federation, *Strategiya izucheniya i osvoeniya neftegazovogo potentsiala kontinental'nogo shelfa RF – proekt*, September 2008, http://www.rsppenergy.ru.

[45] According to Deputy Prime Minister Sergey Ivanov, in Boris Kozyrev, "Arktika meniaet strategiyu," *Transport Rossii*, 29 January 2009.

[46] *Strategiya natsional'noi bezopasnosti RF.*

[47] *Osnovy gosudarstvennoi politiki Rossiiskoi Federatsii v Arktike*, 2001; *Strategiya izucheniya i osvoeniya neftegazovogo potentsiala.*

[48] *Osnovy gosudarstvennoi politiki Rossiiskoi Federatsii v Arktike na period do 2020 goda.*

[49] Danila Bochkarev, "Energy Diversification towards the East – Strategic Imperative and Operational Response to the Uncertainty of Energy Demand," *Baltic Rim Economies*, no.1, 19 February 2010, 28.

thousand kilometers and thirty thousand kilometers long, respectively.[50] In summer 2010, the first high-tonnage Russian tanker carried gas condensate from Murmansk on the Kola Peninsula to China, making the voyage faster than expected – in only twenty-two days. Also, Norilsk-Nickel sent the first cargo vessel to sail the entire NSR without icebreaker assistance from Murmansk to Shanghai and to bring consumer goods on the return voyage. Another Russian company, Sovcomflot, plans to use the NSR to sail with oil from the Varandey terminal in Nenets in the western Arctic to Japan. In 2010 also, the Norwegian "Tschudi Shipping Company", in cooperation with Danish "Nordic Bulk Carriers", transported iron-ore concentrate from Kirkenes in northern Norway to China along the Russian northern coast, saving more than 17 days compared to the traditional southern route.[51] Four or five similar voyages are planned for 2011.[52] The Russian agency operating icebreakers, Rosatomflot, received by September 2010 fifteen subsequent applications for the escort of various ships through the NSR in 2011.[53]

In general terms, the Russian Arctic has high commercial potential, in particular in terms of energy and shipping. Nevertheless, the pace and scope of implementation of the nation's ambitious Arctic plans will depend on a number of domestic and external factors. Although the aforementioned Russian strategies and concepts for development of the region reflect interests and priorities, they do not necessarily indicate what will unfold in reality. One of the major factors deciding the fate of the region's economic future will be the price of energy, as the Arctic remains a high-cost region for exploitation of natural resources.[54] The price of energy is set at the global level and determined by such factors as the relationship between demand and supply, including production from other regions, as well as the prospects for production of alternative fuels, such as unconventional natural gas resources (shale gas from rock formations).[55]

The recent impact of the global recession on Russia's energy development has confirmed this dependency. In the wake of a sharp fall in energy prices and the negative impact of the economic meltdown on domestic and foreign gas demand, development of the Shtokman gas field has been delayed. Likewise, the largest gas field on the Yamal Peninsula, Bovanenkovo, was postponed until 2012.

The pace of development of the Russian Arctic energy industry also will be determined by domestic developments and advances in modernization of the national

---

[50] D. Dimitrienko, "Arktika – Persidskii zaliv XXI vieka."

[51] These developments are monitored by the *Barents Observer*; see, for instance, "Preparing for Next Year's Northern Sea Route Season," *Barents Observer*, 20 October 2010.

[52] Iron ore to break ice toward China, *Barents Observer*, 27 January 2011.

[53] Andrei Diev, "Arktika: igra po krupnomu," *Krasnaya zvezda*, 22 September 2010.

[54] As defined in the Russian Arctic policy document: *Osnovy gosudarstvennoi politiki Rossiiskoi Federatsii v Arktike na period do 2020 goda.*

[55] For a more information on shale gas, see Hanna Mäkinen, "Shale Gas – A Game Changer in the Global Energy Play?", *Baltic Rim Economies*, no. 1, 19 February 2010, 31; Indra Øverland, "The Surge in Unconventional Gas – Implications for Russian Export Strategies," *Baltic Rim Economies*, no. 1, 19 February 2010, 18

economy. Russia has expressed an interest in transfers of Western technology and foreign investments, which are especially necessary in the Arctic. This requirement may provide ample incentive for Russia to cooperate with other nations in the region. Recently, it has been illustrated by interest in joint mapping, management, and resource development in the region expressed by the Russian government after reaching in April 2010 agreement with Norway on maritime delimitation of the Barents Sea and the Arctic Ocean.[56]

RUSSIA'S SYMMETRICAL THREAT PERCEPTIONS IN THE ARCTIC

Uncertainties about the pace and scope of economic development in the Arctic notwithstanding, the region's potential alone stimulates various actors to define and articulate their interests and policies toward the Arctic. In turn, the international focus on the region has an impact on Russia's approaches to regional affairs, including security challenges and threats.

The preliminary assessment of the changing Arctic as a theater of maritime operations has emphasized challenges rather than possible advantages, such as greater operational flexibility between the Northern and Pacific fleets in terms of shorter deployment times. Conversely, the potential increase in foreign naval presence and power projection closer to Russia's northern borders in the opening Arctic Ocean has been viewed as a security concern. The debates on Arctic military security that have flourished in particular in the four other polar rim states, spurred, among others, by increased Russian assertiveness and military activity, have been met in Russia with some level of reserve.[57]

According to the 2010 Russian military doctrine, expansion of any foreign military presence in proximity to the national territory, both on land and at sea, is one of the principal "military threats" and possesses a real possibility of escalating into an armed conflict.[58] Because all other polar countries bordering the Arctic Ocean are members of NATO, which is still perceived as having an anti-Russian bias, Russia is the more intent on keeping a close eye on their military plans for the region.[59] As noted by Dmitry Trenin, in general terms, Russia sees any state or nonstate actor with a substantial military potential – including NATO, the United States, China, and other players – as having the potential to become a threat under certain circumstances.

---

[56] "Russia Ready for Joint Management of the Barents Sea," *Barents Observer*, 30 August 2010. See also the joint statement on maritime delimitation and cooperation in the Barents Sea and the Arctic Ocean, signed by President Dmitry Medvedev and Foreign Minister Jonas Gahr Støre in Oslo, 27 March 2010, http://www.regjeringen.no.

[57] See, e.g., A. Balyberdin, "Arctic in the System of Priorities for Maritime Activities."

[58] The military doctrine distinguishes between a military danger and a military threat. The first is defined as international or domestic developments that may escalate to military threat under favorable circumstances. The second implicates a real possibility of outbreak of a military conflict; *Voennaya doktrina RF*, 2010.

[59] According to Russia's Foreign Ministry spokesperson, Andrei Nesterenko, Moscow, 27 July 2009, http://www.murmannews.ru.

This approach derives from the fact that Russian policy makers focus on a state's military capability rather than political intentions, which may be malleable.[60]

Hence, with a combination of warning and reassurance, Russia has made it eminently clear that any expanded role of NATO in the region is unacceptable. Foreign Minister Sergei Lavrov argued, for instance, that there were no problems in the Arctic that called for a military solution or that could justify the presence of "military-political alliances."[61] Chief of the general staff, Nikolai Makarov, went further and warned after NATO's discussions of security prospects in the High North in Reykjavik in January 2009,[62] that from then on the Russian defense planning would take into account presence of the alliance's warships in the Arctic.[63] At the same time, the Ministry of Foreign Affairs has made assurances that Russia is against an arms race in the region.[64] Repeated regularly, and combined with stronger cooperative signals from Russia, the view that there is no reason to summon NATO to the High North has been gaining stronger ground among the key polar actors.

There is a broad consensus among the Arctic nations that in the region there is no military threat and little scope for conflict, which is regarded as both adverse and undesirable.[65] However, although an armed conflict appears inconceivable today, neither Russia nor other polar states can completely discard limited tensions with an escalation potential from their defense planning. That is likely to be the case as long as uncertainties about the future economic, political, and security developments in the Arctic are part of the decision-making process and security equation.

Challenges that may arise from the growing competition for natural resources between various state and nonstate actors have been one of the topics considered in security scenarios discussed inside Russia. The conviction that future global rivalry for waning natural reserves may lead to greater tension and pose a challenge or even a threat to Russia as a country controlling a vast global share of those resources has been voiced by representatives of political and military circles for many years.[66] These

[60] D. Trenin, "Russia's Threat Perception and Strategic Posture," in *Russian security strategy under Putin: U.S. and Russian Perspectives* (Carlisle, PA: Strategic Studies Institute, Army War College, November 2007), p. 35.

[61] "The Arctic Is No Place for Military Blocks," *Voice of Russia*, 15 October 2009 (Lavrov quotation).

[62] "Security Prospects in the High North," a seminar organized by NATO and the government of Iceland, in cooperation with the NATO Defense College, Reykjavik, Iceland, 28–29 January 2009.

[63] "Rossiiskii VMF siadet na khvost korabiami NATO v Arktike," *Izvestiia*, 24 February 2009; "The Arctic is no place for military blocks"; "Lavrov surprised by NATO exercise," *Barents Observer*, 25 March 2009.

[64] A. Nesterenko, Moscow, 27 July 2009, http://www.murmannews.ru.

[65] Remarks by Russian Minister of Foreign Affairs Sergey Lavrov at Arctic Council Session, Tromsø, 29 April 2009, Ministry of Foreign Affairs of the Russian Federation, http://www.ln.mid.ru.

[66] Head of Department in the General Staff's Centre for Strategic Studies, Colonel Yu, A. Martsenyuk, and the Deputy Head S. G. Chekinov, "Slovo Yubilyaram. O nekatorykh problemakh upravleniya gruppirovkami voisk (sil) na strategicheskikh napravleniyakh," *Voennaya mysl'*, 31 January 2005; Commodore G. Ivanov, "Obespechenie bezopasnosti ekonomicheskoi morskoi deiatel'nosti gosudarstva," *Morskoi sbornik*, March 2007; Rear Admiral V. Vashukov, "Vremya i flot. Voenno-morskoi flot i obespechenie natsional'noi bezopasnosti strany v mirnoe vremya," *Morskoi sbornik*, January 2003.

concerns, however, often refer to "Russian" energy resources, reflecting a rather defensive thinking and the persistent sense of insecurity. In a way characteristic of predominantly continental powers, the fear of threat of external enemies, invasion or encirclement, loss of territory, and internal fragmentation is still a major factor in Russian security analysis. A statement by the First Deputy Chief of the General Staff, Lieutenant General Alexander Burutin, provides an example of this perspective. In October 2009, Burutin suggested that the military security of Russia as an energy superpower will be largely determined by the future intensity of the struggle among leading states and transnational corporations for fuel. Burutin warned that if Russia did not take measures to expand its economic and military capabilities, a number of leading world states would attempt to turn Russia into their appendage for raw materials.[67]

The Arctic region has also been mentioned in the context of the expected growing competition for energy. President Dmitry Medvedev pointed out in June 2010 that "an increasing fight for Arctic resources" was an argument in favor of strengthening the navy and providing support for the crumbling Russian shipbuilding industry.[68] The Deputy Chief of the General Staff and Chair of the General Staff Military-Research Committee, General Anatolii Nogovitsyn, similarly argued that "a struggle for energy resources in the Arctic" is one the most important challenges of Euro-Atlantic security, destined to define the fate of Russia, the United States, and Europe in the twenty-first century.[69] To avoid undesired developments, Nogovitsyn proposed including the region in the revised European security architecture presented by Russia to international partners in 2009.[70]

Dwindling global petroleum and gas reserves have also been defined as a security concern in the 2009 *National Security Strategy*. The document asserts that in a long-term perspective, international policy will focus on access to energy resources, including in the major regions such as the continental shelf in the Barents Sea and other parts of the Arctic, in addition to the Middle East, the Caspian Sea, and Central Asia (article 11). The document maintains that it cannot be excluded that problems related to the competitive struggle for dwindling resources world-wide may be solved with the use of military force, although the statement is made without pointing directly at the Arctic or any of the other aforementioned regions (article 12).[71]

---

[67] A. Burutin, "Threats to Russia's Military Security," *Military Parade*, no. 3 (2008), 12–14.

[68] D. Medvedev, "Vystuplenie na zasedanii Soveta Bezopasnosti po voprosam razvitiya sudostroeniya," 9 June 2010, http://www.kremlin.ru.

[69] Olga Kolesnichenko, "Arktika – prioritet rossiiskoi vneshnei politiki," *Voenno-promyshlennyi kurier*, 26 August 2009; "Arktiku podvedut pod dogovor," *Nezavisimoe voennoe obozrenie* (NVO), 19 June 2009.

[70] An analysis of Russia's proposition for the new security architecture was conducted by Bobo Lo, "Medvedev and the New European Security Architecture," Centre for European Reform Policy Brief, July 2009, http://www.cer.org.uk.

[71] *Strategiya natsional'noi bezopasnosti RF.*

Maintaining a reliable military force capable of providing security in the evolving Arctic environment is a crucial element of Russian security policy.[72] One of the goals listed in the fundamentals of Arctic policy adopted by Russia in 2008 was the establishment of a group of general-purpose forces able to provide security in the region in a variety of military-political scenarios.[73] After a fairly alarmist reaction from the international media, including, among others, speculations about Russian militarization of the region, the Russian Ministry of Foreign Affairs ensured, however, that the country had no intention of enhancing its military presence the in the Arctic.[74] In March 2011, however, the Commander of the Russian Ground Forces, General Aleksander Postnikov informed the Council of Federation that a special Arctic brigade will be established in Pechenga, close to border with Norway and Finland.[75]

The need for providing a credible military presence in the Arctic region is also driven by the necessity to protect the Russian strategic nuclear forces.[76] Antiaircraft defenses, including the S-300 long-range surface-to-air missile system, as well as powerful naval capabilities, are viewed as essential elements for this task.[77] Although the Russian surface shipbuilding programs are not explicitly associated with the Arctic, the Northern and Pacific fleets are identified as the main beneficiaries of the new vessel construction. The naval ambitions include new *Sergei Gorshkov*–class frigates, destroyers, and a handful of aircraft carrier groups – the numbers vary from one to two or three for each fleet – to be built over the coming twenty to thirty years. If these plans are realized, Russia's offensive capabilities in the Arctic would be strengthened considerably.

Still, although we may expect some qualitative and numerical enhancements in Russia's military posture in the Arctic in result of the ongoing military modernization and as a reaction to the increase in human activity of the region, a large military buildup seems unlikely in the near term and midterm. Russia's ability to execute its grand naval ambitions within indicated time frames is questionable because of the limited potential of the national economy, the slow pace of new construction,

---

[72] *Osnovy gosudarstvennoi politiki Rossiiskoi Federatsii v Arktike na period do 2020 goda.* Interview with Nikolai Patrushev, "Sovbez v serdce Arktiki," Russian state TV channel Vesti Nedeli, 14 September 2008; press release from the meeting of the SCRF on 12 September 2008; "Vozmozhnost' voennykh konfliktov v Arktike maloveroyatna – ekspert," *RIA novosti*, 4 June 2008.

[73] *Osnovy gosudarstvennoi politiki Rossiiskoi Federatsii v Arktike na period do 2020 goda.*

[74] "Lavrov: No Enhancement of Russian Military Presence in the North," *Barents Observer*, 30 April 2009.

[75] Victor Myasnikov, "Sukhopytnye voiska raznoi stepeni i tyazhelosti," Nezavisimaya qazete, 16 March 2011.

[76] A. Khramchikhin, "V perspektive – arkticheskii front," NVO, 4 February 2009; Khramchikhin, "Severnyi ledovityi TVD," NVO, 28 April 2010.

[77] "Uchebnye puski S-300 sostayatsya v akvatorii Barentseva morya," *RIA novosti*, 23 August 2010; "Raketnye puski na Severnom flote proshli v shtatnom rezhime," *RIA novosti*, 7 September 2010; L. Sidorenko, "Russian Navy Future Developments."

and uncertainty related to the design capacity of the domestic shipbuilding industry, as well as financial constraints, dysfunctional structures, and the outflow of highly qualified personnel.[78]

The emergence of an existential security threat in the Arctic that could provide a stimulus for a larger military buildup does not seem a plausible scenario in the foreseeable future. Hence, apart from its continued roles in nuclear deterrence, the Northern Fleet is likely to remain focused primarily on littoral missions with a limited capability to conduct strategic deployments as a result of the refit and extension of service of older combatants and gradual introduction of ships of the new generation.

RESPONSES TO NONTRADITIONAL SECURITY CHALLENGES

The transformations in the Arctic natural and security environment have raised the prospect of a variety of nontraditional security challenges emerging in the vast northern territories – areas that otherwise are distant, often uninhabited, and for the most part, unsurveyed. These emerging requirements have generated additional assignments for the Federal Security Service (Federal'naya Sluzhba Bezopasnosti, FSB) and its Border Guard branch (Federal'naya Pogranichnaya Sluzhba, FPS).

The need to strengthen surveillance and defense capabilities in the northern regions appeared not to be a pressing matter in 2006, when the Vorkuta-based Independent Arctic Border Detachment, formed in 1994, was disestablished. The responsibility for border security was subsequently shared between military districts and relied on existing automatic surveillance systems, whereas the detachment's human and material resources were diverted to reinforce security on the troublesome southern border, such as in the North Caucasus.[79]

However, the perceived vulnerability of the northern regions, comprising boundaries that wind for nearly twenty thousand kilometers at sea and eleven thousand kilometers on land, has increased in recent years. In 2008, Russia announced that it had taken steps to strengthen security of the northern borders by reorganizing the FSB to incorporate new mission requirements in the region.[80] The head of the FPS, General Vladimir Pronichev, suggested that the Arctic has become a crossroads of interest for many states. According to Pronichev, joined by other leaders, despite the ongoing international cooperation and dialogue, there is a concern over what is perceived as a sharp rise in the number of individuals and organizations wishing to

[78] A. Khramchikhin, "VMF na zarubezhnykh korabliakh," NVO, 3 July 2009.
[79] Aleksandr Slizhevskii, "Eshchë odna "kholodnaya" voina?," NVO, 26 March 2010; "Budut sformirovany arkticheskie voiska FSB," NVO, 3 April 2009.
[80] Vladimir Popov, "Russia's New Arctic Force to Focus on Border Protection," RIA novosti, 30 March 2009.

develop business activities in the region.[81] Among identified potential threats to the region, the Russian authorities point at maritime terrorism, smuggling of narcotics and other illicit goods, as well as massive poaching and illegal export of flora and fauna.[82] The FSB has also reported cases of illegal migration of citizens from the Commonwealth of Independent States: in 2009, for example, more than six hundred persons were arrested for border violations in the Arctic regions.[83]

The expected growing human activity in the north is likely to give incentives to an increased military presence aimed at support and protection of economic activities, as well as exercising the country's authority in the desolate region. In 2009, Russia reestablished Arctic units within the Arkhangelsk and Murmansk border guard which started patrolling the NSR.[84] In addition, Russia aims to create a comprehensive coastal defense infrastructure in the region by 2017.[85] These plans include development of a network of forward-based airfields and modern military towns situated along the Arctic coast, similar to the Nagurskaya compound, which was opened on the Franz Josef Land archipelago in 2008.[86]

Russia has provided assurances that its plans do not include a radical increase in number of personnel deployed to the region and priority has been given to investments in automatic surveillance systems that can maintain continual monitoring throughout the furthermost reaches of the Russian Arctic. They include stationary and mobile electro-optical and infrared surveillance networks and the "Arktika" space system, composed of four meteorological, communication, and radar satellites, first of which is to be launched in 2014.[87] The FSB also relies on unmanned aerial vehicles, of which seven have been purchased from national manufacturers.[88] Projects for a new ice-class boat for prolonged Arctic endurance patrols and other ships for the coast guard have been under development.[89]

Preparations to meet the new security challenges in the Arctic include SAR, humanitarian assistance, and disaster relief (HA/DR). Russia's intention to improve

---

[81] Interview with the head of the FPS, General Vladimir Pronichev, *Rossiiskaya gazeta*, 2 June 2010.

[82] *Osnovy gosudarstvennoi politiki Rossiiskoi Federatsii v Arktike na period do 2020 goda; Strategiya natsional'noi bezopasnosti RF*.

[83] Aleksandr Slizhevskii, "Eshchë odna "kholodnaya" voina?"; interview with V. Pronichev; "Beregovoi okhranie Pogranichnoi sluzhby FSB Rossii – 5 let!" *Kaspiets*, 21 May 2010.

[84] "Arkticheskaya gruppirovka po zashchite severnykh granits RF sozdana v pogransluzhbe FSB RF," *RIA novosti*, 15 September 2009.

[85] *Osnovy gosudarstvennoi politiki Rossiiskoi Federatsii v Arktike na period do 2020 goda*.

[86] Nagurskaya includes administrative and residential buildings, an Orthodox church, garage, energy block, and other technical buildings, "Vladimir Putin na Zemle Frantsa-Iosifa," *Pogranichnik severo-vostoka*, 5–11 May 2010; V. Popov, "Russia's New Arctic Force to Focus on Border Protection"; Vladislav Kulikov, "Northern Belt," *Rossiiskaya gazeta*, 16 September 2009.

[87] According to head of the Russian Federal Space Agency, Anatoly Perminov, "Russia to launch Arctic satellite monitoring project", *Voice of Russia*, 4 May 2010.

[88] Including ZALA-421-05; Irkut-10, and Orlan; "Beregovoi okhranie Pogranichnoi sluzhby FSB Rossii – 5 let!"; interview with V. Pronichev.

[89] Ibid.

its response capability and play a leading role within the sphere has been also reflected in practice.[90] In May 2010, the FSB and the Ministry of Emergency Situations conducted their first joint exercises under severe Arctic conditions.[91] Advances in implementation of economic development plans in the Russian Arctic are likely to lead to an increase in such activities in the future.

CONCLUSION

Russia is a determined, key Arctic power and has high ambitions for development of the northern regions. Traditional hard security concerns continue to play a crucial role in Russia's approach to polar affairs. Despite uncertainties about the region's future commercial viability and the scope and pace of economic developments, the Arctic is likely to remain of paramount significance to Russia into the foreseeable future as an essential element in the country's nuclear deterrence strategy.

Expanded foreign policy ambitions of the Russian leadership, aimed at restoration of the country's international status and combined with increased defense funding, have led to a greater number of high-profile military exercises, in the north. Apart from the rehearsals connected to maintaining a credible nuclear deterrence, the war games included out-of-area naval operations and long-range deployments with a prominent role of the Northern Fleet. The progress in military modernization over the past few years has improved the state of the Russian armed forces. The exercises and maneuvers in the Arctic indicate that the nation is better prepared to participate in more complex air and sea operations than it was just a few years ago. However, a radical strengthening of Russia's military posture in the region seems unlikely in the near future given resource deficiencies as well as lack of a sound justification by security requirements. Possible high political and diplomatic costs of a military buildup in the region may also be part of the considerations.

However, the asymmetries of power, interests, and activities among the Arctic rim states contribute to shaping the regional strategic environment and give Russia an influential position in the region, despite the country's persistent weaknesses. The Arctic plays a more prominent role in Russia's military strategy than in the defense policies of its peers in the region. Similar conclusions can be drawn about the region's projected role as one of Russia's future economic engines and its place – or lack of thereof – in economic plans of other key actors. Hence, Russia is likely to be both a more active and a more visible actor in the region than other nations in years to come.

Although the risk for confrontation in the Arctic, particularly military conflict, is by no means as high as often portrayed in the media and among some experts and

---

[90] *Osnovy gosudarstvennoi politiki Rossiiskoi Federatsii v Arktike na period do 2020 goda.*
[91] *Vladimir Putin na Zemle Frantsa-Iosifa.*

academics, there are still a number of factors that contribute to nagging uncertainty and that may contribute to fuel mutual mistrust. Military activity, likely to follow the opening Arctic Ocean, is one of the potentially problematic dimensions of Arctic politics. Although regular military patrols in the following two decades seem unlikely, a stronger presence of border guards, coast guards, and similar agencies is more plausible if the economic activity continues to accelerate.[92]

Furthermore, some of the remaining legal issues, including demarcating exclusive economic zones, the outer limits of extended continental shelves, and the legal status of the Northwest Passage and some of the straits along the NSR, add further complexity. Potential disagreements and diplomatic tensions can become entwined with identity politics and assertive rhetorical exchanges. Nationalist overtones can color Arctic diplomacy and serve as a suitable tool for mobilizing the domestic public opinion, as exemplified in the recent past not only in case of Russia but also other Arctic countries – Canada in particular.

In addition, the state of Arctic security will be determined in large part by developments within overarching international political frameworks, including Russia's relations with the United States and NATO. Deterioration in these broader structures may have an impact on Arctic affairs – a fact that was illustrated by a souring of Arctic diplomacy in the wake of the 2008 Russo-Georgian war. Indeed, tensions and potential conflicts in the Arctic appears more likely to be generated as a spillover effect from tension outside the region than to emerge from within.

However, there is a broad international consensus that regional stability is in the interest of all circumpolar powers. An intensified dialogue and enhanced Arctic transparency, including military cooperation that in the future preferably goes also beyond collaboration on SAR and HA/DR and the focus on nontraditional security challenges, are additional factors that may contribute to maintain an armed conflict scenario as a hypothetical option only. Likewise, refraining from military posturing and provocative rhetoric will help avoid fueling the national insecurities.

In the case of Russia, the country's efforts to protect its national security in the Arctic through cooperation and dialogue inherently are tied to elements of broadly defined deterrence strategy. Russia repeatedly has stressed that it has an overriding interest in preserving the Arctic as an area of peaceful international cooperation. At the same time, maintaining a reliable military force capable of dealing with a wide range of both symmetrical and nontraditional security challenges and threats remains one of the basic goals of Russian security policy in the region. A belief that mutually beneficial cooperation is possible only between strong parties is typical of this double-track reasoning.

---

[92] Lance M. Bacon, "Ice Breaker," *Armed Forces Journal*, 147, March 2010, 16–19, http://www.armed forcesjournal.com/2010/03/4437078 (Chief of Naval Operations of the U.S. Navy, Admiral Gary Roughead, assessed that a routine military presence in the Arctic is not expected before 2025).

Hence, one may expect that the Russian leadership will continue to communicate the message of reassurance about Russia's willingness to abide by international law and work through international institutions. At the same time though, the nation will continue to signal its capability and readiness to protect its national interests with various means. Above all, the leadership seeks to ensure that Russia's voice is heard when the rules of the game and the region's future are defined.

7

The Russian Arctic in the Twenty-First Century

Caitlyn L. Antrim

In the summer of 2007, when the Russian flag was placed on the ocean floor at the North Pole and the Arctic ice cover receded to the lowest extent ever recorded, the media sought Arctic story lines that would grab the public's attention. Titles and headlines such as "Arctic Meltdown," "A New Cold War," and "Arctic Land Grab" focused on burgeoning Russian activities in the Arctic all fed a sense of circumpolar competition, conflict, and crisis.[1]

These story lines were effective because they built on geopolitical beliefs that have been with us for more than a century, from the final years of the Russian Empire through the Soviet era and into the first years of the Russian Federation. For all of that time, the core of Western geopolitical thought has held that there is a natural conflict between the landlocked Eurasian heartland and the Western maritime nations. In this analysis, the Arctic has played an essential, yet unrecognized, role as the northern wall in the Western strategy to enclose and contain the world's largest land power. Throughout the twentieth century, scant attention was given by the West to changes in Arctic technology, economics, climate, and law that had been under way since the 1930s. Stories of Russian claims to the seabed of the Arctic Ocean and Moscow's control of new sea lanes, interpreted through the old (and by now, creaky) geopolitics of the early twentieth century, heightened fears of conflict.

The geopolitics of the twenty-first century will be different from the days of empire and conflict of the nineteenth and twentieth. The increased accessibility of the Arctic, with its energy and mineral resources, new fisheries, shortened sea routes, and access to rivers flowing north to the Arctic Ocean, is pushing Russia to become an Arctic maritime state. As it progresses, Russia will no longer be susceptible to

---

[1] For examples, see Scott Borgerson, "Arctic Meltdown," *Foreign Affairs* 87, no. 2 (March/April 2008), pp. 63–77 "Russia's Arctic Energy Plans Herald a New Cold War," *Telegraph*, September 18, 2008, http://www.telegraph.co.uk/comment/telegraph-view/3562236/Russias-Arctic-energy-plans-herald-a-new-Cold-War.html; James Graff, "Fight for the Top of the World," *Time*, September 13, 2007, http://www.time.com/time/world/article/0,8599,1663445,00.html.

geographic isolation or strategic encirclement. At the same time, these changes will have a liberalizing influence on Moscow, requiring Russia to become more closely integrated into global commercial and financial networks; to welcome international business involvement; and to participate in international bodies that harmonize international shipping, safety, security, and environmental regulations.

These changes are already opening the way for a new geostrategy that has its roots in the geopolitical thinking of the twentieth century but addresses the changes that are turning the Arctic from an afterthought into a central front in a new geopolitical order. In this new geostrategy, Russia assumes a role as one of the principal maritime powers of the "rimland," and the Russian Arctic becomes a new geographical pivot among the great powers. Decades will pass before Russia can fully make the shift from Eurasian heartland to Arctic coastal state, but the process already is unfolding. Moscow is already integrating policies to this end through new strategies published by its Security Council and federal ministries, and the nation shows every indication that it expects to seize its future seat among the major maritime states of the world.

THE ARCTIC IN TWENTIETH-CENTURY GEOPOLITICS

The twentieth century began with Alfred Thayer Mahan's geopolitical study *The Problem of Asia*.[2] In this classic study, Mahan addressed the competition between the land power of the Russian Empire and the colonial and trading nations whose interests lay along the periphery of the Asian continent, from the Near East to China. Mahan saw Russia as a land power that was limited in its ability to bring its strength to bear through the "debatable lands" that separated Russia from the Western powers in southern Asia, particularly the British Empire and the United States, which could maintain their dominance along the Asian coast by way of maritime trade and sea power. Maintenance of Western power in southern Asia depended on Russia's inability to mount a naval front from the south, in addition to a lack of capability to exploit the potential land approach from the north. To challenge the West, Russia needed either access to the sea from its own ports or an overland route to other ports, a possibility that gave rise to the "great game" of the nineteenth century and the armed and political conflicts in twentieth-century Afghanistan and Iran.

In assessing Russia's access to the open sea, Mahan emphasized the geographical limitations on Russian sea power. From St. Petersburg, Russia had to pass through the Baltic Sea, facing the sea power of the Nordic states in the Gulf of Finland and the Danish straits. From the Crimea on the Black Sea, Russian ships had to pass through the Dardanelles and either the Strait of Gibraltar or the Suez Canal. Ocean access from the far eastern port of Vladivostok was possible, but its distance from the economic, political, and military center of Russia and the growing maritime

---

[2] Alfred Thayer Mahan, *The Problem of Asia and Its Effect upon International Policies* (Boston: Little, Brown, 1900).

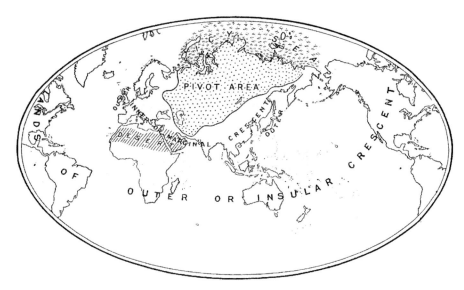

FIGURE 7.1. Mackinder's Geographic Pivot and the Icy Seas. *Source*: Image courtesy of Naval War College Press.

challenge of Japan made that outpost only a limited threat to Western interests in Asia.

Four years after the publication of Mahan's work on Asia, Halford Mackinder laid the groundwork for East-West geopolitics in the twentieth century. In a presentation to the Royal Geographical Society titled "The Geographical Pivot of History," Mackinder identified the southwestern region of the Russian empire as the crossroads of power between East Asia and Western Europe.[3] He viewed the steppes and plains of this region as an avenue by which a central land power, with internal lines of communication, could come to dominate the crescent from the coasts of China and South Asia westward through the Balkans and up to the English Channel.

Mackinder saw technological change, in the form of the railroad, as increasing the power of the heartland and amplifying the historical role of the steppes of Central Asia as the route by which for millennia invading peoples had moved from Asia into Europe. He suggested that control of this region, with its wealth of agricultural production and industrial raw materials, and with the power of movement provided by the railroad, was the pivot around which the conflict between the heartland and the crescent of maritime states revolved (see Figure 7.1).

Thus, in the opening years of the twentieth century, Mahan and Mackinder established the essential framework for the most enduring geopolitical perspective on the century of conflict yet to come: land power versus sea power, the contest

---

[3] Halford Mackinder, "The Geographical Pivot of History," *Geographical Journal* 170, no. 4 (December 1, 2004), pp. 298–22 (originally presented to the Royal Geographical Society on January 25, 1904).

between the Eurasian heartland and Great Britain and the United States for access to the marginal crescent from China to Western Europe.

Containment of Russia and the Eurasian heartland became the geostrategic theme of the century. Mackinder's vision was refined in the early 1940s by the Yale University professor Nicolas Spykman.[4] Spykman died in 1943, but his ideas of enclosure and containment were to be put into practice in the postwar era in response to Soviet expansion of control over Eastern Europe and the Soviet Union's short-lived alliance with communist China. Spykman, like Mahan and Mackinder before him, did not address Russian access to the Arctic Ocean. The significance of this omission is hinted at by the crucial role of the port of Murmansk as the eastern terminus for supplies from the West in World War II, as well as by the establishment of the Soviet Navy's Northern Fleet in 1933 and the growing importance of sea routes linking ports along the Eurasian Arctic coast to the Soviet Union.

Even as late as 1997, Zbigniew Brzezinski (who had been President Jimmy Carter's national security adviser) presented a view of an enclosable Russia bounded by Europe to the west; by former Soviet republics to the southwest; and by India, China, and Japan to the south and east.[5] Although the former national security adviser updated the geopolitical situation to reflect the breakup of the Soviet Union, his geostrategic approach remained one of enclosure and containment, with new relationships being established with the former Soviet republics and client states by the United States and NATO. Once again, the northern enclosure of Russia, the "fourth wall," was assumed but not addressed – and so the twentieth century was closing with the same blind spot that had been introduced one hundred years before.

By the end of the twentieth century, the enclosure and containment of Russia seemed complete, with NATO and the European Union to the west, Western military involvement in Iraq and Afghanistan, the U.S. alliance with Japan in the east, and the rise of India and China as substantial powers on land and sea. The strategy of enclosure and containment, which rested on the belief that geography and political power could permanently enclose Russia, appeared to have endured. But change was coming to the Arctic, the frozen north was changing, and the geopolitical wall to the north already was beginning to crumble.

RUSSIA AND THE ARCTIC

Most of the attention paid to the benefits of Arctic warming and retreat of the polar ice pack has focused on the economic potential of offshore oil and gas deposits and the savings of time and fuel made possible by new transarctic shipping routes. These benefits are significant, but for Russia there are other even greater interests

---

[4] Nicholas J. Spykman and Helen R. Nicholl, *The Geography of the Peace* (1944; rpt., Hamden, CT: Archon Books, 1969).
[5] Zbigniew Brzezinski, *The Grand Chessboard* (New York: Basic Books, 1997), pp. 197–208.

related to the increased accessibility of the Arctic Ocean, including securing a newly opened Arctic frontier and increasing access to the Siberian rivers that reach throughout the interior of the country and empty into the Arctic Ocean. Russia's perception of its Arctic interests can be grouped into four categories: economics, security, transportation, and development.

RUSSIA'S ARCTIC SEAS AND THEIR ECONOMIC IMPORTANCE

Russia's Arctic encompasses the northern seas, islands, continental shelf, and the coast of the Eurasian continent; in addition, it is closely linked to the vast watershed that flows to the sea. The Arctic coast of Russia spans from its border with Norway on the Kola Peninsula eastward to the Bering Strait. Along the coast is a wide continental shelf, running eastward from the Barents Sea in the west to the Kara Sea, the Laptev Sea, the East Siberian Sea, and the Chukchi Sea. Of these seas, only the Barents is largely ice-free throughout the year, a result of the Gulf Stream returning from the Atlantic Ocean and into the Arctic. The Russian continental shelf extends northward far beyond Moscow's two-hundred-nautical-mile exclusive economic zone (EEZ). When free of ice, the coastline along the Arctic stretches almost forty thousand kilometers (including the coasts of the northern islands), which must be patrolled and protected. The Russian Arctic coast drains a watershed of 13 million square kilometers, equal to about three-quarters of the total land area of Russia and an area larger than any country on the earth, save Russia itself.

Russia has long been a major producer of oil and gas from land-based resources. The resources of the Arctic continental shelf are attracting increasing attention. Deposits in the Barents Sea are already being developed, with other known deposits in both the Barents and the Kara seas being eyed for future exploitation. Yet still more energy resources are awaiting discovery. In 2008 the U.S. Geological Survey estimated that of the undiscovered oil and gas in the Arctic, more than 60 percent was located in Russian territory – equivalent to about 412 billion barrels of oil. All but a very small percentage of these resources are on shore or inside the Russian EEZ.[6] The area of greatest potential is in the Kara Sea basin, with smaller, yet still respectable, prospects in the Laptev and East Siberian seas.

SECURITY AND NAVAL OPERATIONS

Russia's Northern Fleet has been based on the Kola Peninsula, on the southwest shore of the Barents Sea, since 1933. The fleet is the largest and most powerful

[6] Kenneth J. Bird, Ronald R. Charpentier, Donald L. Gautier, David W. Houseknecht, Timothy R. Klett, Janet K. Pitman, Thomas E. Moore, Christopher J. Schenk, Marilyn E. Tennyson, and Craig J. Wandrey, *Circum-Arctic Resource Appraisal: Estimates of Undiscovered Oil and Gas North of the Arctic Circle*, USGS Fact Sheet 2008-3049 (Washington, D.C.: U.S. Geological Survey, 2008).

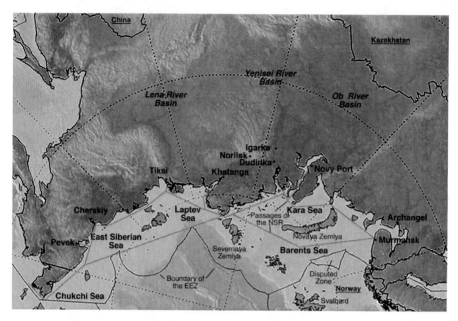

FIGURE 7.2. Seas, Coastlines, and Watersheds of Siberia. *Source:* Image courtesy of Naval War College Press.

component of the Russian navy. From its bases, the fleet's ballistic-missile sub-marines deploy under the Arctic ice. The Northern Fleet is also well situated to deploy year-round to the North and South Atlantic and to escort commercial ship-ping to or from ports in northwest Russia. Although the Northern Fleet could be kept within the Arctic in the case of unrestricted naval warfare, at other times, Russian warships operating from Murmansk have free access to the ocean. An ice-diminished Arctic helps Moscow achieve permanent access to the open ocean, an objective of imperial Russia for centuries.

If Western geostrategists had a blind spot with regard to the fourth wall of Russia's enclosure, the potential for change was apparent to others even before World War II. In a 1938 article in *Foreign Affairs*, H. P. Smolka offered a prescient outlook for Russia in the Arctic. He addressed the basing of the Northern Fleet on the Kola Peninsula and examined the role of the newly formed Central Administration of the Northern Sea Route (NSR) as the development agency for the Russian Arctic coast in Asia, even comparing the administration to the British East India Company.[7] In spite of this prominent discussion, no hint of reconsideration of the strategy of enclosure was to appear in the work of the prominent geostrategists who followed in the footsteps of Mahan and Mackinder, including Spykman and Brzezinski.

[7] H. P. Smolka, "Soviet Strategy in the Arctic," *Foreign Affairs* 16, no. 2 (1938), pp. 272–78.

Smolka identified the military benefit of northern development activities by addressing Mahan's points about Russia's lack of access to the high seas. He argued that the fleet based in Murmansk would gain access to the open ocean: "Russia would thus be bottled up on three sides: west, south and east. But in the North – and there only – there is an independent, continuous and all-Russian coastline, unassailable by anyone."[8]

The retreat of polar ice is opening vast expanses of coastline and offshore waters to access and exploitation. Russia's Coastal Border Guard has evolved from the maritime division of the Soviet-era KGB into a modern coast guard that is responsible for monitoring maritime activities along the coast and in the EEZ and for enforcing national maritime laws and regulations. It is a small service with assets that include conventional frigates and corvettes assigned to the Pacific and Black Sea fleets, several fisheries and EEZ patrol vessels, and lighter vessels intended for near-coast operations. Only a handful of the ships are designed for Arctic conditions or ice operations. Russia's ability to patrol and monitor its increasingly accessible Arctic EEZ has not kept pace with the receding summer ice cover.[9]

THE NORTHEAST PASSAGE AND THE NORTHERN SEA ROUTE

The first single-season transit of the Northeast Passage (i.e., along the full length of the Arctic coast of Russia) was not completed until 1932, coinciding with the Soviet Union's recognition of the north as a new and critical dimension of its national security. The Central Administration of the Northern Sea Route was created that same year with the mission of developing the resources of the north. Sea routes were charted and icebreakers were built to make it possible to reach ports from the Kara Gate (the passage between the island of Novaya Zemlya and the mainland, which separates the seas north of Europe from those of Asia) eastward to the Bering Strait. This section of the Northeast Passage is defined as the Northern Sea Route (NSR). Military bases and closed industrial cities, as well as some of the infamous gulags, were established along this northern frontier in the 1930s and 1940s, and air bases and monitoring stations were operated along the Arctic periphery during the Cold War era. Port facilities to support access to the interior were maintained near the mouths of the major rivers feeding into the Arctic Ocean. Traffic along the NSR grew slowly but continuously through the rest of the Soviet era.

The economic disruption accompanying the transition from the Soviet Union to the Russian Federation led to a decade of neglect of the NSR and of the port facilities that had supported it. Cargo along the NSR declined precipitously during

[8] Ibid., pp. 85–94.
[9] *Naval Institute Guide to Combat Fleets of the World: Their Ships, Aircraft, and Systems*, 15th ed. (Annapolis, MD: U.S. Naval Institute Press, 2007), p. 669.

the 1990s. In 2000, then president Vladimir Putin brought renewed attention to the Northern Sea Route as part of a new national economic strategy that marked the end of the decline. The new vision of the NSR elevated it to the status of a core component of Russia's economic development strategy.[10]

The NSR serves both as a set of regional sea lanes and as a transarctic passage. There is a natural divide at the Taymyr Peninsula, which separates the Kara Sea to the west from the Laptev Sea to the east. This is the northernmost point of Asia and the last point that opens during the summer ice melt. The passage is constrained by the Vilkitskiy Strait, which separates the mainland from the island of Severnaya Zemlya, where shallow depth and retention of ice late into the summer limit the transit of ships between east and west. Partial, regional routes continue to operate even when transit along the full length of the Northeast Passage is prevented by the freezing of the several narrow straits along the way.

The NSR provides access to regional ports such as Novy Port, which is located near the mouth of the Ob River; Dikson, Dudinka, and Igarka (towns on the Yenisei that have served as loading points for Siberian mineral and timber resources); and Tiksi, at the mouth of the Lena River. These ports also support coastal shipping during the summer season, when ice cover is at its minimum.

Beyond providing a national route connecting northern ports and access to the interior, the NSR is of interest to global shipping firms as an alternative to the longer southern route between the Far East and Europe. The journey from Yokohama to Rotterdam can be reduced by about four thousand miles by way of the NSR. Even with reduced speeds in a northern passage, the shortened distance translates into a quicker voyage and decreased fuel consumption, with substantial financial savings to the shipper. At present, the Arctic shipping season is of unpredictable length, dependent on changing climate patterns. Sea and ice conditions require ships designed specifically for passage through the icy waters. The NSR will not appeal to major shipping firms as a regular route until more experience is gained and the route is upgraded with modern aids to navigation, port facilities, and search-and-rescue capabilities. Over time, those developments, with or without further retreat of the polar ice, will make the Northeast Passage a more attractive route. The increase in the number of ice-capable vessels will magnify the trend.

The NSR depends on powerful icebreakers to open routes though the ice and to escort shipping, even in summertime. Six nuclear icebreakers, four of the heavy *Arktika* class and two of the shallow-draft *Taymyr* class, maintain the NSR. Major Russian commercial enterprises have begun acquiring their own ice-breaking cargo ships. In 2009, the fleet operated by Norilsk Nickel MMC, in north-central Siberia, accounted for nearly a million tons of shipping from Dudinka through the Kara Sea

---

[10] Vladimir Putin, statement on board the nuclear icebreaker *Arktika*, April 2000, cited in Yuri Golotyuk, "Safeguarding the Arctic," *Russia in Global Affairs* 3 (July–September 2008), http://eng.globalaffairs .ru/number/n_11281.

and on to the Kola Peninsula. Norilsk's success is leading to the design of similar vessels for unescorted transport of oil and natural gas in the Arctic.[11]

In theory, the NSR can also serve as a sea corridor by which the Northern Fleet could reach the Pacific Ocean, but such passage remains hazardous because naval vessels are not designed to ice-class standards. Passage through ice-infested waters, even with icebreaker escorts, is potentially dangerous to the hulls and propulsion systems of warships, whose complex superstructures are also susceptible to icing, to the detriment of stability.[12]

THE ARCTIC WATERSHED

Russia's Arctic watershed comprises the Eurasian heartland and the northern coastal regions that, until recently, served as the fourth wall enclosing Russia and limiting its communication and commerce with the rest of the world. The Asian watershed alone, which constitutes what Mackinder defined as the "Pivot Area" and Spykman called the "Heartland," accounts for about two-thirds of the land area of Russia.

Russia's Arctic watershed is richly endowed. The southern part of western Siberia is a highly productive agricultural area. The region is rich in oil and coal, and the Ob and Yenisei rivers provide abundant hydroelectric power. Large deposits of iron and bauxite provide the raw materials for steel and aluminum production. The central Siberian plateau in the north is home to Norilsk Nickel, the world's largest producer of nickel and palladium. The Lena River provides access to productive gold and diamond mines. The watershed is also home to the largest forest in the world, stretching across Siberia from the northwest to the southeast.

Vast distances, rugged terrain, and severe climate preclude the construction of highways and railroads in the north, but the three major river systems – Ob, Yenisei, and Lena – reach throughout the watershed, from the Ural Mountains in the west, Mongolia and Kazakhstan in the south, and the mountains bordering the Pacific Ocean in the east. The potential of these rivers to support the development of the watershed can be seen in comparison to the importance of the Mississippi River for the United States (see Table 7.1). At present, this potential has been blocked by the Arctic climate, which opens the rivers in the north for only a couple of months each year.

The climate of the Eurasian coast is one of the most extreme and inhospitable in the world, with winter temperatures reaching minus forty degrees centigrade, and ice on the sea as thick as two meters. The climate takes a severe toll on port

---

[11] "Russia to Start Eastward Oil, Gas Shipments via Arctic in 2010," *RIA Novosti*, December 26, 2009, http://en.rian.ru/russia/20091226/157382462.html. Russia's largest shipping firm, Sovcomflot, announced its intent to ship oil eastward over the NSR and on to Japan in the summer of 2010 using one of its new double-acting seventy-thousand deadweight-ton shuttle tankers.

[12] R. Douglas Brubaker and Willy Østreng, "The Northern Sea Route Regime: Exquisite Superpower Subterfuge," *Ocean Development and International Law* 30, no. 4 (1999), p. 305.

TABLE 7.1. *Comparison of Siberian River Systems with the Mississippi River System*

River System	Greatest Length (km)	Basin (sq. km)	Average Discharge (m³/sec)
Ob	5,410	2,972,497	12,500
Yenisei	5,539	2,580,000	19,600
Lena	4,472	2,490,000	17,000
Comparison			
Mississippi	6,300	3,225,000	16,200

facilities, producing extreme fluctuations in river depth and flow during the summer melting season. Resupply to sustain human habitation during the long and frigid winters is expensive. Costs that were borne as security expenses during the Cold War have to be justified on commercial grounds. As a result, many old facilities have deteriorated or been abandoned over the past two decades and need to be rebuilt from scratch. Maintenance of facilities in the region has been complicated by seasonal warming, which causes melting and refreezing of the permafrost. The temperature fluctuations make soil structurally unstable for construction. Only when commercial traffic provides economic incentives to maintain facilities near or on the Arctic coast do ports (such as Dudinka, which services Norilsk Nickel) manage to operate at their former capacities.

CHANGE IN THE ARCTIC: BREACHING THE FOURTH WALL OF CONTAINMENT

In all of the geostrategic analyses that guided Western strategy in the twentieth century, the Arctic played a critical but unrecognized role as the fourth wall enclosing Russia. Western geostrategists, from Mahan and Mackinder to Spykman and Brzezinski, saw the frozen rivers and seas of the Arctic Ocean as completing the containment of Russia. The assumption of an impervious North was reasonable for the analysts of the early twentieth century, who, in the words of Nicholas Spykman, were convinced that "geography is the most fundamental factor in foreign policy because it is the most permanent."[13] This seemingly obvious maxim proved incorrect during the first decade of the twenty-first century, as changing climatic conditions led to a string of summers that set record lows for ice cover – losses of 30 percent of average ice cover in the late summer and declines in maximum ice cover in the winter of more than 10 percent.

Had geostrategists in the mid- to late twentieth century examined the evolution of the Arctic in Russia, they would have recognized that the role of the Arctic

---

[13] N. J. Spykman, *The Geography of the Peace* (New York: Harcourt, Brace, 1944), p. 41.

in completing the enclosure of the heartland rested on four factors: technology, economics, climate, and law. Changes in those factors went unnoticed in the West, even though evidence that they were subject to varying levels of change began to appear as early as the 1930s.

ARCTIC TECHNOLOGY

Russia has fought the barrier of the polar ice for more than a century, building an impressive fleet of icebreakers and ice-strengthened vessels. In the four and a half decades between World War II and the breakup of the Soviet Union, traffic along the route rose from less than a half million tons per year in 1945 to 6.6 million tons in 1989. During that time, the technology of Arctic transportation evolved from simple reinforced bows and strengthened hulls to specialized hull designs and coatings, ballast-shifting capability, nuclear power, pod-mounted directional thrusters, and other remarkable capabilities.

Russia's commitment to the development of ice-covered regions is illustrated by its investment in icebreakers. The current fleet includes six second-generation nuclear-powered icebreakers, four heavy-duty dual-reactor ships for use along the length of the NSR, and two smaller single-reactor icebreakers capable of clearing routes and escorting ships into ports and rivers. A focus on nuclear icebreakers, however, fails to reflect the full Russian commitment to shipping in the Arctic. Diesel-electric icebreakers that support regional operations and maintain port and river access are being constructed to replace and expand the aging fleet of Soviet-era vessels. The recent introduction of tankers and cargo vessels of the "double-acting" type – with azimuthal pod propulsion, cruising bows (for good performance in open water while steaming ahead), and ice-breaking hulls aft (for ice breaking while steaming astern) – is helping privatize Arctic routes. Norilsk Nickel's five ice-breaking cargo ships run throughout the year. In 2009 the ships carried almost 1 million tons of cargo between Dudinka and Murmansk. The state-owned shipping firm Sovcomflot just commissioned for use along the NSR its third seventy-thousand-deadweight-ton (dwt) double-acting tanker.

Oil and gas technology developed for the Gulf of Mexico and the North Sea is improving access to offshore oil and gas deposits in the Arctic. Advanced offshore techniques, including remote-exploration technology, directional drilling that allows a single well site to reach through the seafloor to tap deposits many kilometers away, and seabed-based production technology, are making development in the Arctic seas more attractive. New ships and advances in oil and gas technology are only part of the key to opening the Russian Arctic watershed. Development of ports and river transport systems are necessary to connect the NSR to currently isolated regions of the Eurasian heartland. Winter freezing of the northern reaches of rivers will require both new ice-breaking capabilities and improvements to ports and waterways to extend the period during which shipping can reach the sea.

ENERGY ECONOMICS

Economic containment of the Soviet Union began to crumble in the early 1980s, when European nations decided to facilitate the construction of a pipeline to bring natural gas from western Siberia to Western Europe. The pipeline had been opposed by the United States because it put control over the most strategic of materials, energy, in Soviet hands, and because it provided funds and technology to the struggling Soviet economic system. American proponents of using trade as a tool to influence the Soviet Union lost out to European policies that favored East-West trade for mutual benefit.[14] A decade later, with the breakup of the Soviet Union and the rapid privatization of state enterprises, fears of trade and interdependence with Russia declined further. Rising oil and gas prices, the discovery of oil and gas deposits in the Barents Sea, and demonstration of deepwater and cold-weather exploration and exploitation technology made Arctic deposits attractive candidates for development. By the beginning of the twenty-first century, with energy supplies already flowing to Europe, there was little concern about the shift to new Russian sources in the Arctic. Finally, although the Russian Federation still sends mixed messages about foreign investment, particularly in strategic sectors of the economy, opportunities for foreign participation in oil and gas development and transportation draw Western attention and investment at levels unheard of only two decades ago.

CHANGING CLIMATE

Over the last two decades of the twentieth century, scientists plotted a slow reduction in the extent of ice cover in the Arctic. In the past ten years, this trend has accelerated. Scientists are contemplating a continuation of the decline that could lead to a complete seasonal loss of ice cover toward the middle of the century.[15] Arctic winters, however, will continue to be long and harsh, and there is no projection of a complete loss of ice cover in wintertime, although ice will not extend as far and likely will be thinner and less dense first-year ice.

RosHydroMet, Russia's hydrometeorological agency, has projected a winter increase of up to four degrees centigrade along Russia's Arctic coast by 2040.[16] Base temperatures near minus forty degrees centigrade, however, mean that the winter

---

[14] U.S. Congress, *Technology and East-West Trade: An Update* (Washington, D.C.: Office of Technology Assessment, May 1983), p. 70.

[15] "Ice-Free Arctic Possible in 30 Years, Not 90 as Previously Estimated," *Science Daily*, April 2, 2009, http://www.sciencedaily.com. See also National Snow and Ice Data Center, http://nsidc.org/news/press/20091005_minimumpr.html. Although the term *ice-free* generally means that no more than 10–15 percent of the ocean surface is covered with ice, climate experts are forecasting a summer in which the entire Arctic Ocean is free of ice at some point within a few decades.

[16] Federal Service for Hydrometeorology and Environmental Monitoring (ROSHYDROMET), *Assessment Report on Climate Change and Its Consequences in Russian Federation: General Summary* (Moscow: ROSHYDROMET, 2008), p. 13 (my translation).

ice of the coastal sea and rivers and extremely low temperatures will continue to be a challenge. Still, such a change in temperature would be significant, because it would lead to a shorter and less bitterly cold winter in the north, with less time for ice to spread and thicken. Warming in the southern Arctic region of the watershed, estimated at two degrees centigrade, will gradually increase growing periods and lead to the melting of permafrost, slowly moving northward the lands available to human development.

CHANGES OF INTERNATIONAL LAW

Just as Arctic technology, economics, and climate evolved over the twentieth century, so, too, did international law as it applies to the Arctic. At the beginning of the twentieth century, when the Arctic Ocean was an ice-locked and unexplored realm, there was little need for a sophisticated international legal regime. In the 1920s, Russia proposed that the coastal states simply divide the northern area into sectors bounded by lines drawn from the North Pole to the coastal borders between states, but this proposal was not accepted by the other Arctic states, and eventually it was dropped by Russia as well.

It was not until a comprehensive law of the sea was negotiated and implemented in the 1982 UN Convention on the Law of the Sea (UNCLOS) that rules applicable to the Arctic Ocean were adopted. Other laws and agreements, including the 1990 U.S.–U.S.S.R. Maritime Boundary Delimitation Agreement, the 1995 Agreement on High Seas and Straddling Stocks, and conventions and guidelines of the International Maritime Organization, have further extended the legal regime of the Arctic.[17] The Arctic Council, established in 1996, provides a forum for collaborative study of sustainable development in the Arctic. The Ilulissat Declaration of 2008 commits the five Arctic coastal states (Russia, the United States, Canada, Norway, and Denmark) to resolve issues through diplomatic channels.[18] Significant progress has been made on the resolution of disputes over maritime boundaries and access rights between Russia and Norway, and Oslo and Moscow have far more to gain from each other by acting amicably than they could hope to gain through open conflict. The two nations are formalizing their boundary in the Barents Sea, but sovereignty issues around the Svalbard Archipelago will require additional effort.

[17] 1982 UN Convention on the Law of the Sea (UNCLOS), 1995 UN Agreement for the Implementation of the Provisions of the United Nations Convention on the Law of the Sea of 10 December 1982 relating to the Conservation and Management of Straddling Fish Stocks and Highly Migratory Fish Stocks; Agreement between the United States of American and the Union of Soviet Socialist Republics on the Maritime Boundary with Annex, signed at Washington, D.C., June 1, 1990; International Maritime Organization, Guidelines for Ships Operation in Ice-Covered Waters, MSC Circ. 1056, December 23, 2002.

[18] The Ilulissat Declaration, Arctic Ocean Conference, Ilulissat, Greenland, May 28, 2008, http://www.oceanlaw.org/downloads/arctic/Ilulissat_Declaration.pdf.

From the perspective of Russia's interests in the Arctic, the most important aspects of UNCLOS were its creation of the exclusive economic zone (EEZ), recognition of national jurisdiction over the continental shelf beyond the EEZ, and establishment of the right of coastal states bordering ice-covered waters to establish and enforce regulations to protect the marine environment within the EEZ. These provisions give Russia a basis for jurisdiction over shipping in the NSR, fisheries in the EEZ, and seabed minerals to the outer limit of the continental shelf, all subject to a responsibility to observe the rights of other states as specified in UNCLOS. Under the convention, Russia proposed boundaries of its extended continental shelf drawn on the basis of scientific data and a complex formula in article 76 of UNCLOS, which accounts for distance from shore, depth of seafloor, thickness of sediment, slope of seabed, and the nature of underlying rock. The boundary proposal was submitted in 2001 to the Commission on the Limits of the Continental Shelf (CLCS), an international body that comprises experts in marine geology and related fields. The CLCS returned the proposal to Russia, stating that additional evidence would be needed before the commission could provide an opinion on the merits of the claim.[19]

Under the convention's provisions governing navigation in ice-covered seas, Russia is allowed to establish and enforce regulations applicable to the protection of the Northern Sea Route as long as that route is "ice covered" for most of the year and the regulations are related to protection of the marine environment. The regulations also must be based on scientific evidence and not discriminate among ships on the basis of national registry.[20]

RUSSIA'S ARCTIC VISION

The Kremlin has had long involvement in the development of the Russian Arctic, from the establishment of the Northern Sea Route Administration in 1932 to the recent statement of Russia's strategy for the Arctic. In September 2008, the Security Council of the Russian Federation laid out its vision of Russia's Arctic future, which captured the nation's basic interests in the Arctic:

- Use of the Arctic zone of Russia as a strategic resource base of Russia to tackle socioeconomic development of the country
- Preservation of the Arctic as a zone of peace and cooperation
- Conservation of unique ecosystems of the Arctic
- Use of the Northern Sea Route as a national integrated transport communications line in Arctic Russia[21]

[19] UNCLOS, art. 76.
[20] UNCLOS, art. 234.
[21] *Foundations of State Policy in the Arctic of the Russian Federation for the Period to 2020 and Beyond*, September 18, 2008 (my translation, from the original, "Основы государственной политики Российской Федерации в Арктике на период до 2020 года и дальнейшую перспективу"), http://www.scrf.gov.ru/documents/98.html.

The document *Foundations of State Policy of Russia in the Arctic for the Period up to 2020 and Beyond* focuses on priorities for Arctic policy, many of them incorporated into more specific strategies and concepts in other functional areas. From a functional perspective, the key provisions can be grouped into foreign policy, military security, economic development, and transportation and maritime policy.

FOREIGN POLICY

In seeking to establish the Arctic as a "zone of peace and cooperation," the Russian Arctic policy emphasized mutually beneficial bilateral and multilateral cooperation between Russia other Arctic states on the basis of international treaties and agreements. Underlying all Russian policies toward the Arctic is support for regional collaboration in the Arctic and commitment to UNCLOS and multilateral organizations and approaches, including the International Maritime Organization and the Arctic Council. Russia also was supportive of the meeting of the five Arctic coastal states that met in Ilulissat, Greenland, in 2008 to issue a declaration on management of the Arctic. The key foreign policy point in the Ilulissat Declaration – that the Arctic coastal states will resolve disputes peacefully in line with the law of the sea – reflects the goals of the Russian Arctic policy.[22]

MILITARY SECURITY

In military terms, Russia's Arctic policy focuses on the protection of the nation and its borders, which run north into the Arctic Ocean. The document also is geared toward achieving a favorable political and legal operating regime in the Russian Arctic for the Russian Federation's armed forces and other organizations needed in the region, particularly the Federal Security Service's Coastal Border Guard.

The opening of the Arctic raises four issues of military security: the protection of the ballistic-missile submarine fleet; protection of trade routes along the Arctic and from the Arctic to other parts of the world; defense of coasts, ports, and shipping; and the movement of warships between the Atlantic and Pacific oceans.

The protection of the ballistic-missile submarine fleet, which is part of the traditional naval and strategic security of the region, is not addressed by the Russian Arctic policy. The majority of Russia's strategic missile submarines are based in the Kola Peninsula, from where they can deploy quickly in times of tension to safe operating stations under the polar ice cap. The thick and noisy ice pack provides security and eliminates the need to pass through the closely watched Bering Strait and the gap between Greenland, Iceland, and the United Kingdom. Surface ships and the attack and patrol submarines of the Northern Fleet can provide additional security as the strategic submarines cross the relatively shallow continental shelf on

---

[22] Ilulissat Declaration.

the way to deep and ice-covered waters. The Northern Fleet also has the traditional roles of ensuring freedom of navigation for shipping and showing the flag overseas. Instead of concern over deepwater naval operations, the military-security issue on which the Russian Arctic policy primarily focuses is the defense and protection of the borders and area of the Russian Arctic zone. The primary border activities are the following:

- Creation of a functioning coast guard in the Arctic from the Federal Security Service and effective interaction with the coast guards of other Arctic coastal states in combating terrorism at sea, preventing smuggling and illegal migration, and protecting biological resources
- Development the border infrastructure in the Russian border zone and reequipping of the border guard
- Implementation of an integrated system for the monitoring of surface activities and oversight of fishing activities in the Russian Arctic[23]

Arctic change will put an increasingly heavy burden on the Coastal Border Guard. The force has fewer than nine thousand personnel and only about a half dozen 3,710-ton patrol icebreakers. These aging ships were built almost thirty years ago, and only two are reported to be in service in the Arctic. Although naval vessels may supplement some activities of the border patrol, the small patrol icebreakers and a few lightly armed patrol tugs are the only ice-capable armed vessels in either the Coastal Border Guard or the navy. The assets are spread thin: in addition to the Arctic Ocean, the Coastal Border Guard patrols the Baltic, Black, and Caspian seas; the Amur and Ussuri rivers; and the coastal Pacific Ocean.[24] Nor are ice-capable ships, other than the large icebreakers, available to provide quick search-and-rescue response along the northern shipping lanes. The sudden addition of the newly opened Arctic coast and the vast tract of EEZ and continental shelf resources in the strenuous Arctic environment adds a heavy responsibility. Management of shipping, enforcement of environmental regulation and fisheries policies, and provision of search-and-rescue capabilities taxes the small force. It is not clear that Moscow fully understands the new demands placed upon the Coastal Border Guard. When the emerging requirements finally are grasped, the service will need to increase its size and resources quickly to meet its growing responsibilities. The Coastal Border Guard also will need to collaborate with the navies and coast guards of other Arctic states to meet all of its responsibilities.

---

[23] *Foundations of State Policy in the Arctic of the Russian Federation for the Period to 2020 and Beyond.*
[24] *Naval Institute Guide to Combat Fleets of the World: Their Ships, Aircraft, and Systems,* 15th ed. (Annapolis, MD: U.S. Naval Institute Press, 2007), p. 669.

ECONOMIC DEVELOPMENT

Socioeconomic development is the core element of Russia's Arctic policy. Expanding the resource base of the Arctic zone of Russia would do much to fill the nation's needs for hydrocarbon resources, living marine resources, and other strategic raw materials. These vast living and nonliving resources also provide virtually all of Russia's foreign exchange, which fund domestic development and economic growth.

The Ministry for Regional Development has prepared a paper on sustainable development in the Arctic for the Arctic Council,[25] and the ministry was tasked with preparing a regional development plan for the Arctic land for the Russian Security Council. The development plan will also address revision of the state subsidies for activities that support Arctic development.

TRANSPORTATION AND MARITIME POLICY

In 1987, General Secretary Mikhail Gorbachev broached the possibility of opening the Northern Sea Route to foreign commercial shipping traffic.[26] In 1991, this initiative was implemented by new rules governing the NSR. Finally, in the summer of 2009, the German ships M/V *Beluga Fraternity* and M/V *Beluga Foresight* were among the first foreign vessels to transit the length of the Northern Sea Route. The ships passed from Uslan, South Korea, through the Arctic Ocean and on to the Netherlands, with a stop to offload heavy cargo at Novy Port near the mouth of the Ob River. A revised set of rules to govern such traffic is anticipated to be released in the near future, with the expectation that the NSR will be open to international traffic on terms similar to those of the Panama and Suez canals.[27]

The identification of the Arctic as an area of strategic national interest has been incorporated into other national policies and plans. *Transportation Strategy to 2030* established objectives for strengthening the NSR and the river network that links the route to the interior.[28] The strategy sets a specific goal of building three new "linear" icebreakers that will begin, after 2015, to replace the aging *Arktika*-class heavy nuclear

---

[25] Concept paper on preparation of the Arctic Council's Sustainable Development Action Plan, Sustainable Development Working Group, Arctic Council, presented in Svartsengi, Iceland, October 22, 2003.

[26] Mikhail S. Gorbachev, speech on the presentation of the Order of Lenin and the Gold Star Medal to the city of Murmansk, October 1, 1987, excerpted in Lawson W. Brigham, ed., *The Soviet Maritime Arctic* (Annapolis, MD: U.S. Naval Institute Press, 1991), p. 309.

[27] "Artur Chilingarov: 'Russia Has Obvious Advantages in the Arctic,'" *Голос России* [Voice of Russia], February 11, 2010, http://rus.ruvr.ru. Chilingarov anticipates that regulations will soon be issued establishing the Northern Sea Route as a transportation backbone for Russia, regulating the route along the lines of the Suez and Panama canals and charging fees to cover the cost of operation of the ice-breaking fleet.

[28] Ministry of Transportation of the Russian Federation, "Transport Strategy of the Russian Federation to 2030," November 22, 2008 (my translation, from the original, **ТРАНСПОРТНАЯ**

icebreakers. The *Arktika*-class ships were constructed in the 1970s and are due for retirement.[29] The strategy also calls for building conventionally powered icebreakers to support regional development, river ice breaking, and port maintenance. Finally, *Transportation Strategy to 2030* anticipates a focus on developing ports and inland waterways along the NSR in the period 2015–30.

Russia's maritime policy emphasizes increasing capacity to conduct maritime trade. This can be seen in the Arctic in the introduction of sophisticated ice-capable cargo ships and tankers built both in Russia and in foreign shipyards. The dual-acting Norilsk ships are proving their worth in the Kara Sea, and in the summer of 2010, Sovcomflot demonstrated the capability of its own dual-acting tankers to move crude oil from the Kara Sea eastward to Japan.[30]

The relationship between maritime power and economic strength, a staple of American and British global strategies, has become manifest in Russia as well. Reflecting on increasing globalization and the role of the Russian navy, Fleet Admiral V. I. Kuroyedov, then the service's commander in chief, wrote in 2005:

> We understand very well that the 21st century is a century of the World Ocean, and this country should be ready for this if it is going to participate, on a par with other countries, in the competition for access to their resources and international trade routes. Only a modern, advanced fleet, above all its naval component, can ensure Russia's full-fledged participation in the sustained use of natural resources of the seas in the interest of advancing the State's economic development.[31]

AN ARCTIC GEOGRAPHICAL PIVOT: IMPLICATIONS AND OPPORTUNITIES

Mackinder's original concept of the "geographical pivot" presented Central Asia as the region through which peoples and armies had for centuries moved westward to threaten European civilization. Over time, his concept evolved into the proposition that a powerful heartland could threaten Western interests across the southern rim of Asia and up through Central Europe. Concurrently, Mahan saw in southern Asia a potential battleground between the land power of the heartland and the maritime power of the British Empire and the United States over the resources of the coast of Asia.

Things have changed. Russia has lost its territories to the south and the independent nations along the southern rim of Asia are able to defend their own interests.

СТРАТЕГИЯ Российской Федерации на период до 2030 года), http://doc.rzd.ru/isvp/public/doc?STRUCTURE_ID=5102&layer_id=3368&refererLayerId=3368&id=3771.

[29] The nuclear icebreakers *Arktika* and *Siber* were retired in 2008, leaving four of the *Arktika* class of heavy nuclear icebreakers in service, along with two of the single-reactor, shallower-draft river icebreakers.

[30] "Russia to Start Eastward Oil, Gas Shipments via Arctic in 2010," *RIA Novosti*, http://en.rian.ru; "SCF to Test Northern Sea Route," *Lloyd's List*, http://www.lloydslist.com.

[31] Adm. V. I. Kuroyedov, "War Experience and the Outlook for the Development and Employment of the Navy in Future Wars and Armed Conflicts," *Military Thought*, April 1, 2005, pp. 38–45.

Any latent imperial designs on reaching the Indian Ocean or Persian Gulf by force appear forgotten. In the twenty-first century, an accessible Arctic will lead Russia to turn northward, not just to exploit Arctic resources but also to connect its Asian interior to the rest of the world through maritime trade. A new perspective, looking toward Russia over the North Pole, brings the new geographic pivot into clear focus (see Figure 7.2).

The old geostrategy of enclosure and containment of Russia is gone for good. In the new geopolitical vision for the twenty-first century, Russia takes a role not of a renewed heartland but of a maritime state that draws its strength from its Arctic coast and watershed. Even if the Arctic ice melt were to stall, advances in technology for Arctic shipping and resource development, combined with the economic return for development of the energy resources in the Arctic, would ensure increased connections and commerce between the Russian Arctic and the rest of the world. By midcentury, the Northern Sea Route is likely to be a regular shipping route, beginning with seasonal service based on ice-class vessels and later expanding as climate and ice conditions allow. As the Arctic becomes more accessible, the northern coast of Eurasia may take the place of Mackinder's pivot, as both a route of passage and an area of exploitable resources.

This geographical pivot of the twenty-first century will not be without conflict, but with commitment to international law and respect for the rights of the coastal and distant states, the conflicts can be political rather than military. Unlike the "great game" of Asian geopolitics of the nineteenth century and the heartland-versus-rimland contest of the twentieth, the groundwork has been laid through the Law of the Sea and the Ilulissat Declaration to ensure peaceful development of the Arctic sea routes and to recognize coastal state rights to manage, develop, and protect the living and mineral resources in and under the Arctic coastal seas.[32]

Several sovereignty issues have yet to be resolved. Russia and Norway have complex resource-access issues in the Barents Sea and Svalbard archipelago, the United States may yet again challenge some of Russia's internal waters claims along the NSR, and the Commission on the Limits of the Continental Shelf has yet to render a recommendation concerning Russia's expansive continental shelf claim to much of the seabed on the Eurasian side of the Arctic Ocean. These are legal and diplomatic matters that, though important, do not touch on the survival of the state or outweigh the overall benefits of maintaining peace and stability in the Arctic. As such, the disagreements that exist are unlikely to lead to more than demonstrations of interest through ship patrols and occasional harassment or detention of accused violators of jurisdiction claimed by Russia and other states. These lower-level disputes are manageable.

[32] The Ilulissat Declaration intentionally referred to the "Law of the Sea" instead of UNCLOS or the "Law of the Sea Convention" because the United States is not yet party to the Convention. While the wording may seem clumsy, it was intentional. In spite of not referring to the Convention, "Law" and "Sea" were capitalized in the Declaration.

As a maritime state with interests in sustaining freedom of navigation on a global stage and in maintaining safety and security in its offshore waters, in the twenty-first century Russia will increasingly share interests long held by the United States and other traditional maritime powers. Russia's interests in its Arctic will foster a maritime policy that embraces coastal resource management and freedom of international navigation, though likely with a greater emphasis on offshore sovereignty and less focus on distant water-power projection. Strategic security policy will be a continuation of past efforts. The U.S.-Russia maritime boundary is resolved de facto (pending ratification of a treaty by the Russian Duma), and current and potential boundary disputes between Russia and U.S. allies Norway, Denmark, and Canada are likely to be resolved through peaceful means. The United States and Russia also have an agreement that maritime boundary and navigation disputes will be resolved diplomatically rather than by resort to arms.[33] The conflicts that do arise will be focused on matters of commercial navigation, boundary delimitation, fisheries management, energy development, environmental protection, and ocean science, all the subject of international diplomacy and regulatory enforcement rather than warfare.

Russia, with its newly accessible Arctic waters, will need to focus on further developing its regulatory and enforcement capability to manage activities in a region that will more than double the current area of responsibility of the Coastal Border Guard.

The West, including the United States, can gain from the evolution of Russia's Arctic watershed from an isolated heartland of limited economic activity, a geopolitical "black hole," in the words of Zbigniew Brzezinski, to a bustling maritime region trading large amounts of raw materials and agricultural and industrial goods. The U.S. Arctic Policy, issued as a national security directive in early 2009, explicitly addressed military issues that Russia omitted from its Arctic policy framework.[34] But the full range of U.S. Arctic interests finds counterparts in Russia's policy objectives. Strategic defense issues aside, Russia's objective of establishing the Arctic as a "zone of peace and cooperation" is equally applicable to the United States and its allies.

Mutual gain is the goal of U.S. and Russian policy that seeks to "reset" U.S.-Russian relations. Arctic cooperation consistent with the Global Maritime Partnership initiative and the capabilities and priorities identified in the 2007 *Cooperative Strategy for 21st Century Seapower*[35] can promote the peaceful use of the Arctic while building

[33] Union of Soviet Socialist Republics–United States: Joint Statement with Attached Uniform Interpretation of Rules of International Law Governing Innocent Passage, entered into at Jackson Hole, Wyoming, September 23, 1989, reprinted in 28 I.L.M. 1444 (1989).

[34] U.S. National Security Presidential Directive NSDP 66/Homeland Security Presidential Directive HSPD 25, January 9, 2009, http://www.fas.org.

[35] A *Cooperative Strategy for 21st Century Seapower*, October 2007. Elements of the cooperative strategy include "foster[ing] and sustain[ing] cooperative relationships with more international partners" and "prevent[ing] or contain[ing] local disruptions before they impact the global system" and capabilities relevant to the implementation of the strategy in the Arctic, including maritime security and humanitarian assistance and disaster response.

familiarity among maritime users of the Arctic and demonstrating the potential to cooperate in an area of increasing geopolitical importance. The mechanisms toward this goal will be diplomatic engagement, information sharing, business promotion, and cooperation between the Coastal Border Guard and the coast guards and navies of the other Arctic coastal states.

The best course is to address Russia's evolving maritime role with an Arctic regional maritime partnership based on the model of the Global Maritime Partnership Initiative, which addresses both military and civilian interests in climate change, maritime resource conservation, marine scientific research, and marine industry. The U.S. objective should be to work collaboratively to resolve disputes over extended continental shelf and fisheries claims, to negotiate a regional high-seas fisheries management plan for the Arctic Ocean, and to develop a regional Arctic maritime transportation plan that includes assignment of Arctic Ocean search-and-rescue responsibilities. The United States can work with Russia to better coordinate security and safety policies on the ocean and ice surface and in the air, fulfilling the goals of the U.S. Arctic Region policy and the sea services' *Cooperative Strategy*.

An Arctic regional maritime partnership could support beneficial maritime collaborations to enhance the prospects that the Arctic geographical pivot will be an area of peaceful collaboration rather than simply shifting conflict from the south and west of Eurasia to the north. Elements of such a partnership should include the following:

Reinforce the rule of law: Russia and the United States need to take the lead in strengthening the rule of law in the Arctic. Russia should finally ratify the maritime boundary agreement with the United States. For its part, the United States should accede to UNCLOS. A firm commitment to a common understanding of UNCLOS will promote peaceful resolution of issues among Arctic states and aid in broad acceptance of regulations by non-Arctic states that seek to transit the Arctic Ocean, exploit its resources, and conduct polar research.

Military cooperation and emergency response: Application of the Global Maritime Partnership to the Arctic region can improve the capability of all Arctic states to respond to accidents and natural disasters. Increased activity in the Arctic need not require each Arctic state to maintain a full spectrum of ships, aircraft, satellites and observation stations, or emergency supplies. Shared awareness of assets and combined exercises would benefit all users of the Arctic by providing greater capacity for aid and assistance.

Maritime safety and security: The Arctic states, with Russia and the United States in the lead, should be prepared to provide response to maritime emergencies, from search and rescue to responses to major disasters at sea, such as oil spills. Leadership by the Arctic states in the International Maritime Organization can help avoid different, perhaps conflicting, national design specifications and operating regulations for transarctic shipping and collaboration on regional fisheries management can lead to sustainable fisheries rather than overexploitation.

Arctic domain awareness: Maritime security, resource management, and marine environmental protection will all depend on accurate and up-to-date information regarding human activities and ocean, ice, and climate data. Joint observation, identification, and tracking of ships and aircraft, particularly those of non-Arctic states, will be needed to maximize the effectiveness of the limited air and sea assets available in the Arctic. Although military security will limit access to some information, particularly regarding submarines, shared knowledge and expertise will be the framework on which most collaborative work will be undertaken and collective decisions will be made.

Arctic science: Fostering cooperative Arctic research by all interested parties and promoting sharing of results should be a priority for engagement. Successful multilateral polar science programs should ensure that nonsecurity, noncommercial data from national sources is shared with all researchers.

Arctic policies of regional and transiting states: Distant parties have interests and rights in Arctic waters and indigenous people have interests in maintaining and developing their culture both through traditional activities and through trade and economic development made possible by a warming Arctic. These two groups must be involved in Arctic management activities that touch their substantive interests, not just in the Arctic Council but also in other organizations and agreements that address Arctic issues.

The opening of the Arctic in twenty-first century will afford Russia the opportunity to develop and grow as a maritime power, first in the Arctic region and eventually extending to wherever else its merchant fleet carries Russian goods and returns with foreign products. This transformation of the threatening heartland of Mackinder and Spykman to a constructive member of the maritime powers will require extensive effort to bring the new maritime Russia into closer collaboration and partnership. Commitment to the rule of law, shared Arctic domain awareness, joint security and safety operations and collaboration in developing policies for the future can maintain the Arctic as a region of peace even while the coastal states develop new naval and law enforcement capabilities for the region.

8

The Rise of the Arctic on the Global Stage

Pauli Järvenpää and Tomas Ries

The Arctic is rapidly emerging as a major playing field in world politics. Prior to the Cold War, it was a *terra nullius* to all but the indigenous populations. During the Cold War, it became of massive importance in the strategic nuclear relationship between the United States and the Soviet Union. This had a tangential political impact on the adjacent regions, notably the Nordic states, including Finland, but it occupied a very narrow margin of world affairs as a whole, and one that, in peacetime, largely took place behind the veil of highly specialized strategic submarine and air preparations and operations.

With the end of the Cold War, the Arctic again became dormant in world affairs. However, in the past few years, it has been woken up again and is now rapidly emerging with full force on the world stage. One could almost say that there has been a paradigm shift in how we look at the region. There is a growing recognition that the Arctic, instead of staying a backwater of politics, is rapidly moving to the limelight of attention.

We face two major challenges. From a global perspective, we must ensure that this process of change takes place in a politically and ecologically harmonious manner. If we fail, then the Arctic could emerge as a region with considerable political tensions and massive ecological crises. From a Nordic regional perspective, we must address the consequences of our northern Arctic quadrant shifting from having been a political void to becoming a focal point of global economic and political interest and activity.

This chapter examines the emergence of the Arctic on the world political arena and the critical challenges this poses, and it finally takes a look at the consequences for the Nordic region and for Finland in particular.

1. DRIVERS OF CHANGE

Three deep trends are currently opening up the Arctic, enabling expanded human activity in the region. The first is global warming. It appears beyond doubt that global warming is taking place and that it is taking place particularly rapidly at both poles. As a result, the Arctic ice cap is shrinking and at a far more rapid rate than forecast. According to recent estimates, the Arctic ice cap is now only half the size it was fifty years ago. This is opening up the Arctic Ocean sea areas and expanding human access and activities ever deeper into the Arctic. The second deep trend is technological advances in extraction and communications technology. This increases the human capability for industrial activity in difficult Arctic conditions, making it both physically feasible and economically viable. The third deep trend is the gradually increasing global scarcity of vital natural resources, including some key commodities available in the Arctic, such as oil, natural gas, rare minerals, and fish. As demand and prices increase, the higher costs of Arctic industrial activity will become economically bearable.

These three trends can be considered enablers, as they allow for greater human activity in the Arctic. In addition, however, the interests and will to exploit the Arctic are also increasing. This is directly related to the last trend, the rising global scarcity of vital raw materials. This drives the interest of regional and global actors to exploit the Arctic in two crucial ways. The first is financial. Extracting and refining scarce natural resources is a vast source of revenue, crucial for both business corporations and for states. The second is political power. Controlling key parts of the global economic production chain provides decisive political power, something that particularly Russia is acutely aware of.

These two factors mean that the geopolitical stakes in the Arctic are increasing significantly and will in all likelihood transform our far northern neighborhood into a major global geopolitical playing field in the coming years. This will likely attract interest on a global scale, beyond the littoral states, with not only states but also transnational corporations becoming major actors.

2. EFFECT

Future economic activity in the Arctic can be divided into two major categories. The first is raw material exploitation – extracting and possibly refining natural resources, such as oil, natural gas, fish, and probably rare minerals from the seabed. The second is maritime transportation – exploiting the transarctic sea lines of communication (SLOC) for shipping between the economic powerhouses in North Asia and the North Atlantic.

On the whole, both fields are still in very early stages of development. Two major exceptions in the field of raw material exploitation are fisheries and oil and natural gas:

• A significant fishing industry has emerged in the Barents Sea area over the past fifty years. This is one of the fifteen key fish-producing areas in the world's oceans, and it is in many respects a success story in terms of sustainable exploitation. Thanks to strong, effective, and sustained Norwegian efforts, the fish stocks have been protected in the face of very strong exploitation pressures. Today, the Barents remains one of the four out of fifteen remaining sea areas with thriving fish stocks. As world food scarcity continues to increase, we can expect a great pressure to exploit Arctic marine sources of nourishment. This will be compounded by the shrinking sea ice and the warming of the Arctic waters, which will both open up more of the Arctic to fishing vessels, as well as leading fish stocks to migrate and perhaps spawn further north.

- The second major extraction industry already active on the Arctic mainland is oil and gas, on a very large scale in the Russian Arctic mainland and Alaska, and now emerging offshore in the Barents Sea. Although the exact size and location of Arctic oil and gas deposits remains unclear, it appears likely that significant deposits lie under the seabed in various other parts of the Arctic Ocean, including north of Greenland. As these resources become mapped with greater certainty, they will likely generate a very great increase in oil and gas exploitation in the Arctic. In addition, because the transportation of natural gas is most flexible in its liquid form (as opposed to fixed pipelines), refineries for producing liquefied natural gas (LNG) and loading it on LNG shipping will also likely emerge on adjacent Arctic land areas. One such hypermodern facility is already in operation, on the island of Melkøya near Hammerfest on the Norwegian coast of the Barents Sea, developed and run by Norwegian industry to serve the huge Snøhvit gas fields.

In the field of communications, the use of Arctic sea lanes is only just beginning. The sea lanes are attractive from a shipping perspective, as they offer the shortest SLOC between North Asia and the North Atlantic, potentially linking three of the world's most vibrant economic zones (China-Korea-Japan, the European Union, and the eastern United States). Hitherto, however, the difficult ice conditions have precluded any serious commercial use of the Arctic shipping lanes. Such commercial shipping as has taken place has been along the Northeast Passage, running along the Russian Arctic coastline, and the Northwest Passage, running through the Canadian Arctic archipelago. However, traffic along these lanes has been very limited and local, restricted to two or three late-summer months when, or if, ice conditions have made it possible.

With the melting Arctic ice, this is now changing. In the summer of 2009, the first cargo ship transit took place connecting Asia to Europe through the Northeast Passage. The Russians had for years hauled goods and energy products along their Siberian coastline, lately assisted by Finnish and Latvian icebreakers, but the two German ships transiting from South Korea to the Netherlands marked a new era. The Northeast Passage shortens the distance between the Asian and Western European ports by more than seven thousand kilometers and thus provides summer competition with the Suez Canal.

It is expected that in coming years, the SLOC could become commercially viable for certain categories of shipping, such as bulk cargo. However, for much of the shipping industry, notably the vast volumes of global container traffic that depend on just-in-time-delivery schedules, the uncertain ice conditions will still preclude the use of Arctic SLOC for some time.

The most dramatic potential Arctic shipping lane is, however, the direct transarctic SLOC, taking the shortest transpolar route right across the Arctic. Because of the ice conditions, this was unthinkable as recently as ten years ago, but the accelerating melting of the ice is becoming a serious consideration for certain shipping categories that do not depend on just-in-time-delivery. Estimates as to when the Arctic SLOC could become viable range from one to three decades, obviously depending on what sort of shipping is envisaged. However, the likelihood that the Arctic will emerge as one of the key global SLOC is no longer contested.

Such shipping activity will also in all likelihood spawn a number of tangential commercial activities in the Arctic. Most important among these could be transit harbors, where cargo is transferred from regular shipping to special ice-reinforced ships that take the cargo across the Arctic. Such harbors would need to be placed at both the Atlantic and the Pacific entrances to the Arctic and could potentially become vast enterprises. Further related activity would be the port and support facilities for the icebreaker fleets that would need to accompany the commercial convoys, as well as a host of other support activities such as search-and-rescue (SAR) and all other onshore support facilities.

Finally, three further potential Arctic industries need to be kept in mind. The first is Arctic tourism, especially on cruise liners, which is already increasing and will likely grow considerably. This calls for special support facilities, notably in SAR. The second is the exploitation of rare minerals off the Arctic seabed, in the form of mineral nodules. The third is basing platforms for data-processing centers to support the global cybersphere. Google and other actors are already examining the possibility of placing huge data-processing and storage centers on remote (security) and cool (machine-heat) locations, for which the Arctic may prove suitable. Although the ecological footprint of such facilities might be limited, they could be of major geopolitical significance given their vital importance for the global information infrastructure.

Although the exact contours remain unclear, the net effect of all this will be significantly increased human activity in the Arctic, a great increase in the geopolitical significance of the Arctic, and a major impact on the Arctic ecosystem.

3. STRATEGIC CONSEQUENCES

The foregoing developments are likely to have three key strategic consequences. The most profound is ecological, with a massive regional impact and possible global ramifications, some of them severe. The second consequence is regional and consists of the socioeconomic impact on the local societies. This may also have regional Arctic political consequences. The third consequence is geopolitical and consists of how the Arctic states and other parties engaged in Arctic activity are affected by the Arctic development and how they react to the new Arctic "great game" that will emerge. The impact here can range from the soft multilateral agenda to hard realpolitik, including the threat or use of military force, and could have global consequences.

The first and most fundamental strategic consequence is the impact on the Arctic ecology. Here we can discern three key drivers:

1. The first and deepest impact is from global warming, which is fundamentally transforming the Arctic ecosystem and biosphere. The exact consequences remain impossible to predict, but they range from the most obvious – the shrinking ice cap – to uncertain but drastic potential tipping points, such as a reversal of the Gulf Stream, which in turn could affect the entire global oceanic conveyor belt with massive global systemic consequences.
2. The second ecological impact is from the consequences of increased economic and social activity that will multiply the human footprint in the Arctic, with a host of consequences from exploitation and pollution, leading to the degradation of local and regional biotopes and the disruption of regional ecosystems.
3. The third ecological impact is from the consequences of potential but almost inevitable industrial and other accidents, such as oil spills or other toxic releases. This could lead to sudden catastrophic ecological damage on the local or regional level. It can also lead to significant economic and political tensions, dealt with herein.

The second strategic consequence is socioeconomic. The economic exploitation of the Arctic will have two major effects:

1. First, on the global geopolitical level, the states owning the Arctic resources and the enterprises exploiting them will benefit from massively increased revenues. The resulting economic power will be on a strategic scale. For the states concerned, the control of access to the resources and the revenues they generate imply increased political power both at home and abroad. For the corporations, it implies massive gains in revenue and profit.
2. The second socioeconomic consequence is regional. For the local populations, the Arctic economic boom will – in one way or another – fundamentally transform their societies and living conditions. The impact will be both direct, from the actual exploitation activity itself, and indirect, from the significant logistic support infrastructure that will ensue over wide-reaching adjacent areas. To take just one pinpoint example, it is estimated that the initial infrastructure development needed to exploit potential oil and gas resources north

of Greenland could lead to the temporary influx of up to three hundred thousand workers during a five- to ten-year period. With a local population of some fifty-eight thousand in Greenland, this migratory inflow alone will have a massive social and cultural impact. A second important regional impact is political. If the indigenous populations are able to gain authority over part or all of the economic activity in their homelands, it will also fundamentally affect their political empowerment. Here again, Greenland is a key example. Hitherto, decades of declarations in favor of full independence from Denmark have been tempered by the realization that the local population has been totally dependent on Denmark's economic subsidies. Should oil and gas exploitation provide Greenland with a significant independent source of revenue, the aspirations to independence could be realized, thus transforming the Arctic political map.

The third strategic consequence is on global power politics. This is a function of how the key actors choose to manage the Arctic great game that will emerge as part and parcel of the ecological, economic, and social transformation of the Arctic. Here, one can discern two critical areas.

The first is the question of control – who owns what? This is a vital national strategic interest for the Arctic littoral states because of the huge economic and political stakes and the wealth and power they engender. It is also of major ecological significance, as delimitation may affect how ecological standards, oversight, and enforcement can be applied to regulate human activity and protect the environment. This issue encompasses both ownership of natural resources and control of Arctic SLOC. It is compounded by the fact that some major non-Arctic powers – such as China, Japan, South Korea, and others – will have major Arctic economic interests. For China and Japan, access to Arctic oil and natural gas could become an existential issue. Finally, most of the states concerned will depend on Western transnational corporations to finance and actually exploit the Arctic resources, as the funds, but especially the technical know-how and technologies, are largely in their hands. Thus, we may expect the key transnational corporations to become major players as well.

The second key geopolitical factor is the potential for political tensions in how the previously described game is played out. Here, three major areas of potential friction can be identified.

The first is political. The key issue here is ownership. Currently the delimitation of significant parts of the Arctic is contested among the littoral states. Although they have all declared their intent to settle their differences peacefully through the UN Convention on the Law of the Sea (UNCLOS), it remains to be seen whether this will be accomplished. If the soft multilateral agenda fails, we could face competing claims to ownership of natural resources and to the right to exploit and regulate significant parts of the Arctic Ocean. A second major political issue has been mentioned earlier and is the question of whether newly found wealth will lead to pressures for independence among the indigenous peoples. Greenland is a case where this is both likely and could have significant consequences, but also other peoples may explore this opportunity. How this will affect the Arctic political map, and with what domestic and international consequences, is still largely unexplored.

The second major area of potential friction is over the protection (or otherwise) and management of the Arctic ecology. Here, two key sources of tension can be identified:

1. First, we will almost certainly see a clash between the postmodern emphasis on supranational universal values, in this case prioritizing protection of the environment, against the modern hard national values emphasizing exploitation of natural resources and sovereign rights. The latter hard approach applies clearly to one of the great Arctic powers, Russia, but that it is not restricted to Russia alone was amply demonstrated at the Copenhagen Summit in the fall of 2009. This leaves the potential for significant political tensions between those emphasizing ecological norms, regulation, and enforcement and those emphasizing sovereign rights and exploitation – both within states and between states. This tension could become particularly acute if we fail to reach multilateral agreements on both the delimitation of the Arctic and the ecological standards.

2. Second, even if we do reach such agreements, tensions could emerge between declared policy and implementation, and particularly over policing and enforcing. Who will have the right to oversee that ecological standards are respected, and even more difficult, to enforce their implementation, if the respect is lacking? Finally, tensions could erupt suddenly in the wake of ecological disasters. This can emerge during the disaster where both information sharing and disaster management can lead to tensions. Even more tense could be the postdisaster tensions over who is to blame and particularly who is to pay for the potentially astronomic cleanup costs – a game of high political and economic stakes, fueled by multiple domestic pressures and attention.

Third, there is the military dimension. The question is what role the Arctic will play in the littoral powers' military planning and how their regional military posture will develop. Here, two major interest areas can be distinguished:

1. The first is strategic nuclear policy and primarily includes the United States and Russia. This area dominated the Arctic during the Cold War but has since receded to the shadows as the bilateral relationship has become less overtly tense. However, Russia is acutely aware that it has only two real claims to superpower fame today – oil and gas resources and revenues thereof on the one hand, and the strategic nuclear arsenal on the other hand – and Russia has consistently prioritized its strategic nuclear forces in both word and deed even after the end of the Cold War. Its Arctic focus has diminished

for technical reasons, as Russia has had difficulty modernizing its strategic nuclear submarine (SSBN) fleet and has failed to modernize its sea-launched ballistic-missile (SLBM) arsenal. However, this is not for lack of trying, and should Russia manage to overcome those technological obstacles, we may expect a revival of its SSBN basing on the Kola Peninsula, which could also lead to a renewed buildup of her conventional forces there. Overall, however, the strategic nuclear relevance of the Arctic will be a function of how the U.S.-Russian relationship develops in coming years.

2. The second major military impact on the Arctic is conventional and regional, and it consists of the extent to which the littoral powers feel the need to back up their Arctic claims and activity with a military presence. Currently, only two states have developed and maintained a serious Arctic conventional military capability, in terms of surface vessels and units that can operate in the Arctic in any strength. The most powerful, in terms of ice-breaking capability, is Russia, which operates the only large-scale icebreaker fleet in the Arctic. Russia also maintains a ragged vestige of its former amphibious capability deployed with the Northern Fleet based on the Kola and associated support forces. The other state is Norway, which over some fifty years has developed both the resources and skills for effective Coast Guard fisheries protection operations in the Barents, and whose Coast Guard vessels and new fleet of frigates constitute the most modern naval fleet with Arctic operational potential. A third traditional Arctic military presence, very small and specialized comprising just a handful of soldiers, but with a strategic function and unique capability, is the Danish Sirius Patrol. They operate small dogsled patrols along Greenland's uninhabited eastern coast, lasting several months at a time. This is primarily a political and legal exercise to demonstrate sovereignty, dating back to the interwar years when Denmark feared possible Norwegian ambitions in the area. Although this is no longer a factor, the patrol has been kept in existence, and though very small, it remains the foremost military unit capable of sustained ground operations in the most extreme Arctic conditions.

On the rhetorical level, this condition changed following the planting of the Russian flag on the seabed at the North Pole at the depth of about four kilometers in summer 2007. Although the Russians themselves acknowledged that the flag planting does not represent a legal claim to the North Pole and its environs, it was a reminder of their claim that the Lomonosov Ridge is a part of the Siberian shelf and thus Russian territory. Though purely symbolic, with no legal significance, the Russian action was a strong political statement and released a spurt of bellicose signals from other Arctic littoral states. Even countries normally seen as benign champions of peace and soft power, such as Canada and Denmark, suddenly announced military programs directed at strengthening their Arctic presence, including building new Arctic bases, fleets of icebreakers and ice-strengthened naval vessels, reinforced military units on the ground, and so forth. So far, the actual implementation of these statements has lagged far behind, but it indicates the underlying tensions and potential for a military buildup. Most serious in this regard is the Russian rhetoric. The Russian government's formal strategy was announced in 2009 in a document titled *The Russian Federation's National Security Strategy until 2020*. In that document, the Russian government highlighted the long-term significance of energy policy focused on possessing energy resources in the Middle East, the Barents Sea, the Arctic area, the Caspian Basin, and Central Asia. The government also noted that, "amid competitive struggle for resources, attempts to use military force to solve emerging problems cannot be excluded." Although Russia, like Canada and to some extent Denmark, still needs to match deeds to words, the hostile nonzero sum of the Russian statements is cause for genuine concern.

In May 2008, the five coastal states met in Ilulissat, Greenland, to adopt the Ilulissat Declaration, in which Canada, Denmark, Norway, Russia, and the United States bound themselves to ecologically friendly ways of natural resource exploration and peaceful means for handling disputes while at the same time acknowledging the legitimacy of UNCLOS. The declaration was, however, a symbolic gesture, as it was legally nonbinding.

The net conclusion of all of this is that, even though the conventional Arctic military presence currently remains limited, there is considerable potential for an increase in forces and tensions, particularly if the states concerned fail to reach a negotiated multilateral agreement over who owns what. Second, and independent of this, the need to police and enforce unilateral or multilateral Arctic ecological standards will become very much stronger and then lead to the increasing deployment of paramilitary and military naval and air units capable of doing so. This can form a second area of significant tension, particularly if the delimitation of sovereign jurisdiction remains unclear and following major ecological disasters.

4. RUSSIA

All Arctic states except Russia belong to the globalizing, or Western, community. However, tensions over Arctic affairs have arisen among them (Iceland–Great Britain, Canada–United States, Canada–Denmark). All of them, it is interesting to note, are founding members of the NATO alliance. As a result, however, barring radical shocks, we can assume that these countries can probably solve their differences in a reasonable manner, because they share the same basic interests and a way of doing business, based on a non-zero-sum worldview.

Russia is regrettably not part of this postmodern community. Economically, socially, and politically, Russia remains an early- to mid-modern state. The worldview of the Kremlin is also fundamentally different from the Atlantic community; on the basis of on a zero-sum logic, it seems to prioritize power politics over soft relations. At the same time, the Russian leadership and the political system have demonstrated clear nonchalance with issues that we in Western societies take seriously – such as liberal governance and protecting the environment.

Russia has a lot at stake in the Arctic region, perhaps more than any other Arctic nation. Of the five states adjacent to the Arctic Ocean, Russia has by far the longest shoreline, about 17,500 kilometers long, and the largest Arctic population. Economically, the region is of vital importance to Russia. It is estimated that as much as one-fifth of Russian gross domestic product derives from north of the Arctic Circle. Furthermore, according to recent estimations (by the U.S. Geological Survey in 2009), the Arctic area contains some 30 percent of the world's undiscovered natural gas and about 13 percent of the world's undiscovered oil. The undiscovered natural gas is believed to be mainly found in Russia. In some estimates, as much as 70 percent of the gas is concentrated in the Russian sector. Siberia alone is estimated to hold oil reserves equal to the Middle East. As for the minerals, it is estimated that Russia is extracting up to 90 percent of the nickel and cobalt in the Arctic, 60 percent of the copper, 96 percent of platinoids, and 100 percent of apatite concentrate. Also, the oil and gas pipelines in northern and northwestern Russia, ranging from the Baltic Pipeline System (BPS), launched in 2001, to the Nord Stream gas pipeline connecting Vyborg to Germany and to be laid along the bottom of the Baltic Sea, will make Russia a strong player in the European energy business.

Climate change, as foreseen, will also strongly affect Russia and its interests. Global warming is opening up new sea lanes of communication: the Northern Sea Route hugging the northern coastline of Russia from the Barents Sea to the Bering Strait and the Northwest Passage through the Canadian Archipelago. A direct route across the Arctic Ocean over the North Pole is also a possibility. Estimates differ on how soon this all will happen, but whether it will happen as early as 2030 or in around 2050 is a moot point. What is important is that the lanes will be of great economic significance. The sailing time from China, South Korea, and Japan to Europe and North America will be drastically shortened – by several days to some weeks even – and new economic opportunities will be created. At the same time, the newly ice-free routes also offer potential problems: piracy, terrorism, illegal immigrants, incidents at sea. Especially oil shipments and Arctic tourism have the potential to create havoc in the new sea routes of communication and the adjacent shores with their vulnerable ecosystems.

Hence, there is a high potential for serious differences between Russia and other Arctic states over Arctic affairs, especially given the profoundly different power political perception of international relations in Russia. Also, the Russian disregard for issues we take seriously and the Russian proclivity for using various forms of coercion make an increased Russian military presence likely, with the strong possibility of military pressure in Arctic crises. This is further reinforced by the revived Russian focus on the Kola Peninsula and Arctic strategic nuclear SSBN operations as part of the Russian strategic nuclear posture.

Supported by the huge revenues from oil and gas, Russia is on its way to becoming a world player again. The collapse of the late 1980s and the 1990s is over, and the

Russians feel that they "are back." It is not an accident that Russian leaders have repeatedly emphasized the importance of the Arctic as a strategic resource base for Russia in the twenty-first century. For example, President Dmitry Medvedev was clear in his address to the Russian Security Council in September 2008 that the Arctic had a special place in solving the long-term challenges of the country and increasing Russian competitiveness in global markets. Likewise, *The Russian Federation's National Security Strategy until 2020* identifies the Arctic region as a potential area of conflict and refers to the possibility of military means to be used to resolve crises in the region. Conflict over energy resources is, therefore, seen by Russian military and policy analysts as a significant, realistic concern over the coming decade. Furthermore, Russia claims that an extension of its continental shelf covers territory leading right up to the North Pole, this claim conflicting directly with continental shelf claims by Canada, Denmark, and Norway.

In *The Military Doctrine of the Russian Federation 2010*, published on 5 February 2010, the provision for use of Russian forces overseas "to defend the interests of the Russian Federation and its citizens, and to protect international peace and security" is repeated. Operations overseas to remove threats or suppress aggression can also be undertaken at the instigation of the United Nations "or other bodies." The reference to "other bodies" can be assumed to apply mainly to the Collective Security Treaty Organization (CSTO), in which Russia is the most prominent member. Although it can be assumed that these stipulations in the doctrine are meant for other areas than the Arctic, it is possible that by extension they can also be applied in contingencies in the Arctic region.

Perhaps the Russian behavior, with increased military activities giving it support, is just a show of strength to get better deals in the future, but it is clear that in the minds of the Russian political leadership, military force is a strong element of Russia's policy arsenal. This is shown by the robustness of the Russian 2006–15 military procurement program, and by the large military exercises the country carried out in its western and northwestern parts in the summer and fall of 2009. The establishment of a special Arctic military capability is a development in this same direction. The decadelong hibernation is over also in how the Russians use their military capabilities. There has been a show of force through its long-range aviation capabilities, witness the renewal of Russian strategic bomber flights, supported by tankers, escort fighters, and reconnaissance aircraft, as far as to the Atlantic as Iceland and Scotland. The well-publicized Russian expedition under the North Pole and the symbolic planting of the Russian national flag there on 2 August 2007 is yet another demonstration of strong Russian interests in the region.

However, it would be a mistaken conclusion to draw from all of this that Russia is there to willfully threaten Arctic security. What the Russian behavior means, first and foremost, is that those who at the end of the Cold War were hastening to proclaim that the era of geopolitics was over in the Arctic regions were just plain wrong. What we witness is that geopolitics is back, and it is back with vengeance. At the same time, we should also see Russia as an opportunity, not only as a spoiler in the game of Arctic politics. Wherever possible, we should try to draw Russia to be a responsible shareholder. And it should not be overlooked that, in many ways, the Russians are also dependent on the West. This applies with particular force to their need to obtain Western technology for their exploitation of the abundant gas and oil reserves in the Arctic regions.

The great game over the Arctic has already begun. We will need to find multilateral solutions if we are to avoid serious ecological degradation as well as political and military tensions. This diplomatic effort will, however, also need to be backed up by a capability to police and – if need be – to protect our vital interests in the Arctic.

5. CONSEQUENCES FOR THE NORDIC REGION AND FINLAND

As a consequence of what is happening in the Arctic region, Finland's northern neighborhood is shifting from having been a quiet backwater to becoming a focal point of world politics and economy. The Arctic will be an area in which military security, economic security, and environmental security overlap. In fact, it is an example of a postmodern arena of world politics, where short-term national interests clash with long-term global objectives. The question is whether the national interests can be reined in so that they will not jeopardize the overriding global objective, the maintenance of security and stability in the Arctic.

One acute area for Arctic cooperation overriding narrow national interests should be maritime safety. As more and more ships venture into the Arctic, the demand for route control management, ice and wave information, and search-and-rescue capabilities will continue to increase, and the resources available to meet this increased demand should be found. The Baltic Sea maritime shipping regime could provide a useful model. There is a requirement for ships entering the Baltic Sea through the Kattegat and the Great Belt or the Sound to report themselves, and there are commonly accepted norms for information systems, shipping guidance regulations, and incident response in the Baltic.

According to *The Arctic Marine Shipping Assessment 2009 Report*, published by the Arctic Council, the Baltic Sea area has some of the densest maritime traffic in the world, with more than two thousand ships en route on an average day, not including ferries, smaller fishing boats, or pleasure craft. Among those two thousand ships, some two hundred are oil tankers with a cargo up to 150,000 gross tons. Furthermore, a mandatory reporting system has been introduced in the Gulf of Finland called the Gulf of Finland Mandatory Reporting System (GOFREP). Finland, Estonia, and Russia require that all vessels exceeding three hundred gross tons are required to participate in the GOFREP system when sailing in the international waters in the Gulf of Finland.

On top of that, countries in the Baltic Sea basin have joined each other in an effort to produce a common recognized maritime picture. This started with cooperation between Finland and Sweden (Sea Surveillance Cooperation between

Finland and Sweden, or SUCFIS), in which both countries feed in information to each other's data systems from various different sensors to produce a common recognized maritime picture (primary sensors in Finland, for example, belonging to the navy, border guards, and Maritime Administration, and secondary ones to the Environmental Centre, customs service, police, and rescue service). It makes imminent sense in an area, where the imaginary line between Helsinki and Tallinn is crossed on an annual basis by more than 7,600 tankers, 17,500 passenger ships, and 25,000 other vessels. By extension, as the volumes of Russian energy products are rapidly growing and are carried to the European and world markets via the Baltic Sea, the Baltic states – Estonia, Latvia, and Lithuania – can be considered Arctic states. At least they are strongly affected by the oil and gas trade that originates from the Russian parts of the Arctic.

The bilateral SUCFIS cooperation in 2009 was extended to all countries in the Baltic Sea area, including one outsider, Norway. Only Russia has so far declined to join what is now called the Sea Surveillance Cooperation Baltic Sea (SUCBAS). This same model of cooperation is in the process of being introduced on the European Union level as Maritime Surveillance (MARSUR) to support the EU Security and Defence Policy maritime dimension.

The main objectives, which obviously could apply in the Arctic region as well, of this multilateral cooperation are to support maritime safety, to control environmental hazards, to support the border authorities, to improve maritime situational awareness, and to strengthen bilateral and multilateral interoperability. This is all the more necessary when it is known that the number of tankers sailing to such huge ports as Primorsk and Ust Luga at the end of the Gulf of Finland will keep increasing year by year. The same is true also in the Arctic, where the estimated volumes of maritime traffic in the Northern Sea Route are expected to be about 40 million tons of oil and gas per year by 2020.

Active measures to improve defenses in the Arctic area have been quite modest and, as such, do not give cause for alarm. However, it is interesting to note some recent developments in the military field as well. One of the most noteworthy is the suggestion contained in the Russian *Security Strategy to 2020*, signed by President Medvedev in May 2009, to create a special Arctic military force based on units from the Leningrad, Siberian, and Far Eastern military districts. The general economic downturn and the collapse of the price of oil have postponed the establishment of the force until a later date. There is no doubt, however, that the idea of such a force will live on in the Russian military-planning circles.

Meanwhile, military cooperation among the five Nordic countries – Sweden, Norway, Finland, Denmark, and Iceland – is growing, and it has been consolidated under the umbrella of the Nordic Defence Cooperation (NORDEFCO) by the decision of the Nordic defense ministers in their meeting in Helsinki in November 2009. The cooperation will range from military education and training to exercises and common purchases of matériel. The Nordic chiefs of defense have combed through all possible areas of interest, and they have come up with more than 140 different areas of potential cooperation, out of which almost 50 areas have been named as "low hanging fruit," ready to be exploited today.

Another interesting set of ideas highlighting the possibilities for Nordic cooperation was presented in February 2009 by Thorvald Stoltenberg, former Norwegian foreign minister, at the behest of the Nordic foreign ministers. His report, *Nordic Cooperation on Foreign and Security Policy*, contains thirteen specific proposals aiming to enhance Nordic cooperation in the fields of foreign and security policy. One of the starting points for his work was the observation that "there is a widely held view that the Nordic region is becoming increasingly important in geopolitical and strategic terms. This is a result of the role of the Nordic seas as a production and transit area for gas for European markets and of the changes taking place in the Arctic." And, furthermore, "The Nordic countries are responsible for the management of large sea areas. Climate change and melting of the sea ice will open the way for considerable activity in these areas, including new shipping routes through Arctic waters to the Pacific Ocean. This means that Nordic cooperation in the northern seas and the Arctic is highly relevant."

On the basis of the foregoing, Stoltenberg proposed that the Nordic countries should take on themselves part of the responsibility for air surveillance and air patrolling over Iceland. He also argued that a Nordic system should be established for monitoring and early warning in the Nordic sea areas. Such a system could have two pillars, one for the Baltic Sea (Baltic Watch) and one for the North Atlantic, with parts of the Arctic Ocean and the Barents Sea (Barents Watch) under a common overall system. Once a Nordic maritime monitoring system is in place, a Nordic maritime response force should be established, consisting of elements from the Nordic countries' coast guards and rescue services. It should patrol regularly in the Nordic seas, and one of its main responsibilities should be search and rescue. By 2020, a Nordic polar orbit-satellite system should be established in connection with the development of a Nordic maritime monitoring system. Finally, Stoltenberg argued that the Nordic countries, which all are members of the Arctic Council, should develop cooperation on Arctic issues focusing on practical matters. He saw the environment, climate change, maritime safety, and search-and-rescue services as appropriate areas for such cooperation.

Militarily, perhaps the most ambitious proposal by Stoltenberg was his idea that a Nordic amphibious unit should be established based on existing units and the cooperation already existing between Sweden and Finland. The unit could be deployed in international operations. According to Stoltenberg, the unit should also develop its Arctic experience. Politically, the most controversial proposal was his thirteenth proposal, which stated that the Nordic governments should issue a mutual declaration of solidarity, in which they commit themselves to clarifying how they would respond if a Nordic country were subject to external attack or undue pressure. Such a declaration would, according to Stoltenberg, complement, not replace, the Nordic countries' existing foreign and security policy allegiances.

As far as the soft policy tools are concerned, one such potential tool to deal with the Arctic security issues could be the Arctic Council, established in 1996 by the "Arctic Eight" (Finland, Sweden, Norway, Denmark, Iceland, Russia, the United States, and Canada). Its establishment had its roots in the signing in 1991 of the Declaration and Strategy for the Protection of the Arctic Environment by the same eight states.

The "Rovaniemi process" that started after the signing of the declaration, as well as the work conducted in the Arctic Council, have proved the council to be an important platform for discussing key issues relating to the Arctic region to protect the region's unique environment. But the process has clearly shown the limits of the council in that there are clear haves and have-nots within the council. If nothing before, then at least the Ilulissat conference demonstrated that difference: the Arctic Council members that do not have direct access to the Arctic seas were not invited to the conference.

Another problem widely identified with the Arctic Council is that it is a soft law instrument, with no powers to establish internationally legally binding obligations for the participating states. Besides the council, another way to tackle the issues could be through the EU Northern Dimension policy, launched by Finland in the late 1990s. It could provide a platform to harmonize the interests of the countries of the region.

CONCLUSIONS – THE ARCTIC SECURITY AGENDA

What we see, on the basis of the discussion here, is both a deep and a broad transformation of the Arctic security environment. This in turn generates a broad security agenda. It can be broken down into two key parts:

The first deep agenda point is the need to improve our understanding of the ecological consequences of the human impact on the Arctic. This is the scientific agenda. It includes both the need to understand what is happening and the need – and of equal importance – to develop a sufficient consensus among the scientific community to lend political weight to the conclusions. The second part of the scientific agenda is to propose solutions to sustain the Arctic ecosystem and, together with industry and with strong government backing, to develop eco-friendly technology capable of reducing the damage to the Arctic.

This part of the agenda could be called the scientific high ground. It is important because knowledge will, in this case, provide considerable political power, both in negotiations and in shaping the mood – and hence domestic political pressures – of global civil society. The technological angle will in turn be important economically, providing highly sought-after and lucrative new industries.

The second deep agenda point is the political one – the need to manage the various interests in the Arctic region. This includes two key subcomponents. The first is the multilateral agenda – the arena of soft politics. This is clearly the ideal way to regulate behavior in the Arctic region and to settle eventual differences. It includes three key areas: first, delimitation and ownership; second, regulation of industrial and other activity in the Arctic to protect the environment; and third, various governance mechanisms for managing the evolving issues in the political, economic, social, and ecological domains.

The second political agenda point is how to manage potential hard security challenges. This is the arena of power politics and could become necessary should attempts to find soft multilateral solutions fail. This includes at least three subcomponents. First is the need to oversee whatever ecological rules that are set – either multilaterally or nationally. Second is the need to enforce the rules in the event breaches are perceived. This policing component provides considerably more scope for tension. Finally, the need to manage conflicting interests should they emerge, including outright confrontations. These can range from diplomatic disputes to, in the worst case, outright military pressure and even use of military force.

For a small country such as Finland, located next to the emerging Arctic great game and a neighbor to one of the key Arctic players, Russia, the stakes are obviously high. Key areas where Finland could become active include the following:

1. The scientific agenda: Ensuring that Finland develops sufficient expertise in Arctic ecological and related technological domains, so that Finland can at a minimum protect its vital interests in multilateral fora, and eventually – if it chooses – take the high ground in Arctic ecological multilateral negotiations. As noted already, the maxim that knowledge is power will apply particularly to the Arctic.

2. The technological agenda: Ensure that Finland develops niche technology critical for Arctic activity. This will both provide economic benefits and strengthen Finland's political negotiating position.

3. The multilateral agenda: Ensure that Finland develops the diplomatic networks that allow it to secure its vital interests in the Arctic soft power game.

4. The hard power agenda: Ensure that Finland has protected its interests and developed capabilities in case conflicts and confrontations emerge along its northern Arctic neighborhood. For this, Finland is too small and its resources much too limited. This argues for a comprehensive, collaborative, and cooperative approach with those states sharing its basic values and goals as a member of the Arctic community.

9

The Arctic Challenge to Danish Foreign and Security Policy

Nikolaj Petersen

DENMARK'S AWAKENING AWARENESS OF THE ARCTIC

In May 2008, Danish Foreign Minister Per Stig Møller gathered colleagues from the four other states bordering the Arctic Ocean for a successful conference in Ilulissat, Greenland, on the future governance of the region.[1] In the so-called Ilulissat Declaration adopted at the conference, the Arctic Five stated the following:

> The Arctic stands at the threshold of significant changes. Climate change and the melting of ice have a potential impact on vulnerable ecosystems, the livelihoods of local populations and indigenous communities, and the potential exploitation of natural resources. By virtue of their sovereignty, sovereign rights and jurisdiction in large areas of the Arctic Ocean, the five coastal states are in a unique position to address these possibilities and challenges. In this regard we recall that an extensive legal framework applies to the Arctic Ocean. . . . Notably, the law of the sea provides for important rights and obligations. . . . This framework provides a solid foundation for responsible management by the five coastal states and other users of this Ocean through national implementation and application of relevant provisions. We therefore see no need to develop a new comprehensive international legal scheme to govern the Arctic Ocean.[2]

A few weeks earlier, the Danish Ministry of Foreign Affairs (MFA) and the home-rule government of Greenland published a joint strategy paper, "Arktis i en brydningstid" ("The Arctic in a Time of Change"), which spelled out Denmark's and Greenland's joint Arctic interests in the face of new economic-political developments in the

---

[1] The participants were Foreign Minister Jonas Gahr Støre, Norway; Foreign Minister Sergei Lavrov, Russia; Minister of Natural Resources Gary Lund, Canada; Deputy Secretary of State John Negroponte, United States; Foreign Minister Per Stig Møller, Denmark; and Premier Hans Enoksen, Greenland.

[2] The Ilulissat Declaration, 28 May 2008, in *Danish Foreign Policy Yearbook 2009* (Copenhagen; Danish Institute for International Studies), pp. 154–55.

region.[3] Moreover, an official Defense Commission was set up in early 2008, with a remit including an analysis of the implications of recent and future Arctic developments. On the basis of the commission's report, a broad parliamentary majority adopted a defense plan for 2010–2014 in June 2009, which staked out guidelines for Denmark's future security policy in the Arctic.[4] These three events reflect an awakening Danish awareness of the Arctic as a "new," semiautonomous region in international politics and represent a first attempt to formulate relevant policies at the multilateral, bilateral, and unilateral levels. This awareness has been spawned by a cluster of novel developments such as global warming, new prospects for oil and gas extraction north of the Arctic Circle, and the upcoming partition of the Arctic Ocean among the coastal states' extended continental shelves. An additional factor is the introduction of Greenlandic self-government (*selvstyre*) in June 2009.

The notion of an Arctic political-strategic region in its own right, where Denmark and Greenland have important interests, is new to Danish political thinking. Of course, the significant geopolitical role of the Arctic and Greenland during the Cold War was understood in Copenhagen. But this had very little to do with Denmark or Greenland itself, as it resulted from an extraregional factor, namely the strategic confrontation between the United States and the Soviet Union. With the end of the Cold War, strategic interest in Greenland declined until it was revived for a while by U.S. plans for missile defense against "rogue states," or the "axis of evil." In December 2002, the Bush administration requested permission from Denmark to upgrade the Ballistic Missile Early Warning System (BMEWS) radar at Thule Air Base in northwestern Greenland to advanced missile-defense standards. Such permission was given in 2004 in the so-called Igaliku Agreement. Technically a supplement to the 1951 Defense Agreement between Denmark and the United States concerning Greenland, the agreement was cosigned on the Danish side by the home-rule government of Greenland. In addition, joint declarations on economic, technical, and environmental cooperation between the United States and Greenland were signed as part of the deal.[5] The particular interest in missile defense has weakened under the Obama administration. Instead, the Arctic agenda is crowded with a number of endogenous or intraregional developments, to which Denmark is only beginning to respond.

This chapter first briefly discusses the setting of Danish Arctic policy, including regional warming, prospects for oil and gas development, the policies of other Arctic actors, and Greenland's new self-government status. Next, it turns toward a discussion

---

[3] Namminersorlutik Oqartussat and Udenrigsministeriet (2008), *Arktis i en brydningstid: Forslag til strategi for aktiviteter i det arktiske område*, May 2008, http://www.um.dk.

[4] *Forsvarsforlig, Juni 24*, 2009, http://www.um.dk.

[5] The 1951 agreement allowed the United States to operate three air bases in Greenland, of which Thule Air Base is the only one left. DUPI (Dansk Udenrigspolitisk Institut), *Grønland under den kolde krig*, vol. 2, pp. 144–53. For the Igaliku Agreement, see "Aftalekompleks i tilknytning til opgradering af Thule-radaren, August 6, 2004," http://www.um.dk.

of Denmark's security policy for the Arctic under varying conditions of cooperation and conflict, with an emphasis on the Arctic tasks, present and future, of the Danish defense forces.

RECENT POLITICAL AND ECONOMIC DEVELOPMENTS

Greenland: From Home Rule to Self-Government

The Kingdom of Denmark is a peculiar political entity, in fact what is left of an eighteenth-century empire comprising the Kingdom of Denmark with scattered colonial possessions in the West Indies, Africa, and India; the duchies of Schleswig and Holstein; and the Kingdom of Norway, with its dependencies: the Faeroe Islands, Iceland, and Greenland. Today only the Faeroe Islands and Greenland, which have become self-governing communities, are left to constitute the so-called Rigsfællesskab ("realm" or "commonwealth") together with metropolitan Denmark (including half of Schleswig). Greenland's self-government status was proclaimed on 21 June 2009, exactly thirty years after the introduction of home rule in 1979. The self-government "constitution" recognized the people of Greenland as a distinct people under international law who possess an inherent right to independence if and when they so desire.[6] Furthermore, the document gave the self-government authorities sole ownership of Greenland's underground riches, including the offshore seabed, and the option to take over domestic policy areas, mainly in the judicial field, which still are managed and financed by the Danish state. But the new rights come with a price tag. Denmark's annual financial block grant to Greenland of more than 3 billion kroner will be reduced by half of Greenland's future net income from minerals and hydrocarbons, and the transfer of new policy areas will have to be financed fully by the self-government's budget.

Compared to home rule, self-government does not include significant new competences in the field of foreign affairs, as Greenland has had to accept that there is little formal scope for this in the Danish constitution. Defense, foreign policy, sovereignty control, and most other authority tasks therefore remain Danish prerogatives. On the other hand, there is a general Danish-Greenlandic understanding, codified in the self-government statute, that the informal process should continue in which Greenland has gradually gained an important say over Danish foreign policy concerning Greenland.

Greenland's takeover of its underground wealth coincides with the publication of new and more reliable estimates of oil and gas reserves on its continental shelf, as well as increasing interest in its mineral wealth. This is certain to whet Greenlandic appetites for independence. However, if the Arctic does in fact become an important economic-political region, the defense of Greenland's interests will require

---

[6] The Faeroe Islands also have the option of independence.

physical and human as well as political-diplomatic resources, which a small nation of fifty-seven thousand people inhabiting an area four times that of France, can hardly muster. Greenland's self-government is therefore likely to continue its basic dependency on Denmark, whereas Denmark's physical presence in the Arctic will increase rather than diminish under the new dispensation. The precondition, however, is a close coordination of Danish and Greenlandic interests and a strong Danish defense of Greenland's particular interests.

A start has been made by the previously mentioned Danish-Greenlandic strategy paper from May 2008. The main thrust of the paper represents a significant paradigm change in Danish and Greenlandic policy away from an emphasis on sustainable development and protection of the vulnerable Arctic environment to "a growing awareness that the consolidation and development of the Arctic societies must rest on economic development."[7] Thus there has been a shift from a defensive, protective response to climate and other changes to a more offensive, exploitative approach. With respect to foreign policy in the Arctic, the paper states that "Denmark and Greenland . . . have a clear foreign and security policy interest, that the new challenges and possibilities, which . . . climate changes may create in the Arctic, are handled in accordance with international legal principles and existing treaties, that is, by dialogue, cooperation and negotiation."[8]

In connection with the transition to self-government, an election to the Greenland parliament (Landsting) ravaged the two parties, which had dominated the home-rule period. The centrist Siumut and the moderate Atassut were removed from power, and a government dominated by the leftist IA (Inuit Ataqatigiit) party was installed. The government shift has not led to any significant shift in Greenland's economic and foreign policy, however, as the new government, led by Premier Kuupik Kleist, has consolidated the economic modernization policy and so far has dampened ambitions for Greenlandic independence in the near future.

Global Warming and Prospects for Arctic Economic Development

Global warming is the single most important process that is propelling the Arctic onto the global political scene. The warming process is particularly fast in the Arctic, which is leading some scientists to speculate on the possibility of an approaching tipping point at which climate change suddenly accelerates. As far as Greenland is concerned, comprehensive measurements of a wide range of indicators over the past decade at the Zackenberg Research Station in northeastern Greenland already document significant changes toward a warmer climate.

Economic activities in Greenland are likely to be affected directly by the expected rise in air and ocean temperatures, as well as indirectly by the melting of the

[7] *Arktis i en brydningstid* (note 3), p. 7
[8] *Ibid.*

Greenlandic ice cap and the Arctic Ocean ice cover. In contrast to most other world regions, many regional effects of Arctic warning are likely to be beneficial, which, of course, is partly a reflection of the forbidding nature of the present polar climate. Thus, rising air temperatures will benefit farming and gardening in Greenland and especially facilitate the budding mining industry by reducing prospecting and transportation costs. In addition, rising ocean temperatures will probably benefit the fishing industry by the return of cod to Greenlandic waters and the growth of stocks of catfish, halibut, and herring. In contrast, shrimp fishery, Greenland's main industry, is likely to suffer, as will also hunting and small-scale fishing – that is, the traditional Inuit way of life.

In a short-term perspective, the main effect of rising ocean temperatures is likely to be diminished ice coverage of the Arctic Ocean. Summer ice coverage has retreated significantly in the past decade, thus leading to predictions of a seasonally ice-free Arctic Ocean sometime this century. If, or rather when, the Arctic waterways become navigable on a regular but still only seasonal basis, shipping patterns around Greenland are likely to change. An opening of the Northwest Passage through Arctic Canada will increase shipping in the Davis Strait and Baffin Bay, and the possible opening of an Arctic "highway" right across the North Pole will introduce shipping to the Greenland Sea and the Fram Strait off Greenland's northeastern coast. Other increases in shipping volume are likely to come from cruise ships (already fairly common in Greenland), and not least from ships servicing offshore oil and gas production sites to the west and eventually the east of Greenland.

Greenland as a New Petroleum Region

During 2007–08, concrete but essentially uncertain estimates of so-called undiscovered oil and gas reserves in the Arctic were published in the U.S. Geological Survey's *Circum-Arctic Resource Appraisal*.[9] Its main conclusion was a mean estimate of 412 billion barrels of oil equivalents (BBOE) of undiscovered hydrocarbons north of the Arctic Circle. The mean estimate for oil was about 90 BBOE, amounting to about 13 percent of the world's undiscovered oil reserves, whereas the total estimate for natural gas is 1,669 trillion cubic feet. The four largest reserves were estimated to be the West Siberian Basin (132 BBOE), Arctic Alaska (72 BBOE), the East Barents Basin (61 BBOE), and the East Greenland Rift Basins (31 BBOE). Further down the list came the East Canada and West Greenland province (17 BBOE) and the North Greenland Sheared Margin (3.3 BBOE).

Although the Arctic is a promising oil and gas region, it is also a problematic one. The harsh climate of low temperatures and strong winds, and especially the ocean ice, whether as firm ice cover or as drifting ice floes and icebergs, make oil and gas

---

[9] U.S. Geological Survey, *Circum-Arctic Resource Appraisal: Estimates of Undiscovered Oil and Gas North of the Arctic Circle*, U.S. Geological Survey Fact Sheet 2008-3049, July 2008, http://www.usgs.gov.

prospecting, drilling, and production extremely difficult and hazardous, especially off eastern Greenland. The development of producing oil fields off Greenland is therefore highly dependent on the pace and magnitude of ice melting in the Arctic Ocean and adjoining seas.

However, political decisions also matter. In the aftermath of the Deepwater Horizon oil-spill disaster in the Gulf of Mexico in 2010, concerns rose as to the safety of Arctic drilling, and as a result Canada, the United States, and Norway put new deepwater drilling on hold. But not the Greenland self-government, which in June 2010 gave the Scottish firm Cairns Energy licenses for two exploratory drillings in Baffin Bay starting in July 2010. The Greenland authorities contend that Greenland applies the world's strictest safety rules (i.e., Norwegian ones) and demands the world's highest disaster guarantee – a fund of 60 billion Danish kroner – from prospecting companies. Even so, the question remains as to which resources Greenland can mobilize in case of a major disaster. As a consequence of the self-government's arrangement, Denmark has not been in on the decision to allow drilling, but the buck is likely to stop at the Danish government's desk.

ARCTIC SECURITY IN THE FUTURE

The Arctic Conflict Potential

As a minor player, Denmark's Arctic policy is sensitive to future patterns of conflict and cooperation between the coastal states and other interested parties. Territorial issues are obvious potential sources of conflict. The long-standing Norwegian-Russian disagreement about the delimitation of zones in the Barents Sea was peacefully solved during President Medvedev's visit to Norway in April 2010, but other disputes, such the U.S. disputes with Canada and Russia over the status of the Northwest Passage and the Northern Sea Route, may escalate with increasing economic and political interests in the region. Denmark's dispute with Canada over the minuscule Hans Island in the Nares Strait is a reflection less of its importance than of the intractability of territorial conflicts.

More serious conflicts could be unleashed in the wake of the upcoming partition of the extended continental shelf in the Arctic Ocean, popularly (but somewhat misleadingly) called the race for the North Pole. In accordance with the 1982 UN Convention on the Law of the Sea (UNCLOS), all coastal states situated around the Arctic Ocean have declared an exclusive economic zone (EEZ) stretching two hundred nautical miles seaward from their coastal base lines. In addition, article 76 of the convention stipulates that for a ten-year period after accession to the treaty, state parties may raise documented claims before the UN Commission on the Limits of the Continental Shelf (CLCS) to those parts of the extended continental shelf that reach up to 150 nautical miles beyond their EEZ or, depending on various technical details, up to 100 nautical miles beyond the 2,500 meter isobath. This is the so-called extended or outer continental shelf (OCS). The most coveted prize is the undersea Lomonosov Ridge, which stretches from north of Greenland across the Arctic Ocean to Siberia, and that Russia, Canada, and Denmark claim is a natural extension of their continental shelves. It is still an open question as to how the CLCS will treat the individual, potentially overlapping demands as they are presented, and whether there will be a possibility of interstate agreements on partition lines. Denmark has agreed to initiate negotiations with Norway as soon as the CLCS decides on the Danish claim. Copenhagen also is interested in a similar agreement with Canada. Russia and Denmark are due to submit their claims in 2011 and 2014, respectively, and the possibility of a territorial conflict over the seabed of the North Pole area cannot be excluded.

Another important ingredient in the Danish Arctic equation is the regional policies of the other members of the Arctic Five, especially as they relate to the "militarization" of the Arctic, understood as the growth in military capabilities and activities in the region. So far, the most active states in this regard have been Canada and Russia. Thus, Canada's Conservative Party Prime Minister Stephen Harper has repeatedly stated the need for Ottawa to promote an increased military presence in the north under the motto "use it [i.e., sovereignty] or lose it." Accordingly, Canada has adopted plans for military and naval bases in the Northwest Passage and has reacted strongly to alleged Russian violations of Canada's airspace and Air Defense Identification Zone. The crucial player is the Russian Federation, which has by far the longest coast line on the Arctic Ocean and stands to gain a major part of the OCS above the Arctic circle. As a power whose economic development and political status is intimately linked to oil and gas extraction, the prospect of significant finds on the relatively shallow North Russian and Siberian offshore is all-important. About 20 percent of Russia's gross domestic product and 22 percent of its exports are produced in the area, according to President Medvedev. Russia was the first country to stake its claim to part of the Arctic Ocean when, in 2001, it presented the CLCS with a claim to a chunk of 1.2 million square kilometers (roughly the combined areas of France, Italy, and Germany) including a major part of the Lomonosov Ridge. However, the CLCS did not accept the claim and has demanded additional data and documentation, to be provided by 2011.

Russia has stepped up its patrols in the Arctic since August 2007, when it demonstrated its power and will by planting a Russian flag on the ocean floor four thousand meters below the North Pole. Moscow also deployed an icebreaker to the region.[10] The episode was garnered with martial statements by activist officers and gave rise to nervousness among the other coastal states, that also worry about the 2009 announcement that Russia will build a special Arctic force in the next decade. In contrast,

---

[10] At the Ilulissat conference in May 2008, Foreign Minister Lavrov explained that the operation was undertaken because Russia was able to do so and because it wanted to demonstrate to others that it could.

Russia's adherence to the Ilulissat Declaration and authoritative statements that Russia will respect UNCLOS procedures for the partition of the Arctic continental shelf, as well as the recent agreement with Norway, point to a Russian interest in cooperating with the other coastal states in exploiting the economic potentials of the Arctic.

Compared to Russia and Canada, the United States has held a low profile in Arctic politics. The reluctance to play a more active role may be because the United States is not a party to UNCLOS. This is likely to change, however. One of the very last actions of the Bush administration was to release a new directive on Arctic policy, which since then has been adopted by the Obama administration. The U.S. Arctic region policy foreshadows "a more active and influential national presence to protect its Arctic interests and to project sea power throughout the region."[11] It will take some time, however, before the regional balance of power tips in favor of the United States.

In addition to intraregional conflict potential, Arctic politics will be sensitive to spillover from extraregional conflicts, such as the 2008 crisis between Russia and Georgia. Spillover from NATO-Russian conflicts elsewhere is probably the single most destabilizing factor in the Arctic equation. Denmark's general relations with the other members of the Arctic Five are relevant in this context. Briefly, Denmark has excellent relations with the United States, as witnessed by its substantial participation in the wars in Iraq and Afghanistan, and Copenhagen is determined to keep those relations so, despite concrete disagreements over the U.S. approach to global warming; and despite the dispute about Hans Island, relations with Canada are traditionally close. Norway is a close ally as well, although the two countries to some extent parted ways after the Cold War. In the Arctic, though, Denmark and Norway tend to agree in substance but not always in tactics. For obvious reasons, Norway is more occupied than Denmark with Russia's Arctic activities. Nevertheless, Denmark's post–Cold War relations with Russia have been marred by disputes over Russia's policies vis-à-vis the Baltic states, Kaliningrad, Chechnya, and Georgia, as well as over NATO enlargement, which Denmark has actively promoted. As a result, Denmark was for a long time viewed in Moscow as one of the least friendly members of NATO. However, President Medvedev's state visit to Copenhagen in April 2010 – the first since 1964 – may be the beginning of a new, more cooperative relationship.

The Potential for Arctic Cooperation

Balancing the Arctic potential for conflict, there are also a number of incentives to cooperate between the Arctic Five and other interested actors. First, by their very

---

[11] White House, National Security Presidential Directive (NSPD-66/HSPD-25), 9 January 2009, Sec. B,3.

TABLE 9.1. *Potential Arctic Tasks for Danish Foreign and Security Policy*

Cooperation pole			Conflict pole
Regime tasks	Authority tasks	Sovereignty tasks	Military tasks
Follow-up on Ilulissat	Charting	Continental shelf	Interdiction
Charting	GREENPOS	claim	Crisis management
Ship reporting system	reporting system	Air surveillance	Territorial defense
Search and rescue	Search and rescue	Sea surveillance	Defense
Ship certification	Police tasks	Land surveillance	cooperation
Ice and weather	Ice and weather		
services	services		
Environmental	Environmental		
control	control		
Fishery inspection	Fishery inspection		

nature, transborder problems like pollution from oil and gas production rigs and the regulation of international shipping call for international management. Second, the general shortage of infrastructure and material resources in the Arctic, in combination with high costs, serves to make joint solutions more attractive than national ones. Third, pressure from outside actors for influence can best be accommodated in cooperative regimes. Finally, there is a strong incentive to cooperate (or at least avoid conflict), in that the full exploitation of economic opportunities requires a nonconflictual environment.

Areas where a need or possibility for cooperation and regime formation can be identified include functions like the charting (mapping) of often shallow coastal waters, a reporting system for ships entering Arctic waters, safety regulations for cruise ships, certification of ships for Arctic navigation, search-and-rescue (SAR) readiness, weather and ice services, and the provision of ice-breaking capabilities. Although most of these functions relate to the management of an increased volume of Arctic shipping, improved regional weather and ice services also will be of vital interest to oil and gas companies working in Arctic environments, as will disaster readiness and pollution control.[12]

FUTURE NONMILITARY TASKS FOR DENMARK

Despite these incentives for cooperation in the Arctic, Danish policy also must calculate the possibility of increased conflict and the eventual need for a proper defense of Greenland. Table 9.1 summarizes a number of relevant future tasks within a mixed cooperative-conflictual environment. So far, Danish efforts in

[12] These possible regimes are discussed in greater detail in Nikolaj Petersen, "The Arctic as a New Arena for Danish Foreign Policy: The Ilulissat Initiative and Its Implications," in *Danish Foreign Policy Yearbook 2009*, (Copenhagen: Danish Institute for International Studies), pp. 35–78.

Greenland have focused on authority and sovereignty tasks, that is, on policing and controlling civilian activities offshore and on guarding Greenland's sea and land territory against intrusion by other powers. In the absence of a special coast guard, these tasks are handled by the Danish Armed Forces, with the exception of minor control functions, which are performed by Greenland's self-government authorities. However, with growing activities in the Arctic region, new policy tasks will present themselves at either pole of the cooperation-conflict dimension. If regional cooperation comes to prevail, many authority tasks may be wholly or partially regionalized in international regimes and other cooperative schemes. If, however, conflict becomes the dominant feature, proper defense tasks will present themselves.

Regime Policy

From the Danish perspective, the framework for future regime formation in the Arctic already exists, in the shape of the Ilulissat Declaration of May 2008. The idea of committing the Arctic coastal states to a code of Arctic conduct was hatched in September 2007 by Foreign Minister Per Stig Møller (of the Conservative People's Party) as a reaction to the Russian power demonstration the previous month – and to a somewhat similar idea floated by his Norwegian colleague Jonas Gahr Støre. The initiative was foreshadowed by the foreign minister in a speech at Chatham House on June 26, 2007, "Climate Change, Foreign and Security Policy," in which Møller specifically dwelled on Arctic melting and its wider geostrategic implications, such as "competition over new accessible natural resources, rights to new shipping routes and disputes over maritime zones and territories formerly covered by ice." And he added, half joking: "We will soon have to discuss and decide: who owns the North Pole. That, by the way, I think we do!"[13]

But the Ilulissat initiative was also embedded in the broader context of an ambitious international climate policy. According to an internal MFA document of September 2007, the conference would market Denmark as an active international actor with respect to peaceful international crisis management, the strengthening of international law, and the handling of the Arctic challenges. Specifically, it would highlight Denmark's role in the integration of climate and foreign policy, "where Denmark is an international front runner."[14]

This integration of climate and foreign policy dates back to 2004, when Per Stig Møller's close political ally Connie Hedegaard (Conservative People's Party), was appointed minister of the environment. In August 2005, Hedegaard launched the so-called Greenland dialogue by calling an informal ministerial conference

[13] Per Stig Møller, "Climate Change: Politics versus Economics," Chatham House, 26 June 2007, *Danish Foreign Policy Yearbook* 2007, pp. 142–51 (p. 144)
[14] Departmental note to the foreign minister, 3 September 2007, MFA (Ministry of Foreign Affairs) file 46.C.62.

at Ilulissat to discuss the implications of climate change and to further a common understanding of the problem.[15] The dialogue continued in meetings in South Africa (2006), Sweden (2007), and Argentina (2008), returning to Ilulissat in the summer of 2009 with the participation of twenty-nine delegations. In another initiative, Denmark canvassed successfully for Copenhagen as the venue for the Fifteenth Conference of Parties (COP-15), the UN Conference on Climate Change, which was held in December 2009. The meeting was meant to result in an international agreement to succeed the Kyoto protocol. By that time, Prime Minister Anders Fogh Rasmussen (Liberal Party), whose government started out in 2002 promoting Bjørn Lomborg's climate skepticism, had been convinced during the so-called cartoon crisis of 2005–06 of the need to make the West independent of (Middle Eastern) oil. Until he was appointed secretary-general of NATO in the spring of 2009, Anders Fogh Rasmussen was an energetic spokesperson for international carbon dioxide reduction.[16] This nexus between climate and energy was cemented in 2007, when Connie Hedegaard was appointed the world's first minister for climate and energy. By 2010, Hedegaard likewise resigned from Danish politics to become the European Union's climate commissioner.

Considering the high hopes and significant economic and political investments in COP-15, its outcome was a deep disappointment. The result of the conference led to some questioning of Denmark's handling of the preparation and management of the conference. By a very active role as host of the conference, Denmark had to bear some of the onus for its meager outcome, even though the main responsibility had to be laid at the doorsteps of the United States; China; and regional powers like India, Brazil, and South Africa.

The basic approach of the COP process is the mitigation of the warming process by reducing carbon dioxide emissions. The difficulties of this strategy make a supplementary adaptation approach more important than before, that is, a strategy designed to cope with the effects (rather than the causes) of global (and Arctic) warming. One such strategy is embedded in the Ilulissat initiative of Foreign Minister Per Stig Møller, from the summer of 2007.

The idea of the Ilulissat conference in May 2008 was to commit the Arctic Five to manage the new Arctic challenges through "dialogue, cooperation and negotiation" and to confirm the UNCLOS regime as the framework for the partition of the continental shelf, as well as for the future management of Arctic Ocean issues in general. The corollary to this insistence on the UNCLOS machinery

[15] Ilulissat, on the western coast of Greenland, is the site of the world's most productive glacier. The dramatic retreat of the glacier front has become an icon of global warming, and the Danish government has used the small settlement as a popular, exotic venue of several conferences and meetings on international climate change.

[16] In the cartoon crisis, Denmark became the scapegoat of the Muslim world with consumer boycotts of Danish products, anti-Danish street demonstrations, and embassy burnings. In 2008, the Danish embassy in Islamabad was damaged by a suicide bomber. See, e.g., Jytte Klausen, *The Cartoons That Shook the World* (New Haven, CT: Yale University Press, 2009).

was the rejection of any need for a new legal framework, such as a specific Arctic treaty or internationalization of the region. The result was quite the opposite: the Ilulissat Declaration gave the Arctic Five a special responsibility for Arctic affairs, an attribution that was resented by outsiders to the process, such as Iceland and Sweden.

To assuage criticism, Denmark claimed that the Ilulissat initiative was a singular event and not the beginning of an exclusive coastal state cooperation. Thus, when Denmark took over the chairmanship of the Arctic Council in April 2009, Per Stig Møller in his inaugural speech referred to the Ilulissat Declaration and went on to say that "the task of carrying the issues forward and developing common solution lies to a large part with the Arctic Council." As concrete tasks, he mentioned search and rescue, guidelines for tourism, and the effort to make mandatory the International Maritime Organization's polar code guidelines for Arctic shipping.[17]

Denmark took no further initiative, and when Canada invited them to a follow-up foreign minister's meeting of the Arctic Five near Ottawa on 29 March 2010, Per Stig Møller gave a positive but somewhat guarded response. In a letter of 5 February to Canadian Foreign Minister Lawrence Cannon, he confirmed that he and Kuupik Kleist, Greenland's premier, would attend the meeting, which "will provide a useful occasion for the Arctic Ocean states to reconfirm the strong commitments we made in Ilulissat on the law of the sea and the orderly settlement of any possible overlapping claims." But he also cautioned "that we should all remain committed to the Arctic Council as the preeminent organization for international cooperation in the Arctic." It was therefore "decisive" that the meeting did not create dividing lines within the council and that any result of the meeting would be viewed by its other members as "constructive and complementary to the cooperation taking place."[18]

In a government reshuffle later in February 2010, Møller was succeeded – much against his will – by the Conservative Party leader Lene Espersen, who promptly cancelled her participation in the meeting. The reason – it collided with a family holiday in Mallorca – raised a formidable press campaign against the minister, which did not abate until she apologized and called the decision the worst in her political career. In the government's inner cabinet, Møller, now minister of culture, reportedly complained that the cancellation would totally compromise his own Arctic policy. But this context was largely ignored by the campaign, which only scratched the surface by focusing on the minister's priorities and her failure to grab the opportunity for an early get-together with U.S. Secretary of State Clinton.[19]

As it were, the Arctic Five meeting was fairly uneventful. Although it was agreed that the Arctic Council should remain the central platform for discussing Arctic problems, it was likewise agreed that the Arctic Five was a legitimate forum for

---

[17] Speech by Danish minister for foreign affairs at the Arctic Council, 29 April 2009, http://www.um.dk.
[18] MFA, Ministerprotokollen (Ministry of Foreign Affairs, Minister's Protocol), 5 February 2010.
[19] Mrs. Espersen's Arctic faux-pas eventually contributed to her downfall in January 2011 as party leader. She remained foreign minister, though.

discussions of problems that concerned only the five coastal states. The group should not be formalized but should continue as a forum for senior officials.[20]

Authority Tasks

As shown in Table 9.1, there is a considerable overlap between what is here called regime tasks and national authority tasks. Whether a particular function will be performed in the future by an international regime or continue on a national basis, it is a safe assumption that more resources will have to be allotted to these functions. Costs and efficiency may favor international solutions, and some functions like ship certification or guidelines for Arctic shipping make sense only in an international setting. To take an example, Denmark presently operates the so-called GREENPOS reporting system, which is obligatory for all ships entering Greenland's territorial waters. However, there is no enforcement mechanism, and cruise ships often fail to report their presence. An international reporting regime could probably be made more efficient by a fine system. In contrast, functions like policing and various environmental or fishery controls are likely to remain in national hands.

Sovereignty Policy

Even before Denmark ratified UNCLOS in 2004, the government had launched a scientific project together with the Greenlandic and Faeroese governments with a view to present documented claims to the outer continental shelves of the two North Atlantic parts of the commonwealth before the expiration of the ten-year deadline.[21] Such claims must be documented by seismic and echo-sounder data, which are extremely difficult to collect in the ice-bound waters north of Greenland. Here, Denmark is working together with Canada to find evidence of a geological connection between the Greenlandic-Canadian continental shelf and the Lomonosov Ridge. Apart from the continental shelf north of Greenland, Denmark also collects data for claims to the shelf to the northeast and south of Greenland, as well as to the north and south of the Faeroe Islands. Whether the UN commission will accept the Danish claims in toto, the essential sovereignty tasks of surveillance and sovereignty enforcement will have to cover significantly larger stretches of the northern seas than they do today.

DEFENSE TASKS IN AND AROUND GREENLAND

If Arctic politics should veer toward conflict, new defense tasks will present themselves, such as interception readiness, crisis management capabilities, and even

---

[20] Report (heavily sanitized) on Ottawa conference by the Danish embassy in Ottawa, 30 March 2010, MFA file 46.B.2. YOW, DOK705387.

[21] See "Kontinentalsokkelprojektet," http:// www.a76.dk.

proper defense capabilities. Such measures may be undertaken as a reaction to (Russian) violations of Greenland's airspace or in response to regional crises with a limited use of force. Both contingencies are imaginable, though not likely, whereas conflict levels that call for substantial defense capabilities in Greenland are even less plausible. As a matter of fact, there has never been a traditional defense capability in Greenland, even during the Cold War. The very limited Danish military presence has been exclusively occupied with authority and sovereignty functions. And even though the 1951 Danish-American Defense Agreement is formally about the defense of Greenland, the U.S. presence has never been concerned with creating a traditional territorial defense of the island. Thus, Thule Air Base has been without an active defense since 1965.

Denmark's Military Presence in Greenland in 2010

In 1995, the Danish forces in Greenland were brought together in the Greenland Command (Grønlands Kommando, or GLK), which like the Faeroe Command (and the three service commands) is directly subordinate to the Danish Defense Command. The command (whose personnel counts some one hundred people) carries out its missions with delegated units from the navy and air force. As mentioned, these tasks comprise surveillance, enforcement of sovereignty, and a number of authority tasks. The Greenland Command is headquartered at Grønnedal Naval Station in southwestern Greenland and has facilities at the former Sondrestrom Air Force Base, now Kangerlussuaq, in mid-Greenland, where Air Group West is stationed as well as a weather station with a landing strip at Station Nord in faraway northeastern Greenland and a landing strip in Mestersvig, East Greenland. By far the largest defense facility in Greenland, Thule Air Base in northwestern Greenland is operated by the United States according to the 1951 defense agreement. The base hosts the large BMEWS radar, built in 1960 (and modernized in the 1980s) as the hub of the U.S. BMEWS system, which is being upgraded for inclusion in the U.S. missile-defense system. Another important facility at Thule is a satellite-tracking station for communication with U.S. military satellites. With military personnel in the low hundreds, Thule is only a fraction of its size in the late 1950s, when it was manned by more than seven thousand personnel.[22] Denmark uses Thule for supply flights to Station Nord but has only a liaison officer stationed at the base.

As for matériel, the Danish navy has four *Thetis*-class inspection frigates (3,500 tons) specially built for operations in the North Atlantic. One of these is permanently assigned to the Greenland Command and another to the Faeroe Command. In 2002, a third frigate, which had been assigned to geological research around Greenland, was made the command and flag ship of the Danish navy and withdrawn

[22] On Thule, see Nikolaj Petersen, "SAC at Thule: Greenland in the Polar Strategy," *Journal of Cold War Studies* (forthcoming spring 2011).

from the North Atlantic. This weakening of the Greenland assignment was redressed in 2008–09 with the introduction of two modern inspection vessels of the *Knud Rasmussen* class (1,720 tons), which replace two of three smallish *Agdlek*-class inspection cutters. Furthermore, the Greenland Command can use a *Challenger* surveillance purposes for about a week each month. Finally, the legendary Sirius dog-sled patrol has surveyed the vast coastal stretches of northeastern and northern Greenland since World War II.

VIEWS ON ARCTIC DEFENSE AFTER 2010

Is this modest effort enough in view of the expected expansion of authority and sovereignty tasks? And will a proper defense capability be needed in the future? In a recent report from the independent Danish Institute for Military Studies, titled *Hold hovedet koldt!* (Keep cool!), future defense needs in Greenland are analyzed under the assumption that a militarization of the Arctic is highly improbable, because Russia has neither the capabilities needed for nor interest in a confrontation with the West in the extreme north.[23] If Russia is to exploit its vast resources in the Arctic, it needs a peaceful and cooperative environment.

Considering the obvious Danish interest in avoiding militarization of the Arctic, the report warns that Denmark should be careful not to increase its military presence unnecessarily, so as to appear threatening to potential enemy powers (i.e., Russia). On the contrary, Denmark should invest energy and resources in developing debating fora with the participation of these states. The report concedes that there is a need to strengthen existing Danish capabilities in Greenland but recommends that this should be done primarily by organizational reform and a stronger prioritizing of its tasks. If this is not enough, Denmark may increase its Arctic capabilities, but only cautiously and hesitantly. At the political level, Denmark should refrain from "problematizing" the Arctic in NATO, so as not to contribute to Russian feelings of threat.

Former foreign minister Uffe Ellemann-Jensen has a more hardheaded analysis. In an opinion editorial, he criticizes what he calls "frightened comments to the effect that Denmark risks provoking Russia if we arm ourselves in the Arctic." First, he points to the manifest potential for conflict in the region despite mutual promises to respect existing rules, which is why a Danish military presence is quite "legitimate." Second, Denmark has a constitutional responsibility to defend Greenland's self-government and its interests. And third, Denmark has a solidary obligation not to free ride at the cost of the other NATO coastal states. Therefore, "We must also have troops and ships and aircraft which can operate in the Arctic."[24]

---

[23] Henrik Jedig Jørgensen and Jon Rahbek-Clemmensen, *Hold hovedet koldt! En scenariebaseret undersøgelse af forsvarets opgaver i Grønland frem mod 2030* (Copenhagen: DIMS, Dansk Institut for Militære Studier, 2009).

[24] Uffe Ellemann-Jensen, "Derfor skal vi have dansk militær i Grønland," *Berlingske Tidende*, July 24, 2009.

These two views indicate the extremes of a debate, which is still in its infancy. As such, they represent two opposing views of Denmark's international role. One is the small power tradition of nonprovocation, which was dominant before World War II and put its stamp on Denmark's Cold War policy. The other view, which has prevailed since the end of the Cold War, sees Denmark as a strategic actor that can and must make a difference outside its own borders. This hardheaded policy was initiated by Ellemann-Jensen in the early 1990s and has made Denmark a self-conscious participant in the Iraq War and the intervention in Afghanistan, where Danish troops are presently heavily tasked with fighting Taliban warriors in Helmand Province.

ARCTIC SECURITY POLICY, 2010–2014

Since the 1960s, Danish defense policy has been laid down in broad parliamentary agreements, normally for four-year periods. In June 2009, the latest such agreement was signed by the broadest parliamentary majority ever and with the longest duration ever, namely five years (2010–14).[25] The agreement continued the process of internationalizing and deterritorializing the Danish defense forces, which has been under way for the past two decades. This outcome is predicated on the analysis that the territorial threat to Denmark ceased with the end of the Cold War and is unlikely to reappear in the foreseeable future. Instead, Danish threat perceptions are focused on international terrorism, the spread of weapons of mass destruction, and the problem of failed and weak states, that is, threats to international order rather than to national security.

Climate change is discussed in two contexts. First, global warming is assumed to have negative effects on international order, particularly in Africa, which is seen as both the most exposed region and the one least prepared to handle climate change. Denmark is therefore likely to become increasingly involved in operations on the African continent, as in disaster relief missions. The overall conclusion is that there will be an unchanged demand for Danish military interventions worldwide but also a greater diversification of tasks than today, when the emphasis is almost entirely on combat operations.

In addition, the agreement acknowledges and addresses the increasing geostrategic importance of the Arctic, but without discussing the inherent contradiction between the unchanged level of overseas missions and the new Arctic ones. The agreement is explicitly based on the conclusion of the 2008 Defense Commission that increasing economic activity in the Arctic will result in new and growing authority and sovereignty tasks.[26] The agreement also seems to be in accordance with the

[25] See *supra* note 4.
[26] Forsvarskommissionen, "Dansk Forsvar: Global engagement," *Beretning fra Forsvarskommissionen af 2008* [Report of the 2008 Defense Commission], March 2009, pp. 77–90, http://www.fmn.dk.

2009 risk assessment by the Defense Intelligence Service, which notes a growing risk of intentional or unintentional conflicts in the Arctic as a consequence of growing strategic interests and a greater military presence there. In particular, Russia's interest in expanding its domain and its proven will to use military power is seen as a potential problem. The assessment finds it unlikely, however, that the present strengthening of military presence in the Arctic will lead to military conflicts. In a longer time perspective there is, though, a risk of minor clashes and diplomatic crises, in which essential strategic and energy interests collide. These confrontations might take the form of military harassment of other states' military forces or of their civilian exploitation of natural resources in the contested areas.[27]

The military threat assessment for the Arctic is not alarmist, at least in the short term, and the defense agreement is correspondingly vague on the scope and character of Denmark's future military presence there. The main emphasis is clearly on strengthening the capability for authority and sovereignty tasks.

The agreement introduces planning, organizational, and matériel novelties with respect to the Arctic. Thus, two major planning exercises are announced. One is a risk analysis of the marine environment in view of the expected increase in shipping volume and activity levels over the coming five years. This reflects an official expectation that increased shipping will be the first tangible effect of Arctic warming, with associated pollution risks, search-and-rescue needs, and other tasks.

Another exercise will be a comprehensive general analysis of future defense tasks in the Arctic, including the benefits of closer cooperation with other Nordic countries, the United States, Canada, the United Kingdom, and even Russia, with respect to surveillance and the variety of additional missions in the region. In particular, the analysis is tasked to look into the use of combat aircraft for surveillance and sovereignty control around Greenland and into ways to strengthen airborne inspection capabilities in the short run. The latter reference is probably to the potential use of piston-engined aircraft for fishery and other control purposes. The decision to conduct a comprehensive defense analysis reflects a basic uncertainty as to how to handle the new Arctic dimension of defense. The problem is simply so new that the necessary informational and analytical basis for major decisions is absent. Furthermore, the pressure for major long-term decisions is still weak, apart from the necessary improvement of airborne surveillance and inspection capabilities. As a result both projected analyses were still under preparation in early 2011.

Other factors are probably at play as well. One problem, which has been neglected so far, are the implications of a strengthened military presence in the Arctic on Denmark's international operations. Because the international operations are already straining defense resources to the breaking point, any significant expansion of tasks will require a painful prioritization of old and new missions. The Defense

---

[27] Forsvarets Efterretningstjeneste, FE. *Efterretningsmæssig risikovurdering 2009* [Defense Intelligence Service, Intelligence Risk Assessment 2009](Copenhagen:·FE).

Commission dodged the issue, and so does the defense plan for 2010–14. To further complicate things, such a discussion might conjure interservice rivalries. In short, although the present international operations put the army into focus, a relative shift of focus to the north would shift attention to the navy and air force, to the detriment of the hard-pressed army.

Another unexplored problem is the interaction between overseas operations and Arctic politics. The internationalization of Denmark's defense forces rests on the assumption of a threat-free European environment, but this situation may not endure if conflicts from the Arctic spill over to the European scene. A conflict with Russia in the north might easily be transformed into a territorial threat against Denmark, and so undermine the premise of the present internationalist security policy.

The defense agreement introduces three organizational novelties. First, it proposes amalgamating the Greenland and Faeroe commands into a joint Arctic Command, presumably to be headquartered in Nuuk, the capital of Greenland. This unification of the two North Atlantic commands has, in fact, been discussed for some time under another heading, namely that of rationalization and savings. Moving the headquarters from Grønnedal, an isolated locality in southwestern Greenland, which can be reached only by helicopter and boat, to Nuuk would save money and improve coordination between the command and the self-government authorities of shared inspection and SAR tasks and will ease the future takeover of additional authority by the self-government. Furthermore, the merger, which was still under scrutiny in early 2011, will allow some greater operational flexibility between missions in Faeroese and Greenlandic waters.

The second novelty concerns the prospective formation of an Arctic reaction force (*indsatsstyrke*) composed of units from all three services with an Arctic capability, which can be activated in certain situations. "The reaction force will contribute to a generally larger competence in the area and be employed in Greenland or in international tasks in an Arctic environment." Which units and for what purposes is, however, entirely unclear, as there has been no public discussion, and probably no internal discussion, of this. In fact, military spokespersons are slightly embarrassed by the "militaristic" overtones of the concept.

A third novelty is the suggestion to include Thule Air Base in the solution of Danish defense tasks "in cooperation with other countries," which refers to the United States and possibly to Canada, which uses Thule for supply flights to Alert on Ellesmere Island. According to the 1951 defense agreement, Thule is operated by the United States, but in article II,4c Denmark "reserves the right to use [the base] in cooperation with the United States of America for the defense of Greenland and the rest of the Atlantic Treaty Area" and "to construct such facilities and undertake such activities therein as will not impede the activities" of the United States. Although this article has never been invoked, it seems a handy basis for including Thule in the future management of Danish defense tasks in Greenland. For one thing, Thule's harbor facilities could be used as a base for naval patrols in Baffin Bay and eventually (when the Nares Strait becomes navigable) north of Greenland. Similarly, the air base could be used for surveillance flights north of Greenland. A modest beginning was made in the fall of 2010 when a joint U.S.-Canadian-Danish search and rescue exercise in Baffin Bay was held out of Thule. Finally, the agreement announces certain procurement decisions, which also point to a concentration in the short run on the improvement of inspection and surveillance capabilities. Over the following five years, new and more powerful helicopters will replace the present *Lynx* helicopters on the inspection frigates, and a third *Knud Rasmussen*–class inspection ship will be commissioned in 2017. The immediate aim of the new defense agreement is therefore to create a better and more effective management of authority and sovereignty tasks in the expectation of growing shipping and other economic activities around Greenland in the near future. With respect to defense measures proper, the agreement is cautious, and no further decisions are likely to be made before the end of the five-year period. At that time, the announced comprehensive analysis of Arctic defense needs will probably be the basis for further decisions.

CONCLUSION

Denmark's role in the new Arctic policy arena is still not well defined. Copenhagen's fear of a race to the North Pole gave rise to the significant Ilulissat initiative in 2007 and the resulting Ilulissat Declaration of May 2008, which commits the Arctic Five to act responsibly and within the bounds of the existing international maritime regime – UNCLOS. This commitment has since been the core of Denmark's Arctic policy. However, Denmark's ownership and investment in the Ilulissat initiative has not yet given rise to new initiatives. Rather, the emphasis has been on action within the wider Arctic Council, which Denmark has chaired from 2009 to 2011 in IMO, the International Maritime Organization, and UNCLOS.

It seems safe to say that Arctic authority and sovereignty tasks will grow in the future, most likely as a mix of a national task expansion and the establishment of international regimes. This development will require both an active Danish diplomacy in Arctic affairs and the procurement of relevant matériel resources. On both counts, some uncertainty prevails. The affair about Foreign Minister Espersen's not attending the Arctic Five meeting in March 2010 has left some questions as to the present government's awareness of and commitment to Arctic politics. On the matériel side, some requirements are addressed in the new defense agreement. But the question of a larger Danish military presence in the Arctic has been postponed until after 2014, at which time a clearer picture of the direction of Arctic politics may obtain.

The uncertainty about the future of Denmark's Arctic policies contrasts against the oft-forgotten fact that Denmark has more at stake in the Arctic than other players. Future developments there pose not only questions concerning interstate cooperation and conflict but also questions concerning the survival of the Danish state as we know it, that is, as a multinational commonwealth (*rigsfællesskab*) of the Kingdom of Denmark and its self-governing parts, Greenland and the Faeroe Islands. Both North Atlantic nations have gained wide-ranging internal autonomy under their home-rule and self-government arrangements, as well as increasing say over their external relations. For example, both stand outside the European Union. Both nations have been promised independence, if they so wish, and several trends point in that direction.

Today, however, the pressure is (still) weak in Greenland, because independence and the withdrawal of the hefty Danish subsidy of the self-rule government would mean a drastic fall in living standards. But this may change in the future. The present Greenlandic government has abandoned its protection of traditional hunting and small-scale fishery and has set its hopes on economic modernization, especially the exploitation of Greenland's mineral wealth[28] and the development of expected hydrocarbon reserves, both of which will be aided by Arctic warming. It will take huge investments before royalties begin to fill the self-government's coffers, but once that happens, Greenland may become an extremely wealthy community. In that case, pressures for independence will increase, but so might also be the case with external pressures on Greenland, either arising as needs for Arctic cooperation or as threats from a hostile environment.

Greenland will remain a very small community of only fifty-seven thousand people, and it is likely to continue to lack many of those human, matériel, and institutional resources necessary to handle the challenges of a future Arctic Ocean coastal state.[29] Basically, Greenland may face the choice of seeking some form of protection from either the United States or Denmark, and historical affinity and economic and cultural ties make it more likely that it will choose the latter. The most likely development, therefore, is a continuation and gradual intensification of the present informal foreign policy cooperation between Denmark and Greenland based on mutual trust and common interests – a kind of *status quo plus*. This could involve Greenland taking over if not operations then the financing of those authority tasks that follow naturally from the self-rule division of responsibilities. This outcome would be especially relevant with respect to the control of the fishery and

---

[28] Presently, much interest is directed at Greenland's deposits of so-called rare earth elements, a group of some fifteen elements which have unique magnetic, fluorescent, and chemical properties which make them indispensable in the manufacture of many modern products such as laptops, rechargeable batteries, magnets, mobile phones, and catalytic converters. China presently has a near-monopoly on the international marketplace by supplying 92–94 percent of world demand. Recently China's beginning export restrictions have caused companies to look for non-Chinese suppliers such as Greenland and Australia. The Kvanefjeld complex on the southern tip of Greenland may hold up to one-third of the world's reserves of rare earth elements and is presently intensively surveyed and prospected.

[29] The Faeroe Islands have a similar recognized right to independence as that of Greenland. Oil exploration in Faeroese waters is intense, with good prospects of exploitable finds. If there are finds, Faeroese independence is very likely.

oil and gas industries, which are fully under the political control of self-rule. Even then, Denmark would have to shoulder the main burden of providing the resources necessary to play an equal part in the future management of Arctic problems. On the positive side, this would be a powerful guarantee of the preservation of the *Rigsfællesskab* and so of Denmark's identity as a European–North Atlantic state with a strong bond with the United States.

10

Arctic Security

A *Greenlandic Perspective*

Adam Worm

CONSTITUTIONAL FRAMEWORK

Since 1979, Greenland has had a system of local autonomy, known as home rule,[1] which in June 2009 by a new act on Greenland Self-Government was updated to self-government.[2] The system of self-government means that it is possible for the Greenland government to assume authority over almost all areas of public life in Greenland. According to the Act on Self-Government, Greenland's Parliament has full legislative power in areas in which responsibility has been taken over by Greenland.

According to the Danish constitution and the Act on Self-Government, however, some areas cannot be taken over and have to remain with the Danish government. Those areas are the following:

- The Constitution
- Foreign affairs
- Defense and security policy
- The Supreme Court
- Currency and monetary policy

Defense and security policy is thus a prerogative of the government of Denmark. However, according to the Act on Self-Government,[3] and practice developed over thirty years, the government of Greenland is in fact involved in issues of foreign

---

[1] Act No. 577 of November 29, 1978, on Greenland Home Rule (repealed by the Act on Self-Government).
[2] Act No. 473 of June 12, 2009, on Greenland Self-Government and Executive Summary of the Greenland-Danish Self-Government Commission's Report on Self-Government in Greenland, http://www.stm.dk (for an English version, see http://www.nanoq.gl).
[3] Chapter 4 of the Act no. 473 of June 12, 2009 on Greenland Self-Government.

policy, defense policy, and security policy relating to Greenland.[4] Because of this authority reserved for Copenhagen, the government of Greenland has been engaged in negotiations on security policy concerning Greenland, and thus has a natural interest in the general issue of Arctic security policy.

POLITICAL BACKGROUND

Self-government is not the same as independence. Self-government is based on the Danish constitution, and thus Denmark still has sovereignty over Greenland. Independence, however, is a long-term goal of the government of Greenland. It is a precondition to independence that Greenland has a sustainable economy. This is currently not the case, as roughly 57 percent of the budget of the government of Greenland or 30 percent of the gross domestic product (GDP) of Greenland is financed by a block grant from Denmark.[5]

It is the goal of the government of Greenland to reduce its dependency on the block grant. Therefore, the government of Greenland is striving to diversify the economy and to promote new industries as an alternative to fishing and hunting.

In this respect, Greenland's subsoil resources are obviously interesting. In recent years, even after the financial crisis, the mining and oil industries have shown increasing interest in exploring for resources on the land and continental shelf of Greenland. Up until now, however, only the mining of hard minerals has been commercialized. None of the explorations for oil has succeeded, but the U.S. Geological Survey estimates that the areas northeast of Greenland contain roughly 31 billion barrels of oil.[6] If minerals or oil are discovered, the government of Greenland will have the authority to issue licenses. If Greenland receives income from royalties or taxation from resource development, the government of Greenland would receive DKK 75 million, and it must use half of the rest of that income to reduce the block grant.[7]

U.S. MILITARY PRESENCE

In 1951, Denmark and the United States concluded the Agreement Pursuant to the North Atlantic Treaty concerning the Defense of Greenland.[8] The agreement

---

[4] Circular, November 7, 2005, from Danish Ministry of Foreign Affairs to the Diplomatic Missions in Copenhagen concerning conclusion of agreements under international law by the government of the Faeroes and by the government of Greenland. The note and the attached remarks to Act No. 578 of June 24, 2005, concerning the concluding of agreements under international law by the government of Greenland contains a description of practice concerning Greenland's international affairs since 1979.

[5] See http://www.stat.gl (partly in English).

[6] Information in English on the oil and mining exploration activities in Greenland can be found at the website of the Greenlandic government's Bureau of Minerals and Petroleum (http://www.bmp.gl).

[7] Section 8(1) of Act No. 473 of June 12, 2009, on Greenland Self-Government.

[8] Agreement of April 27, 1951, between the U.S. government and the government of Denmark, pursuant to the North Atlantic Treaty, concerning the defense of Greenland.

stipulates that the United States, as a party to the NATO treaty, may assist Denmark in the defense of Greenland by establishing such designated defense areas or military bases as the two governments may agree. A defense area is principally Danish territory, but under the treaty, the United States is granted the right by Copenhagen to operate the facility virtually without Danish interference.[9] As regards termination, the agreement will remain in force as long as the NATO treaty exists. Any modifications to the agreement shall be by mutual consent. Needless to say, these terms reflect the balance of power between a strong United States and a weakened Denmark in the years immediately following World War II. Three such defense areas and four installations form part of the distant early warning (DEW) line and were established during the 1950s and 1960s. Since 1991, however, Thule Air Base has been the only remaining defense area, and the DEW line installations have been disestablished.[10] The United States does not pay rent to use the base, but there are agreements concerning the employment of Danish and Greenlandic labor and the purchase of other services.

During the early part of the Cold War, Thule Air Base was intended as a stepping-stone for long-range flights in defense against the Soviet Union. Later on, the main purpose of Thule has been to serve as a radar station and satellite tracking installation. Today U.S. personnel number roughly 100 persons, and the civilian Danish-Greenlandic service personnel include 450 personnel – a number that expands during the summer period.[11] The Danish defense has a liaison officer stationed at the base.[12]

Besides Thule Air Base, the most spectacular evidence of the U.S. military presence in Greenland is the operation of Air National Guard 109.[13] From March to August of each year, the 109 unit conducts exercises with C-130 aircraft operating under Arctic conditions. As a part of the exercises, unit 109 moves equipment and personnel in support of scientific projects in Greenland. In 2004, the U.S. government and Denmark and Greenland concluded negotiations on the upgrading of radar for use in the missile defense system, which was finished in 2010. At the same time, the two nations agreed on modernization of the defense agreement, a declaration concerning environmental cooperation, and a declaration on economic and technical cooperation (i.e., cooperation concerning nonmilitary issues).[14]

---

[9] Articles 2, 4, 6(3), 7, 8, and 9 of the defense agreement of April 27, 1951.

[10] Dansk Udenrigspolitisk Institut, *Grønland under den kolde krig – dansk og amerikansk sikkerhedspolitik 1945–68* (Copenhagen: Dansk Udenrigspolitisk Institut, 1997). An English summary is available: Greenland during the Cold War – Danish and American Security Policy 1945–68 (Copenhagen: Dansk Udenrigspolitisk Institut, 1997).

[11] Further information concerning the base is found at the websites of the base (http://www.thule.af. mil) and of the civilian Danish service company at the base Greenland Contractors (http: www .greenlandcontractors.dk).

[12] Article 2(3)(a) of the defense agreement of April 27, 1951, *supra* note 8.

[13] http://www.109aw.ang.af.mil/history/index.asp.

[14] http://www.state.gov/r/pa/ho/trvl/ls/8515.htm.

During the almost sixty years of its existence, the Thule Air Base has from time to time been an issue in Greenlandic politics. There are several reasons that the base is a domestic factor. First, the base was established by a joint U.S.-Danish decision without Greenlandic participation and therefore has a legacy of the colonial spirit of the time immediately after World War II. Second, an Inuit settlement was moved to make space for the base. Third, a U.S. Air Force B-52 bomber carrying hydrogen bombs crashed in Greenland in 1968. Fourth, the generally secretive atmosphere and exclusiveness of the base tends to cause resentment.[15] The agreements of 2004 have, to some extent, cleared the table. Greenland participated in the new agreements, which helped strengthen general political consensus on the issue of the base.

DANISH MILITARY PRESENCE IN GREENLAND

In general terms, the purpose of the Danish defense in and around Greenland is primarily to claim Danish sovereignty by presence and surveillance. At the same time, Danish forces perform search-and-rescue (SAR) missions; fisheries inspection; and other tasks in support of local society, such as ice surveillance and maritime environmental cleanup.[16] The military authority is vested in the Greenland Command, which is situated at Naval Station Grønnedal (Kangilinnguit) in southern Greenland. The Greenland Command comprises some sixty military personnel and civilians. The Greenland Command has authority over the following units in Greenland:

- The Sledge Patrol Sirius (dog sleds), stationed at Daneborg, in northeastern Greenland: Twelve men patrol the northern and northeastern regions of Greenland, ensuring sovereignty and providing police authority
- Station North, in northeastern Greenland: Five men maintain a runway; claim sovereignty for Greenland; support the Sirius patrol, SAR expeditions, and scientific missions; and collect meteorological data and other tasks as assigned
- Danish liaison officer at Thule Air Base: The liaison officer and two non-commissioned officers attend to the interests of Denmark in cooperation with the U.S. military personnel at the base and support the Danish-Greenlandic civilian personnel at the base in various civilian matters
- Station Mestersvig, eastern Greenland: Two noncommissioned officers maintain a runway and support the Sirius patrol, support and control civilian expeditions in the area, collect meteorological data, and serve other functions as assigned
- Group West, Kangerlussuaq (previously known as Sondre Strom): Three military persons support the deployment of military aircraft to Greenland

---

[15] For a description of the resettlement of the Inuit village and the B-52 crash, see Dansk Udenrigspolitisk Institut, *Grønland under den kolde krig* (note 10 supra).

[16] For a description of the mission and capabilities of the Danish defense in Greenland, see the website of Greenland Command, http://www.forsvaret.dk/glk.

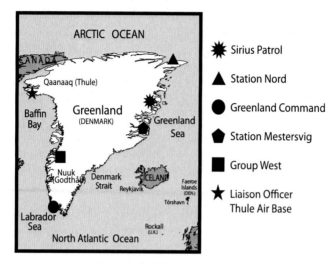

FIGURE 10.1. Location of Greenland Command Units.

To accomplish these missions, Greenland has available three inspection ships of the *Thetis* class, capable of embarking a Lynx helicopter and a fifty-two-person crew. The ships are being phased out and replaced by new, larger ships of the *Rasmussen* class, which also are equipped with a helicopter. Some elder and smaller cutters with fourteen crew members are being phased out. These ships and the cutters are specially designed and built for operations in Arctic waters. The Danish defense force maintains three Challengers (CL-604), small jet aircraft, at its disposal. The force, among other tasks, is deployed in Greenland (and completes about four hundred flight hours per year) for surveillance, fisheries inspection, passenger transportation, and other missions. The military personnel in Greenland consist mostly of Danes stationed for one to three years. Only a few Greenlanders are engaged in defense. The government of Greenland and the Danish defense force are cooperating for more Greenlanders to join the defense. The total costs for defense operations are roughly $70 million per year.

DANISH DEFENSE AGREEMENT FOR THE YEARS 2010–2014

In May 2009, the parties of the Danish Parliament, except for one, concluded an agreement for the period 2010–14.[17] The agreement is remarkable in that it provides a great deal of attention to the Arctic. First, the agreement recognizes that higher energy prices will make exploration of oil and gas in the Arctic more interesting for business. At the same time, the expected melting of ice will in the long run provide increased opportunities for shipping in the Arctic. The rising level

---

[17] Danish Defense Agreement 2010–2014, June 24, 2009, available in English at the website of the Ministry of Defense, http://www.fmn.dk/eng/Pages/Front%20page.aspx.

of activity will change the significance of the region and thus entail more tasks for the Danish defense. Second, the document recognizes that the other Arctic coastal states have prioritized the Arctic, among other things, by maintaining a maritime presence. Third, the agreement recognizes that Arctic coastal states have stated that the UN Convention on the Law of the Sea (UNCLOS) is the appropriate legal framework for maritime delimitation in the Arctic. Accordingly, the Danish political parties see no need for a special treaty for the Arctic along the lines of the Antarctic Treaty. The parties agree that the legal delimitation of the boundaries shall be established according to the rules of international law. On this basis, the parties agreed that the Greenland Command and the Faeroese Command should be streamlined and combined into a joint Arctic Command, located in Greenland. The modification of the commands will be implemented in a dialogue with the self-government authorities of Greenland and the Faeroe Islands. A comprehensive analysis of the future tasks of the Danish defense in the Arctic shall be performed, including an analysis of the possibilities of closer cooperation with other Nordic countries, the United States, Canada, Russia, and the United Kingdom regarding marine surveillance and other similar tasks. The analysis also will have to establish whether surveillance and other similar systems could also be implemented with regard to shipping near Greenland. The phaseout of small cutters and the introduction of larger inspection ships of the *Rasmussen* class will be continued.

The parties agreed to examine the possibility of strengthening the capacity of aircraft inspection. Consideration can also be given to using combat aircraft in the occasional performance of surveillance and sovereignty missions in and around Greenland. In addition, unmanned aircraft systems and satellite-based surveillance systems may be capable of supplementing manned aircraft over the long term. If Thule Air Force Base may come to play a bigger role in solving the tasks of the Danish defense in cooperation with other partners, which presumably includes the United States, then the parties also agreed that an Arctic response force should be designated – it could be established and composed of units from all of the armed services that possess Arctic capacity. Finally, as a consequence of the expected increase in shipping in the Arctic, a proper risk analysis concerning the marine environment surrounding Greenland should be conducted. Thus, most Danish politicians have agreed to some essential facts and declarations of national intentions relating to the Arctic and Greenland. The Greenlandic and Faeroese authorities were represented in the commission that prepared the agreement, and they also support the proposals.

POSSIBLE DISPUTE: THE CONTINENTAL SHELF

Since 2001, the Danish government, the government of the Faeroe Islands and the government of Greenland have been cooperating to file a submission for an extended continental-shelf claim in accordance with article 76 of UNCLOS.[18] Research and marine surveys are being conducted in three areas around Greenland – to the north, northeast, and south of Greenland – and in two areas north and south of the Faeroe Islands. A submission for the area north of the Faeroe Islands has been presented to the UN Commission on the Continental Shelf (CLCS), and submissions for the other areas are expected during the years 2011–14. It is well known that, from time to time, a so-called race for the North Pole is discussed. The understanding of Greenland's self-government is that, by concluding the Ilulissat Declaration of May 28, 2008,[19] the Arctic coastal states have committed themselves to the rules reflected in the law of the sea in this respect. Thus, states declared that "the law of the sea provides for important rights and obligations concerning the delineation of the outer limits of the continental shelf. . . . We remain committed to this legal framework and to the orderly settlement of any possible overlapping claims."[20] At the same time, the Arctic coastal states are in fact acting according to the rules set forth in the law of the sea, foremost by conducting research to present submissions that claim an extended continental shelf. Consequently, the government of Greenland does not see a need for an Arctic treaty, as some institutions, such as the European Parliament, have called for. The Arctic is not a *terra nullius*. An extensive legal framework, including UNCLOS, already applies to the Arctic.

THE DISPUTE WITH CANADA CONCERNING HANS ISLAND

Canada and Denmark agreed in 1973 on the median line of the Davis Strait, but they failed to agree on delimitation of Hans Island, which sits astride the channel.[21] Thus, the median line stops on each side of the island. From time to time, the two parties have raised their flags on the island. In 2005, however, the foreign ministers of Canada and Denmark agreed to disagree on the legal status of Hans Island. In a joint statement on September 19, 2005,[22] the two nations acknowledged the different views on the sovereignty of the island and committed themselves to reach a long-term solution to the Hans Islands dispute that would be based on the principles of the United Nations. In the meantime, the parties will inform each other of activities relating to Hans Island, and those activities shall be carried out in a low-key and restrained manner. Thus, Greenland regards the outstanding question of sovereignty

[18] The English-language website of the Danish-Greenlandic-Faeroese Continental Shelf Project, http://www.a76.dk.
[19] The declaration is available at the website of the Danish Ministry of Foreign Affairs, http://www.um.dk/NR/rdonlyres/BE00B850-D278-4489A6BEAE230415546/0/ArcticOceanConference.pdf.
[20] cf. note 19 supra.
[21] Agreement of December 17, 1973, between the government of the Kingdom of Denmark and the government of Canada relating to the delimitation of the continental shelf between Greenland and Canada.
[22] The joint statement is available at the website of the Canadian Ministry of Foreign Affairs, http://www.lac-bac.gc.ca/webarchives/20060208024054.

over the small island not as a security problem but as a diplomatic problem. The Hans Island issue has not been a hindrance to closer cooperation between the Danish and the Canadian geological surveys concerning research on the continental shelf relating to article 76 of UNCLOS. In the same spirit of good-neighborliness, the Canadian forces (represented by the chief of the defense staff) and Defense Command Denmark (represented by the chief of defense) signed a memorandum of understanding concerning Arctic defense, security, and operational cooperation on May 14, 2010.

PERSPECTIVES AND CONCLUSIONS

Greenland is under the military security umbrella of Denmark, the United States, and NATO. The government of Greenland, however, does not define Arctic security in purely military terms. At present, Greenland's government cannot imagine that possible conflicts, such as disagreements over the continental shelf and its possible resources, could develop into armed conflict or outright war in the Arctic. Although the government is aware of the fact that disputes may develop, there is a high degree of confidence that they will be solved according to international law, including the law of the sea. But Greenland's government does not rule out the possibility that the general security situation is subject to change. Thus, Arctic security has to be interpreted more broadly. More cooperation is needed among interested states. In recent years, cooperation among coast guards has been strengthened, which is a positive development, but there is also a need for cooperation concerning the regulation of shipping, surveillance, protection of the Arctic environment, and SAR. For instance, regulation of international shipping in the Arctic is not a military issue, but rather must take place under the rules developed at the International Maritime Organization. The issues of cooperation on issues such as SAR and maritime safety are also developed in other forums, such as the Arctic Council.

Why do we then discuss these issues in military terms? Primarily because we have to have a military presence in the area performing surveillance and exercising sovereignty. And these capabilities have to be used for a range of purposes that are not primarily of the military but in the general interest of society.

11

Territorial Discourses and Identity Politics

Iceland's Role in the Arctic

Valur Ingimundarson

INTRODUCTION

A domestic political consensus on prioritizing the Arctic in Iceland's foreign and security policy reflects awareness that the emerging territorialization of the region will refocus geopolitical attention on the north. To be sure, there are no illusions about Iceland recapturing its former role as a Cold War prize. But Iceland's approach is based on its strategic location, for material rewards, and Arctic identity politics. This is not to say that multilateral aspects of the Arctic, such as environmental protection, the rights of so-called indigenous people, or international legal norms have been sidelined. There is, indeed, a tension between the north as a high-stakes resource base and a geopolitical arena,[1] on the one hand, and as an ecological frontier to be regulated by an international regime, on the other hand. On balance, however, the strategic dimension has been given more weight as a result of the growing geopolitical importance of the Arctic because of climate change and the prospects for a seasonal ice-free Arctic; the geopolitics of natural resources; the jurisdictional division of the Arctic Ocean's outer continental shelf; and the prospects of the opening of new sea lanes.

Thus, Iceland is grappling with the same question as other Arctic states: how to reconcile sovereign state interests with international governance or stewardship norms designed to stave off future conflicts over jurisdictional and maritime boundaries and access to natural resources? Current Arctic sovereignty discourses are made up of disparate, if interrelated, historical genealogies: sovereignty or territorial controls; a return to the language of nineteenth-century "great power" geopolitics;

[1] On northern discourses, see, for example, Lassi Heininen and Heather N. Nicol, "The Importance of Northern Dimension Foreign Policies in the Geopolitics of the Circumpolar North," *Geopolitics* 12 (2007), 133–65.

I would like to thank EDDA – Center of Excellence in Critical Contemporary Research and the University of Iceland Research Fund for supporting my research on Arctic geopolitics.

a romanticized "true north" ideology, exalting a frontier mentality of possession and conquest; and recycled Cold War military narratives. With respect to governance, the five Arctic littoral states, Canada, Russia, the United States, Denmark (on behalf of Greenland), and Norway, have issued statements, pledging loyalty to the UN Convention on the Law of the Sea (UNCLOS).[2] Yet their public commitment to international rules and regulations over Arctic jurisdiction has not prevented them from initiating a quiet and incremental military preparedness in the region. In addition, they share, together with the three other Arctic states, Iceland, Finland, and Sweden, profound skepticism toward proposals – espoused by nongovernmental organizations and other transnational bodies – for concluding an agreement on Arctic governance,[3] an Arctic Treaty along the lines of the 1959 Antarctica Treaty, making the region a scientific preserve and sanctuary, with a ban on military activity. In short, the Arctic coastal states want to have a privileged role in managing the region, which they interpret as being consistent with UNCLOS, on the basis of their geographic location, sovereign rights, and economic and political interests.

In this chapter, I explore how Iceland is responding to these conflicting Arctic discourses and practices. The focus is on how the following regional and transnational developments have influenced and shaped Icelandic approaches: the end of a fifty-five-year U.S. military presence in Iceland; Russian geopolitics and resumption of strategic aviation in the North Atlantic; Arctic ice melting and the prospects for the opening of new sea lanes and transportation routes; the Norwegian High North strategy, and Iceland's EU membership bid. Because Iceland makes no territorial or resource-based claims in the region – which according to estimates contains 13 percent of the world's unexploited oil reserves and 30 percent of its gas[4] – it is not involved in any disputes with other Arctic countries over jurisdiction or access to natural resources. Nonetheless, it is investigating the possibilities of oil exploration in its exclusive economic zone near Jan Mayen – in the so-called Dragon Zone.

I show that, as a result of its geographic position, Iceland is claiming a stakeholder role based on contemporary geopolitical developments mixed with a discourse on historical rights and mythological references. Apart from rejuvenating old ideas about Iceland's strategic location in an "Arctic Mediterranean," it has firmly resisted the

[2] See, for example, the Ilulissat Declaration, issued by Arctic states at the Arctic Ocean Conference in Ilulissat, Greenland, 27–29 May 2008, accessed on 1 February 2011, http://www.oceanlaw.org/downloads/arctic/Ilulissat_Declaration.pdf.

[3] See Oran R. Young, "Whither the Arctic? Conflict or Cooperation in the Circumpolar North," *Polar Record* 45 (232), 73–82.

[4] See U.S. Geological Survey, "Circum-Arctic Resource Appraisal: Estimates of Undiscovered Oil and Gas North of the Arctic Circle" (Washington, D.C.: U.S. Government Printing Office, 2008), accessed on 1 February 2011 at http://www.usgs.gov; see "USGS Arctic Oil and Gas Report: Estimates of Undiscovered Oil and Gas North of the Arctic Circle," accessed on 1 February 2011, http://geology.com/usgs/arctic-oil-and-gasreport.shtml; "New Survey of Arctic's Mineral Riches Could Stoke International Strife," *Guardian*, 29 May 2009; see also Valur Ingimundarson, *The Geopolitics of Arctic Natural Resources* (Brussels: European Parliament, 2010).

development of a hegemony exercised by the five Arctic littoral states and insisted, together with Finland and Sweden, on the primary importance of the eight members of the Arctic Council.

Like the other Arctic states, Iceland has reacted negatively to outside initiatives regarding regional policy for the negotiation of an international treaty on the Arctic. It does not, however, oppose a limited presence of alliances or supranational organizations in the region. Consistent with its EU membership application, Iceland has been supportive of the European Union's bid for observer status in the Arctic Council. And although it has traditionally warned against Arctic militarization, it followed Norway's lead in advocating a "soft" NATO monitoring and surveillance mission. Thus, Iceland is seeking ways to make room for outside players in the region – in an effort to elevate its status as an Arctic state – without jeopardizing the privileged status of the Arctic Eight.

THE ARCTIC IMAGINATION: HISTORICAL MYTHS
AS POLITICAL INSTRUMENTS

The phrase "scramble for the Arctic" has not only been used by the global media to highlight potential conflict scenarios or to underscore the need for some sort of an international order in the Arctic. It has also produced countereffects, neocolonial spin-offs, serving the purpose of using history to address present-day problems. To be sure, this does not apply equally to all Arctic states. Irrespective of the flurry of geopolitical and propaganda activities of other Arctic stakeholders, the United States has so far not shown much military interest in the region,[5] even if it has reaffirmed its territorial claim (Alaska) and its support for the U.S. Senate's ratification of UNC-LOS – a prerequisite for an international recognition. To the U.S. government – preoccupied with Iraq and Afghanistan – it is a waste of money and resources to engage in Arctic sovereignty controls. The catchphrase is "scientific time line" – to know when to intervene and to start investing in the Arctic at some unspecified future date.

Some realists surely oppose such a wait-and-see attitude. In his 2008 alarmist exhortation to the U.S. political elite – published in *Foreign Affairs* – to abandon its neglect of the Arctic and to assume a global leadership role to prevent the region from "erupting in an armed mad dash for its resources," Scott Borgerson used the nostalgic paraphrase "Go North, Young Man" as a way of drawing, in gendered terms, on a specifically male-bonding American-settler experience.[6] This historical reference was meant to rekindle the spirit of daring and youthful masculine excitement associated with the participation in a frontier-pioneering project based on conquest – on

---

[5] See, for example, Scott G. Borgerson, "Arctic Meltdown: The Economic and Security Implications of Global Warming," *Foreign Affairs* 87, no. 2 (March–April 2008), 63–77; Borgerson, "The Great Game Moves North," *Foreign Affairs*, 25 March 2009, http://foreign_affairs.com.

[6] See Borgerson, "Arctic Meltdown"; Borgerson, "The Great Game Moves North."

desires to colonize a "virgin space." Thus, the Arctic was portrayed in the same way as the colonization of the American West: as an aspiring and noble cause for young men. In its contemporary reworking, there is, predictably, no mentioning of the four hundred thousand officially classified "indigenous people" who live in the Arctic. But this evocation of the past is a stark reminder of the continued relevance of such colonial traces in the imagination of realist commentators on the Arctic.

Icelandic Arctic discourses are also rooted historical mythologies, with the past being used to create political narratives in the present. References to the phrase "Arctic Mediterranean" – coined by the explorer Vilhjálmur Stefánsson – are being used to evoke utopian materialist potentials based on the prospective opening of new sea lanes and transarctic trade as a result of Arctic ice melting.[7] Thus, Icelandic officials have appropriated, reformulated, and repacked Stefánsson's early–twentieth-century vision of all-year commercial sea routes around the Arctic, with ports, naval stations, and weather stations on strategically placed islands. According to this scenario, which is conditioned on changed global trade patterns and on the linking of the North Atlantic with the Pacific, Iceland is poised to become a key transarctic commercial hub – a center for reception, distribution, and transshipment.

Despite ice melting – with summer navigation possible in twenty to thirty years – there is no scientific evidence that has been produced to buttress the claim that the Arctic sea routes will be open and readily accessible in winter. Indeed, what has been missing in much of the speculation about new trade routes and transarctic navigation is that the future Arctic Ocean will remain ice covered for much of the year. Moreover, the projection of Iceland as a central location for transshipments is not only open to contestation on economic and environmental grounds. The very notion of the use of shorter routes has also been questioned.[8] This has not prevented the circulation of ideas of establishing an "international monitoring and reaction center" in Iceland in connection with Arctic natural resource management, with Greenland sometimes used as an example, and increased shipping.[9] So far, such proposals have not been taken up by other Arctic states and are not likely to be implemented any time soon.

Such embellished narratives are not limited to Icelanders. Canadian Arctic discourses are also under the spell of northern mythologies, identity politics, and power

---

7 See Icelandic Foreign Ministry, "Fyrir stafni haf. Tækifæri tengd siglingum á norðurslóðum" [Ocean Ahead: Opportunities Linked to Arctic Shipping] (Reykjavik: Ministry of Foreign Affairs, 2005); Icelandic Foreign Ministry, "Ísinn brotinn: Þróun norðurskautssvæðisins og sjóflutningar, horfur í siglingum á Norður-Íshafsleiðinni" [Broken Ice: Arctic Developments and Sea Transports; Prospects for Arctic Shipping] (Reykjavik: Ministry of Foreign Affairs, 2006); Icelandic Foreign Ministry, "Ísland á norðurslóðum" [Iceland and the Arctic] (Reykjavik: Ministry of Foreign Affairs, 2009).

8 See Svend Aage Christensen, "Er de nordlige søruter egentlig kortere? Lidt for rosenrøde billeder af et blåt Polarhav?" Danish Institute for International Studies (DIIS) Brief, February 2009, accessed on 1 February 2011, http://www.diis.dk/sw56039.asp.

9 See Icelandic Foreign Ministry, "Ísland á norðurslóðum."

politics. They center on Canadian "True North" identity – as a way of demarcation and distance from the United States, which is not seen as a "northern power" or an "authentic" Arctic state. When taken to their extremes, Canadian territorial discourses border on "sovereignty fetishism" – as exemplified by the much-quoted remark by Canadian Prime Minister Stephen Harper on the need for controlling the passage through the Canadian archipelago – "Use it or lose it."[10] It reveals what Franklyn Griffiths has termed "possession anxiety,"[11] which has kept Canada at arm's length from the United States in Arctic affairs, even if it wants more U.S. engagement in the area, and traditionally suspicious of Russia – the country that by far has the most to gain from Arctic riches.

The strong feelings of the Norwegians for Svalbard – and its exalted place in the cultural and political imagination – is another example of the idealization of what the Norwegians call the High North, mixed with territorial ambition and economic interests. It also reflects the instrumental use of language – as a way of defining geographic space in political terms – to merge a Norwegian or European High North narrative with broader Arctic perspectives.[12] What the Norwegians are concerned with is, among other things, vying for international support for their position on Svalbard, especially the contested two-hundred-mile "fishery protection zone," to reduce the risk confrontation in the Arctic because of overlapping territorial claims, and to manage their relations with Russia.

Finally, the Russian act of planting a flag on the North Pole seabed in 2007 is a form of what Michel Foucault termed the "ideology of the return"[13] – the reification of the past in the present. The flag episode was hailed as a geopolitical feat and a scientific breakthrough designed to remind the whole world that Russia was a great polar and scientific power. As one Russian spokesperson put it, "It is like putting a flag on the moon."[14] This episode, of course, tells less of Russia's matching American scientific prowess associated with the moon mission than of Cold War memories of superpower competition and space colonization in the late 1950s and 1960s. Thus, this Arctic propaganda display represents, just like other versions discussed here, a quintessential frontier narrative.

[10] See "Time to 'use it or lose it,' Harper declares," *Gazette* (Montreal), 11 August 2007.
[11] Franklyn Griffiths, "Towards a Canadian Arctic Strategy," Canadian International Council, accessed on 1 February 2011, http://www.canadian_internationalcouncil.org, 33.
[12] Jonas Gahr Støre, "Iceland and Norway – Neighbours in the High North," speech given at the University of Iceland, 3 November 2008, accessed on 1 February 2011, http://www.regjeringen.no/en/dep/ud/Whats-new/Speeches-and-articles/speeches_foreign/2008/iceland-and-norway–neighbours-in-the-hi.html?id=534706.
[13] See an interview with Michel Foucault, "Space, Knowledge, and Power," in *Foucault: Reader*, ed. Paul Rabionow (New York: Pantheon, Books, 1984), 250.
[14] See Tom Parfitt, "Russia plants flag on North Pole," *Guardian* (UK), 2 August 2007.

ICELAND'S NEW PLACE: THE AMERICAN WITHDRAWAL
AND RUSSIAN GEOPOLITICS

Although it was an exaggeration to claim – as the Icelandic government did – that a military vacuum had opened up in the North Atlantic following the closure of the U.S. base in 2006, there are linkages between the Arctic question and NATO's air-policing policy and Russian strategic aviation. The Russian decision to resume Cold War–style bomber flights in 2007 was motivated by a desire to restore, symbolically, Russia's military prowess for domestic political consumption and to underscore its geostrategic interests in places such as the Arctic. As a compensation for the U.S. departure, NATO provided Iceland with a temporary air-policing agreement – with individual member states volunteering to assume, on a rotation basis, air surveillance with fighter jets for several weeks a year.

Until September 2008, Russian bombers flew, on average, once a month near Iceland. Since then, the flights, which have more in common with enhanced training than regular Cold War–style patrols, have become less frequent, not least because of the economic crisis.[15] The Russians have never violated Iceland's airspace, even if they have sometimes not shied away from theatrics or what some critics have seen as "primitivism."[16] In 2007, the bombers circled around Iceland several times, coming as close as thirty-five miles to its shores. The Icelandic government issued high-level, public diplomatic protests and ignored informal overtures by Russia on the conclusion of a soft security cooperation agreement. The flights also raised concerns about civilian air-traffic safety given the lack of communications with the bomber pilots, whose planes do not operate with anticollision equipment.[17]

This anti-Russian tone, however, quickly subsided when the economic crisis hit Iceland in the fall of 2008. After being turned down for emergency aid by its Western allies, Iceland turned to Russia for a US $5.4 billion loan.[18] The Russians were initially positive, with Prime Minister Vladimir Putin allegedly approving the deal. But a premature announcement by the Icelandic Central Bank raised suspicions in Moscow that Iceland was using the request to get Western assistance. When Iceland was subsequently forced to ask the International Monetary Fund (IMF) for a bailout, the Russian government saw no reason to bear the brunt of a rescue package. Even if Russia's role proved short lived, Iceland faced Western criticisms for its eagerness to accept aid from Russia.[19] The loan was immediately put in an anti-Western context:

[15] Personal Interview with a high-level Russian official, 22 June 2009.
[16] Personal Interview with a high-level former Norwegian diplomat, 30 June 2008.
[17] See Risk Assessment Commission, "Áhættumatsskýrsla fyrir Ísland" [A Risk Assessment Report for Iceland] (Reykjavik: Icelandic Foreign Ministry, 2009), accessed on 1 February 2011, http://www.utanrikisraduneyti.is/media/Skyrslur/Skyrsla_um_ahattumat_fyrir_Island_a.pdf.
[18] Personal Interview with a high-level Russian official, 22 June 2009.
[19] Personal Interview with a high-ranking Icelandic official, 15 November 2008.

Russia wanted to use Iceland as part of a strategy to bolster its claim to Arctic oil and gas resources.[20] That Russia wanted to expand its geostrategic influence in the North was likely, even if Iceland's Arctic role should not be exaggerated. But this also led to farfetched media speculations about Iceland's intention of offering Russia base rights as a sign of gratitude for a potential loan. What gave them added currency was a criticism voiced by Icelandic President Ólafur Ragnar Grímsson, who sharply criticized Iceland's traditional allies, especially Britain, but also the United States and the Nordic countries, for not coming to Iceland's rescue.

It would, of course, not have been the first time that Iceland – which topped the list of U.S. per capita foreign aid from the late 1940s until the mid-1960s[21] – would use its strategic importance to play off East against the West. In the 1950s, NATO decided to provide Iceland – in a first for a member country – with economic aid to prevent it from accepting a huge loan offer from the Soviet Union.[22] But Iceland was in no situation, in 2008, to play such political games for economic benefit. And there were never any plans to offer the Russians base rights in Iceland. To accept a loan that amounted to one-third of Iceland's gross domestic product was certainly open to debate. But Iceland would not have jeopardized its Western political, trade, and cultural ties by joining a Russian alliance. There are practically no trade ties between Iceland and Russia, and even if bilateral political relations have traditionally been good, they have never been close. In addition, the Russians did not act – as part of an Arctic strategy – on a proposal to construct an oil refinery in the West Fjords of Iceland, an economically weak area with great interest in foreign investment. Nonetheless, the Russian loan episode had spillover effects on Iceland's security policy. The official rhetoric against the Russian bomber flights was abandoned not only because of the overwhelming focus on the economic crisis but also because of the reduction in the flights.

STRATEGIC DISCOURSES VERSUS IDENTITY POLITICS

According to Barry Buzan and Ole Waever, and the proponents of the so-called Copenhagen school in European security studies, the securitization of an "existential threat" – whether "real" or only presented as such – is accomplished through a speech act. The success of such an act, which requires exceptional political means, is not only contingent on the authority of those who proclaim it but also on the credibility

[20] Brownen Maddox, "Cold shoulder for Iceland rival," *Times* (London), 10 October 2008; "The High North: The Arctic contest heats up. What is Russia up to in the seas above Europe," *Economist* (UK), 9 October 2008.
[21] "Foreign Aid – Size and Composition," n.d. [1965], Dennis Fitzgerald Papers, 1945–1969, Box 44, Dwight D. Eisenhower Library, Abilene, Kansas.
[22] See Valur Ingimundarson, "Buttressing the West in the North: The Atlantic Alliance, Economic Warfare, and the Soviet Challenge in Iceland, 1956–1959," *International History Review* 21, no. 1 (March 1999), 80–103.

of their case.[23] The Icelandic government was never in a position to respond to the U.S. departure or to seek to exploit a future great-power rivalry over Arctic territory and oil and gas resources through a speech act. It was impossible to evoke a state of exception because there were no signs – or public acceptance – of any military threats and because the United States and other NATO governments, which exercised far more authority as securitizing actors, would not have endorsed it. For that reason, the Icelandic government was in no position to securitize the Russian bomber flights. Iceland's limited inclusion in NATO's air-policing policy was more of an act of routinization based on the Baltic precedent than a response to increased risk levels.

A sociopolitical theory developed by what has been dubbed the "Paris school,"[24] especially by Didier Bigo, in critical security studies offers a more promising way of analyzing the Icelandic case than a state-of-exception discourse. Rejecting the notion of security as a speech act, the theory stresses how bureaucratic actors construct security as part of routine practices of categorization and definition. This approach illuminates well how Icelandic officials attempted to "naturalize" instead of "securitize" a post-American policy agenda and the emerging Arctic question. It was rationalized not by referring to any threat scenarios, even if there was, for a time, an anti-Russian component to it, but by referring to Iceland's security obligations (especially vis-à-vis NATO); to its position as an Arctic player; and, less convincingly, as a prospective central transarctic commercial hub.[25] Thus, the discourses on the Arctic were not only about geopolitics, economic and social development, and environmental concerns; they were as much about competing bureaucratic interests, especially between the Foreign Ministry – with its emphasis on NATO, air policing, and its own institutional defense setup – and the Justice Ministry, which was more concerned with coast guard interests, including oil and gas transports in Icelandic waters and the danger posed to cruise ships, with thousands of passengers on board, if hit by an iceberg in Arctic waters. All these security scenarios, however, lacked urgency and could be justified only on functional security grounds – institutional preparedness for various contingencies.

Nonetheless, the focus on the north following the U.S. departure was partly seen as a way of drawing NATO's attention to Iceland and, by implication, strengthening

---

[23] See Barry Buzan, Ole Waever, and Jaap de Wilde, *Security: A New Framework for Analysis* (Boulder, CO: Lynne Rienner Publishers, 1998), 22–26.

[24] See Didier Bigo, *Polices en réseaux: L'expérience européene* (Paris: Presses Sciences, Po, 1996).

[25] See, for example, "Breaking the Ice: Arctic Developments and Maritime Transportation: Prospects of the Transarctic Route – Impact and Opportunities," 27–28 March 2007, accessed on 1 February 2011, http://www.mfa.is/media/Utgafa/Breaking_The_Ice_Conference_Report.pdf. Some skepticism has been voiced about the revolutionary potential of the new sea lines. See Fréderic Lassarre, "High North Shipping: Myths and Realities," in *Security Prospects in the High North: Geostrategic Thaw or Freeze?*, eds. Sven G. Holtsmark and Brooke A. Smith-Windsor (Rome: NATO Defense College, 2009), 179–99. Svend Aage Christensen, "Er de nordlige søruter egentlig kortere? Lidt for rosenrøde billeder af et blåt Polarhav?" Danish Institute for International Studies (DIIS) Brief, February 2009, accessed on 1 February 2011, http://www.diis.kd/sac.

the argument for air policing. From an external perspective, the policy was under the influence of Norway's High North strategy, which is, at bottom, about its relations with Russia, climate change, and oil and gas. Iceland's Arctic stakes are far more limited than those of Norway. But Iceland supported the Norwegian government's push for a NATO surveillance role in the north, an initiative that led to a declaration in the name of NATO's secretary-general in 2009 to commit the alliance to limited regional soft security issues, such as search and rescue at sea and marine pollution management in the Arctic.[26] An expanded NATO role in the Arctic is not shared by all alliance members, and some resist a proposal for using the NATO-Russia Council to discuss Arctic affairs. Because four of the five Arctic littoral states are NATO members, the need for the Council has been questioned. And Arctic states, such as Canada, prefer dealing with Russia outside a NATO framework.[27]

The EU Commission's application for an observer status in the Arctic Council has enjoyed Iceland's full backing. The European Union could see Iceland's EU membership as a strategic asset – together with the Arctic member states Denmark, Sweden, and Finland – because of its geographic position. Even if Iceland is not an Arctic littoral state, its exclusive economic zone extends to the Greenland Sea bordering the Arctic Ocean. Although Denmark belongs to the Arctic Five, its role is conditioned by Greenland's autonomy and by its obligation to recognize its independence, if it opts for it in the future. Finally, Sweden and Finland play a more limited geostrategic role in Arctic affairs than Iceland.

Yet the presence of NATO and the European Union in the Arctic remains controversial, with notably Canada and Russia voicing the most vocal opposition. Some Arctic proposals, which have been floated by the European Council of Ministers and, especially, by the European Parliament, have been rejected by the Arctic states, such as a temporary ban on fishing in the Arctic high seas and the conclusion of a legally binding Arctic governing regime modeled on the Antarctica Treaty. Both NATO and the European Union have so far been nonconfrontational in their Arctic approaches. Yet they are bound to show more strategic interest in this region-to-be, whose borders remain fuzzy and whose governance is still marked by ambiguity.[28]

---

[26] This decision was made public at a NATO seminar on the High North in Iceland in January 2009. On the seminar, see Sven G. Holtsmark and Brooke A. Smith-Windsor, eds., *Security Prospects in the High North: Geostrategic Thaw or Freeze?* (Rome: NATO Defense College, 2009).

[27] Personal Interviews with Western officials, 15 December 2009.

[28] The UN Convention on the Law of the Sea (UNCLOS) permits the Arctic states to make additional territorial claims if it is proved – and accepted by the UN Commission on the Limits of the Continental Shelf – that certain areas reach beyond their respective continental shelves. Although the UN commission can determine the size of the continental shelf, it has no power to resolve disputes between nations. The Russians, who stand to gain the most in the Arctic, argue that the waters off Russia's northern coast extending to the North Pole belong to its maritime territory because an underwater feature, the Lomonosov Ridge, is an extension of its continental territory. This claim has been contested by the other Arctic states and was not accepted by the UN commission pending further research.

Although the UN Commission on the Limits of the Continental Shelf can determine the size of the continental shelf, it has no power to resolve disputes between
states. After issuing recommendations, it will most likely be up to the five parties
to negotiate with one another with regard to setting maritime boundaries and rival
claims. They have an incentive to do so in a peaceful and orderly manner, but
interstate conflicts cannot, of course, be ruled out.

Direct stakeholders, such as Russia and Canada and Norway,[29] have slowly
increased their military preparedness. The United States has not ruled out unilateralism to protect what it terms *sovereign interests*.[30] Even Denmark, which has, generally, refrained from actions that could be construed as a "hard security" approach
toward the region is contemplating the creation of a military contingent specifically for the Arctic.[31] This development raises questions about the credibility of the
commitment by all five Arctic states at the Ilulissat meeting in Greenland in 2008
to clinging to international norms when dealing with territorial claims beyond the
two-hundred-mile exclusive economic zone.[32]

Given the potential for confrontation, the political rhetoric and posturing on the
Arctic should not be discounted. There are several conflict scenarios. First is a U.S.-
Canadian dispute over the maritime boundary in the Beaufort Sea; the United States
also rejects Canada's claim to the Northwestern Passage. Second is Russia's claim
to the Lomonosov Ridge, which is contested by Denmark and Canada, which have
been working together to find evidence of a connection between the Greenland-
Canada continental shelf and the Lomonosov Ridge. Third, the Norwegians are
seeking international acceptance of their position on Svalbard, in particular the two-
hundred-nautical-mile "fishery protection zone" declared around the archipelago.
It is not accepted by Russia and many other states and is not recognized by Norway's
allies, including Iceland. Norway's Svalbard sovereignty claims are based on the

---

[29] See, for example, Canada's Department of Foreign Affairs and International Trade, "Defining
Canada's Extended Continental Shelf," 14 August 2008; Dmitry Medvedev, "Protecting Russia's
National Interests in the Arctic," speech given at a meeting of the Russian Security Council, 17 Septem-
ber 2008, accessed on 1 February 2011, http//www.kremlin.ru/eng/text/speeches/20078/0917/1945;
Russian Security Council, "Foundations of the Russian Federation National Policy in the Arctic
Until 2020 and Beyond," 27 March 2009, accessed on 1 February 2011, http://www.scrf.gov.ru.

[30] See George W. Bush, "U.S. National Security Presidential Directive and Homeland Security
Presidential Directive (NSPD-66/HSPD-25)," 9 January 2009, accessed on 1 February 2011, http:
//www.fas.org/irp/offdocs/nspd/nspd-66.htm.

[31] This was recommended by the Danish Defense Commission; see "Danish Defence – Global
Engagement," March 2009, 68, accessed on 1 February 2011, http://www.fmn.dk/eng/Defence%
20Commission/Pages/Defence%20commission.aspx; see also Jens Ejsing, "Danmark opruster i Arktis" [Denmark rearms in the Arctic], *Berlinske Tidende*, 14 July 2009; see also "Denmark plans on
increasing Arctic presence," *Arctic Focus*, 28 July 2009, accessed on 1 February 2011, http://arcticfocus
.com/2009/07/28/denmark-plans-on-increasing-arctic-presence/.

[32] See, for example, the Ilulissat Declaration, issued by Arctic states at the Arctic Ocean Conference
in Ilulissat, Greenland, 27–29 May 2008, accessed on 1 February 2011, http://www.oceanlaw.org/
downloads/arctic/Ilulissat_Declaration.pdf.

1920 Svalbard Treaty; but what restricts them is that the nondiscriminatory rights to practice peaceful economic activities of the parties of the 1920 Svalbard Treaty apply. Fourth is Canadian-Danish disagreement over the tiny Hans Island, which is located in the center of the Kennedy Channel of the Nares Strait, which separates Ellesmere Island from northern Greenland and connects Baffin Bay with the Lincoln Sea. The dispute is about the island itself – not about the waters, seabed, or the control of navigation. The island has played some role in the new Canadian Arctic policy by being considered the guardian of the northeastern access route to the Northwest Passage. But after a highly symbolic and politically charged flag-planting war, which culminated in a visit by the Canadian defense minister to Hans Island in 2005, the two countries decided to opt for a diplomatic solution. In 2007, Canada conceded that the border line went right across the island, but Denmark has kept up its claim to the entire island.[33]

The solution of these problems is not a matter of urgency. Territorial disputes usually delay natural resource exploitation instead of leading to securitization or military confrontation. A worst-case scenario in the Arctic requires a drastic deterioration of relations between the United States and/or NATO and Russia, which is unlikely given the desires and actions of both sides to improve them as part of U.S. President Obama's "reset" agenda or linkages to other international disputes (an example would be the Georgian war, which did, however, not have long-term impact on the relations between Russia and the West). Nonetheless, external realities can be created and re-created irrespective of whether they correspond to scientific time lines, to climate change or the opening of sea lines, or to geopolitical logic. Even if the Russian North Pole flag planting mainly served internal political aims – within the context of Russia's presidential succession after Putin and parliamentary elections in 2007 – it had deep impact on other Arctic stakeholders. It spurred intense nationalistic reaction in Canada, speeded up the development of the U.S. presidential directive on the Arctic, and contributed to the Ilulissat initiative.

Mikhail Gorbachev's "Arctic Zone of Peace" speech in 1987 provided the groundwork for decoupling confrontational hard security politics – as the hegemonic approach toward the Arctic during the Cold War – from soft security issues, such as scientific cooperation and environmental protection.[34] Despite its Cold War connotations, it paved, in some sense, the way for the Copenhagen school in security studies – and the extended concept of security – in the 1990s and beyond. The establishment of the Arctic Council was the product of such soft security discourses. The trend now, however, is more toward preparations for a slow or "silent" securitization.

Rejecting the likelihood of great-power confrontational scenarios, the Icelandic government has been more concerned with Arctic identity politics – the prevention

[33] Nanna Hvidt and Hans Mouritzen, eds., "Danish Foreign Policy Yearbook 2009" (Copenhagen: Danish Institute for International Studies, 2009), 52.

[34] Kristian Åtland, "Mikhail Gorbachev, the Murmansk Initiative, and the Desecuritization of Interstate Relations in the Arctic," *Cooperation and Conflict*, 43, no. 3 (2009), 289–311.

of a development of an Arctic Five decision-making forum. It saw the Ilulissat meeting as an attempt on the part of the Arctic coastal states to bypass the Arctic Council and to exclude the other Arctic nations from their deliberations. It protested vocally against its exclusion, more so than the Swedes and Finns, who also voiced their displeasure.[35] Even if the Ilulissat meeting was projected as a onetime affair, the Canadian government convened a follow-up meeting,[36] which was held at the end of March 2010 in Chelsea, Canada. This meeting can be characterized as a failure, and not only because it produced no new results but because it prompted renewed protests by the three other Arctic states and by the representatives of Arctic indigenous peoples. Hillary Clinton, U.S. secretary of state, publicly reprimanded the host, the Canadian government, for not inviting those stakeholders. The rebuke forced the Canadian foreign minister, Lawrence Cannon, to declare publicly – as his Danish counterpart had done following the Ilulissat meeting – that the forum was not meant to be a permanent institution.[37]

At this stage, it is too early to tell whether the Arctic Ocean states will continue their exclusive deliberations on Arctic governance. Iceland is bound to continue resistance to any such effort – with or without Sweden and Finland, whose interests are more focused on the Baltic Sea rather than on the Arctic. This does not mean that the Arctic Council is going to be a decision-making body on Arctic governance. Although it remains the main venue for Arctic affairs, its limited and nonpolitical mandate prevents it from settling territorial disputes. Thus, the underlying tension between Arctic state interests, especially oil and gas, and an emphasis on multilateral regulatory authority, such as UNCLOS, remains unresolved.

There are arguments to be made for increased cooperation between the Arctic Ocean states as part of efforts to prevent territorial disputes from escalating. Yet prospects for joint rules concerning oil and gas exploitation are not likely. And experience from shared oil regions, such as the North Sea, indicate that states prefer national to international regulation.[38] In contrast, there are incentives for international solutions relating to disaster readiness or pollution control. A case in point is the initiative by the Arctic states – under the aegis of the Arctic Council – on formalized and legally-binding cooperation in aeronautical and maritime search-and-rescue operations.[39]

---

[35] Interview with Icelandic officials, 2 December 2009. See also Hvidt and Moritzen, "Danish Foreign Policy Yearbook 2009," 58.

[36] Personal Interviews with Icelandic officials, 9 December 2009.

[37] "Clinton Rebuke Overshadows Canada's Arctic Meeting," Reuters, 29 March 2010, accessed on 1 February 2011, http://www.reuters.com/article/2010/03/30/us-arctic-idUSTRE62S4ZP20100330.

[38] Hvidt and Mouritzen, "Danish Foreign Policy Yearbook 2009," 65.

[39] Anton Vasiliev (the senior Russian Arctic official in the Arctic Council), "Is the Ilulissat Declaration Adequate?" presentation at the conference Arctic – Changing Realities, sponsored by the Nordic Council of Ministers, 26 May 2010.

Thus, there is bound to be more international pressure from non-Arctic states or the European Union for some kind of internationalization of the Arctic or at least the establishment of regimes over which they can have some influence designed to protect their interests, for example with respect to the effects of climate change and maritime issues.[40] And even if the Arctic states are reluctant to open up the Arctic for outside regulations, except for UNCLOS, they differ among themselves on how non-Arctic states and organizations should be allowed to have a voice in Arctic affairs. Russia's policy is that the less external involvement in the Arctic, the better. It has used the Ilulissat Declaration to stress that the Arctic littoral states are responsible for governance of Arctic areas under their jurisdiction and that other states or organizations have no legal basis for such claims. It is against EU and NATO involvement in the Arctic. Canada has also used sovereignty rhetoric to stress the rights of Arctic Ocean states. It has stood in the way of the European Commission's application for observer status in the Arctic Council, not least because of its ban on the sale of seal products. And in contrast to the United States, Canada has been resistant to using the NATO-Russia Council as a forum for discussing Arctic matters.

The Nordic states are, however, far more open to EU influence in the Arctic, as can be expected, given the EU membership of three Arctic states, Denmark, Sweden, and Finland. There are limiting factors, to be sure. Finland and Sweden do not border the Arctic Ocean and are the only Arctic countries without jurisdictional claims in the Arctic Ocean and adjacent seas. Denmark is the only Arctic Ocean state, and it is an EU member. But it is acting on behalf of Greenland, which left the European Union in 1985. It is an open question whether Greenland will secede from Denmark on the basis of the independence clause contained in the Home Rule Act, if its rich natural resources will be developed within the coming decades.[41] Like the Nordic EU members, Iceland – together with Norway – supports, as noted, the EU Commission's application for observer status in the Arctic Council. If Iceland becomes a member of the European Union, it could strengthen EU presence in the region. Yet, while seeing the EU Commission's commitment to UNCLOS as a valuable asset, the Nordic Arctic states are opposed to the resolution passed if later abandoned by the European Parliament on an Arctic Treaty and to a proposal, which has not been approved, for a moratorium on commercial exploitation of Arctic resources.

Thus, the involvement of international organizations remains controversial among Arctic states. The same applies to the prospective role of China, which has shown much interest in the Arctic. Its application – together with those of Japan and South Korea – for observer status in the Arctic Council is facing hurdles. What explains China's interest is the prospect for the opening of new shipping lanes and transportation routes linking the Pacific and the North Atlantic. To be sure, China is hamstrung by the fact that United States and Russia control the Bering Strait or the

[40] Hvidt and Mouritzen, "Danish Foreign Policy Yearbook 2009," 64.
[41] Ibid., 67–68.

Pacific entryway to the Arctic Ocean, the Northern Sea Route and the Northwest Passage. But as a great power, China – like the European Union – is bound to have more influence on future Arctic developments. If these powerful actors will be excluded by the Arctic states, they will probably – in the name of their political and economic influence – eventually force through a stakeholder role.

CONCLUSION

The Icelandic government is framing its response to new Arctic geopolitical realities through a more proactive policy. It is an attempt to draw attention to the North Atlantic – and to itself – and is also consistent, if pursued with less intensity, with Norway's hyperfocus on the High North. It also reflects the belief that Iceland is poised to attain more geostrategic importance as a result of future scenarios, such as climate change and state-centered and commercial activities in the north. It is too early to define Iceland's role in future transatlantic and transarctic interactions. If the region will be remilitarized, Iceland – just as in the Cold War – will, again, assume strategic importance, even if the shifting of boundaries to the Arctic suggests that it will be less central. There are, however, bound to be conflicts in Iceland between the potential material benefits offered by natural resource extraction and concerns about the environmental detrimental impact on marine life given the central role of the fishery sector in its economy.

Iceland's support for maintaining a privileged role of the Arctic states in managing the Arctic has not prevented it from backing international legal frameworks for settling territorial claims in the region, especially UNCLOS. It has also dismissed propaganda displays associated with Arctic politics – such as the Russian North Pole flag planting – and been critical of what it sees as exaggerated Arctic sovereignty discourses by some stakeholders.[42] Finally, it has, as noted, put much emphasis on retaining the central role of the Arctic Council. The approach fits within the framework of an extended post–Cold War concept of security, whereby sovereign "national interests," such as territorial and resource claims, mix with transnational processes. But more important, the approach reflects Icelandic determination to be part of an Arctic club of eight and to cling to a place of strategic relevance.

As I have shown here, Iceland has been trying to come to grips with several external and internal developments, such as the withdrawal of the U.S. military forces, a renewed Russian geopolitical role, an EU membership application, and a rupture generated by a domestic economic collapse. From 2006 until 2008, Iceland's security approach continued to be driven by – and contingent on – Cold War parameters: territory and potential state threats.[43] Icelandic officials used Russia's resumption of

[42] Griffiths, "Towards a Canadian Arctic Strategy," 33.
[43] See Barry Buzan, *People, States and Fear: An Agenda for International Security Studies in the Post-Cold War Era* (Boulder, CO: Lynne Rienner Publishers, 1991); see also Buzan, Waever, and de Wilde, *Security*, 195, 204; Barry Buzan and Ole Waever, *Regions and Powers: The Structure of International*

bomber flights, NATO's air-policing policy, and the emerging Arctic discourse to rationalize a territorial defense agenda and to legitimize new institutional security structures in the domestic domain. This involved a commitment to the continuation of the U.S. defense relationship – in the form of the 1951 U.S.-Icelandic Defense Agreement – if in a far weaker deterritorialized form. More important, efforts were made to strengthen Iceland's ties with NATO, and bilateral, nonbinding, security cooperation arrangements were negotiated with Norway,[44] Denmark,[45] and Britain.[46] Iceland sought to keep Russia at a distance by dealing with it through multilateral frameworks such as NATO and the Arctic Council and by shunning bilateral arrangements.[47]

This policy is currently being tested and contested by a dramatic shift of domestic political priorities after Iceland became the first casualty of the international financial crisis. There is still much political support in Iceland for engaging the northern dimension, even if the discourse is still couched in too-optimistic materialist terms. The economic crash exposed ambivalence about the real need for the institutionalization of air policing, whose aim is mostly symbolic: to show that a demilitarized Iceland is a NATO member. Thus, the government quickly scaled down those missions in late 2008 as a cost-cutting measure. On the surface, the bomber flights and NATO's air-policing arrangements constitute links between a Cold War past and an Arctic future. Still, although the acts represent recycled military symbolism, Russian strategic aviation is not seen as posing a territorial threat. And the willingness to approach Russia for an emergency loan shows that the the Icelanders do not view the bilateral relationship in traditional Cold War adversarial terms.

With Iceland grappling with the effects of an unprecedented economic disaster, an IMF rescue package, and deep-seated political changes, there is an overwhelming focus on societal security. Iceland's EU membership bid is geared toward achieving more financial and economic stability. If successful, which is by no means certain

Security (Cambridge: Cambridge University Press, 2003); Ole Waever, "Insecurity, Security, and Asecurity in the West European Non-War Community," in Security Communities, eds. Emmanuel Adler and Michael Barnett (Cambridge: Cambridge University Press, 1998), 88; Ken Booth, Theory of World Security (Cambridge: Cambridge University Press, 2007).

44 "Samkomulag Noregs og Íslands um samstarf á sviði öryggismála, varnarmála og viðbúnaðar" [Memorandum of Understanding between Norway and Iceland on Security Policy Cooperation], April 2007, accessed on 1 February 2011, http://www.utanrikisraduneyti.is/media/Frettatilkynning/MOU_-_undirritun.pdf.

45 "Yfirlýsing Danmerkur og Íslands um samstarf um öryggis- og varnarmál og almannavarnir" [Joint Declaration between Denmark and Iceland on Security Cooperation], April 2007, accessed on 1 February 2011, http://www.utanrikisraduneyti.is/media/Frettatilkynning/Yfirlysing_Islands_og_Danmerkur.pdf.

46 "Samkomulag Bretlands og Íslands um samstarf á sviði varnar- og öryggismála" [Agreement between the United Kingdom and Iceland in Defense and Security], May 2008), accessed on 1 February 2011, http://www.utanrikisraduneyti.is/media/PDF/UK-Iceland_MoU_-Icelandic.pdf.

47 See Valur Ingimundarson, "Iceland's Security Policy and Geopolitics of the North," in Emerging from the Frost: Security in the 21st Century Arctic, ed. Kjetil Skogrand (Oslo: Institutt for Forsvarsstudier, 2008), 80–87; see also, Ingimundarson, "Iceland's Post-American Security Policy, Russian Geopolitics, and the Arctic Question," RUSI Journal 154, no. 4 (2009), 74–81.

given the high level of domestic political resistance to it in Iceland, it would offer other types of security guarantees, such as the mutual solidarity declaration in the case of a terrorist attack or natural disasters. And despite the current focus on "post-affluent reconstruction," Iceland's security discourse is still contingent on territory as underscored by the continued emphasis on a northern dimension. Hence the Icelandic emphasis on carving out a specific role and not being shut out of the decision-making process in the region. Indeed, Arctic power games are about identity politics – about exclusion and inclusion – whereby states and organizations are classified on the basis of power and legitimacy as those on the inside and those on the outside. The inbuilt logic of such a constellation is the reproduction of confrontational discourses rather than cooperative ones.

PART III

North American Security Interests in the Arctic

12

Canada and the Newly Emerging International Arctic Security Regime

Rob Huebert

INTRODUCTION

Canada is in the midst of a massive transformation of the Arctic. Never before in recorded history have so many elements come together to literally redraw the face of the Arctic. The impact of climate change on the Arctic is perhaps the best known. Increasing global temperatures are causing the ice cover to melt. The resulting accessibility of the previously inaccessible Arctic Ocean has captured the world's attention. The Arctic is believed to contain vast amounts of untapped natural resources; in particular, some estimates suggest that the Arctic may have 30 percent of the world's undiscovered gas resources and 13 percent of its oil.[1] Canada has already become the world's third-largest diamond producer on the basis of three mines in the Northwest Territories.[2] A third major factor is a rapidly changing geopolitical environment. As the ice melts, and as expectations rise regarding the new mineral potential, both the circumpolar states and other members of the international community are increasingly looking to the Arctic as a new zone of opportunity. Whereas the previously inhospitable Arctic prevented operations in the region, this will soon be changing.

The most important question is what the new international Arctic regime will look like. What will be the impact of the new geopolitical realities on the Arctic and on Canada? Will the Arctic become a region of cooperation, or will it become a region of increasing competition and conflict? Furthermore, what policies and actions will the circumpolar states implement to protect and promote their interests? For countries such as Canada, which has historically posited itself as an Arctic state, the

---

[1] Kenneth J. Bird, Ronald R. Charpentier, Donald L. Gautier (CARA Project Chief), David W. Houseknecht, Timothy R. Klett, Janet K. Pitman, Thomas E. Moore, Christopher J. Schenk, Marilyn E. Tennyson, and Craig J. Wandrey, "Circum-Arctic Resource Appraisal; Estimates of Undiscovered Oil and Gas North of the Arctic Circle," U.S. Geological Survey Fact Sheet 2008-3049 (2008), June 5, 2009, http://pubs.usgs.gov/fs/2008/3049/.

[2] Statistics Canada, "Study: Diamonds Are Adding Lustre to the Canadian Economy," *The Daily*, January 13, 2004, http://www.statcan.gc.ca/daily-quotidien/040113/dq040113a-eng.htm.

entry of new states and other bodies into the Arctic region with interests that do not align with Canadian interests will be unsettling. Until now Canada has been able to protect its interests simply given the inaccessible nature of the region. Now that this is changing, what is Canada prepared to do to secure its Arctic?

UNDERSTANDING CANADIAN ARCTIC SECURITY AND SOVEREIGNTY

Any discussion of Canadian Arctic security is inevitably linked to the issue of Arctic sovereignty. For Canadians, Arctic sovereignty has been the dominant issue in the international system. It has dominated and has overshadowed most discussions pertaining to Arctic security. Canadians had ongoing concerns that the United States had intentions to "take over" elements of the Canadian north.[3] Although few of those suspicions actually transpired,[4] the United States has consistently maintained that the Canadian Northwest Passage is an international strait.[5] This issue is the main sovereignty challenge facing Canada. Canada has needed to protect its Arctic security since the end of the Second World War.[6] But the irony is that the United States has been willing and able to carry the lion's share of the work regarding North American Arctic security. Canadian governments have provided some resources when necessary, such as for the shared protection of North American Arctic aerospace.[7] But they were always happy to keep those efforts to a minimum.

For Canadians, *Arctic sovereignty* is an all-encompassing term for all international challenges in the Arctic. When Canadian leaders call for the protection of Canadian Arctic sovereignty, they may be talking about international challenges to the status of the Northwest Passage, but they could just as easily be talking about Arctic security or Arctic boundary disputes. The different manner in which the term *Arctic sovereignty* is used confounds efforts to understand current Canadian Arctic security needs. Therefore, the question that needs to be addressed is, What is Canadian Arctic sovereignty and security?

As a concept, sovereignty has numerous understandings.[8] At its core are four major elements. The first aspect of sovereignty refers to defined borders. Historically, the drawing of borders focused on land – where one state began and where one ended.

[3] Shelagh Grant, *Sovereignty or Security: Government Policy in the Canadian North, 1936–1950* (Vancouver: University of British Columbia Press, 1988); Edgar Dosman, ed., *The Arctic in Question* (Toronto: Oxford University Press, 1976).
[4] Whitney Lackenbauer and Peter Kikkert, *The Canadian Forces and Arctic Sovereignty* (Waterloo: Wilfrid Laurier Press, 2010).
[5] Rob Huebert, "The Shipping News Part II: How Canada's Arctic Sovereignty Is on Thinning Ice," *International Journal* 58, no. 3 (Summer 2003): 295–308
[6] Rob Huebert, "Renaissance in Canadian Arctic Security," *Canadian Military Journal* 6, no. 4 (2005–06): 17–29.
[7] Joseph Jockel, *No Boundaries Upstairs* (Vancouver: University of British Columbia, 1987).
[8] For good discussions on the concept, see Jens Bartelson, *A Genealogy of Sovereignty* (Cambridge: Cambridge University Press, 1995); James Allan, *Sovereign Statehood* (London: Allen and Unwin, 1986).

The issue of borders became much more complicated as states moved to claim control over their adjacent maritime zones. A new concept of maritime regions began to emerge over time. These zones provide different types of sovereign control for the coastal states. Borders are still important, but as one moves away from the coastline, they provide for different levels of control. The second major component of sovereignty is a population. A state's people need to be contained within the borders. Thus, Antarctica, which has no indigenous population, is not a state. The third element of sovereignty is the existence of a government that makes the final authoritative decisions for the population contained within the established borders. The government has the right to make decisions and to enforce them, with coercive power if necessary. The fourth element of sovereignty requires that the international community recognize the sovereignty of the state.

With the exception of one small island, Hans Island, located between Greenland and northern Canada, Canada faces no challenge to its sovereignty over its Arctic lands.[9] However, Canada does face international challenges to its sovereignty over maritime regions of its Arctic. The United States and the European Union have both taken positions claiming that the Northwest Passage is an international strait and not Canadian internal waters.[10] Both the United States and the European Union are of the position that this means that Canada does not have the right to unilaterally control international shipping as it enters those waters. Canada also disagrees with the United States on the division of the maritime boundary north of Alaska and the Yukon. There are also two small disagreements with Denmark about the division of the Lincoln Sea.[11] Though too early to know with certainty, there may be disagreement among Canada, Russia, Denmark, and the United States concerning extended continental shelf claims in the Arctic Ocean. Given that none of these countries have submitted its final claim, it is unknown whether there is any overlap of extended continental shelf claims.

It is equally difficult to understand current conceptualizations of Canadian Arctic security. *Security* is itself a term in transition. Traditional security is understood to be the protection of the state from the threats – normally understood in military terms[12] – from other states. With the rising danger posed by international terrorist organizations, traditional security has also begun to include nonstate actors. The means to counter those threats is normally understood to require military action by the state itself or in cooperation with its allies. During the Cold War, the main threat

9   Don McRae, "Arctic Sovereignty: What Is at Stake?" *Behind the Headlines* 64 (2007): 1–23.
10 Rob Huebert, "Polar Vision or Tunnel Vision: The Making of Canadian Arctic Waters Policy," *Marine Policy* 19, no. 4 (July 1995): 343–63.
11 David Gray, "Canada's Unresolved Maritime Boundaries," *IBRU Boundary and Security Bulletin* (1997): 1–10.
12 For the best collection of articles that addresses the entire discussion on the nature of security, see John Baylis, James Wirtz, Colin Gray, and Eliot Cohen, eds., *Strategy in the Contemporary World*, 2nd ed. (Oxford: Oxford University Press, 2007): 1–392; Allan Collins, ed., *Contemporary Security Studies* (Oxford: Oxford University Press, 2007): 1–444.

to Canadian Arctic security was the Soviet Union. But that threat largely dissipated when the Soviet Union collapsed. A new understanding of security emerged in the 1990s when it was recognized that the Arctic faced significant environmental challenges. These included transboundary pollutants such as mercury and persistent organic pollutants.[13] It was soon determined that, although the pollutants did not originate in the Arctic, they were accumulating in dangerous quantities in the Arctic food chain. These pollutants posed a serious threat to the well-being of all northern Canadians but in particular the indigenous populations who depended on food caught in the wild. Therefore, environmental security became a primary concern following the end of the Cold War.

In this way, security and the Canadian Arctic includes both traditional and non-traditional security components. Traditional security is normally provided for by the military and diplomatic arms of the federal government. Nontraditional security needs are met by the environmental, scientific, and economic branches of government. Although there is no comprehensive understanding in Canada about the interaction between these different types of security (as they tend to be described in either-or terms), both types of security require the Canadian government to take action against a foreign actor to provide for the security of Canadians.

In discussions about Arctic sovereignty and security sovereignty, the point that is often lost is that it is a means not an end. Stating that a region in the Arctic is Canadian may appeal to nationalistic tendencies, but unless it provides something for Canadians, it remains an expensive pursuit. Sovereignty needs to be the first step to provide for Canadians' protection and promotion of their interests, and hence their security. Canadian governments need to have sovereign control of their Arctic regions so that the Canadian populations within those boundaries can benefit from Canadian laws, rules, and regulations that promote and protect Canadian interests. In this capacity, Canadian Arctic sovereignty is a requirement to allow for Canadian Arctic security. The understanding is that sovereignty and security are linked as one concept. Sovereignty is required to give the state the right to act. Security is what the state is providing for its population. Thus, Canada wants to have Arctic sovereignty so that it is able to provide for both traditional and environmental security needs of Canadians in the Arctic region. In the modern era, what are the challenges to Canadian Arctic sovereignty and security?

THE SECURITY AND SOVEREIGNTY CHALLENGES
AND TO THE CANADIAN ARCTIC

The understanding of Canadian Arctic security is complicated by the current lack of traditional threats, that is, direct military threats to the Canadian Arctic. However,

---

[13] David Downie and Terry Fenge, eds., *Lights against POPs: Combating Toxic Threats in the Arctic* (Montreal: McGill-Queen's University Press, 2003).

troubling developments may change this in the future. Several trends suggest that many Arctic and non-Arctic states are rebuilding their combat-capable forces in the Arctic. Although this does not mean that military conflict is imminent, it does suggest that the states have concerns sufficient enough to allocate scarce resources to improve their military capabilities in the Arctic. The threats that are understood to exist are almost entirely focused on sovereignty. As discussed earlier, these include the American and European position that the Northwest Passage is a strait used for international navigation; the boundary dispute between Canada and the United States regarding the division of the Beaufort Sea; and the dispute between Denmark and Canada regarding the division of the Lincoln Sea and Hans Island. This is a small island measuring only one kilometer by four kilometers, with no trees, no habitation, and no known resources. In addition, Denmark and Canada settled the maritime boundary in 1974. So, no matter which country ultimately successfully claims the island, the maritime boundary will not change.[14]

The continental shelf claims of Canada, Russia, Denmark, and the United States may also overlap. However, as none of these countries has yet to finalize its claims, it is uncertain as to whether there will be conflicting claims. A clearly established process is in place to peacefully resolve any differences in the event of a dispute regarding the claims. All five of the Arctic states (including Norway) that will be claiming an extended continental shelf met in Greenland in May 2008 and pledged to follow the international rules on settling the issue.[15]

Nevertheless, the unresolved issues do involve important interests. The boundary disputes remain unresolved because the stakes are important. The disputed zone of the Beaufort Sea may contain significant amounts of oil and gas. Thus, whichever country is able to establish its claim may be the beneficiary of significant resources. There is also an issue pertaining to the right to determine environmental standards in the region. The Canadian position is further complicated by the fact that it has used the position it has taken to determine the boundary of a land claims agreement. The western section of the land claims area for the 1984 Western Inuvialuit Land Claims Agreement follows the Canadian claim.[16] Should Canada have to surrender its claim, it will need to redraw the boundary for the agreement, which will be politically sensitive.

Other international boundary issues remain unresolved among the other Arctic states. It had appeared that the Russians and the Americans had settled the boundary dividing the Bering Strait, but the Russian Duma has refused to ratify the

---

[14] Rob Huebert, "Return of the 'Vikings': The Canadian-Danish Dispute over Hans Island – New Challenges for the Control of the Canadian North," in *Breaking Ice – Renewable Resource and Ocean Management in the Canadian North*, eds. Fikret Berkes, Rob Huebert, Helen Fast, Micheline Manseau, and Alan Diduck (Calgary: University of Calgary Press, 2005): 343–63.

[15] *The Ilulissat Declaration: Arctic Ocean Conference*, Ilulissat, Greenland, May 27–29, 2008, http://www.oceanlaw.org/downloads/arctic/Ilulissat_Declaration.pdf.

[16] Rob Huebert, *Canadian Arctic Sovereignty and Security in a Transforming Circumpolar World – Foreign Policy for Canada's Tomorrow*, no. 4 (Toronto: Canadian International Council, May 2009).

agreement.[17] Some Russian parliamentarians expressed concern that the agreement was made at a time of severe Russian weakness. As such, some Russians have come to believe that the agreement is skewed toward American interests at the expense of Russia's. In contrast, Russia and Norway have resolved a forty-year disagreement over the division of the Barents Sea.[18] Most observers were surprised that the Russians and the Norwegians were ultimately able to reach agreement.

In general, the issues facing Canada and the entire circumpolar region are viewed as diplomatic challenges at a low to medium complexity, and not as overtly threatening to international peace and security. When leaders talk of threats in the Arctic, the focus is generally on societal health and environmental threats, with the acknowledgment that the northern population and, in particular, the indigenous populations of the north, face tremendous social and economic challenges. As the ice melts, many members of the indigenous communities are facing severe challenges to maintain their way of life. Tremendous new difficulties face those who wish to continue to hunt and fish. Traditional knowledge is being confounded by the new climate. Stocks of terrestrial and marine animals are also coming under increased challenges. Climate change, in conjunction with transboundary pollutants, threatens the traditional way of life for most northern indigenous peoples in all Arctic states. The youths of these peoples are increasingly being exposed to the lifestyle of the southern population through new forms of technology. Many are looking southward rather than to participate in a traditional way of life. The Internet, Facebook, and other new forms of communication present new options and opportunities. But at the same time, there is a serious lack of economic opportunities for most indigenous youths.[19] Although they know what their southern counterparts are doing, they often do not have the same resources to do the same. In this manner, societal security is emerging as one of the most significant threats facing the Arctic.

THE CHANGING ARCTIC

When the Arctic remained largely inaccessible to the international community (with the exception of the submarine forces of the United States and the Soviet Union), Canada was able to position itself as caring about protecting Canadian Arctic sovereignty and security by limiting its actions to the creation of innovative new policy directives and by publicly stating how much it valued its north. It seldom found

---

[17] Vlad M. Kaczynski, "US-Russian Bering Sea Marine Border Dispute: Conflict over Strategic Assets, Fisheries and Energy Resources," *Russian Analytical Digest*, May 1 2007: 2–4.

[18] Walter Gibbs, "Russia and Norway Reach Accord on Barents Sea," *New York Times*, April 10, 2010, A10.

[19] Frances Abele, "Northern Development: Past, Present and Future," in *Northern Exposure: Peoples, Powers and Prospects for Canada's North*, eds. Frances Abele, Thomas J. Courchene, F. Leslie Seidle, and France St.-Hilaire (Montreal: Institute for Research on Public Policy, 2009): 19–68.

it necessary to allocate significant resources to consolidate its policies.[20] However, Canada can no longer rely on the Arctic's formidable environment as a barrier to the international community. The physical changes brought about by climate change, driven by the potential of great economic wealth and facilitated by new technologies that increase the ability of southerners to enter the Arctic, have all accelerated international interest. In addition, new international legal rules are leading to greater accessibility of the Arctic. This means that a new Arctic geopolitical region is developing. Most observers hope that the core element of this new region will be based on cooperation and good relations. Notwithstanding the hope that cooperation will be the hallmark of the region, the fact that states are strengthening their military capabilities in the region suggests that steps are being taken in the event that relationships become competitive in the region.

CHANGES IN THE CLIMATE

Work conducted by the Arctic Council – a body that was very much a Canadian creation[21] – has been most instrumental in understanding the problems posed by climate change. As the changes began to be observed, the Arctic Council commissioned two of its working groups – the Arctic Monitoring and Assessment Programme (AMAP) and the Conservation of Arctic Flora and Fauna (CAFF) – and the International Arctic Science Committee (IASC) to undertake an extensive and exhaustive study of the impact of climate change on the Arctic in 2000. After four years, the Arctic Climate Impact Assessment (ACIA) was released.[22] Its findings are both troubling and overwhelming. Perhaps the most important finding of the ACIA is the magnitude of the problem. The assessment starkly outlines the enormity of the threat that is facing not only the Arctic region but also the entire world. As temperatures increase, the entire Arctic ecosystem is being transformed. The key findings for the Arctic environment are the following:[23]

1.   The Arctic climate is warming rapidly and greater changes are projected. Annual average Arctic temperatures have increased at almost twice the rate of the rest of the world over the past few decades; increasing precipitation, shorter and warmer winters, and substantial decreases in ice and snow cover will likely persist for centuries, and unexpected and larger shifts and fluctuations are possible.

---

[20] Whitney Lackenbauer, *From Polar Race to Polar Saga: An Integrated Strategy for Canada and the Circumpolar World. Foreign Policy for Canada's Tomorrow*, no. 3 (Toronto: Canadian International Council, July 2009).

[21] Rob Huebert, "New Directions in Circumpolar Cooperation: Canada, the Arctic Environmental Protection Strategy and the Arctic Council," *Canadian Foreign Policy* 5, no. 2 (Winter 1998): 7–58.

[22] Arctic Climate Impact Assessment, *Impacts of a Warming Arctic* (Cambridge: Cambridge University Press: 2004).

[23] Ibid., pp.10–11.

2. Arctic warming and its consequences have worldwide implications. These include the melting of highly reflective snow and ice cover, which will in turn lead to a greater warming of the planet, an increase in glacial melt and river runoff that will result in rising sea levels, and the possible slowing of the world's ocean current circulation system.

3. Animal species' diversity ranges and distribution will change. Reduction in sea ice will drastically shrink marine habitat for species such as polar bears, ice-habiting seals, and some seabirds; species' ranges will shift northward, bringing new species to the Arctic and limiting some already present; some marine fisheries will become more productive, whereas freshwater fisheries are likely to decline.

4. Many coastal communities and facilities face increasing exposure to storms. Severe coastal erosion will continue to be a problem, as rising sea ice and reduction of sea ice allows for higher waves and storm surges to reach the shore; some coastlines will face increased permafrost melt, thus adding to their vulnerability; risk of flooding in coastal wetlands can increase; and some communities are already facing significant threats to the coastline.

5. Reduced sea ice is very likely to increase marine transport and access to resources. Continued reduction of sea ice is likely to extend the navigation season and increase marine access to the Arctic's marine resources; reduced sea ice is likely to increase offshore oil and gas extraction projects; and sovereignty, security, and safety issues, as well as social, cultural, and environmental concerns, are likely to arise as marine access increases.

6. Thawing ground will disrupt transportation building and other infrastructure. Transportation and industry on land, including oil and gas extraction, will increasingly be disrupted as the periods during which ice roads and tundra are frozen sufficiently to allow travel are reduced. This could mean a greater shift to marine transport; as frozen ground thaws, many buildings, roads, and so on, will become destabilized, thus causing a need for substantial maintenance and rebuilding; and permafrost degradation will affect natural ecosystems through the collapsing of ground surface, the draining of lakes, wetland development, and the toppling of trees.

7. Indigenous communities are facing major economic and cultural impacts. Many indigenous peoples depend on food sources that are threatened; and changes in species' ranges and availability, access to those species, and perceived and real changes in travel safety because of changing ice and weather conditions will create serious challenges to human health and food security.

8. Elevated ultraviolet radiation levels will affect people, plants, and animals. The stratospheric ozone layer over the Arctic is not expected to improve for at least a few decades, largely due to the effect of greenhouse gases on stratospheric

temperatures; the current generation of Arctic young people is likely to receive a lifetime dose of ultraviolet radiation that is 30 percent higher than any prior generation; elevated ultraviolet radiation can disrupt photosynthesis in plants and have detrimental effects on the early life stages of fish and amphibians; and risks to some Arctic ecosystems are likely as the largest increases in ultraviolet radiation occur in spring, when sensitive species are most vulnerable.

9. Multiple influences interact to affect people and ecosystems. Changes in climate are occurring in the context of many other stresses, including chemical pollution, overfishing, land use changes, habitat fragmentation, human population increases, and economic changes; the multiple stresses can combine to amplify impacts on human and ecosystem health and well-being. In many cases, the total impact is greater than the sum of its parts. Decreased ice cover in the Arctic will result in drastic changes in the Arctic. These will range from the microscopic to the international. The changes in sea ice are introducing changes in the algae that live on the bottom of the ice. In turn, change in the algae affects the entire food chain in the Arctic.

These changes are occurring now and will transform the entire Arctic in ways that cannot yet be fully appreciated. But as if this were not enough, the impacts of climate change are occurring at the same time as there is a vastly increasing renewed interest in the resources of the Canadian north and the circumpolar region in general.

CHANGES IN RESOURCE EXPECTATIONS

The expectations for the region are huge. In 2008, the U.S. Geological Survey estimated that the Arctic potentially holds up to 30 percent of the world's undiscovered gas reserves and 13 percent of the world's undiscovered oil reserves.[24] This is estimation. It will require actual exploration to determine whether these estimates are correct. Nevertheless, the expectations are that there are substantial resources of oil and gas in the region.[25] Most of the major oil companies continued to look for oil in the Beaufort Sea even during the recession from 2008 to 2010.

Unconventional resources, known as gas hydrates, are also potentially located in the Arctic.[26] Gas hydrates are a recently discovered source of gas found in a jellylike state and are found in either very deep waters or very cold waters or in a

[24] Bird et al., "Circum-Arctic Resource Appraisal, http://pubs.usgs.gov/fs/2008/3049/.
[25] Jeffrey Jones, "Update 2- Imperial, Exxon, Mobil Win Beaufort Sea Acreage," Reuters, July 19, 2007, http://www.reuters.com/article/companyNewsAndPR/idUSN1942038220070719; CBC, "Ottawa Awards BP $1.2 Billion in Exploration Permits in Beaufort Sea," CBC News, July 8, 2008, http://www.cbc.ca/canada/north/story/2008/06/09/beaufort-leases.html.
[26] S. R. Dallimore and T. S. Elliot, eds., *Scientific Results from the Mallik 2002 Gas Hydrate Production Research Well Program, MacKenzie Delta, Northwest Territories, Canada*, Geological Survey of Canada Bulletin 585 (Ottawa: 2005).

combination of both. They are believed to have formed as gas seeps through porous rocks and form as a precipitate on the ocean bottom. Large amounts of gas hydrates have been located in the Beaufort Sea. To date, there are no economically viable means of exploiting this new resource. However, numerous studies are attempting to determine the feasibility of using the hydrates.

Although oil and gas are the primary focus of most states with respect to the Arctic, there are other significant mineral deposits in the region. On the basis of three new northern mines, Canada has moved from producing no diamonds to becoming the world's third-largest producer of diamonds.[27] Possibly the world's largest and purest deposit of iron ore is being prepared for development in Nunavut, Canada.[28] These are only a few of the many examples of actual and potential resources located in Canada's north.

The Arctic is also increasingly becoming a destination choice for tourism. The number of cruise ship vessels sailing to the waters around Alaska and recently to the waters around Greenland has increased substantially.[29] Although the excursions are expensive, it seems likely that as the ice continues to melt and the region becomes more accessible, tourism in the Arctic will increase.

One of the most controversial economic potentials of the Arctic is the prospect of new northern shipping routes. The debate as to when and if the Arctic will emerge as a transit point for international shipping is extensive.[30] There are three potential routes that may be taken: the Northwest Passage, the Northern Sea Route and Northeast Passage, and over the North Pole. In 2010, the Russians have been encouraging international shipping through the Northern Sea Route. Canada has experienced some increase in ship traffic in the Northwest Passage, but at this point, most of the shipping is destination based and not transit shipping. Although international shipping through northern routes may occur, it remains more theoretical than practical at this time. Nevertheless, both Canada and Russia are taking active steps to assert their control of the waterways.

At the same time that knowledge about Arctic resources is growing, newer technologies are being developed to facilitate the exploitation of those resources. South Korean shipyards are developing the means to build ice-strengthened oil and gas carriers. Several ice-strengthened oil tankers are already in use in Russian northern waters.[31] It is expected that similar gas carriers will soon be built.

[27] Statistics Canada, "Study: Diamonds."

[28] Fox Business, "Bafflinland Provides Update on Mary Rivers Project," December 5, 2008, http://www.foxbusiness.com/story/markets/industries/industrials/baffinland-provides-update-mary-river-project-2086450117/.

[29] Protection of the Arctic Marine Environment (PAME), Arctic Council, *Arctic Marine Shipping Assessment 2009 Report*, http://pame.is/images/stories/PDF_Files/AMSA_2009_Report_2nd_print.pdf.

[30] The *Arctic Marine Shipping Assessment Report* provides the best assessment of the possibilities of Arctic shipping through all routes.

[31] Rob Huebert, *The Newly Emerging Arctic Security Environment* (Calgary: Canadian Defence and Foreign Affairs Institute, March 2010).

CHANGING INTERNATIONAL REGIME

Perhaps one of the most important sources of changes in the Arctic is the changing nature of the international legal regime. In 1996, the UN Convention on the Law of the Sea (UNCLOS) came into force. As with the Arctic Council, Canada also played a central role in its creation.[32] The convention, often described as the constitution of the oceans, has emerged as one of the most significant international treaties of the modern era.[33] It codified existing maritime law and created new elements to provide for the improved utilization of the oceans. One of the most significant new elements of UNCLOS was to provide coastal states with the right to extend their control of their continental shelf beyond both their territorial seas and the economic exclusive zone (EEZ) through article 76.[34] If a state is able to scientifically demonstrate that it has a continental shelf that extends beyond its two-hundred-mile EEZ, it may claim the rights to its soil and subsoil. However, it cannot claim rights over the water column over the region. In effect, this gives the coastal state the rights to the resources on and below the seabed. This is clearly understood to be resources such as oil and gas deposits.

This right, codified in article 76, has worldwide ramifications. However, its impact is being particularly felt in the Arctic.[35] It is suspected that almost the entire Arctic Ocean may be claimed by the coastal states – Canada, the United States, Russia, Denmark, and Norway. The process created by UNCLOS gives the prospective states ten years from the point of their ratification of the convention to then embark on the necessary hydrographic studies to determine whether they are able to make a claim. Once they have completed their study, then they must submit their claim to a UN body – the Commission on the Limits of the Continental Shelf (CLCS).[36] This body will determine whether the claim is scientifically correct. If the submission is endorsed, then the submitting state must enter into negotiations with any neighbors whose claim overlaps with its own. The process is long and strenuous. Nevertheless, all of the Arctic states have been dedicating substantial resources to the process and have been taking it very seriously.

The prospect of creating new boundaries in the Arctic has resulted in some of the greatest concerns about the prospects of a land grab. Of course, the land that

---

[32] Robert E. Hage, *The Third United Nations Conference on the Law of the Sea: A Canadian Retrospective* (Toronto: Canadian Institute of International Affairs, 1983).

[33] R. R. Churchill and A. V. Lowe, *The Law of the Sea*, 3rd ed. (Manchester: Manchester University Press, 2002).

[34] United Nations, *The Law of the Sea, United Nations Convention on the Law of the Sea with final Index and Final Act of the Third United Nations Conference on the Law of the Sea* (New York: United Nations, 1983).

[35] Ron Macnab, "Nationalizing the Arctic Maritime Commons: UNCLOS Article 76 and the Polar Sea," *Yearbook of Polar Law* 2 (2010): 171–88.

[36] United Nations, Oceans and Law of the Sea, Division for Ocean Affairs and Law of the Sea, "Commission on the Limits of the Continental Shelf (CLCS)," 2007, http://www.un.org/Depts/los/clcs_new/clcs_home.htm.

is being grabbed is under water. To minimize concerns that the process may result in conflict, the five Arctic states met in Ilulissat, Greenland, in May 2008. At the meeting, the five Arctic states (the Arctic Five, or A5) reaffirmed their commitment to resolving their claims peacefully and in accordance with international law (and specifically the dispute settlement mechanism provided by the convention itself).[37]

But in spite of the efforts to cooperate, complicating factors may interfere with the intent to develop the new borders in a peaceful and orderly fashion. The first problem is that the United States has not signed or ratified the convention.[38] Enough Republican Senators have opposed the treaty over the years to prevent the two-thirds majority needed in the Senate to ratify the treaty. Following Obama's victory and the success of Democrats in the Senate, the hope was that the Americans would immediately accede to the treaty. But this did not happened. Instead the Obama administration made the passage of the Strategic Arms Reduction Treaty (START) its major priority devoting all of its political efforts to that task. Following the successful ratification of START, the Obama administration announced early in 2011 that it will now be focusing its efforts on the ratification of UNCLOS.[39] However, there have been no official statement yet from the administration and it remains uncertain as to when it will move on ratifying UNCLOS. Thus the expectation is that the United States will remain a nonparty to the convention for the time being.

The second complicating factor is that while the A5 has agreed to act cooperatively in the region, this commitment was made before the actual claims had been made. Only the Russians had gone public with their claim, which was returned by the CLCS as lacking in scientific evidence.[40] Thus, it is not yet known whether the other Arctic states, in particular the United States, Canada, and Denmark, will have overlaps with Russia or with one another. The hope is that the spirit of cooperation will continue if and when overlaps are found. But what will happen when real interests become challenged remains unknown. The convention allows for the extension of new ocean boundaries. This will result in the redrawing of the boundaries dividing the seabed of the Arctic Ocean. At this point, all of the Arctic states have committed to the peaceful and orderly delineation of those borders. However, what resources, if any, are at stake is not understood. Nor is it clear what the final map will look like.

[37] *The Ilulissat Declaration: Arctic Ocean Conference.*
[38] Rob Huebert, "The United States Arctic Policy: The Reluctant Arctic Power," *School of Public Policy Briefing Papers Focus on the United States* 2, no. 2 (May 2009): 1–26, http://www.policy school.ucalgary.ca/files/policystudies/SPP%20Briefing%20-%20HUEBERT%20online_2.pdf.
[39] InsideDefence.com, "Obama Administration To Push Law Of The Sea Treaty In Senate This Year," February 4, 2011 http://insidedefense.com/.
[40] United Nations, Oceans and Law of the Sea, Division for Ocean Affairs and Law of the Sea, "Commission on the Limits of the Continental Shelf (CLCS): Outer Limits of the Continental Shelf beyond 200 Nautical Miles from the Baselines: Submissions to the Commission: Submission by the Russian Federation," http://www.un.org/Depts/los/clcs_new/submissions_files/submission_rus.htm.

This is yet another part of the uncertainty surrounding the transformation of the Arctic.

THE NEW GEOPOLITICS OF THE ARCTIC

The Arctic is melting, which makes it more accessible. As it becomes more accessible, more resources are being discovered in the region. As more resources are discovered, new means of exploiting these resources are being developed, which will speed up the means by which the resources can be developed. At the same time, new developments in international law are changing what coastal states can claim as their own, which will transform the means by which the Arctic states can assert control of the region. When considered in its entirety, it is clear that the Arctic is about to be a much more significant region in the international system.

As a result of these transformations, the circumpolar states are beginning to develop new security policies and capabilities. A new geopolitical reality is taking shape in the Arctic region. The assessment of this new geopolitical reality is difficult to make because so many new actions and policies are in transition. As in any transitory period many of the indicators of this transformation remain unclear. Furthermore, unlike the Cold War era, this period includes efforts to improve cooperation at the same time that the various state actors are beginning to improve their military capabilities to engage in unilateral actions to protect their Arctic interests. It would appear that the circumpolar states are hoping for the best but are beginning to prepare for something different. These actions have also started to attract the attention of non-Arctic states and actors such as China and the European Union, who have also begun to develop Arctic policies.[41] So the security steps that the Arctic states are taking must be addressed.

DENMARK

Denmark's link to the Arctic is through its relationship with Greenland. Though Greenland, a former Danish colony, was given home rule in 1979, Copenhagen retains certain administrative responsibilities over Greenland, notably in foreign and defense issues. In the summer of 2009, Denmark announced that it will be establishing an Arctic military command and task group. It is also creating an Arctic response force that will include combat aircraft.[42] The main focus of Denmark's Arctic security concerns has been on homeland security for Greenland in terms of

[41] Space limitations prevent an examination of the security policies of the non-Arctic states. For this and an in-depth examination of the security policies and actions of the Arctic states, see Rob Huebert, *The Newly Emerging Arctic Security Environment* (Calgary: Canadian Defence and Foreign Affairs Institute, March 2010).

[42] "Arctic Rivalry Heats Up," *Copenhagen Post*, July 15, 2009, http://www.cphpost.dk/news/national/88-national/46275-Arctic-rivalry-heating-up.html.

search and rescue, surveillance and maintenance of territorial sovereignty, fishery protection, and oil-spill reaction. However, Denmark retains strong relations with the other Nordic countries and has aligned its Arctic policies with those of NATO and the European Union (which Greenland is not a member of).

The Danish armed forces are currently going through a modernization of their capabilities. Their navy took delivery of three ice-strengthened frigates (*Thetis* class) in the early 1990s. In the mid-2000s, the navy took command of two new Combat/Flexible Support Ships (*Absalon* class). These vessels are designed to be assigned a multiple range of tasks and are relatively large (6,300 metric tons).

FINLAND

Like Sweden and Denmark, Finland does not have an independent Arctic policy, but it chooses to influence and endorse the policies of the European Union, the Nordic Council, and the Barents Euro-Arctic Council. Finland has been more engaged than Sweden in circumpolar affairs, having initiated the Arctic Environmental Protection Strategy in 1991 (the precursor to the Arctic Council). Significantly, it also proposed the Northern Dimension for the European Union, which was subsequently adopted soon after the 1999 Finnish European Union presidency spearheaded the formulation of a new Northern Dimension policy during its 2006 European Union presidency.

Finland's long border and history with Russia explains its relative activity in Arctic affairs. Perhaps more than any other country, Finland is vulnerable to the social and environmental problems faced by Russia in its northwest region, which the European Union's Northern Dimension policies are meant to mitigate. It is also strongly interested in promoting links and cooperation between Russia and the west so as not to repeat the tensions of the Cold War era, felt so acutely in Helsinki.

Although Finland is not a member of NATO, it preserves the option of joining that organization in the future and describes its objectives, tasks, and obligations as analogous with the foreign and security policy goals of NATO and the European Union. Its reluctance to join is related to the fact that it does not want to antagonize Russia over its membership. Through the Partnership for Peace Program, Finland has begun to conduct military operations with NATO in the region.[43]

ICELAND

The importance of the High North was outlined in a report delivered to the Icelandic parliament in November 2007, whereby the foreign minister declared that the

[43] Tom Sullivan, "In Sweden's Far North, a Convergence of Fighter Jets, Reindeer, and Hurt Feelings," *Christian Science Monitor*, June 9, 2009, http://www.csmonitor.com/2009/0611/p06s10-woeu.html.

High North is a new core feature of Icelandic foreign policy.[44] Iceland's interests in the changing Arctic are especially related to the economic opportunities presented by transarctic shipping, for which it would hope to become a hub.

From 1951 to 2006, the United States provided for the defense of Iceland through the Iceland Defence Force (IDF), headquartered in Keflavík, through the deployment of American air assets including fighter aircraft. In 2006, these were withdrawn by the United States. The U.S.-Icelandic Defense Agreement was established at the urging of NATO during the Cold War, when Iceland was situated in a particularly strategic location in the North Atlantic. Given the new security realities of the twenty-first century, the United States unexpectedly announced its decision to withdraw the IDF in March 2006, a task that was completed by September of that year. Iceland has no military force of its own. The Icelandic coast guard is responsible for security, search-and-rescue, and law enforcement activities at sea. Along with Norway, Iceland has been particularly active in encouraging a stronger NATO presence in the Arctic region.

Although the bilateral defense agreement with the United States remains in effect, Iceland has sought other partnerships to ensure that its defense and security needs are met. The cornerstone of its new security policy is its membership in NATO, which has offered Iceland a limited air policing arrangement from 2008 until 2011. Iceland has further signed political declarations on cooperation on security matters in the North Atlantic, with Denmark and Norway, respectively.[45] Discussions with Canada, Germany, the United Kingdom, and the Nordic Council (Nordic Supportive Defence Structures [NORDSUP] Cooperation) are in progress. Commitments from Norway and the United Kingdom have been particularly important. Iceland has also been seeking closer relations with China in terms of international shipping. At this point, it is uncertain what shape this relationship will look like.[46]

NORWAY

Of the European countries, Norway has the most developed Arctic policy, and its involvement in circumpolar affairs has been high, particularly during its 2006–09 chairmanship of the Arctic Council. The Soria Moria Declaration,[47] a government manifesto issued in 2005 by the Norwegian governing coalition parties, established a holistic "northern areas" strategy. It regarded "the Northern Areas as Norway's most

[44] Address by Minister of Foreign Affairs Ingibjörg Sólrún Gísladóttir, November 8, 2007, http://www.iceland.org/media/rom/speech_of_foreign_minister.pdf.

[45] Iceland Minister for Foreign Affairs, *Changed Security Environment – New Perspectives in Defence*, November 27, 2007, http://www.mfa.is/speeches-and-articles/nr/4095.

[46] "Iceland Invites China to Arctic Shipping," *Barents Observer*, September 22, 2010, http://www.barentsobserver.com/iceland-invites-china-to-Arctic-shipping.4821566.html.

[47] *The Soria Moria Declaration on International Policy* (Norway), http://www.regjeringen.no/en/dep/smk/documents/Reports-and-action-plans/rapporter/2005/The-Soria-Moria-Declaration-on-Internati.html?id=438515.

important strategic target area in the years to come" and iterated that "the handling of Norwegian economic interests, environmental interests and security policy interests in the North are to be given high priority and are to be seen as being closely linked."

To that end, the Norwegian government's High North Strategy was issued on December 1, 2006.[48] Although the seven primary political priorities include such issues as environmental stewardship, resource development, international cooperation, cooperation with Russia, and cultural safeguarding, the first priority states that Norway "will exercise [its] authority in the High North in a credible, consistent and predictable way" and focuses on the exercising of sovereignty and the presence of armed forces.

The 2008 Norwegian defense document[49] reinforces that commitment, stating, "The northern regions are Norway's prime area for strategic investment."[50] Their importance is linked to "Norway's position as a significant energy exporter and as a country responsible for the administration of important natural resources extending over large sea areas."[51] To that end, Norway has been busy modernizing its coast guard and is establishing radar stations and open-water monitoring facilities in the Barents and Norwegian seas as a response to Russia's heightened military activities in the region. Norway is also one of only a handful of countries that boosted its defense spending in 2009. The defense budget, delivered in October 2008, continues the government's ongoing resolution to strengthen Norway's naval, land, and air defense capabilities in the High North and particularly in areas bordering Russia.[52] In particular, the Norwegian government has focused on improving both its maritime and its air force capabilities. This includes the construction of five new frigates built in Spanish shipyards that have been given an Aegis combat system,[53] and the decision to buy forty-eight F-35 strike fighters announced in November 2008.[54] In the summer of 2010, the Norwegian defense minister met with the head of the American navy. At the meeting, discussions were held on the sale of advanced antiship missiles for the F-35 and American training in northern Norway.[55] Norway has also developed

---

[48] *The Norwegian Government's High North Strategy*, December 2006, http://www.regjeringen.no/upload/UD/Vedlegg/strategien.pdf.

[49] Norway Ministry of Defense, *Norwegian Defence 2008*, http://www.regjeringen.no/upload/FD/Dokumenter/Fakta2008_eng.pdf.

[50] Ibid., 7.

[51] Ibid.

[52] Gerard O'Dwyer, "Norway to Boost 2009 Defense Spending," *Defense News*, October 15, 2008, http://www.defensenews.com/story.php?i=3772512.

[53] Endre Lunde, "Norway's New Nansen Class Frigates: Capabilities and Controversies," *Defence Industry Daily*, June 7, 2006, http://www.defenseindustrydaily.com/norways-new-nansen-class-frigates-capabilities-and-controversies-02329/.

[54] Robert Wall and Graham Warwick, "Norway Picking F-35 over Gripen NG," *Aviation Week*, November 20, 2008, http://www.aviationweek.com/aw/generic/story_channel.jsp?channel=defense&id=news/NORWAY11208.xml.

[55] Forsvars Departementet, "Looking for Cooperation in the North," August 19, 2010, http://www.regjeringen.no/nb/dep/fd/aktuelt/nyheter/2010/onsker-godt-samarbeid-i-nord.html?id=612522.

and built a class of six very fast (faster than one hundred knots) small missile boats. The *Skjold*-class missile fast-patrol boats are designed for antiship and antiaircraft combat missions in coastal waters.[56]

RUSSIA

Russia is the world's largest Arctic state and, with roughly 2 million inhabitants, it possesses by far the largest northern population. The Arctic region has been an important contributor to the Russian economy since the discovery of Siberian oil in the 1960s. In large measure, the recovery of the Russian economy over the past decade, as well as its continued health, has been and remains directly related to the export of oil and gas. By law, Russian oil and gas is a strategic resource and development is heavily controlled by the central government. All told, the industry accounts for roughly 20 percent of the country's gross domestic product, with fully 22 percent of the nation's export earnings being produced in the Arctic. The tax revenue from the state-owned gas company Gazprom alone makes up roughly 25 percent of Russian federal tax revenues.

The principal thrust of Russian Arctic policy has thus been the protection and expansion of its northern resource base. Russian President Dmitry Medvedev, a former head of Gazprom, has publicly described the use of Arctic resources as central to the country's energy security, stating, "Our first and main task is to turn the Arctic into Russia's resource base of the 21 century."[57] Both the state's new Arctic policy (adopted by the Russian Security Council in September 2008)[58] and the state security policy (approved in May 2009)[59] emphasize the growing energy potential of the north and the importance of its development.

The majority of the Arctic's undeveloped hydrocarbons, which Russian companies are investing billions of dollars developing, are located in the offshore areas on the continental shelf. The Russian shelf is estimated to possess vast amounts of oil and gas and Moscow is sparing no effort to map the region and claim as much undersea territory as possible. A number of expeditions have been made to this effect with the most dramatic being the planting of a Russian flag on the seafloor of the North Pole. Russia is attempting to make its claim to an extended continental shelf under the guidelines of UNCLOS and the government has claimed it will make its submission sometime in 2010 or 2011.

---

[56] "Skjold Class Missile Fast Patrol Boats, Norway," *Naval Technology*, http://www.naval-technology.com/projects/skjold/.

[57] "Medvedev: Arctic Resources Are Key to Russia's Future," *Seattle Times*, (September 18, 2008), http://seattletimes.nwsource.com/html/nationworld/2008187217_russia18.html.

[58] Russian Security Council, *Fundamentals of Public Policy of the Russian Federation in the Arctic up to 2020 and Beyond*, September 2008, http://www.scrf.gov.ru/documents/98.html.

[59] Arctic Focus, "Russian Security Strategy Released" (May 15, 2009), http://Arcticfocus.com/2009/05/15/new-russian-security-strategy-released/.

Russia's Transport Minister Igor Levitin has also stated Moscow's desire to substantially increase maritime traffic along the Northern Sea Route, otherwise known as the Northeast Passage.[60] The potential for increased shipping generated by the Arctic's thinning ice is reflected in ship orders. A large number of Arctic liquid natural gas and oil tankers with ice-breaking capacity have been ordered by oil and gas companies, and the government has announced plans to order four to six nuclear-powered icebreakers by the year 2020.

Russia has been working within the boundaries of international law in its attempts to expand its continental shelf and, through the Ilulissat Declaration and other public pronouncements,[61] has expressed a desire to resolve Arctic disputes through diplomatic channels. However, recent policy documents and pronouncements by both political and military leaders make it plain that Russia considers military force an acceptable means of defending what it considers its Arctic interests.

To this end, Russia has increased its military presence in the North over the past five years. Strategic bomber flights have been resumed over the Arctic Ocean and the Norwegian Sea, whereas in 2008, the Russian navy announced that its fleet had "resumed a warship presence in the Arctic."[62] Moscow has also declared an increase in the operational radius of its northern submarine fleet to include much of the Arctic Ocean. These Arctic naval patrols include the area off the Spitsbergen archipelago, where Russia and Norway have a dispute over the extent of Norway's exclusive economic zone. This is in keeping with the high priority placed on the Arctic by the maritime doctrine adopted under former president Vladimir Putin.[63]

The Russian ability to project power into the Arctic has strengthened over the past five years and will likely increase in the near future. The 2009 Russian budget called for a 25 percent hike in defense spending.[64] In 2010, the government announced an even larger defense budget increase to support its new capital programs.[65] A large portion of this is earmarked for the navy, which is currently building its next-generation *Borey-* and *Yasen*-class nuclear submarines, laid down as part of a state armaments program through 2015.[66] Select army and special forces units have

[60] "Northern Sea Route to Charge Shipping Companies," *Barents Observer*, March 2009, http://www.barentsobserver.com/index.php?id=4563114&xxforceredir=1&noredir=1.

[61] Arctic Council, *Ilulissat Declaration*, May 2008, http://Arctic-council.org/filearchive/Ilulissat-declaration.pdf.

[62] "Russian Navy Resumes Arctic Warship Patrols," *Javno*, July 2008, http://www.javno.com/en-world/russian-navy-says-resumes-Arctic-warship-patrols_164326.

[63] *Maritime Doctrine of Russian Federation 2020*, July 2001, http://www.oceanlaw.org/downloads/Arctic/Russian_Maritime_Policy_2020.pdf.

[64] "Russian Defence Increased 25%," *Pravda*, September 2008, http://english.pravda.ru/news/russia/19-09-2008/106406-russia_defense_budget-0.

[65] "New Heights for Russian Defence Spending," *Barents Observer*, September 23, 2010, http://www.barentsobserver.com/index.php?id=4821994&xxforceredir=1&noredir=1.

[66] "Reactor on Russia's Newest Nuclear Submarine Fired Up," *RIA Novosti*, November 2008, http://en.rian.ru/russia/20081121/118453947.html.

also begun increased training in Arctic warfare.[67] In 2009, Russia deployed several nuclear-missile-carrying submarines (*Delta-IVs*) escorted by nuclear-powered attack submarines to Arctic waters, where they launched several missiles in a test.[68] In September 2010, a large portion of both the submarine and the surface forces of the Northern Fleet exercised in the Barents Sea.[69] The exercises included more than four thousand troops and tested a wide range of Russian missiles. They had also announced that in the spring of 2010 that they would land paratroopers at the North Pole.[70] However, for reasons unknown, this was canceled. In October 2010, the head of the Russian navy, Admiral Vladimir Vysotsky, announced that, "in accordance with the Russian Armed Forces plan of strategic deterrence, we will continue to take measures aimed at demonstrating military presence in the Arctic."[71] To this end, he announced that in 2010 the Russian navy had conducted more than ten military patrols in the Arctic and that the air force had conducted sixteen bomber flights over the northern parts of the Atlantic and Arctic oceans. In September, a bizarre incident involving an American frigate, the USS *Taylor*, occurred in the Barents Sea. The American vessel had just concluded an official port visit to Murmansk and was headed home. While in international waters, a Russian maritime patrol aircraft made two low passes with its bomb bay open over the American ship. The incident was officially closed when the head of the American navy, Admiral Gary Roughead, received a "satisfying explanation" about the incident. However, the content of the explanation was not made public.[72]

In part to support its position in the region, Moscow has become increasingly assertive in its relations with the West. The state's national security policy has labeled the United States a "main rival" of Russia, whereas Russian state-owned newspapers have increasingly criticized the United States and NATO, accusing the West of coveting Russian resources and of attempting to militarize the north.[73]

The security and development of the Arctic's resources, particularly the oil and gas reserves, is the principal aim of Russian Arctic policy. Concurrently, Moscow's increasingly assertive foreign policy generally has been made possible by the wealth

[67] "Russia to Deploy Special Arctic Force by 2020," *RIA Novosti*, http://www.globalsecurity.org/wmd/library/news/russia/2009/russia-090327-rianovosti02.htm.

[68] "Russia Outwitted US Strategic Defences with Missile Test," *RIA Novosti*, July 15, 2009, http://en.rian.ru/mlitary_news/20090715/155530936.html.

[69] Ministry of Defense of the Russian Federation, "News," September 7, 2010, http://www.mil.ru/info/1069/details/index.shtml?id=75615.

[70] "Russia Paratroopers Head towards North Pole," *Barents Observer*, July 29 2009, http://www.barentsobserver.com/russia-paratroopers-head-towards-north-pole.4615739–116320.html.

[71] "Russia Increases Combat Capabilities in Arctic," *Barents Observer*, October 4, 2010, http://www.barentsobserver.com/russia-increases-combat-capabilities-in-Arctic.4826505–58932.html.

[72] "Bomb Bay Doors Open over US Frigate," *Barents Observer*, September 9, 2010, http://www.barentsobserver.com/index.php?id=4819811&xxforceredir=1&noredir=1.

[73] Azeri-Press Agency (APA), "Russian National Security Strategy until 2020: Main Rival Is the United States Again in the Next 12 Years," APA, December 2008, http://en.apa.az/news.php?id=94381.

generated by those same reserves. Although Russian action in the Arctic has remained within the boundaries of international law, the state is certainly prepared to act unilaterally if it supposes its interest to be at risk.

SWEDEN

Of all the Arctic states, Sweden has been the least engaged in matters of circumpolar relations and Arctic security, and it has not articulated an Arctic or High North foreign policy. The reasons for this may be linked to geography. Sweden does not share a border with Russia or a coastline with the Arctic Ocean. Thus, Sweden has fewer security and economic interests in its northern area.

Although its participation in the Arctic Council has been limited, Sweden has been active in other regional organizations, including the Nordic Council, the Barents Euro-Arctic Council, and the European Union. Its defense and security policy emphasizes cooperation with the Nordic countries and the European Union, as well as NATO, despite the fact that it is not a member. There is broad political support in Sweden for the further development of bilateral and multilateral Nordic military cooperation. However, no Swedish strategy has been announced related to the new security challenges facing the Arctic.

There are some signs that Sweden is moving toward greater cooperation with NATO, thus causing some observers to speculate that it may be moving toward joining the alliance.[74] In June 2009, Sweden hosted a large NATO military exercise – Loyal Arrow – under the terms of the Partnership for Peace Programme in its northern region of Lapland.[75] It involved more than fifty aircraft and two thousand troops, including those from Finland, Germany, the United Kingdom, and the United States (also through NATO's Partnership for Peace).

The Swedish government is also investing in the development of a very technologically advanced warship. The *Visby*-class corvette is one of the world's first stealth warships. Made of advanced composite materials and capable of speeds of more than thirty-five knots, it is a small vessel that has been given a very powerful antisubmarine, antiaircraft, and antiship capability.[76] Five such vessels will be produced.

Sweden has also recently eliminated its draft and is moving to a smaller and more professional armed forces. In a recent interview, the Swedish chief of defense staff explained that the move was designed to give the Swedish forces greater international mobility, including a greater ability to operate in the High North.[77]

[74] Peter Vinthagen Simpson, "Liberals: Sweden Must Join NATO," *The Local: Sweden's News in English*, May 13, 2009, http://www.thelocal.se/19406/20090513/.
[75] Sullivan, "In Sweden's Far North," http://www.csmonitor.com/2009/0611/p06s10-woeu.html.
[76] "Visby Class Corvettes, Sweden," *Naval Technology*, http://www.naval-technology.com/projects/visby/.
[77] "General Sverker Goranson, Sweden's Chief of Defence Staff," *Defence News*, November 2, 2009, http://www.defensenews.com/story.php?i=4354246&c=FEA&s=INT.

UNITED STATES

In January 2009, the United States released a comprehensive Arctic policy, prioritizing the state's interest in protecting the region's environment, developing its natural resources, and maintaining national security.[78] This policy replaced the 1994 Arctic Policy.[79] The new policy statement illustrates the growing importance of the Arctic in American policy, driven principally by the increasing accessibility of the Arctic waters and the improving prospects for gas and oil extraction.

This sentiment is echoed by the military, which plans to increase surveillance with both unmanned aerial vehicles (UAVs) and manned aircraft. Since the 1950s, the U.S. Navy has maintained the capability to operate in the Arctic waters and the thinning of the ice has made an expansion of its operations there increasingly likely. Dating back to 2000, the navy has been examining the possibility of an ice-free Arctic and the potential and challenges that such a development would create.[80] As maritime traffic and resource extraction increase, the navy will likely increase the tempo of its submarine patrols and perhaps even deploy surface assets to the northern waters – a scenario that the navy has studied.

American military leaders have also recently expressed concern about the growing potential threats to the Arctic and have begun to call for increased American awareness and capability. General Victor Renuart, commander of the Northern Command, has publicly discussed what he sees as a growing security problem in the Arctic.[81] In October 2009, the U.S. Navy released its *Navy Arctic Roadmap*, which argues that the navy must begin to rebuild its capacity to act in the Arctic because of the coming international interests and challenges in the region.[82]

The United States continued to send nuclear-powered submarines to Arctic waters throughout the post–Cold War era. It had sent only *Los Angeles* and *Sea Wolf* attack submarines to the Arctic. Many observers had assumed that their newest class of submarines were not capable of under-ice operations. This suggested that the U.S. Navy was moving away from Arctic operations in the long term. However in November 2009, the navy publicly announced that the USS *Texas* – one of the first *Virginia*-class submarines – had reached the North Pole.[83] It is clear that all classes of American submarines can go to northern waters.

[78] U.S. Department of State, *National Security Presidential Directive and Homeland Security Presidential Directive*, January 2009, http://www.fas.org/irp/offdocs/nspd/nspd-66.htm.

[79] U.S. Department of State, "Fact Sheet: US Arctic Policy," *Dispatch*, December 26, 1994, http://findarticles.com/p/articles/mi_m1584/is_/ai_16709524.

[80] U.S. Office of Naval Research, *Operations in an Ice-Free Arctic*, http://www.natice.noaa.gov/icefree/finalArcticreport.pdf.

[81] John Bennett, "Renuart: New President Faces Cyber, Arctic Threats," *Defense News*, August 21, 2008, http://www.defensenews.com/story.php?i=3684947.

[82] Task Force Climate Change/Oceanographer of the U.S. Navy, *U.S. Navy Arctic Roadmap*, October 2009.

[83] "USS *Texas* Pays Icy Visit to Arctic," *Honolulu Advertiser*, November 8, 2009, http://www.honoluluadvertiser.com/article/20091108/COLUMNISTS32/911080383/0/COLUMNISTS32/USS-Texas-pays-icy-visit-to-Arctic.

Despite the capability and stated willingness to act unilaterally in defense of American interests, U.S. policy considers multilateral cooperation as the most desirable means of dealing with most Arctic issues. The United States is a signatory of the Ilulissat Declaration (Greenland, May 2008), pledged to resolve boundary difficulties within the legal framework of UNCLOS, and government policy statements have emphasized this cooperative approach.[84] American policy also recognizes the utility of international cooperation in the realm of Arctic research, with regards to environmental protection and through the Arctic Council. However, U.S. policy emphasizes that the council should stay "within its limited mandate of environmental protection and sustainable development" and not become involved in matters of defense or state policy.

American Arctic policy is largely governed by the state's desire to see an orderly and environmentally nonintrusive development of the region's hydrocarbon reserves; the establishment of transit rights through the Arctic straits; and the assurance of national security from terrorist, criminal, or state-based threats in the region. However, the policy makes it clear that as much as it wishes to see the region developed in a cooperative fashion, its core interests will be defended by unilateral action if necessary.

CANADA

So where does this leave Canada? Like its northern neighbors, for the past eight years, Canada has been rethinking its Arctic security policies. Although it continues to speak in terms of defending its "Arctic sovereignty," it is increasingly taking action that bolsters its ability to provide security. Over the past decade, and particularly since 2005, the Arctic has come to play an increasingly prominent role in Canadian policy as the Prime Minister's Office, the Department of National Defense, the Department of Foreign Affairs, and a host of other federal departments have promoted the region to the top of their agendas. In large measure, this has been a result of the improved accessibility of the north, the enhanced potential of hydrocarbon extraction and the reemergence of traditional questions of sovereignty.

Ottawa's concern over its position in the Arctic has been demonstrated by a series of new projects, begun or announced since 2005, which seek to improve the ability of Canadian military and civilian authorities to operate in the region. The Royal Canadian Navy is slated to receive new *Polar*-class patrol ships (Arctic offshore patrol ships, AOPS), capable of sustained Arctic operations,[85] and the coast guard icebreaker *Louis St. Laurent* is scheduled to be replaced by a new large

---

[84] Arctic Council, *Ilulissat Declaration*, May 2008, http://Arctic-council.org/filearchive/Ilulissat-declaration.pdf.

[85] Canadian Department of National Defense, *PMO Arctic/Offshore Patrol Ship*, http://www.forces.gc.ca/admmat/aops-npea/home-accueil-eng.asp.

icebreaker, the $720 million *John G. Diefenbaker* in 2017.[86] To supply those vessels, a new military and civilian deepwater resupply center is also being constructed at Nanisivik, on Baffin Island.[87] As of October 2010, there had been no word on when construction would actually begin for the AOPS and new icebreaker. Work has been progressing on the resupply center. Interestingly, the Department of Defense has begun to use purchases initially made for Afghanistan in the north, but it has not really discussed this in the public sphere. The recently acquired C-17 strategic lift aircraft landed for the first time in Alert in April 2010.[88] The aircraft were used again for an exercise conducted in Resolute in August 2010. Given the vast improvement that this aircraft provides over the rest of the Canadian airlift, this is a very significant improvement in the Canadian Forces' ability to move equipment.

Prime Minister Stephen Harper has also announced an Arctic Training Centre in Resolute Bay for the army, which is intended to support regional military and civilian emergency operations, to increase capabilities and to quicken response times.[89] The Canadian Rangers force is also being augmented and a new army reserve unit is being established in Yellowknife.

In addition, the Canadian military is actively seeking to increase its surveillance capability over the region with UAVs and manned aircraft. It is also in the process of establishing its Northern Watch system, which uses both land-based and underwater sensors to detect vessels passing through choke points in the Northwest Passage.[90] In March 2009, the Polar Epsilon project came on line. It is a space-based surveillance system involving Canada's new RADARSAT 2 satellite, designed in part to monitor the ocean approaches of the Arctic.[91] The Canadian government has also announced plans to develop the next generation of satellites called RADARSAT Constellation.

In a further attempt to increase Canadian control over the Arctic waters, the government announced in August 2008 that the coast guard's northern reporting system (NORDREG) will be mandatory for all vessels in the Canadian Arctic.[92] Previously, the Canadian government only requested that foreign vessels notify the Canadian government when they entered Canadian northern waters. This meant that a foreign vessel could enter these waters without the Canadian government being

---

[86] Prime Minister of Canada, *The John G. Diefenbaker National Icebreaker Project*, http://pm.gc.ca/eng/media.asp?id=2252.

[87] Royal Canadian Navy, *Arctic Deepwater Port*, http://www.navy.forces.gc.ca/cms/3/3-a_eng.asp?category=7&id=623.

[88] Jerome Lessard, "8 Wing Pilot Performed World's First C-17 Landings in Alert," *Trentonian*, April 17 2010, http://www.trentonian.ca/ArticleDisplay.aspx?e=2552914.

[89] Prime Minster of Canada, *Canadian Forces Arctic Training Centre*, http://pm.gc.ca/eng/media.asp?id=1785.

[90] Defence Research and Development Canada, *Northern Watch TD*, http://www.ottawa.drdc-rddc.gc.ca/html/background-eng.html.

[91] Canadian Department of Defense, *Polar Epsilon Project*, http://www.mdn.ca/site/news-nouvelles/view-news-afficher-nouvelles-eng.asp?id=2931.

[92] Prime Minister of Canada, *Backgrounder – Extending the Jurisdiction of Canadian Environment and Shipping Laws in the Arctic*, August 2008, http://pm.gc.ca/eng/media.asp?id=2246.

aware that it was there. Therefore Canada did not have real control over the vessels. This changed in 2010; since then, all foreign vessels are required to report their presence. At the same time, Ottawa announced the extension of its jurisdictional limit under the Arctic Waters Pollution Prevention Act from one hundred to two hundred nautical miles.[93]

CONCLUSION

Canada is rediscovering itself as a circumpolar nation. Although the concept of the "True North strong and free" has always been integrated into the psyche of the country, in truth, as a country, Canada has seldom dedicated much attention or resources to its northern region. Historically, its international focus was always directed either south toward the United States or east toward Europe, whereas the Arctic was largely ignored. However, the rapid development of events in the Arctic region is forcing Canada to sit up and take serious notice of its northern area. The combined impact of climate change, resource development, technology advancement, and a changing geopolitical environment is transforming the fundamental nature of the circumpolar world. This transformation is resulting in an Arctic that is becoming increasingly accessible to the rest of the world, with ramifications that are not yet fully understood. What is understood is that with greater accessibility of the Arctic, new questions are emerging as to the role that it will play in the international system. As such, each of the states that border the region has begun the process of reexamining its northern policies.

As with the other Arctic states, Canada has been wrestling with its role in the Arctic. In particular, it has been addressing two core issues: how does it control the region, and how does it make the region secure? In Canada, the first challenge is referred to as the defense of Canada's Arctic sovereignty. This is the issue that attracts the most attention in Canada. It revolves around the control of international shipping through the Northwest Passage and the determination of the maritime boundaries framing the Canadian Arctic. However, in Canada, the term *Arctic sovereignty* has become synonymous with efforts to control the entire maritime and land region that Canada claims in the Arctic. The second issue that follows the control of this region is the means by which Canada then attempts to secure the regions. There are two main challenges that Canada faces as it adapts to a rapidly international Arctic.

Successive Canadian governments have wrestled with the balance between unilateral and multilateral means to achieve Arctic security. This has meant that careful attention must be paid to the balance required between the development of both diplomatic and military means to achieve Canadian Arctic security. At the heart of the debate is understanding what Canadian Arctic security is. It is not at

[93] Canadian Department of Transportation, *Arctic Waters Pollution Prevention Act*, http://www.tc.gc.ca/Acts-Regulations/acts/1985cA-12/menu.htm.

all clear what the term actually means – it has different meanings for different people.

Historically, Canadian governments have never made hard decisions based on their understanding of Arctic security. Rather, since the end of the 1960s, to appeal to a wide range of Canadians, they were able to offer innovative policies to "secure" the Canadian north without ever backing them with any substantial expenditure.

Canadian policy makers were able to get away with the policy of talking loudly but carrying a very small stick because of two factors. First, the extremely inhospitable climatic conditions of the north made it completely inaccessible but for a few. Only a small number of states actually possessed the technological capabilities to build and operate nuclear-powered submarines, icebreakers, and long-range aircraft that could venture into the region. In this context, Canada had to contend only with the actions of non-Canadians in a small but very significant range of activities. The most significant was the development of the Arctic Ocean as a major front of the Cold War.

Climate change is melting the Arctic. What had previously been a region of stark beauty that was barred to all but northern indigenous people, the most intrepid of explorers, and more recently icebreakers and nuclear-powered submarines is opening to the world. The promise of new resource development, new shipping routes, and other economic opportunity now beckons. New technologies are being developed that will speed the opening of the Arctic as a "new" international region. In the face of this opening, the Arctic states are attempting to ensure that cooperation and international law provide the rules governing international interaction in the region. But as much all states proclaim their commitment to the peaceful and cooperative development of the Arctic, all are rebuilding their military capabilities to operate in the region. Although it would appear that all of the Arctic states are hoping that cooperation is the defining feature of the region, they are preparing and training in case that does not happen.

It is in such an environment that Canada now finds itself. Long accustomed to being able to proclaim itself an Arctic state but without really having to do much, it now finds itself having to make difficult and expensive decisions to ensure that it is able to defend and protect its Arctic interests. In an era where the Arctic is opening to the world, Canada is finding it necessary to take the steps that truly defend the "True North strong and free." It may be free, but it will not be cheap.

13

Polar Race or Polar Saga?

Canada and the Circumpolar World

P. Whitney Lackenbauer

Climate change is transforming the Arctic. The ice cover on the Arctic Ocean is shrinking in breadth and depth, permafrost is melting, and indigenous flora and fauna are threatened. Questions abound about what these changes will mean for northern peoples and for stability and security in the circumpolar world. Political rhetoric in Canada has heated up, prompted by uncertainty about Canada's hold on its Arctic. Much of this discourse affirms just how little southern Canadians actually know about the north. Although Canadians pay reverence to "the True North strong and free" in our national anthem, the stark reality is that the vast majority lived huddled along the southern boundary with the United States. Ignorance about the Arctic breeds alarmism. The promise of cooperation and dialogue with northern Canadians and our circumpolar neighbors, which seemed to frame government plans in the 1990s, is often jettisoned in recent political pledges to "stand up for Canada." If many academics and journalists are to be believed, the circumpolar agenda is dominated by a "polar race," with a concomitant sovereignty and security crisis precipitated by climate change and competing interests in "our" Arctic.

After the last round of frenzied debate over Canadian sovereignty in the wake of the 1985 *Polar Sea* voyage, Franklyn Griffiths suggested that the Arctic states had to decide whether they wanted the region to be one of enhanced civility or one of military competition. In his view, accepting "an integrated concept of security – one in which military requirements are combined with an awareness of the need to act for ecological, economic, cultural, and social security," would allow northerners to play a more direct role in setting agendas and fostering cooperation and dialogue.[1] In the early twenty-first century, amid rhetoric about a "new Cold War" in the Arctic, commentators like Rob Huebert suggest that cooperative arrangements are less credible. In a supposed race for resources, the Russians, Americans, Danes, and

---

[1] Franklyn Griffiths, "Civility in the Arctic," in *Arctic Alternatives: Civility or Militarism in the Circumpolar North*, ed. Franklyn Griffiths (Toronto: Science for Peace and Samuel Stevens, 1992), 279–309.

other energy-hungry nations are alleged to threaten Canada's northern inheritance. Since coming to office in 2006, the Conservative government's initiatives have emphasized the primacy of security (albeit couched in the language of sovereignty) through its commitments to enhance Canadian northern defense capabilities. By extension, northern indigenous leaders are frustrated that their voices have been pushed to the margins.[2]

The time for Canadian action in the Arctic has indeed come, but it should not be justified by partisan political rhetoric rooted in alarmism or paranoia. A crisis mentality is more conducive to symbolic reactions and hollow commitments, designed to serve positive short-term optics rather than sustained investment in Canadian capabilities and northern development. Although outside forces have typically driven the northern foreign policy agenda, the twenty-first century demands new thinking that carefully integrates domestic and international priorities if Canada wants to seize opportunities and take a leadership role in a rapidly evolving circumpolar world.

BACKGROUND

The current Arctic sovereignty and security "crisis" in Canada is predicated on the idea that previous governments have failed to protect Canadian interests. A more careful reading of the historical record suggests that the expansion and entrenchment of Canada's Arctic sovereignty through the twentieth century – albeit in an ad hoc and reactive manner – was a remarkable success given our parsimonious and halfhearted national commitment to investing in the region. Indeed, anxiety about "using or losing" our Arctic inheritance is more revealing of the Canadian psyche – particularly our chronic lack of confidence – than of objective realities. This anxiety also encourages a disproportionate emphasis on national defense at the expense of a broader suite of social, economic, and diplomatic initiatives.

Crisis rhetoric conceals a history of diplomacy and successful working relationships that helps to explain how and why Canada's security and sovereignty interests have been upheld over the past half century. A careful reading of historical lessons learned suggests that quiet diplomacy and practical, bilateral solutions have allayed most of the acute crisis concerns that precipitated government reactions since the Second World War. If Canada's goal has simply been to hang on to the north, expand its claims to include archipelagic waters, and incrementally entrench its claims in international law, then twentieth-century politicians and civil servants deserve modest praise. Over the past half century, Canada's most successful unilateral actions have been backed up by negotiations with our American allies: we have long-standing precedent in agreeing to disagree with the United States while safeguarding our essential interests. Legal scholar Donat Pharand's latest analysis

---

[2] See, for example, Mary Simon, "Inuit Say Budget Falls Far Short of Throne Speech promises," Inuit Tapiriit Kanatami (ITK) press release, 27 February 2008.

of Canada's sovereignty case is grounds for optimism, not pessimism: our internal waters case is strong.[3]

One hundred thirty years ago, Canada's sovereignty over the Arctic lands and waters was far from secure. The young Dominion inherited the islands of the high Arctic archipelago from Britain in 1880 not because it asked for them, but because Britain wanted to transfer responsibility for its nebulous rights after it received "two apparently innocent requests for concessions of arctic territory in 1874."[4] Canada proceeded to ignore the Arctic for the following quarter century, until the Klondike Gold Rush encouraged it to look north. In the early twentieth century, the government sent official missions to the Arctic to explore and to collect customs duties and licensing fees from whalers – a modest assertion of Canadian legal authority. In the interwar years, Royal Canadian Mounted Police (RCMP) posts dotted the northern landscape, suggesting a continuous presence.[5] There was little cause for worry about lands and islands once Canadian negotiators reached agreements with Denmark and Norway to settle terrestrial sovereignty claims. American explorers complied with Canadian regulations, and geography seemed to preclude any military threat; Canada was a "fireproof house" insulated from European and Asian conflagrations by distance and isolation.

The Second World War brought the Canadian north into new strategic focus. The Americans were worried about overland and air routes to Alaska, and they entered into agreements with Canada to build airfields, a highway, and an oil pipeline in the northwest. When American personnel swept into the region to complete these tasks, Prime Minister William Lyon Mackenzie King became paranoid that American developments, taken in the name of military security, would undermine Canadian sovereignty.[6] They did not. The Americans pulled out of Canada at war's end, and at Ottawa's request, the ownership of permanent facilities in the north passed into Canadian hands. Canada emerged unscathed in terms of territorial ownership, but senior officials certainly took note of the interdependency between security and sovereignty.[7]

The onset of the Cold War renewed pressures on Canada to balance sovereignty concerns with continental security imperatives. Polar projection maps revealed how

---

3 Donat Pharand, "Arctic Waters and the Northwest Passage: A Final Revisit," *Ocean Development and International Law* 38, nos. 1–2 (2007): 58–59.

4 Gordon W. Smith, "The Transfer of Arctic Territories from Great Britain to Canada in 1880, and Some Related Matters, as Seen in Official Correspondence," *Arctic* 14, no. 1 (1961): 53–73.

5 William R. Morrison, *Showing the Flag: The Mounted Police and Canadian Sovereignty in the North, 1894–1925* (Vancouver: University of British Columbia Press, 1985).

6 Shelagh Grant, *Sovereignty or Security? Government Policy in the Canadian North, 1936–1950* (Vancouver: University of British Columbia Press, 1988).

7 P. Whitney Lackenbauer, "Right and Honourable: Mackenzie King, Canadian-American Bilateral Relations, and Canadian Sovereignty in the Northwest, 1943–1948," in *Mackenzie King: Citizenship and Community*, eds. John English, Kenneth McLaughlin, and P. W. Lackenbauer (Toronto: Robin Brass Studios, 2002), 151–68.

Canada's strategic situation had changed when the United States and the Soviet Union became rivals. Arctic defenses were inextricably linked to American security, and the United States pushed for access to Canada's far north to build airfields and weather stations. Canadian officials grew apprehensive and cautious in authorizing new installations, whereas the Americans were anxious to proceed. Journalists began to talk about a looming sovereignty crisis, and scholars cite the era as further evidence that the Americans were willing to encroach on Canadian sovereignty to achieve their ends.[8] Discussion of this encroachment is distorted. "The Americans showed throughout a remarkable tolerance of the requirements the Canadians imposed upon them, even when some of these must have seemed rather picayune," the historian Gordon Smith concludes, "and they demonstrated a genuine willingness to observe Canadian regulations and generally accepted Canadian proprietorship." It was a "striking illustration of successful international cooperation and collaboration," with the United States officially acknowledging Canadian ownership of the entire Arctic archipelago.[9] The Joint Arctic Weather Station Agreement "thus ended the last potential legal threat to Canadian sovereignty over its Arctic *lands*."[10]

As the Cold War heated up in the 1950s, however, the Americans sought extensive air-defense systems extending to the northernmost reaches of the continent, launching yet another round of "crisis" rhetoric. The Distant Early Warning (DEW) Line, built across the seventieth parallel to detect Soviet bombers, was the boldest megaproject in Arctic history, dramatically altering the military, logistic, and demographic characteristics of the Canadian Arctic. The United States designed and paid for it. The Canadian military was already stretched thin by the North Atlantic Treaty Organization's (NATO) commitments in Europe, and Canada could not afford the kind of installations that the Americans wanted. Once again, Canadian officials negotiated a very favorable agreement that protected Canada's sovereignty and secured economic benefits for Canadian companies. Regardless, journalists and opposition politicians suggested throughout the construction and operational phases that Canada lacked practical control over its northland, and that the DEW Line, in the words of *Maclean's* editor Ralph Allen, "is the charter under which a tenth of Canada may very well become the world's most northerly banana republic."[11] Such an eventuality did not come to pass. Canada had concerns, and there were minor indiscretions, but those were managed effectively and the United States again proved an accommodating and respectful ally. The DEW Line was a major coup for Canadian sovereignty, reaffirming that the Arctic islands explicitly belonged to Canada and that the United States, as an ally, accommodated Canadian interests

---

8 See, for example, Grant, *Sovereignty or Security?*
9 Gordon W. Smith, "Weather Stations in the Canadian North and Sovereignty," *Journal of Military and Strategic Studies* 11, no. 3 (2009): 72–73.
10 N. D. Bankes, "Forty Years of Canadian Sovereignty Assertion in the Arctic, 1947–87," *Arctic* 40, no. 4 (December 1987): 287.
11 Ralph Allen, "Will DEW Line Cost Canada Its Northland?" *Maclean's*, 26 May 1956, 16–17, 68–72.

and sought harmony rather than relying on coercion to get its way. "Indeed we might be tempted to congratulate ourselves . . . for enjoying a 'free ride' at least in this area of our defense activities on our own soil, without any unpleasant side effects," Eric Wang of the Department of National Defense's (DND) legal department noted in a 1969 report.[12] Although there were no side effects in terms of sovereignty, there certainly were lasting cultural and environmental impacts.

During the Cold War, NATO and bilateral agreements with the United States guaranteed Canadian security at relatively little expense to the federal government. "Defending against help" from our allies meant that Canada needed only modest defense capabilities to ensure that the Americans did not take unilateral action to defend the northern approaches to North America. Canada could instead focus on being "providers" rather than "consumers" of security.[13] At various intervals, Canadian journalists and politicians panicked about Canada becoming too dependent on the United States and thus abdicating our de facto sovereignty. These concerns had some merit, but solid diplomacy produced sound agreements that preserved (and indeed extended) Canadian sovereignty. Conventional military threats were possible but not probable, and Canada was spared the expense of trying to defend its remote regions alone.

The legal status of the Northwest Passage (NWP) posed a more intractable dilemma than questions of terrestrial sovereignty. American and Soviet submarine activity in the Arctic raised concerns about what was going on under the sea ice in the waters of Canada's Arctic archipelago, but Canadian politicians sent mixed messages in the late 1950s about whether it formally claimed the waters. Canadian officials discussed issuing a more decisive claim in the 1960s. In 1965, the government introduced legislation to institute an exclusive fishing zone based on straight baselines along the east and west coasts, but it did not make a similar move in the Arctic, fearing U.S. objection. Canadians hoped that the Americans might support an extension of Canada's claim to Arctic waters for reasons of defense and national security, but the United States disagreed. In the view of the U.S. Navy, any such move could set a dangerous international precedent. Archipelagic states in Asia, such as Indonesia and the Philippines, could use the NWP as a pretext to unilaterally restrict the freedom of the seas in strategically sensitive areas. This could affect merchant shipping and naval mobility and heighten the potential for international controversy and conflict.[14] "We can't concede [Canada] the principle of territoriality

[12] E. B. Wang, "The Dew Line and Canadian Sovereignty," 26 May 1969, Library and Archives Canada (LAC), Record Group (RG) 25, file 27-10-2-2, part 1. See also R. J. Sutherland, "The Strategic Significance of the Canadian Arctic," in *The Arctic Frontier*, ed. R. St. J. MacDonald (Toronto: University of Toronto Press, 1966), 271.
[13] Desmond Morton, "Providing and Consuming Security in Canada's Century," *Canadian Historical Review* 81, no. 1 (2000): 1–28.
[14] See, for example, David L. Larson, "United States Interests in the Arctic Region," *Ocean Development and International Law* 20 (1989): 179.

[in the NWP] or we'd be setting a precedent for trouble elsewhere in the world," a Department of State official explained in 1969.[15] Ottawa retreated from its plans.[16]

The issue came to a head at the end of the decade. In 1969, American-owned Humble Oil sent the *Manhattan* icebreaker through the NWP to determine whether it was a viable commercial shipping route for oil and gas from the Beaufort Sea. The Canadian media reported the voyage as a direct challenge to Canada's Arctic sovereignty. "The legal status of the waters of Canada's Arctic archipelago is not at issue in the proposed transit of the Northwest Passage by the ships involved in the Manhattan project," Prime Minister Pierre Trudeau reassured the House of Commons on 15 May 1969. His government "welcomed the *Manhattan* exercise, has concurred in it and will participate in it."[17] After all, Humble Oil's request for Canadian cooperation implied that the passage was Canadian, even if the U.S. State Department would not say so specifically.[18] Panic followed. According to Maxwell Cohen in 1970, the *Manhattan* voyages "made Canadians feel that they were on the edge of another American [theft] of Canadian resources and rights which had to be dealt with at once by firm governmental action."[19]

Putting aside but not renouncing any claim to sovereignty, the Liberal government announced its "functional" approach to Canadian sovereignty in 1970. It cast the Arctic as an ecologically delicate region: Canada needed to extend its jurisdiction northward to ensure that foreign vessels did not pollute Canadian waters. The Arctic Waters Pollution Prevention Act (AWPPA) allowed Canada to regulate and control future tanker traffic through the NWP by creating a pollution prevention zone one hundred nautical miles outside the archipelago as well as the waters between the islands. The Territorial Sea and Fishing Zone Act extended Canada's territorial sea to twelve miles, subjecting the waters leading into the passage to Canadian control. Trudeau considered this a show of "legal moderation," but the Americans were furious, announced that Canada's unilateral actions were unjustified in international law, and consequently cut oil imports from Canada in retaliation.[20] While Canada increased its tempo of military activities in the North during the 1970s to "show the flag," it also set to work to consolidate its new regulations in international law. Although initially opposed to the AWPPA, in 1982, the United States supported the Canadian-sponsored article 234 of the UN Convention on the Law of the Sea (UNCLOS), which gave coastal states "the right to adopt and enforce non-discriminatory laws

[15] Milton Viorst, "Arctic Waters Must Be Free," *Toronto Star*, 20 September 1969, 16.
[16] Margaret W. Morris, "Boundary Problems Relating to the Sovereignty of the Canadian Arctic," in *Canada's Changing North*, ed. William C. Wonders (Toronto: McClelland and Stewart, 1971), 322; Smith, "Sovereignty in the North," 236–37; and Elizabeth B. Elliot-Meisel, *Arctic Diplomacy: Canada and the United States in the Northwest Passage* (New York: Peter Lang, 1998), 140.
[17] Canada, House of Commons, *Debates*, 15 May 1969, 8720–1.
[18] Elliot-Meisel, *Arctic Diplomacy*, 141.
[19] Maxwell Cohen, "The Arctic and the National Interest," *International Journal* 26, no. 1 (1970–71): 72.
[20] Elliot-Meisel, *Arctic Diplomacy*, 143.

and regulations for the prevention, reduction and control of marine pollution from vessels in ice-covered areas within the limits of the exclusive economic zone."[21]

The August 1985 voyage of the U.S. Coast Guard icebreaker *Polar Sea*, for reasonable operational reasons relating to the resupply of the American base at Thule, in Greenland, launched another Canadian crisis over the NWP. The Americans refused to seek official permission from Canada, recognizing that this would prejudice their own legal position. In response, the Mulroney government announced that Canada was officially implementing straight baselines around the Arctic archipelago effective 1 January 1986, thus claiming full sovereignty over the NWP as "historic, internal waters." Concurrently, it outlined an aggressive plan to exercise control over its waters and assert its Arctic sovereignty, including a Polar 8 icebreaker, new maritime patrol aircraft, a new northern training center, improved northern airfields, a dozen nuclear-powered attack submarines, and a fixed sonar-detection system at the entrances to the passage. It also promised to negotiate with the United States — a prudent move that, owing to Mulroney's close relationship with President Ronald Reagan, yielded the 1988 Arctic Cooperation Agreement requiring Canadian consent for U.S. icebreaker transits. By agreeing to disagree on the legal status of the passage, the two countries reached "a pragmatic solution based on our special bilateral relationship, our common interest in cooperating on Arctic matters, and the nature of the area" that did not prejudice either country's legal position nor set a precedent for other areas of the world.[22]

Neither the *Manhattan* nor the *Polar Sea* voyages challenged Canadian ownership of the waters. They related to Canada's right to restrict transit passage by foreign commercial or naval vessels. When the federal government perceived Canadian sovereignty as threatened, however, it adopted unilateral legal measures to assert jurisdiction. It also demonstrated its commitment to defending Canadian sovereignty by ordering the Canadian Forces to "show the flag" and make a demonstration of Canada's presence in the north. Given that our closest military and economic ally was also our main challenger, this was a symbolic show of control. Canada could devote resources to a presence precisely because we knew that, in the end, the United States could be relied on to offer us security.[23] When the short-term crises faded, the government's willingness to deliver on its promised investments in Arctic security also melted away. Instead, Canada sought multilateral or bilateral agreements to lessen the likelihood that its claims would be challenged in the future.

---

[21] UN Convention on the Law of the Sea (UNCLOS), part 12, "Protection and Preservation of the Marine Environment," section 8, "Ice-Covered Areas," article 234 "Ice-Covered Areas," 10 December 1982. On the background to article 234, see D. M. McRae and D. J. Goundrey, "Environmental Jurisdiction in the Arctic Waters: The Extent of Article 234," *UBC Law Review* 16, no. 2 (1982): 215–22.

[22] Larson, "United States Interests," 183.

[23] Joseph T. Jockel, *Security to the North: Canada-U.S. Defense Relationships in the 1990s* (East Lansing: Michigan State University Press, 1991), 193.

With the end of the Cold War, budget pressures, promises of a "peace dividend," and few military threats on the northern horizon, Canadian Forces' capabilities in the north were allowed to atrophy. The House of Commons Standing Committee on Foreign Affairs and International Trade approved a 1997 document that recommended Canada's relations focus on international Arctic cooperation through multilateral governance (particularly the Arctic Council) to address pressing "human security" and environmental challenges in the region. "Nothing illustrates more dramatically the link between domestic and foreign factors than the state of the Arctic environment," committee chair Bill Graham stated in the report. "That environment, so special and so fragile, is particularly sensitive to foreign influences." The report, *Canada and the Circumpolar World*, accepted that the concept of security had broadened from military issues to encompass an array of social and environmental issues. "This new agenda for security cooperation is inextricably linked to the aims of environmentally sustainable human development," the report noted. "Meeting these challenges is essential to the long-term foundation for assuring circumpolar security, with priority being given to the well-being of Arctic peoples and to safeguarding northern habitants from intrusions which have impinged aggressively on them."[24]

The Liberal government under Jean Chrétien embraced this emphasis on international cooperation and reconfigured Canada's approach to Arctic sovereignty accordingly. Although the government rejected the committee's recommendation that the Arctic should become a nuclear-free zone, it did not perceive any security crisis that warranted an increased military presence beyond a modest expansion in the number of northerners serving with the Canadian Rangers.[25] In 2000, the Department of Foreign Affairs and International Trade issued *The Northern Dimension of Canada's Foreign Policy* (NDFP), which revealed how environmental and social challenges were predominant. "Whereas the politics of the Cold War dictated that the Arctic region be treated as part of a broader strategy of exclusion and confrontation," the document noted, "now the politics of globalization and power diffusion highlight the importance of the circumpolar world as an area for inclusion and co-operation." Framed by principles of Canadian leadership, partnership, and ongoing dialogue with northerners, this new northern foreign policy was rooted in four overarching objectives: to enhance the security and prosperity of Canadians, especially northerners and Aboriginal peoples; to assert and ensure the preservation of Canada's sovereignty in the north; to establish the circumpolar region as

---

[24] House of Commons Standing Committee on Foreign Affairs and International Trade (HCSCFAIT), *Canada and the Circumpolar World: Meeting the Challenges of Cooperation into the Twenty-First Century* (1997): ix, 100.

[25] Department of Foreign Affairs and International Trade, *Government Response to Standing Committee on Foreign Affairs and International Trade Report "Canada and the Circumpolar World: Meeting the Challenges of Cooperation Into the Twenty-First Century* (Ottawa: Department of Foreign Affairs and International Trade, 1998).

a vibrant geopolitical entity integrated into a rules-based international system; and to promote the human security of northerners and the sustainable development of the Arctic.[26] The focus on diplomacy and circumpolar cooperation meant that traditional preoccupations with "defending" sovereignty slipped to the back burner.

Growing concerns about climate change, the opening of the NWP, global demands for Arctic resources, and security in the post-9/11 world have since conspired to put the Arctic back on the national and international agenda. The 2000 Canadian Forces' *Arctic Capabilities Study* recognized that northern security had evolved to include environmental, social, and economic aspects, but it argued that the coming decades would make the north even more vulnerable to "asymmetric" security and sovereignty threats. The Canadian Forces had to be prepared to respond to challenges related to environmental protection, increased shipping as Arctic sea lanes opened as a result of climate change, heightened commercial airline activity, and "trans-national criminal activity" that would accompany resource development such as diamond mining.[27] Recent laments reflect a new alarmism: urgent action is again necessary because Canada's paltry capabilities are insufficient to project control over its Arctic lands and waters at a time when our sovereignty is likely to be challenged. In a break with past practice, this latest sovereignty crisis is in anticipation of what may lie ahead. Nevertheless, our assessment of the past is colored by anticipation of a future that, in the eyes of many commentators, does not look friendly.

A sober analysis of historical developments yields an unexpected set of lessons learned. First, Canadian sovereignty is not in serious jeopardy. This is most certain in terms of the Arctic archipelagic islands and mainland. Canada addressed potential challenges to de facto sovereignty over its territory through quiet diplomacy and managed to successfully balance continental security priorities with its national interests. In terms of its Arctic waters, Canada has incrementally expanded its claims and, with the application of straight baselines in 1986, has established "that no right of innocent passage exists in the new internal waters of the Northwest Passage."[28] Although foreign countries disagree with Canada's position on the legal status of the passage, this issue has been managed successfully on an agree-to-disagree basis with the United States. History does not support the nationalist myth that the United States has deliberately and systematically sought to undermine Canadian sovereignty. Both the Canadians and the Americans have strong reasons for their legal positions, and they have sensibly managed this issue without prejudice to their respective legal positions. Indeed, seeking greater clarity may place Canada, and its principal ally, in a lose-lose situation.

---

[26] Department of Foreign Affairs and International Trade, *The Northern Dimension of Canada's Foreign Policy* (Ottawa: Department of Foreign Affairs and International Trade, 2000).

[27] Canadian Forces Northern Area (CFNA), *Arctic Capabilities Study* (Yellowknife: Canadian Forces Northern Area, 2000).

[28] Pharand, "Arctic Waters and the Northwest Passage," 43.

Historical trends also demonstrate that alarmism and reactionism lack staying power. They help to get Northern issues onto the political agenda, but when anticipated threats or crises do not materialize as the alarmists anticipate, the political will to carry through dissipates quickly. This explains why Canadian governments have often made bold proclamations to invest in Northern sovereignty and security but have largely failed to deliver on an integrated, proactive Arctic strategy. Although Canada's passive-reactive approach has been successful insofar as it allowed Canada to expand and entrench its sovereignty in the twentieth century, this approach is not appropriate for the twenty-first century. First, it has failed to stimulate Canadian investment in northern social and economic development. Second, numerous commentators suggest that new challenges precipitated by climate change, heightening pressures for access to Canadian waters and arctic resources, may lead to "loss by dereliction."[29]

Since coming to office in early 2006, Prime Minister Stephen Harper's "use it or lose it" refrain has become the dominant political message. Tapping into primordial national anxieties about sovereignty, this threatening phrase resonates with southern Canadians who have taken little interest in their Arctic but have been led to believe that military capabilities will shield Canada from "the perfect storm" brewing in the circumpolar north.[30] The logic of defending sovereignty from foreign challenges has also brought a shift from past governments that favored recognition – persuading others to accept our claims without demonstrating a capacity to enforce them – to a Harper government that favors enactment.[31] Its instrument of choice is the Canadian Forces, which fits within the "Canada First" vision that pledges to defend "our vast territory and three ocean areas" through increased defense spending and more regular and reserve forces.[32] This posturing, although it has international implications, is clearly directed at a domestic audience that Harper hopes will grant him a majority government on the basis of strong, decisive leadership.

Scenario-Based Thinking

A forward-thinking Arctic strategy is inherently predicated on future scenarios: plausible stories about future environments in which current decisions play out. Even

29 Donald M. McRae, "Arctic Sovereignty: Loss by Dereliction?" [Canadian Arctic Resources Committee] *CARC – Northern Perspectives* 22, no. 4 (1994–95), 4–9.
30 Rob Huebert, "Canada and the Changing International Arctic: At the Crossroads of Cooperation and Conflict," in *Northern Exposure: Peoples, Powers and Prospects for Canada's North*, eds. Frances Abele, Thomas J. Courchene, F. Leslie Seidle, and France St-Hilaire (Ottawa: Institute for Research on Public Policy, 2009), 77.
31 Franklyn Griffiths, "Canadian Arctic Sovereignty: Time to Take Yes for an Answer on the Northwest Passage," in *Northern Exposure: Peoples, Powers and Prospects for Canada's North*, eds. Frances Abele et al. (Ottawa: Institute for Research on Public Policy), 109–10.
32 Prime Minister's Office (PMO), "PM Unveils Canada First Defense Strategy," 12 May 2008.

when these are not explicit, they underlie the rationale for a particular course of action.

The academic debate between Rob Huebert and Franklyn Griffiths is a good illustration of how anticipated scenarios influence the ways that commentators frame the issues and help to set priorities. Huebert sees the Arctic as a potential battleground. Since the late 1990s, he has forecast a perfect storm brewing over climate change; newly accessible Arctic resources; shortened transportation routes; and competing national claims to Arctic waters, the seabed, and islands. Canada is at a "crossroads" and must choose between "scal[ing] back or abandon[ing] some of their unilateral objectives and develop[ing] a multilateral framework for new governance."[33] His writings assert that the "soft law" in the region and the U.S. unwillingness to ratify UNCLOS makes the legal regime a tenuous basis for solving problems while global competition for resources and incompatible national interests bring circumpolar countries and other stakeholders into growing conflict. By extension, in this hostile world, where only the strong will survive, Canada must take unilateral action to assert control and defend its sovereignty or its claims will be overwhelmed by rival powers.[34]

By contrast, Griffiths has emphasized that Canadian sovereignty is "well in hand" and the government should focus on stewardship – "the enactment of sovereignty" – in light of uncertainty related to climate and geopolitical change.[35] By downplaying the immediacy or probability of the northern military and commercial threats emphasized by Huebert, Griffiths emphasizes the need for ongoing dialogue between southern stakeholders and northern residents on agenda setting and priority setting.[36] Concurrently, if Canada sees the United States as an ally rather than a polar adversary, this offers the prospect of a working bilateral compromise on the NWP, the issue "that continues to tower above all other of our Arctic sovereignty concerns."[37] In short, by asserting the improbability of an existential threat to Canada's possession of its Arctic waters, Griffiths provides the conceptual space to envision schemes for constructive international engagement and cooperative management.

"The Future of Arctic Marine Navigation in Mid-Century," a series of scenario narratives produced by the Global Business Network for the Arctic Council's Protection of the Arctic Marine Environment (PAME) working group, provides a framework to devise and analyze plausible futures for Arctic marine navigation. Much of the alarmist rhetoric swirling in the Canadian media suggests a looming Arctic "race": more demand for resources and trade and less stable governance. The

---

[33] Huebert, "Canada and the Changing International Arctic," 78.

[34] Ibid.; Huebert, "The Shipping News Part II: How Canada's Arctic Sovereignty Is on Thinning Ice," *International Journal* 58, no. 3 (2003): 295–308; Huebert, "Renaissance in Canadian Arctic security?" *Canadian Military Journal* 6, no. 4 (2005–06): 17–29.

[35] Franklyn Griffiths, "Our Arctic Sovereignty Is Well in Hand," *Globe and Mail*, 8 November 2006.

[36] Griffiths, "The Shipping News: Canada's Arctic Sovereignty Not on Thinning Ice," *International Journal* 58, no. 2 (2003): 257–82; "Camels in the Arctic," *Walrus*, 4 January 2008.

[37] Griffiths, "Canadian Arctic Sovereignty," 107.

FIGURE 13.1. Global Business Network Future Arctic Marine Navigation Matrix (2008).

no-holds-barred race for resources in the Arctic frontier presupposes intense competition and a corresponding willingness to violate rules, growing military activity, unilateral action, and political friction over states' willingness to allow transarctic passage. National interests are paramount, shared interests are few and unreliable, and rapid climate change will fuel a feeding frenzy in an anarchic region allegedly devoid of "overarching political or legal structures that can provide for the orderly development... or mediate political disagreements over Arctic resources or sea-lanes."[38] For reasons that will be discussed, Canada cannot thrive in this anarchic scenario – and particularly not through unilateral action – given its low military, political, and economic strength relative to the Russians, the Americans, and the European Union.

[38] Scott G. Borgerson, "Arctic Meltdown: The Economic and Security Implications of Global Warming," *Foreign Affairs*, March–April 2008, 71.

Given the challenges that Canada faces from its circumpolar neighbors, "realists" might assert that this scenario is naive. Even the Russians seem to think that an Arctic race scenario is misguided. The Russian ambassador-at-large Anton Vasilyev, who is also a high-ranking participant in the Arctic Council, told reporters on October 22, 2008, that "media assessments of possible aggression in the Arctic, even a third world war, are seen as extremely alarmist and provocative. In my opinion, there are no grounds for such alarmism. . . . We are following the situation in the region, this also includes the military activity of other countries, but we hope cooperation will be the main feature."[39] The Russians are working to define their extended continental shelf, as are their circumpolar neighbors, including Canada, and President Dmitry Medvedev told a Russian Security Council session in September 17, 2008, that the shelf was "a guarantee of Russia's energy security and that the Arctic should become the resource base for Russia this century."[40] Although pessimists read into such proclamations the possibility of armed conflict over uncertain boundaries and the resources therein, if someone inserted the word *Canada* in place of *Russia* this could be mistaken for one of Prime Minister Harper's speeches.

As James Kraska observes in his chapter in this volume, senior Canadian officials have made some peculiar statements about Arctic security in recent years. When the Russian government announced a new frontier law to define its southern Arctic claim in September 2008, for example, Prime Minister Harper responded that Canada was stepping up its military measures in the region because of the Russians' willingness to flout international law. "We would like to hope that this is, at best, the result of inattentive reading of the materials published by the Russian Security Council," the Russian Foreign Ministry replied, explaining that the new federal law had nothing to do with its continental shelf claim.[41] Indeed, Russian press releases have emphasized the socioeconomic benefits of development, noted that the interests of indigenous peoples and environmental regulations will be taken into account, and reaffirmed that Russia will submit scientific evidence to the United Nations to support its shelf claim. Hyperbolic political responses unfairly accusing the Russians of violating Canadian airspace, which are discussed later, indicate that Canadian officials can be prone to grandstanding without solid grounding in international law. Ironically, Canada has played a role in stimulating the Arctic race that it is accusing others of generating.[42] This is disconcerting.

What Canada can anticipate and should seek is an Arctic "saga": greater demand for resources and trade coupled with more stable governance.[43] Shared economic

---

[39] "Russia Says Media Reports on Possible Arctic Conflict 'Alarmist,'" *RIA Novosti*, 22 October 2008.
[40] Ibid.
[41] "Russia Says Arctic Marking Does Not Imply Territorial Claim," *RIA Novosti*, 23 September 2008.
[42] See, for example, Rick Rozoff, "Arctic: Canada Leads NATO Confrontation with Russia," *Global Research*, 5 August 2009, http://www.globalresearch.ca/index.php?context=va&aid=14657.
[43] Global Business Network, "The Future of Arctic Marine Navigation in Mid-Century," scenario narratives produced for the Protection of the Arctic Marine Environment working

and political interests, global economic prosperity, and systematic resource development will permit a range and variety of maritime activity, with navigational infrastructure and improved technology making marine transport safer, more efficient, and more economically viable. It incorporates what northern stakeholders have identified as key priority areas – sustainable development, constructive circumpolar engagement, and environmental protection – without sacrificing either Canadian sovereignty or security. Canada should frame a new discourse as a confident, sovereign northern nation willing to invest and participate in sustainable development. "If we focus only on losing, then lose we will," Sheila Watt-Cloutier perceptively noted.[44] Simply put, Canada cannot emerge victorious in a polar race.

CANADIAN DEFENSE, SOVEREIGNTY, AND ARCTIC SECURITY

Over the past three years, Prime Minister Harper has announced a spate of new military measures to respond to anticipated sovereignty challenges in the Arctic. This extension of the government's "Canada First" defense strategy[45] is politically sound, but it is unrealistic if it is setting up "Canada-only" expectations for the Arctic region. Canada cannot afford the suite of necessary capabilities to defend our Arctic from any possible aggressor. More important, there is no need to try to achieve total security by ourselves. Despite the hyperbolic media rhetoric about a new cold war brewing, there is no significant conventional military threat to our far north, nor will Canada solve its boundary disputes with the force of arms. Canadians need to invest in military capabilities so that the Canadian Forces can operate in all parts of the country and play a supporting role to civil authorities. As the international lawyer Donald McRae notes, "a responsible government provides proper policing, surveillance, search and rescue and other services throughout its territory."[46] This lacks the political glamour of saving the country from foreign challenges to its territorial and maritime integrity, but it is a sounder rationale on which to base a national sovereignty and security strategy.

Every Arctic country has national interests at stake in the region. This recognition should neither be grounds for Canada to adopt a narrow, unilateralist approach to circumpolar affairs nor a basis for apathy borne of faith that Canada's neighbors will look after the region for us. Simply relying on our allies to protect our interests limits our range of action. Being a good neighbor means having the ability to control your territory and waters so that you do not have to rely entirely on your friends

group, http://arctic-council.org/filearchive/AMSA%20Scenarios%20of%20the%20Future%20-%20%20 20Narratives%20Report.pdf.

[44] Sheila Watt-Cloutier, "Nunavut must think big, not small, on polar bears," *Nunatsiaq News*, 17 January 2007.

[45] *Canada First Defense Strategy*, http://www.forces.gc.ca/site/focus/first-premier/June18_0910_CFDS_english_low-res.pdf.

[46] Donald M. McRae, "Arctic Sovereignty: What Is at Stake?" *Behind the Headlines* 64, no. 1 (2007): 3.

to do so. In Canada's case, having to depend too heavily on our allies, particularly the Americans, for security in the Arctic makes us jittery because it raises concerns about our de facto sovereignty. Even if our de jure sovereignty is solid, primordial Canadian concerns about American intentions tend to launch us into yet another round in the game of sovereignty crisis reaction. Canada must be prepared, at the very least, to defend against needing too much help from its major ally, given that our interests do not always coincide.

Since coming into office in 2006, the Conservatives have made the Canadian Forces the centerpiece of their use-it-or-lose-it approach to Canadian sovereignty. The government has made frequent reference to the "critical role" that the military plays in "protecting Canadian sovereignty." As long as its logic is grounded in functional reasons, and not the flawed notion that military "boots on the ground" strengthens or perfects our legal sovereignty,[47] the Canadian government should be commended for its promises to invest in defense capabilities. Although the Liberals modestly increased the tempo of military operations in the Arctic in the early twenty-first century and promised to augment capabilities in their 2005 Defense Policy Statement, Stephen Harper swept into office with a much stronger resolve to make the Arctic a top priority. "We believe that Canadians are excited about the government asserting Canada's control and sovereignty in the Arctic," the prime minister told a *Toronto Sun* reporter on 23 February 2007:

> We believe that's one of the big reasons why Canadians are excited and support our plan to rebuild the Canadian Forces. I think it's practically and symbolically hugely important, much more important than the dollars spent. And I'm hoping that years from now, Canada's Arctic sovereignty, military and otherwise, will be, frankly, a major legacy of this government.[48]

His government's main military announcements, all announced as sovereignty initiatives, include expanding and enhancing the Canadian Rangers; ordering Arctic/Offshore Patrol Ships; building a deepwater Arctic docking and refueling facility in Nanisivik; launching RadarSat-2 to provide enhanced surveillance and data-gathering capabilities; conducting major military exercises; building a Canadian Forces Arctic Training Centre in Resolute; establishing a new Canadian Forces Reserve unit in Yellowknife; and creating the Arctic Response Company Group.

Overall, the government's commitments to invest in more military capabilities for the north are reasonable and proportionate to probable short- and medium-term threats. Canadians will be well served if the government delivers on the Arctic-oriented promises that it has already made. But investing additional resources in

[47] On "undisciplined rhetoric" along these lines, see James Kraska, "The Law of the Sea Convention and the Northwest Passage," *International Journal of Marine and Coastal Law* 22, no. 2 (2007): 262.
[48] Kathleen Harris, "Laying Claim to Canada's Internal Waters," *Toronto Sun*, 23 February 2007.

defense capabilities will not achieve greater security unless they are rationalized in a whole-of-government strategy that situates Canadian Forces' responsibilities in proper context. Despite political and media intimations, the Canadian Forces are not the lead agency in most domestic incidents and do not have a standing mandate to enforce Canadian laws. They play a supporting role to other departments and agencies with functional responsibilities for security and emergency preparedness in the Arctic. The Canadian Forces may be called on to support activities such as protecting our environment and fisheries or countering organized crime, illegal immigration, and drug interdiction, but their role is secondary.

Expectation management will be key. The Standing Senate Committee on National Defense and Security observes that current level of interjurisdictional collaboration and cooperation in strategic emergency planning and management is inadequate across the country.[49] Canadians demand that the government do everything possible to keep the Arctic pristine, but the vulnerability of ecosystems, coupled with the low population and infrastructure density, makes emergency response management particularly difficult in the region.[50] Canada must establish an effective Arctic action plan with an emergency response framework and a disaster mitigation strategy covering contingencies like a major air disaster in the high Arctic, a massive oil spill in Canada's internal waters, or an infectious disease outbreak. Government messages must resist creating a sense of alarmism (the possibility of a major oil spill, for example, is remote at present) and be realistic about what is feasible to achieve so that federal departments and agencies are not set up to fail.[51]

Similarly, Canada should emphasize the positive relationship that it enjoys with the United States in Arctic security. Since 1957, Canada and the United States have jointly monitored northern North American airspace through the North American Aerospace Defense Command (NORAD). In May 2006, this agreement was expanded to incorporate a maritime warning mission, reflecting the heightened American emphasis on maritime security and continental security more generally.[52] Through constructive diplomacy, Canada should explore the possibility of creating a combined Arctic Command to coordinate Canada's Joint Task Force North and U.S. Northern Command surveillance and response efforts in the Arctic. This

49 Standing Senate Committee on National Security and Defense (SSCNSD), *Emergency Preparedness in Canada: How the Fine Arts of Bafflegab and Procrastination Hobble the People Who Will Be Trying to Save You When Things Get Really Bad* ... (Ottawa: Senate of Canada, 2008), 42.
50 Jonathan Seymour and Associates and Mariport Group, *Canadian Arctic Shipping Assessment Scoping Study*, prepared for Transport Canada Seaway and Domestic Shipping Policy (2005), 2.
51 Operation Nanook exercises, held each August since 2007, are joint operations designed to hone interoperability of Canadian Forces air, land, and sea capabilities. They also include whole-of-government exercises to test what capabilities federal, territorial, and municipal government stakeholders can bring to emergency scenarios.
52 Captain (Navy) Jamie Cotter, "Developing a Coherent Plan to Deal with Canada's Conundrum in the Northwest Passage," *Journal of Military and Strategic Studies* 11, no. 3 (2009): 36.

initiative could include a Canadian-U.S. joint operational planning group, which would include representatives of the Canadian and U.S. navies and coast guards located at Colorado Springs, with access to NORAD planning staff.[53] A more efficient command and control structure would allow us to work with our allies to deal with emergencies in the Arctic in a more timely and effective manner than Canada can hope to accomplish alone.[54] This is also compatible with the agree-to-disagree framework that I lay out in the following section. Rather than emphasizing the perceived sovereignty loss inherent in coordinating efforts, Canadians should acknowledge that our politicians, civil servants, and senior officers have historically succeeded in finding bilateral and multilateral solutions to sovereignty and security dilemmas that protect and project Canada's national interests.

DIPLOMACY

Canadian scholars and media commentators have, for years, been inadvertently building the legal case for foreign countries or multinational corporations which might want to challenge our control over the Northwest Passage (NWP). They have done so with admirable intentions, trying to kick-start Canada into action, but the implications are unfortunate. Canadians have become convinced that our sovereignty is on thinning ice. This provides senior decision makers, based in southern Canada and possessing a distinctly southern worldview, with a convenient pretext to devise "stand up for Canada" strategies that play to a southern audience. Diplomacy and dialogue are marginalized, and a positive short-term outcome – defined as strong political optics with the aura of decisive action – becomes more important than process. This has unfortunate implications for northerners, who, once again, face the prospect of having their voices needlessly and unconscionably relegated to the sidelines. If the Canadian government is going to take a leadership role in promoting regional stability and cooperation, it needs to broaden its "Canada First" strategy to emphasize the benefits of having bilateral and multilateral partnerships. It is too easy for journalists, trying to generate the next catchy headline, to miss the quiet, constructive, sustained engagement that has benefited Canada and the rest of

---

[53] SSCNSD, *Canada's Coastlines: The Longest Under-Defended Borders in the World* (October 2003), 135. This option is consistent with White House, National Security Presidential Directive (NSPD) 66, Homeland Security Presidential Directive (HSPD) 25 – Arctic Region Policy (hereafter U.S. Presidential Directive), 9 January 2009, which notes that "the United States has broad and fundamental national security interests in the Arctic region and is prepared to operate either independently or in conjunction with other states to safeguard these interests. These interests include such matters as missile defense and early warning; deployment of sea and air systems for strategic sealift, strategic deterrence, maritime presence, and maritime security operations; and ensuring freedom of navigation and overflight."

[54] Major Paul Dittmann, "In Defense of Defense: Canadian Arctic Sovereignty and Security," *Journal of Military and Strategic Studies* 11, no. 3 (Spring 2009); Griffiths, "Canadian Arctic Sovereignty," 133.

the circumpolar world. It is also easy for politicians, seeking to distance themselves from previous governments, to ignore past successes and healthy relationships so that they can trumpet their own distinct contributions.

Canada is one Arctic nation among many, and it needs to accept this reality. Rather than casting unsettled boundary disputes as a polar race destined to end in a resource feeding frenzy that will ignore international law and norms, the federal government should make more effort to clarify Canada's actual claims. Although sweeping "stand up for Canada" language can be beneficial politically, it sets up unrealistic expectations. All Arctic states are engaged in a legally established process to delimit their extended continental shelves, identifying the seabed area outside their two-hundred-nautical-mile exclusive economic zones where they have the exclusive right to exploit resources. All five Arctic Ocean littoral states that have the potential for extended continental shelf claims are likely to adhere to the science-based UNCLOS process to determine the geographical extent of their national rights, as pledged in the Ilulissat Declaration.[55]

"Nobody disputes Canada's control over land in the Arctic, where Inuit have lived for countless generations, or over our 200 mile EEZ," Senator Bill Rompkey has explained. "As for the seabed beyond the EEZ, claims go through an international process."[56] This is a sound assessment. The UN Convention on the Law of the Sea defines the rights and responsibilities of states in using the oceans and lays out a process for determining maritime boundaries. Littoral countries are therefore mapping the Arctic to determine the extent of their claims. Canada ratified UNCLOS in November 2003 and has until 2013 to submit evidence for its extended continental shelf outside the existing two-hundred-nautical-mile EEZ.[57] In this light, Ron

[55] Ilulissat Declaration was adopted at the Arctic Ocean Conference hosted by the Government of Denmark and attended by the representatives of the five coastal states bordering on the Arctic Ocean (Canada, Denmark, Norway, the Russian Federation, and the United States), held at Ilulissat, Greenland, 27–29 May 2008. The declaration stated that all states will adhere to the existing legal framework to settle overlapping claims. Although the United States is not a signatory to the convention, there is every reason to anticipate that it will adhere to its provisions in the Arctic.

[56] Bill Rompkey, "Arctic Sovereignty," *Ottawa Citizen*, 17 July 2008.

[57] The 2004 federal budget announced $69 million for seabed surveying and mapping to establish the outer limits of Canada's continental shelves in the Arctic and Atlantic Oceans. In 2007, the government allocated another $20 million to complete the mapping of its shelf to meet the deadline, and Department of Foreign Affairs officials are confident that it will submit its claims on schedule. Standing Senate Committee on Fisheries and Oceans (SSCFO), *The Coast Guard in Canada's Arctic: Interim Report* (June 2008), 13. The UN Commission on the Limits of the Continental Shelf can review and issue recommendations only on the basis of data submitted by states, and negotiations or arbitration over overlapping claims will occur outside of the United Nations. Rather than lamenting this reality or insisting that Canada must never concede an inch (which sets up our diplomats and politicians for failure), Canadians must engage in concerted diplomacy to seek support for our case rather than trying to stand alone. This is best done by sharing expertise and data and looking to areas of mutual interest to "minimize the possibility of disputes and complications" where possible. Michelle Collins, "Unearthing Mysteries under the Arctic Ice," *Embassy*, 6 November 2008. Collaborative data

McNab, a former member of the Canadian Polar Commission, suggests that "an increased investment in science may be the cheapest, and most effective, immediate means of establishing a sovereign base for our northern lands and seas."[58]

But is this scientific research merely a sideshow to the real contest emerging? Pessimists point to the Russian submarine expedition that planted a titanium flag on the seabed at the North Pole in August 2007, coupled with renewed military overflights and its decision to send warships into Arctic waters in July 2008 for the first time in decades, as evidence that they have nefarious intentions.[59] Two Russian military aircraft which flew close to Canadian airspace on the eve of President Barack Obama's visit to Canada in February 2009 are a prime example. National Defense Minister Peter McKay explained that two CF-18 fighter jets were scrambled to intercept the Russian aircraft. "I have expressed at various times the deep concern our government has with increasingly aggressive Russian actions around the globe and Russian intrusion into our airspace," Prime Minister Harper proclaimed. "We will defend our airspace." This tough talk was misplaced. Russian news agencies reported that "the statements from Canada's defense ministry are perplexing to say the least and cannot be called anything other than a farce."[60] Dmitry Trofimov, the head of the Russian embassy's political section in Ottawa, insisted that there was no intrusion on Canadian national airspace or sovereignty, and "from the point of international law, nothing happened, absolutely nothing." Explaining that this was a scheduled air-patrol flight (which, like Canadian military exercises, was planned months in advance), Trofimov said that this was a really a "minor episode" – something proven by the notable absence of any American reaction to flights that adhered to international law – and did not differ from similar NATO practices just beyond Russian airspace.[61]

Canada also faces several unresolved but well-managed bilateral boundary disputes. There is no great urgency to settle the issue of Hans Island with the Danes, nor that related to two tiny disputed zones (thirty-one square nautical miles and thirty-four square nautical miles) in the Lincoln Sea over Greenland's drawing of straight baselines.[62] The Beaufort Sea question with the United States, which involves offshore hydrocarbon reserves in a 6,250-square-nautical-mile disputed zone, is more

collection by Canada and its closest circumpolar neighbors is beneficial on several levels to producing credible submissions and avoiding conflict. Jacob Verhoef and Dick MacDougall, "Delineating Canada's Continental Shelf according to the United Nations Convention on the Law of the Sea," *Ocean Sovereignty* 3, no. 1 (2008): 4–5.

[58] Randy Boswell, "Canada's Arctic Sovereignty Challenged: U.S. Submarines May Chart the Continental Shelf," *Vancouver Sun*, 8 March 2006.
[59] See, for example, "The High North: The Arctic Contest Heats Up," *Economist*, 9 October 2008, 70.
[60] Mike Blanchfield, "Harper Warns Russians after Two Bombers Intercepted," *National Post*, 28 February 2009.
[61] Meagan Fitzpatrick, "Russian Bombers Did Not Breach Canadian Airspace: Diplomat," *Canwest News Service*, 23 March 2009.
[62] David H. Gray, "Canada's Unresolved Maritime Boundaries," *International Boundaries Research Unit Boundary and Security Bulletin* 5, no. 33 (1997): 65.

significant. The legal case is not clear cut, however, and Canada should anticipate a negotiated solution based on established rules of international law and political compromise.[63]

The Northwest Passage is the issue that looms largest in Canada's political consciousness, however, and explains the country's hypersensitivity to its allies' position on the issue – particularly that of the United States. Although the two countries have different perspectives on specific boundary and transit right questions, they also share much in common. For example, no one disputes that the NWP, running from the Davis Strait to the western Beaufort, is "Canadian" insofar as no foreign country claims that it has stronger rights to the airspace, waters, or seabed than Canada. The sovereignty issue in this case is not about rival ownership in the sense of "possession." The issue relates to how much power Canada has over the waters and the air corridor overhead – in short, the debate is over just how Canadian they are, and what this means in practice.

Canada's position is that the NWP is part of Canada's internal waters, where Canada enjoys full sovereignty and the right to regulate and control foreign navigation. In short, foreign ships have no right of transit passage. Although Canada welcomes domestic and foreign shipping in its waters, it retains the legal right to control entry to, and the activities conducted in, its internal waters. The United States and European countries assert that an international strait runs through those Canadian waters, and therefore that the commercial and naval vessels have the right of transit passage. Accordingly, they allege that Canada does not have the right to pass and enforce its own laws and regulations and would be limited to international safety and maritime standards. The United States insists that, if it acquiesces to Canada's claim that the NWP constitutes internal waters, then archipelagic states could use this as a precedent to restrict naval mobility in other parts of the world.[64]

Canadians have trouble accepting that, insofar as we are desirous of having the United States recognize Canada's internal waters claim to the NWP, they are not going to do so. "As long as there is a United States Navy," former American diplomat David Jones insisted, "U.S. government policy will insist on maintaining

---

[63] Donat Pharand, *The Law of the Sea of the Arctic with Special Reference to Canada* (Ottawa: University of Ottawa Press, 1973), 312; Michel Frederick, "La délimitation du plateau continental entre le Canada et les États-Unis dans la mer de Beaufort," *Annuaire Canadien de Droit International 1979* (Vancouver: University of British Columbia Press, 1979), 78, 91; Donald Rothwell, *Maritime Boundaries and Resource Development: Options for the Beaufort Sea* (Calgary: Canadian Institute of Resources Law, 1988), 45–48. This option is consistent with the 9 January 2009 U.S. presidential directive, which notes that the United States should "consider the conservation and management of natural resources during the process of delimiting the extended continental shelf" and "protect United States interests with respect to hydrocarbon reservoirs that may overlap boundaries to mitigate adverse environmental and economic consequences related to their development."

[64] Griffiths, "Our Arctic Sovereignty Is Well in Hand." This argument is also explicit in the 2009 U.S. presidential directive.

international waterways as international."[65] Some Canadian commentators suggest that if Canada demonstrates it has the rules, regulations, and capabilities to better control activities and thus increase continental security in the passage, then the United States will not contest, and may even support, Canada's claims.[66] This is highly unlikely. The United States will act pragmatically to ensure that its international interests are maintained, and it sees global maritime mobility as integral to its economic and national security. Canada might be an accommodating ally in the Arctic, but there is no guarantee that Iran would not use the NWP case as a pretext to assert unilateral control over the Straits of Hormuz, or Indonesia over the Malacca Straits.[67] To Canada, the NWP – as a part of Canada itself – is a special case that warrants unique attention. The United States sees the NWP in global terms and believes that it must defend its position accordingly. This is not a case of Canada flouting international law but of differing with the United States on how it applies to this unique space.

Canada has various options. The status quo, agreeing to disagree with the Americans on the status of the NWP with limited Canadian capabilities to respond to a challenge or an emergency, may be reasonable for the short term, given the very modest tempo of foreign activity in the region.[68] This position, however, will put Canada at a disadvantage if the passage opens to commercial shipping and Canada cannot assert adequate control. Steps must be taken to defend against contingencies, but these should be geared toward probable threats, not all possible threats. It is not worth picking a fight with the United States that involves fundamental legal principles when the threat scenarios are based only on potentialities. Canada is wise not to provoke a crisis and jeopardize its legal claims when, as Franklyn Griffiths asserts, "we are secure in the benefits of de facto control of the Northwest Passage."[69]

Canada can confidently assert that the waters of the Arctic archipelago constitute internal waters on the basis of straight baselines; historical and continuous use by the Inuit; and vital interests related to the marine environment, the Inuit, and national

---

[65] David Jones, "Don't Kid Yourselves, Canada," *Ottawa Citizen*, 15 August 2008.

[66] See, for example, Michael Byers, "Unfrozen Sea: Sailing the Northwest Passage," *Policy Options* 28, no. 5 (2007): 33; Byers, *Who Owns the Arctic?* (Vancouver: Douglas and McIntyre, 2009); SSCFO, *The Coast Guard in Canada's Arctic*, 24; Bill Rompkey, "Arctic Sovereignty," *Ottawa Citizen*, 17 July 2008.

[67] Kraska, "Law of the Sea Convention and the Northwest Passage," 278–79; Jones, "Don't Kid Yourselves, Canada."

[68] Ironically, the Standing Senate Committee on Fisheries and Oceans' June 2008 interim report, *The Coast Guard in Canada's Arctic*, argues, "As long as ice conditions hazardous to international shipping remained, Canada's interests were protected.... Until now, Canada could afford to go on 'agreeing to disagree' with the United States over its legal status" (19). This is a peculiar assertion on several levels. First, ice conditions clearly remain hazardous to international shipping, as numerous Arctic Council and marine shipping studies have amply demonstrated. The use of the past tense in the report is unwarranted. Second, no justification is offered for why agreeing to disagree is no longer a viable option.

[69] Griffiths, *Globe and Mail* article of 8 November 2006, quoted in Paul Kaludjak, "Sovereignty and Inuit in the Canadian Arctic," *Globe and Mail*, 17 November 2006.

security.[70] Pushing for international clarity on the legal status of the NWP, however, may place Canada in a lose-lose situation. First, taking the issue to court runs the risk of an unfavorable judgment. If the passage were determined either to not be internal waters or to constitute an international strait, this would be perceived as a major sovereignty loss (although neither scenario would seriously undermine Canada's legal authority to regulate commercial shipping).[71] In contrast, if Canada secures international recognition that these are internal waters, this could set a precedent in other parts of the world. Our strategic mobility, and that of our allies, could be constrained as a result, with negative impacts on commerce and our ability to project naval power abroad. In short, pushing too hard for American acquiescence on the NWP issue could actually work against Canada's grand strategic interests. If the United States or other countries are not anxious to push the point,[72] Canada should not provoke a battle with lose-lose potential.

Rob Huebert observes that the heart of the matter is about control. "Canada can afford to lose the right to refer to the Northwest Passage as internal waters," he notes, "but it cannot afford to lose control over the regulation of the ships that sail on it."[73] That stated, Griffiths makes a convincing case that agreeing to disagree with the Americans on the legal status of the passage remains a viable strategy. "The Northwest Passage will see an increase in commercial shipping," he predicts, "but it will move in and out of sites in Arctic North America and not between the Atlantic and Pacific in volume any time soon." In his view, we can and should cooperate with the United States to constrain hostile states' access to Canadian Arctic waters, maintaining our legal position that they are internal waters while choosing "to govern the Northwest Passage *as though* it were an international strait."[74] This is eminently sensible and best serves the interests of both countries.

John Noble, a Canadian diplomat assigned to the U.S. Relations Branch, concluded that, "rather than trying to make a big issue out of this matter, [Canada and the United States] should be proclaiming that the Arctic is an area where we do co-operate and have come to a pragmatic solution to a difficult legal problem."[75] By recasting our mind-set from "use it or lose it" to an emphasis on how we want to use the north, rooted in the confidence that our sovereignty is secure, Canadians can manage our internal waters with our allies and free up financial resources to invest in sustainable northern development. Canada should also be mindful that cultivating the United States as a practical ally on the NWP issue (without prejudice to our respective legal positions) is good insurance against a critical mass of foreign countries allying against us and pushing the legal issue.

[70]　See Pharand, "Arctic Waters and the Northwest Passage," 3–69.
[71]　McRae, "Arctic Sovereignty," 18.
[72]　Griffiths, "Canadian Arctic Sovereignty," 122–24.
[73]　Huebert, "Canada and the Changing International Arctic," 93.
[74]　Griffiths, "Canadian Arctic Sovereignty," 121, 129.
[75]　John Noble, "Arctic Solution Already in Place," *Toronto Star*, 8 February 2006.

Although most Canadian public attention on the disputed status of the NWP is directed to the United States, the European Union also views it as an international strait. The member states of the European Union have the world's largest merchant fleet and would benefit from transoceanic transit routes through Arctic waters. "This could considerably shorten trips from Europe to the Pacific, save energy, reduce emissions, promote trade and diminish pressure on the main transcontinental navigation channels," a recent report noted. "But serious obstacles remain including drift ice, lack of infrastructure, environmental risks and uncertainties about future trade patterns," which means that commercial navigation in the region "will require time and effort." In the meantime, the European Union is urged to improve conditions for this possibility. Canada should be a partner in promoting stricter safety and environmental standards, but it will be alarmed by the comment that EU "Member States and the Community should defend the principle of freedom of navigation and the right of innocent passage in the newly opened routes and areas." This is an obvious reference to the NWP, one of the "new" trade routes that the European Union sees as important "to effectively secure its trade and resource interests in the region and may put pressure on its relations with key partners."[76] Canada should not concede its position on internal waters, but − as with the Americans – this does not preclude a working relationship with the Europeans on other issues.

The Russians are more of a wild card in Canadian foreign policy. In 1997, the House of Commons Standing Committee on Foreign Affairs and International Trade described Russia as a "giant jigsaw puzzle of paradoxes, contradictions, ambiguities, and uncertainties."[77] Ten years later, Russia seemed poised to flex its military and economic muscle, buoyed by a wealth of northern resources. Oil and gas revenues allowed it to begin rebuilding its armed forces, to resume northern air and naval operations, and to invest heavily in the offshore sector.[78] The Russian invasion of Georgia coupled with "Russia's increasingly apparent diplomatic opposition to Western interests" has led to talk of a new cold war.[79] Discussions of how Canada could tap into Russian markets, which were central to perceived bilateral opportunities in the 1990s, have been replaced by saber-rattling rhetoric, much of it generated by alarmist readings of Russia's increased military activities in the polar region and its alleged intentions to unilaterally demarcate and defend its borders.[80]

[76] European Commission (EC), *The European Union and the Arctic Region*, COM(2008) 763 (Brussels, 20 November 2008), 8.
[77] House of Commons Standing Committee on Foreign Affairs and International Trade, *Canada and the Circumpolar World*, 227.
[78] Standing Senate Committee on Fisheries and Oceans, *The Coast Guard in Canada's Arctic*, 8.
[79] Matt Gurney, "The New Cold War, a Brief History," *National Post*, 15 August 2008.
[80] Natalie Mychajlyszyn, "The Arctic: Geopolitical Issues," in *The Arctic: Canadian and International Perspectives* (Ottawa: Library of Parliament InfoSeries, October 2008), 3; Peter O'Neil, "Russia's Militarization May Be Just Sabre-Rattling: Expert – Domestic Audience Might Be Intended Target of Military Beefing," *Canwest News Service*, 17 March 2009. "Tough talk" from Canadian Foreign Affairs

Russia faces unique challenges as the only non-NATO member among the five Arctic littoral states. Sven Holtsmark neatly summarizes Russia's unique geopolitical position and the striking reality that up to one-fifth of its gross domestic product is generated in the Arctic.[81] In his apt assessment, Western-Russian cooperation more generally is the real key to Arctic stability. Although Russian rhetoric and domestic practices "give legitimate reasons for concern," Russian foreign policy statements that emphasize the primacy of international law and multilateralism in international relations "should not be routinely dismissed." Russian policy makers may indeed "realise that adherence to international law and collective solutions are in fact in Russia's own vital interest." Of particular note, the Russian Arctic strategy approved in September 2008 supposedly emphasizes maintaining the Arctic "as an area of peace and cooperation" as one of its four main policy aims.[82] Geographical and economic realities mean that Russia has the most to gain if orderly, lawful development occurs. Accordingly, Canadian politicians must be careful not to let political rhetoric, aimed at a domestic audience to show resolve to defend national interests, undermine Canada's support for international legal regimes.[83] After all, Russia does not dispute Canada's position on the NWP as internal waters, and Canada will be prudent to express its security concerns about the Russian regime through NATO.

CONCLUSION: A CANADIAN NORTHERN STRATEGY

When differences between claims related to Arctic waters and the marine seabed are conflated in alarmist media and political statements, they distort the sovereignty picture.[84] Grouping together a series of individual – and manageable – challenges makes the alleged storm brewing on the horizon seem scarier than it is. There is still room, and time, for bilateral and multilateral cooperation.

Despite the saber-rattling and alarmist rhetoric that might be misconstrued as a Canadian propensity for unilateralism and preparations for a polar race, there

Minister Lawrence Cannon, asserting that "Canada will not be bullied" by the Russians in light of reports that the Kremlin was planning to create a dedicated military force for the Arctic, might be best considered political grandstanding. After all, just five days before, Canada had announced that it was creating a "new Arctic force" over the following five years. David Pugliese, "Reserve Units to Form Core of New Arctic Force," *Ottawa Citizen*, 22 March 2009; Philip Authier, "Canada Won't Be Bullied by Russia: Cannon," *Montreal Gazette*, 27 March 2009.

[81] Sven G. Holtsmark, "Towards Cooperation or Confrontation? Security in the High North," Research Paper No. 45, February 2009 (Rome: Research Division, NATO Defense College).

[82] Ibid., 9.

[83] Randy Boswell, "Canada, Russia Play Political Game in Arctic," *National Post*, 16 August 2009. For a fuller discussion, see P. Whitney Lackenbauer, "Mirror Images? Canada, Russia, and the Circumpolar World," *International Journal* 65, no. 4 (2010): 879–97.

[84] Suzanne Lalonde, "Arctic Waters: Cooperation or Conflict?" *Behind the Headlines* 65, no. 4 (2008): 8–14. For a useful chart summarizing competing claims of the five Arctic littoral states, see David Runnalls, "Arctic Sovereignty and Security in a Climate-Changing World," in *Securing Canada's Future in a Climate-Changing World* (Ottawa: National Round Table on the Environment and the Economy, 30 October 2008), 87.

is a parallel discourse in Canada that receives less media fanfare but points more convincingly toward a polar saga. On 11 March 2009, Minister of Foreign Affairs Lawrence Cannon adopted the language of cooperation and relationships in a speech that emphasized the need for constructive international engagement in the Arctic region. The unveiling of the government's long-awaited Northern Strategy in July 2009 reinforced this message of partnership – between the federal government and northern Canadians, and between Canada and its circumpolar neighbors. Two years earlier, the speech from the throne had promised an "integrated northern strategy strengthening Canada's sovereignty, protecting our environmental heritage, promoting economic and social development, and improving and devolving governance, so that northerners have greater control over their destinies." Although the final document reiterated the myriad promises that the government had already made, it provided a more coherent vision that indicates a shift in emphasis away from narrow security concerns and sovereignty. It trumpeted the government's commitment to "putting more boots on the Arctic tundra, more ships in the icy water and a better eye-in-the-sky." Concurrently, it emphasized that Canada's disagreements with its neighbors are "well-managed and pose no sovereignty or defense challenges for Canada" – a rather abrupt change of tone from previous political messaging.[85]

Thankfully, the lamentable "use it or lose it" message that had been so frequently mobilized to justify the government's agenda was absent from Canada's Northern Strategy. Instead, decision makers seemed to finally pay heed to commentators who find space for cooperation in the circumpolar world. The document casts the United States as an "exceptionally valuable partner in the Arctic" with which Canada has managed its differences responsibly since the Second World War. It also emphasizes opportunities for cooperation with Russia and "common interests" with European Arctic states, as well as a shared commitment to international law. Implicitly, this confirms that bilateral and multilateral engagement – not unilateralism – is key to stability and security in the region. If Canada wants to encourage Arctic development and ensure that northern residents are primary beneficiaries of it, then it is prudent to find ways to synchronize aspects of its policy agenda with the United States and enhance its relationships with Russia and European Arctic littoral states. Balancing an Arctic security agenda with domestic imperatives to improve the quality of life of northerners grappling with the challenges and opportunities accompanying climate change remains difficult. Overheated rhetoric about an Arctic race may have put the region back on Canada's political agenda, but the unlikely prospect of a military confrontation over boundaries and resources is unlikely to keep it there.

Canada's Northern Strategy transcends the line between domestic and foreign policy and seems to acknowledge that sovereignty is primarily about not boundary lines but everything that goes on within them. The litmus test of government resolve

[85] *Canada's Northern Strategy: Our North, Our Heritage, Our Future* (Ottawa: Government of Canada, 2009).

will be follow-through. "Policy is only as good as the action it inspires," Minister Cannon noted at the unveiling of the Northern Strategy.[86] Laying out a broad, integrated, and positive strategy is a step in the right direction. Converting the strategy to deliverables that produce a more constructive and secure circumpolar world will be the real challenge.

[86] P. W. Lackenbauer, "New Northern Strategy Trades Sabre-Rattling for Partnership," *Toronto Star*, 29 July 2009.

14

The New Arctic Geography and U.S. Strategy

James Kraska

It is axiomatic that climate change is affecting the Arctic more than any other region. Arctic sea ice continues to decrease. The summer of 2010 had the third-smallest extent of polar ice on record, and the 2010 ice volume was the lowest on record. One study suggests that the water flowing from the North Atlantic into the Arctic Ocean is warmer today than at any time during the past 2,000 years.[1] The polar ice sheet is melting. In August 2010, a giant mass of solid ice broke away from the Petermann Glacier in northwest Greenland – the largest calving from an ice shelf since 1962.[2] Although the cause of the Petermann calving is uncertain, the Arctic Five (A5) – Russia, Canada, the United States, Norway, and Denmark (Greenland) – are bracing for continuous warming and corresponding geophysical changes in the Arctic.

Circumpolar melting ice foreshadows the prospect of associated political-military change. Will a confluence of political rivalries and a changing climate upend the strategic environment just as melting ice transforms the ocean geography? This is not the first time that climate change has had the potential to cause dramatic political effects. The Little Ice Age that lasted from the sixteenth century to the nineteenth century was marked by a period of worldwide cooling.[3] The seventeenth century, in

---

[1] John Collins Rudolf, "Arctic Waters Warmer Than in 2,000 Years," *New York Times*, January 28, 2011. The study found that the waters of the Fram Strait, which runs between Greenland and the Svalbard archipelago have warmed by 3.5 degrees Fahrenheit over the past one hundred years. The water is believed to be 2.5 degrees Fahrenheit warmer than during the Medieval Warm Period, which was a period of elevated warmth between 900–1300.

[2] The break measured 260 square kilometers (or 100 square miles) and reduced the area of Petermann Glacier by 25 percent and its volume by 10 percent.

[3] The term "Little Ice Age" was introduced by François E. Matthes, Report of the committee on glaciers, vol. 20, *Transactions of the American Geophysical Union* (1939), at pp. 518–23. For a contemporary explanation of the term, see Michael E. Mann, Little Ice Age, vol. 1 *The Earth system: physical and chemical dimensions of global environmental change*, Encyclopedia of Global Environmental Change (Michael C. MacCracken and John S. Perry, eds., 2002), pp. 504–09.

particular, faced upheaval and adversity on a monumental scale. The planet cooled in the Little Ice Age following the medieval warm period, freezing Chesapeake Bay and chilling Alexandria, Egypt; rice crops in Japan and wheat in Portugal were killed by the cold. Climate change caused widespread famine, which descended into anarchy, triggering riots, warfare, and chaos throughout much of the world.

In China, the Ming dynasty suffered a violent collapse; the Ottoman Empire was engaged in a bitter struggle with the Holy League; the Dutch Revolt pried the Low Countries from the Spanish Empire. The Thirty Years' War dismembered Central Europe, throwing the continent into the throes of a bloodbath, which ended in the Peace of Westphalia in 1648. The end of the Thirty Years' War ushered into existence the modern nation-state. More warfare afflicted the globe during the hundred years of the seventeenth-century great crisis than at any time until the 1940s.[4] Looking back on the time, Voltaire explained to his mistress Madame du Chatelet in the 1740s: "The period of usurpations almost from one end of the world to the other," he wrote, was "the result of government, religion and the climate."[5]

The Arctic has placed prominently in military security in the more recent past, and it may be destined to do so again in the future. European Union High Representative for the Common Foreign Policy Javier Solana declared in March 2008 that European countries should prepare for the prospect of conflict in the region. But the very first modern Arctic battle was conducted along the frozen sea-shore interface of the Arctic Circle during the Second World War. The German pocket battleship *Admiral Scheer* and German U-boats stalked Soviet shipping around the island of Novaya Zemlya, astride the Kara Gate along the Northeast Passage, and raided as far east as Dikson on the Northern Sea Route.[6] At the same time, German and Finnish armies occupied the Karelian Peninsula in a thrust to cut off Murmansk as a disembarkation port for Allied supplies into the Soviet Union.

Moscow once again features as a central player in the strategic equation of the Arctic. In early 2009, the new Russian national security strategy warned that the Arctic was one of several energy-producing areas of the world that could erupt into conflict over competing resources claims. The Russian strategy states, "With the ongoing competition for resources, attempts to use military force to solve emerging problems cannot be excluded – and this might destroy the balance of forces on Russia's, and its allies', borders . . . " Similarly, Admiral Stavridis, commander of the U.S. European Command, cautioned that the race for oil and minerals in the Arctic region could lead to war.[7]

4 See generally Geoffrey Parker, *The General Crisis of the Seventeenth Century* (New York: Routledge, 1997).

5 Ibid., pp. 2–4.

6 *Battle for the Arctic Continues: Economic Rivalry in Arctic Leads to Increase in Russian Defense Activity*, Krestyanskaya Rus (Open Source Center, June 11, 2008), U.S. Government translation, Moscow CEP20080701358002.

7 "Senior NATO Commander: Climate Change Could Lead to Arctic Conflict," *Barents Observer*, October 12, 2010.

Still, armed conflict in the Arctic is improbable.[8] The National Intelligence Council, for example, suggests that major war in the Arctic is unlikely, although small-scale conflict – the result of spillover from disputes in other areas gravitating into the Arctic region – is possible.[9] All of the A5 are states' parties in good standing with the UN Convention on the Law of the Sea (UNCLOS), except the United States – and even Washington observes almost all of the provisions of the convention. At a conference in Moscow in September 2010, Russian Premier Vladimir Putin stressed that any disagreements in the region can be solved under the framework of UNCLOS, and furthermore that no Russian development projects would proceed in the Arctic without strict measures to ensure the fragile environment is protected.[10] Putin also stated that, although serious geopolitical and economic interests intersect in the Arctic, the prospects were high that the issues could be solved in a spirit of cooperation and partnership. Scenarios for future war in the Arctic have "nothing to do with reality," Putin stressed.[11]

Norwegian Minister of Defense Grete Faremo agreed with Putin's assessment in a speech before the Atlantic Council of the United States on October 28, 2010. In rejecting the idea that the Arctic faced the potential for an emergent "cold" war, she cited three examples of effective international cooperation developed in international law. First, like Putin, she suggested that the 1982 UN Convention on the Law of the Sea provides a universally accepted rule set for resolving disputes. UNCLOS is a framework for oceans governance that applies equally to the Arctic Ocean as it does to the Atlantic Oceans or Indian Ocean, and every Arctic power accepts the rules set forth in the convention. Second, multilateral fisheries agreements that are associated with UNCLOS have reduced the likelihood of a repeat of the Cod Wars between the United Kingdom and Iceland or the Tuna War between the United States and certain South American nations. These conflicts during the 1970s over fishing rights threatened to upend alliance harmony – nearly driving Iceland and the United Kingdom into war. But UNCLOS settled most disputes and the complementary fishing agreements have provided a mechanism for resolving disagreement. Finally, the 2010 treaty between Norway and Russia on the delimitation of their respective exclusive economic zones (EEZs) in the Barents Sea serves as an example of how seemingly intractable disagreements over oceans governance can be overcome through patient dialogue and cooperation.[12] In that case, the two neighbors negotiated for forty years before they came to an agreement over extension of economic rights and jurisdiction in the Barents Sea.

---

[8] Systems Planning and Analysis, Inc., *Naval Arctic Capabilities Based Assessment*, Draft Prepared for Task Force Climate Change, U.S. Navy (August 13, 2010), p. 13.

[9] National Intelligence Council, *Global Trends 2025: A Transformed World* (November 2008), p. 53.

[10] "Putin: Arctic Environment Comes First," *Barents Observer*, September 23, 2010.

[11] Ibid.

[12] "Changing Security Environment in the Arctic," *Barents Observer*, October 29, 2010.

Minister of Defense Grete Faremo might have added another reason for optimism, which is the success of the UN-specialized agency for maritime matters.
The International Maritime Organization (IMO) has served as a venue for Arctic states to adopt guidelines for ships operating in polar waters, and a mandatory polar code, which would set construction, design, equipping, and manning
(CDEM) standards for ships operating in the Arctic and Antarctic regions, is being
developed.[13]

The foundation for each of these reasons for optimism springs from the legal and
political framework of UNCLOS. Being the least predictable of the A5, one might
think that Russia perhaps poses the greatest challenge for ensuring the application
of UNCLOS to the region. But Moscow has repeatedly expressed support for resolving international differences in the Arctic Ocean in accordance with UNCLOS.
Russia has steadfastly adhered to the convention throughout the process of filing its
extended continental shelf claims filed in accordance with article 76 of the treaty,
assiduously collecting marine survey data of the seabed along the Lomonosov Ridge
to support its title. Despite its sometime bellicose language and saber rattling, from
the perspective of international law of the sea in the Arctic, Russia has a creditable
record. Thus, UNCLOS serves as a key mechanism for conflict avoidance in the
polar north, as it provides a widely accepted framework for resolving disagreements
over marine boundary delimitation, resource disputes on the continental shelf, con-
tending theories of coastal state jurisdiction and navigational freedom.

RUSSIA FEDERATION – ARCTIC HEGEMON?

Russia, which wraps 170 degrees around the pole, is the dominant Arctic power
in many ways. Most of the nonindigenous people and economic output above the
Arctic Circle are in Russia, and two-thirds of the oil and gas in the Arctic are
in Russia – mostly lying offshore. One-third of Russian territory is found north of
the Arctic Circle and the Northern Sea Route links these areas to the Siberian
interior via three vast river watersheds. The area is also linked to the national and,
indeed, the world commodity markets. The largest nickel mine in the world, for
example, is located in the area and operated by MMC Norilsk Nickel. Norilsk
operates a fleet of five seventh-class ice-breaking vessels—the highest class awarded
to Arctic vessels. Similarly, Sevmash and Zvezdochka shipyards in Severodvinsk are
engaged in building Prirazlomnaya ice-class oil platforms, the first destined for the
Prirazlomnoe oil field in the Pechora Sea, at the southeastern part of the Barents

---

[13] See, e.g., Guidelines for ships operating in polar waters, IMO Res. A.1024(26), adopted on December
2, 2009, A26/Res.1024, January 18, 2010, IMO Doc. DE 53/18/2, Development of a mandatory code for
ships operating in polar waters: Proposed framework for ships operating in polar waters, November
20, and IMO Doc. DE 53/18/9, Development of mandatory code for ships operating in polar waters:
Principles for proposed mandatory code for ships operating in polar waters, December 18, 2009.

Sea. The yards are also developing the Arkticheskaya jack-up offshore drilling rig. Finally, sidestepping grimaces from foreign diplomats, Moscow awarded Sevmash a contract to begin construction of the first of at least seven floating nuclear power stations to provide electricity to Arctic coastal industry. The project was transferred to Baltic yards in Saint Petersburg in 2008, however.

These steps are part of a concerted program to ensure that Russia is regarded as the first Arctic superpower. In 2001, Russia was the first nation to stake a claim to the seabed of the North Pole by filing a claim for exclusive resource rights with the Commission on the Limits of the Continental Shelf (CLCS), an independent international organization established by UNCLOS. The United States, Norway, Canada and Denmark (Greenland) have protested the Russian claim, and the CLCS has sought additional information from Russia. Moscow's extended continental shelf claims are still under review.

In 2007, Russian scientists planted on the seabed of the North Pole a Russian flag fashioned from titanium, presaging Moscow's entrance into a new geostrategic opera in what Norway calls the High North. Flush with petrodollars, Moscow is focusing on developing the Arctic as a cash cow to provide a future stream of oil, gas, and minerals for the country. Also in 2007, after a fifteen-year suspension, Russia resumed long-range aviation (LRA) strategic bomber flights over the Arctic. In 2007, Moscow boasted that two Tu-95 bombers flew along the coastlines of Alaska and Canada during a seventeen-hour flight and returned to Russia via the North Pole.[14] In 2008, Canadian jets intercepted a Russian LRA flight near Canada's airspace during a visit by Prime Minister Stephen Harper to Inuvik. The next year two Russian bombers were intercepted just beyond the maritime boundary of the Canadian Arctic by two Canadian CF-18s, only hours before the U.S. president visited Ottawa. By early October 2010, Russia already had conducted ten military patrols and sixteen strategic Tu-95 and Tu-160 bomber flights over the North Atlantic and the Arctic oceans for the year. The Arctic reconnaissance flights are mirrored by Russian LRA patrols in other strategic locations, such as operating surveillance flights near U.S. aircraft-carrier strike groups on the high seas and flying TU-95 strategic bomber patrols near the American bases on Guam.

Russia is also increasing its combat capabilities in the Arctic, including con-struction of new surface warships and additional shore stations.[15] Moscow's newest nuclear powered submarine, *Severodvinsk*, a fourth-generation boat of the *Graney* (*Yasen*) class, was launched from the city of its namesake in mid-June, 2010.[16]

---

[14] Brian Lilley, "Russian Bombers Probe Arctic Air Defenses," *Toronto Sun*, July 30, 2010. The incursions along the Canadian coast have strengthened plans for Canada to acquire sixty-five F-35 stealth fighter jets at a cost of US $9 billion. Ibid.

[15] "Russia Increases Combat Capabilities in Arctic," *Barents Observer*, October 4, 2010 (citing interview of Russian Navy Commander Admiral Vladimir Vysotsky).

[16] "New Nuclear Submarine to Be Launched Today," *Barents Observer*, June 15, 2010.

The *Graney* class is reported to be the most silent submarine in the world.[17] The boats can sprint at a maximum speed of sixteen knots surfaced and thirty-one knots submerged, and they are armed with twenty-four SS-NX-26 cruise missiles. Russia's latest fourth-generation strategic ballistic-missile submarine, *Yuri Dolgorukii*, a boat of the *Borey* class, is undergoing tests in the White Sea. The navy also is involved with preparing a proposal to ensure greater security along the Northeast Passage, which may include establishment of temporary bases for naval vessels at ports throughout the route.[18] Nonetheless, the Northern Fleet faces enormous budgetary pressure – as it is sometimes unable to even pay for heat for barracks and administration buildings at its sprawling complex at Severomorsk.[19]

The Northern Sea Route passes north of Russia through a series of international straits cutting between large coastal islands and the Siberian mainland. The Vilkitskiy Strait between the Taymyr Peninsula and Severnaya Zemlya, which has hard multiyear ice, is slightly above 77° north latitude. Overcoming the geophysical challenges, Russia has developed a much more extensive Arctic shipping infrastructure than any other nation. Established in the 1930s, the routes were used to connect the frozen north to the rest of the country. The infrastructure and port facilities deteriorated in the 1990s with the fall of the Berlin Wall and the breakup of the Soviet Union. Usage of the routes plummeted. In recent years, however, the Northern Sea Route and the western or European portion, the Northeast Passage, are experiencing a renaissance, as Russia lavishes attention and resources on its northern strategy. The routes have tremendous potential to promote the natural resources sector of the new Russian economy. The three large rivers in Siberia flow north to the Arctic, providing the best avenue for moving goods over long distances. Caitlyn Antrim speculates in Chapter 7 of this volume that as the climate warms, the rivers and associated oceanic routes will become even more accessible, both for resource development and for industrial transportation.

The routes have fared prominently in Russia's national economic development strategy since 2000, and Moscow has more icebreakers than any nation on earth.

---

[17] Ibid. The *Barents Observer* reports from a Russian-language story in *Prime-TASS*: "The submarines will have a completely new architecture and new types of armament. For the first time in Russian ship building, the torpedo tubes and missile launchers are placed not in the nose section but in the mid-section of the hull." See, Д. Медведев сегодня примет участие в церемонии вывода из стапельного цеха атомной подлодки нового поколения "Северодвинск," http://www.prime-tass.ru/news/0/%7BDBD86B55-C9A1-4734-AFE8-FC1562541F35%7D.uif.

[18] "Russia Increases Combat Capabilities in Arctic," *Barents Observer*, October 4, 2010 (citing interview of Russian Navy Commander Admiral Vladimir Vysotsky), reporting from a Russian-language source, *RIA Novosti*, October 2, 2010, ВМФ России наращивает боевые возможности в Арктике, http://rian.ru/defense_safety/20101002/281520321.html.

[19] In late October, 2010, the Russian Ministry of Defense owed a local heating company a €2.3 million debt for utilities for the base; despite guarantees of payment, the heating company refused to continue to provide service until the debt was paid. "Northern Fleet Is Freezing," *Barents Observer*, October 28, 2010.

Russia published comprehensive regulations for navigation along the Northern Sea Route, which include navigational control, mandatory pilotage, and required ice-breaker escort (through the Vilkitskiy, Dmitry Laptev, Sannikov, and Shokalskiy straits). Most of the vessel traffic along the Northern Sea Route is Russian flagged. Furthermore, most transits are regional cabotage shipping rather than intercontinental voyages. Three heavy, nuclear-powered icebreakers are to be added to the fleet by 2016. These powerful ships can operate along the northern coast throughout the entire year.[20] The nation also plans to construct a variety of ice-strengthened service vessels for offshore port service and search-and rescue operations.[21] Russia asserts the authority to require all vessels using the route to pay a fee to support ice breaking, and the charge can be as much as US $100,000 per transit. The transit fees and other regulations are excessive. Because the transit fees are disconnected from the actual cost of the services rendered, they constitute an impermissible impediment to transit passage through straits used for international navigation under UNCLOS. Some ice-strengthened ships are capable of conducting the transit without icebreaker support, so requiring icebreaker assistance appears to be more about rent seeking and political control than maintaining safety at sea.

In the west, resolution of the long-standing disputes with Norway over areas of the Barents Sea leaves only the more minor issue of Norway's claims surrounding the Svalbard archipelago as a source of contention. Norway claims a two-hundred-nautical-mile EEZ around Svalbard, as around other Norwegian territory. Some other nations disagree with the claim, casting into doubt Norway's right to make and enforce such a maritime zone. The 1920 Svalbard Treaty did not confer such rights, and Russia has been the most vociferous in objecting to Norway's creation of an economic zone around the islands. A larger group of states, including Spain and the United Kingdom, accept Norway's right to claim an EEZ around Svalbard, but hold the position that all state parties to the 1920 treaty are entitled to exploit the resources in the zone. Oslo argues that, because the treaty applies to the land and sea territories of Svalbard, Norway acquires all contemporary meanings of sovereign rights and jurisdiction in an EEZ, even though the term did not exist at the time that the Svalbard treaty was negotiated. Furthermore, Norway suggests that its EEZ claim is enhanced by the fact that the marine area surrounding Svalbard is the same continental shelf as that of northern Norway.

In practice, Norway recognizes rights to foreign fishing in the waters surrounding Spitsbergen based on historical fisheries in the area, thereby not discriminating against foreign vessels that have a long record of operating in the area. As a result, the Norwegian Fisheries Ministry generally has a rosy demeanor about the issue, stating that there has been no conflict arising from Svalbard's EEZ. In contrast,

[20] Caitlyn Antrim, "Russia and the Changing Geopolitics of the Arctic," *World Politics Review*, March 2, 2009, http://www.worldpoliticsreview.com/articles/3380/russia-and-the-changing-geopolitics-of-the-arctic.
[21] Ibid.

this assessment somewhat ignores the occasional tension caused by Russian fishing vessels operating in the area without obeisance to Norwegian fisheries enforcement patrols.

In the east, Moscow has reached agreement with the United States on maritime boundary delimitation along the Bering Strait. The 1990 treaty has not been ratified by the Duma, but the Russian Federation has observed its terms for twenty years. As more vessel traffic plies the Arctic Ocean, both the United States and Russia will acquire greater vessel safety, security, and traffic management responsibilities along the Bering Strait, the gateway connecting the Pacific Ocean to the Arctic Ocean. The strait was known as the Ice Curtain during the Cold War, and is now referred to as the Bering Gate. The narrow choke point is only fifty-two nautical miles wide and has a depth of between thirty and fifty meters. Greater demand will be placed on vessel traffic monitoring and routing, as well as on aids to safe navigation. The United States and Russia maintain effective cooperation in monitoring the Bering Strait, the most functional element of the bilateral relationship.

STRENGTHENING NORTH AMERICAN ARCTIC SECURITY

Most broadly the United States seeks to help create an Arctic region that is stable and secure, where U.S. national interests are safeguarded and the homeland is protected. The 2010 *National Security Strategy* identifies four enduring national security interests of the United States, and each of these has application to the Arctic region:

- The security of the United States, its citizens, and U.S. allies and partners;
- A strong, innovative, and growing U.S. economy in an open international economic system that promotes opportunity and prosperity;
- Respect for universal values at home and around the world;
- An international order advanced by U.S. leadership that promotes peace, security, and opportunity through stronger cooperation to meet global challenges.

The *Strategy* also sets forth enduring U.S. interests in the Arctic: "The United States is an Arctic nation with broad and fundamental interests in the Arctic region, where we seek to meet our national security needs, protect the environment, responsibly manage resources, account for indigenous communities, support scientific research, and strengthen international cooperation on a wide range of issues." The U.S. armed forces began to consider the strategic and policy implications of a warming Arctic, when, as oceans policy adviser on the Joint Staff, I coordinated a dialogue on the Arctic between the Navy staff and U.S. Northern Command, U.S. European Command, and U.S. Pacific Command. Each of the three geographic combatant commanders held operational control (OPCON) over U.S. armed forces in a portion of the Arctic. One of the first issues that we addressed was whether U.S. forces and security interests the Arctic region would be better served if a single geographic combatant commander had OPCON over the region. Although U.S. Northern Command was keen to fill the role, except for Canada and the United States, all other Arctic nations, including Greenland (Denmark), were within the U.S. European Command area of responsibility. As we enter mid-2011, it remains an open question whether the Unified Command Plan will be amended to grant a single combatant commander OPCON over the Arctic.

After Artur N. Chilingarov, a member of the Russian Duma, led an expedition that used a deep-sea submersible to plant the Russian flag at the bottom of the Arctic Ocean, other U.S. departments and agencies scrambled to become more involved in U.S. policy planning for the region. Beginning in 2007, the National Security Council and the Department of State cohosted a series of White House–level meetings to develop a new U.S. Arctic policy. The effort was divided into four working groups, with the group addressing national security and navigational issues co-led by a U.S. Navy judge advocate and a U.S. Coast Guard officer. The new policy, focusing solely on the Arctic, would replace the directive signed by President Bill Clinton in 1994, a document that also included goals for U.S. Antarctic policy.[22] The interagency process included participants from a dozen U.S. government departments. The Department of Defense supported creation of a new policy, so long as it reflected core Pentagon equities in the region. All participating agencies agreed that UNCLOS was the essential point of departure and governance framework for any new policy. Eighteen months later, on January 9, 2009, the White House released National Security Presidential Directive 66 (NSPD-66), "Arctic Region Policy." The foremost purpose of the policy was to set forth U.S. national security and homeland defense interests in the Arctic in light of climate change.

The U.S. Arctic Region Policy is a clear and unflinchingly honest expression of American security prerogatives in the region. The president states: "The Arctic region is primarily a maritime domain. . . . Human activity in the Arctic region is increasing and is projected to increase further in coming years. This requires the United States to assert a more active and influential national presence to protect its Arctic interests and to project sea power throughout the region." The United States has begun to think more carefully about the future of the Arctic.[23] The policy also identifies freedom of the seas as a "top national priority." Preserving the rights and duties relating to navigation and overflight in the Arctic region supports the ability of the United States and its friends and partners to exercise these

---

[22] Presidential Decision Directive 26 (PDD-26), United States Policy on the Arctic and Antarctic Regions, May 10, 1994.

[23] Robert Huebert, "United States Arctic Policy: The Reluctant Arctic Power," School of Public Policy Briefing Paper 2:2 (May 2009), pp. 10–12, 22, http://policyschool.ucalgary.ca/files/publicpolicy/SPPBriefing-HUEBERTonline.pdf.

rights throughout the world, including through strategic straits. The United States' Arctic policy is to:

- Meet national security and homeland security needs relevant to the Arctic region;
- Protect the Arctic environment and conserve its biological resources;
- Ensure natural resource management and economic development are environmentally sustainable;
- Strengthen institutions for cooperation among the eight Arctic nations;
- Involve the Arctic's indigenous communities in decisions affecting them;
- Enhance scientific monitoring and research of environmental issues.

Somewhat obliquely, the United States also suggests that the A5 states bordering the Arctic Ocean have an interest in regulating the access of non-Arctic powers, such as China. The forgoing laundry-list rendition of U.S. equities in the Arctic region belies a lack of interagency consensus on prioritizing U.S. goals in the region.

"Arctic Region Policy" was released at a time of accelerating Arctic resource competition and profound disagreement over navigational regimes in the region. For example, the emphasis on strict marine environmental regulation and regulatory attempts to battle climate change may prove at odds with freedom of navigation for commercial shipping and operational access to the Arctic Ocean by U.S. naval forces. The national security provisions of the policy were coordinated widely throughout the Department of Defense and included input from the navy staff and combatant commanders for Northern Command, European Command, and Pacific Command.

The new policy also indicates that the United States is "prepared to operate either independently or in conjunction with other states to safeguard [U.S.] interests."[24] These interests include the capability to operate sea and air systems for strategic sealift, strategic deterrence, maritime presence, and maritime security operations, and to ensure freedom of navigation and overflight. "Arctic Region Policy" also identifies a national requirement to protect U.S. Arctic homeland security and sovereignty over land territory and territorial seas, and minerals and oil and gas deposits located under the seabed.

The United States will continue to use the Arctic as a domain to strengthen American strategic deterrence.[25] Under the U.S. *Deterrence Operations: Joint Operations Concept*, decisive influence is achieved by "credibly threatening to deny benefits and/or impose costs," by convincing a potential adversary that restraint on their

[24] White House, National Security Presidential Directive-66/Homeland Security Presidential Directive-25, section III.B, paras. 1–5 (January 12, 2009).
[25] National Security Presidential Directive-66/Homeland Security Presidential Directive-25 (January 12, 2009).

behalf will result in an acceptable outcome.[26] The U.S. national security interests in the Arctic are grounded in advancing strategic deterrence, and they include ballistic-missile early warning and ballistic-missile defense. Naval forces depend on global strategic mobility and tactical maritime and aerospace maneuverability to conduct the spectrum of sea, air, and land operations. Freedom of navigation is especially critical to protect mobility for the most survivable component of nuclear deterrence, which is ballistic-missile submarines (SSBNs).[27] Maintaining operational air and sea access and the ability to operate unimpeded in the Arctic Ocean is a corner-stone of U.S. nuclear deterrence. Situated among the continents of North America, Europe, and Asia, and with access to the Pacific and Atlantic oceans, the geographic proximity of the Arctic Ocean makes it an especially attractive area for submarine patrols. Taking refuge near the ice, stationary submarines are virtually undetectable and therefore invulnerable to attack. Furthermore, the tyranny of vast distances and the presence of the hovering ice canopy make antisubmarine surveillance systems particularly inefficient.

The Arctic is an ideal location for ballistic-missile defense systems, and the area is still a potential vector for ballistic-missile attack on North America. The region is a principle trajectory for nuclear or conventional medium-range and intercon-tinental ballistic-missile attack from Russia, China, North Korea, and Iran. Along with upgraded early-warning radar (UEWR) in the Flyingdales, United Kingdom and Beale, California, there is an early warning, tracking, object classification, and cueing data facility in Thule, Greenland. The Greenland UEWR completed the Ballistic Missile Defense System (BMDS) in 2011. All three of the UEWRs transfer to the U.S. Air Forces in 2012. The UEWRs are solid-state, phased-array, long-range radars that provide space surveillance, tactical warning and assessment and mid-course coverage to detect sea-launched and intercontinental ballistic missiles out to a distance of 3,000 miles. The Early Warning Radar in Clear, Alaska is planned to begin UEWR modernization in 2013. The UEWR has two or three faces, with each face providing 120 degrees of coverage.

The U.S. Air Force also operates a powerful Cobra Dane radar, located on the island of Shemya on the western edge of the Aleutian Island chain, and it has been integrated into the BMDS.[28] Upgraded in 2004, the Cobra Dane facility includes a twenty-nine-meter phased array antenna that supports the North American Air Defense Command (NORAD) and the Missile Defense Agency. Cobra Dane has

[26] U.S. Department of Defense, *Deterrence Operations Joint Operating Concept* 2.0 (Washington, D.C.: U.S. Department of Defense), 5 (approved by Secretary of Defense Donald H. Rumsfeld, chair of the Joint Chiefs of Staff General Peter Pace, USMC, and Commander U.S. Strategic Command General James E. Cartwright, USMC).

[27] Admiral Gary Roughead, General James T. Conway, and Admiral Thad W. Allen, *Naval Operations Concept: Implementing the Maritime Strategy*, 2010, p. 75. See also John Norton Moore, "The Regime of Straits and the Third United Nations Conference on the Law of the Sea," *American Journal of International Law* 74 (January 1980): pp. 77, 88.

[28] Missile Defense Agency, Department of Defense, *Testing, Building Confidence* 5 (2009).

one radar face providing 136 degrees of azimuth coverage. The system is used in maintaining deterrence, verification for strategic arms control, and aerospace missions on behalf of the National Aeronautic and Space Administration.

The United States and Canada are party to a number of mutual agreements to maintain surveillance of North American aerospace. Fifty years ago, the two nations created the Distant Early Warning (DEW) line of radar sites and established NORAD to counter Soviet intercontinental ballistic missiles. Modernized in 1985, the DEW line is a series of radar stations spanning the northernmost land boundary of North America from western Alaska to Greenland, and it is now known as the North Warning System. More recently, the United States has constructed installations for ground-based missile defense, accompanying radars and test beds stationed in the region, including twenty-six ground-based interceptors deployed to Alaska and California. Satellites, ground-based radar, and air force airborne radar and fighter jets form a comprehensive network to counter inbound aircraft.[29]

The navy is entering the field of theater ballistic-missile defense after numerous successful demonstrations of the *Arleigh Burke* guided missile destroyer. The Aegis ballistic-missile defense system is the sea-based component of BMDS, and is designed to defeat short- to intermediate-range, unitary and separating, midcourse-phase ballistic-missile threats with the Standard Missile-3 (SM-3), and in the terminal phase with the SM-2. The U.S. Navy operates five cruisers and sixteen guided missile destroyers outfitted with Aegis BMD capabilities. Of the twenty-one ships, sixteen are assigned to the Pacific Fleet and five to the Atlantic Fleet. By 2013, the navy plans to operate thirty-two BMD Aegis warships. The Naval Air and Missile Defense Command (NAMDC) formed to synchronize and integrate joint and combined efforts across the spectrum of aerospace threats, to include air defense, cruise-missile defense, and ballistic-missile defense.[30] Each of these mission sets relies on freedom of the seas in the Arctic. As the next generation of missile defense gravitates toward sea basing, it becomes inextricably connected to maritime mobility and freedom of navigation.

Department of Defense strategic guidance concerning the Arctic was included in the 2010 *Quadrennial Defense Review* (QDR), which established four priority objectives for the Pentagon. First, the armed forces must be able to "prevail in today's wars." Second, U.S. forces should be positioned to "prevent and deter conflict, and third, prepare to defeat adversaries and succeed in a wide range of contingencies. Finally, the United States seeks to preserve and enhance the All-Volunteer Force. Against the backdrop of these priority objectives, the QDR identified the opening of the Arctic waters to summer vessel traffic as "a unique opportunity to work collaboratively in multilateral forums to promote a balanced approach to improving human and environmental security in the region." In order to achieve the Pentagon's objectives, the QDR states that the Department of Defense will have to "work collaboratively with

29 "About NORAD," http://www.norad.mil/about/index.html.
30 "Navy Air and Missile Defense Command Established," *Targeted News Service*, April 30, 2009.

interagency partners to address gaps in Arctic communications, domain awareness, search and rescue, and environmental observation and forecasting capabilities to support both current and future planning and operations." The QDR also reiterates the Pentagon's strong support for U.S. accession to UNCLOS, which would help to protect U.S. Arctic interests and secure support for more cooperative engagement in the Arctic.

But given the United States' faltering attention toward the region, Professor Robert Huebert aptly described America as the reluctant Arctic power.[31] It is unclear, however, how much of a leadership role the United States should consider taking in the Arctic. Despite a multitude of rather hyperbolic media reports of nations rushing headlong into Arctic conflict, it is unlikely that climate change will have a dramatic impact on U.S. national security interests in the coming decades. Although melting ice will open access to greater human activity in the region in the decades ahead, such as increased vessel traffic through the Bering Strait, there are no compelling economic, political, or military threats on the horizon that are beyond the ability of existing institutions to manage. Except for Russia, the A5 is composed of founding members of NATO. The three additional littoral states include Iceland, also a member of NATO, and Finland and Sweden, nations that are friendly to NATO. In 2009, for example, NATO conducted the Loyal Arrow exercise in northern Sweden. The live-fire exercise, which had jet aircraft from ten NATO and non-NATO countries participating, was the largest aviation military exercise ever conducted in Sweden. Similarly, Finland regularly participates in Partnership for Peace exercises, and Finnish forces have supported NATO's International Security Assistance Force (ISAF) by sending one hundred troops to work with a provincial reconstruction team in Afghanistan and four hundred Finnish troops participate in the NATO-led Kosovo Force (KFOR) in Kosovo. Each of these states accepts UNCLOS and has demonstrated a willingness to manage and resolve disputes through the venues of the IMO, the Arctic Council, and the Barents Euro-Arctic Council, and on a bilateral basis. Russia, although sometimes unable to overcome a deep-seated post–Cold War revanchist sensibility, also has promoted Arctic diplomacy.

As a nation, the United States views the Arctic with relatively minimal interest compared to every other Arctic nation, and enjoys a lackadaisical attitude borne from the perspective of a country with strong Arctic allies and partners and the perception of a low-threat environment. Furthermore, the deep fiscal chasm of the U.S. federal budget augurs against great U.S. leadership in the Arctic. Neither the Department of Defense nor other U.S. government agencies are likely to receive new appropriations for Arctic activities, which are viewed by Congress and the American people as peripheral to more pressing domestic and foreign policy needs. A case in point

[31] Rob Huebert, "United States Arctic Policy" *The Reluctant Arctic Power*, SPP Briefing Papers vol. 2, no. 2 (School of Public Policy, University of Calgary, May 2009). Robert Huebert is a preeminent Arctic security scholar in Canada, and author of Chapter 12 of this volume.

is the U.S. Coast Guard's inability to secure funding for sorely needed icebreakers, a cause it has championed for several years, but without success. Even though the Department of Defense has supported the request from the fifth armed service, Congress and the current and former administrations have not funded the ships. An increased presence in the Arctic would require much more than just icebreakers, however. The American Arctic lacks deepwater port facilities, airfields, aids to navigation and maritime domain awareness systems and associated infrastructure, all of which would have to be created to accommodate a greater U.S. military and law enforcement presence in the region.

The United States is not focused on the Arctic, and, for the most part, other countries prefer it to be that way. Interestingly, Americans in general tend to both lack interest in the Arctic and be widely enthusiastic about the efficacy of diplomacy and accommodation to address problems in the region. In contrast, other countries are more reticent about multilateral solutions. Canada, in particular, is described by one public opinion survey as "rather churlish" and much less open to negotiation and compromise in the Arctic.[32] The image of Canada as a champion of consensus and cooperation does not hold true for the Arctic and, particularly, for the issue of the Northwest Passage. It is a paradox that while Canada is the most intransigent Arctic nation, the one country least willing to compromise in the region, Ottawa is still a more preferred partner than the United States among the populations of all other Arctic nations except Russia.[33] United States inattention to the Arctic has not assuaged doubts that the superpower could become an unhelpful presence in the region.

In general, all Arctic nations have a clear preference for working with Scandinavian countries. Scandinavian states are the most preferred Arctic partner among seven of eight Arctic states, with only the United States preferring another country (Canada) as its first choice.[34] The U.S. choice of Canada as the preferred Arctic partner is ironic, since Canadians identify the United States as one of the least desirable Arctic partners. Among the populations of all Arctic states, which nation was considered the least preferred partner in dealing with Arctic issues? China.

In the past two years, China has become more assertive about its "rights" in the Arctic Ocean, principally as a means to exploit natural resources in the region, and this posture has made all of the Arctic Eight nervous.[35] Admiral Yin Zhou of the People's Liberation Army Navy asserted in 2010 that the "Arctic does not belong to any particular nation and is rather the property of all the world's people" and that "China must play an indispensable role in Arctic exploration as it has one-fifth of

[32] *Rethinking the Top of the World: Arctic Security Public Opinion Survey* (Ekos Research Associates, January 2011), at p. viii
[33] *Rethinking the Top of the World*, at p. 36.
[34] *Rethinking the Top of the World*, at p. 36.
[35] See, e.g., Guy Faulconbridge, "Russian Navy Boss Warns of China's Race for Arctic," *Reuters*, October 4, 2010, http://af.reuters.com/article/energyOilNews/idAFLDE6931GL20101004.

the world's population."[36] Beijing elbowed its way into observer status at the Arctic Council and operates the world's largest nonnuclear icebreaker, *Xue Long* (Snow Dragon). China also has the largest embassy in Reykjavik, Iceland and maintains a large scientific research presence in Spitsbergen. Since 1984, China has conducted twenty-six polar expeditions.[37] China is also testing the feasibility of the Northern Sea Route as a major conduit for commercial traffic. At the beginning of the spring thaw in 2011, China will send an ultra-large tanker on the first-ever transit from Murmansk to China.

Yet China is the least preferred Arctic partner among the populations of seven of the eight Arctic states, with only the Russians naming a different country as their least preferred Arctic partner (they named the United States).[38] The United States, however, is the least regarded among the other Arctic states than any other Arctic state, with seven Arctic states selecting the United States as its first, second, or third least preferred Arctic partner. The United States was selected as the first choice of least favorite partner by the Russians, the second choice least favorite partner by people in Denmark, Iceland, Norway, Sweden, and Northern Canada, and a third choice least favorite partner by people in Southern Canada and Finland. Russia, on the other hand is regarded as a second least favorite partner on Arctic issues only by people in Southern Canada and the United States, and a third least favorite partner by respondents in Northern Canada and Iceland.[39] In sum, among the populations of all Arctic states, the United States is clearly the least popular or least preferred partner for addressing Arctic issues after China. At the same time, the United States is being both restrained and rather unaware of its sovereignty claims and rights in the region.[40] With a focus on ground wars in Afghanistan and Iraq, it is no wonder that the American people seemed to have forgotten that the Arctic is an ocean, the United States is a maritime nation, and naval forces are essential for polar security and global stability.

FREEDOM OF THE SEAS

During the Cold War, the U.S. Navy provided Arctic maritime security for Canada and other NATO nations. American patrols in the region – primarily subsurface and

---

[36] David Akin, "Harper Deals with New Arctic Rival: China," *Toronto Sun*, June 23, 2010, http://www.torontosun.com/news/g20/2010/06/22/14484401.html.

[37] Joseph Spears, "The Snow Dragon Moves into the Arctic Ocean Basin," vol. 11. *China Brief*, January 28, 2011, http://www.jamestown.org/programs/chinabrief/single/?tx_ttnews%5Btt_news%5D=37429&cHash=a076c446d9.

[38] *Rethinking the Top of the World*, at p. 37.

[39] *Rethinking the Top of the World*, at p. 37.

[40] For example, concerning the U.S.-Canadian dispute over six thousand square miles of exclusive economic zone in the Beaufort Sea, half of Canadians believe that their country should try to assert full sovereignty rights over the area, whereas only ten percent of Americans hold a similar view. Sixty-two percent of Americans prefer to work to strike a deal over the disputed territory, while forty-three percent of Canadians hold such view. *Rethinking the Top of the World*, at p. 40.

long-range aviation – diminished during the 1990s. Today, however, climate change promises to gradually open up the waters of the Arctic for new resource development and to new shipping routes. The Northwest Passage, the Northern Sea Route, the Bering Strait, and even a transpolar route across the North Pole may reshape the global transport system.[41] The importance of these routes is reflected in the 2009 Arctic Region Policy, which states: "Freedom of the seas is a top national priority."[42] Consequently, the 2009 policy adopted identical language as that found in the 1994 U.S. policy on the Arctic and Antarctic regions, which states: "freedom of the seas is a top national priority." Freedom of navigation is the only U.S. national interest in the area that is singled out for special recognition or independent acknowledgment in the new policy. One reason is that freedom of navigation is not a regional issue but rather has worldwide political, operational, and legal impact. The seas are interconnected and form a single world ocean. Strategic mobility and maneuverability throughout the Arctic Ocean – the fourth largest of the world's oceans – has global implications. Reflecting the spatial global quality of the oceans, the 2009 Arctic policy invokes existing U.S. national-level authorities concerning maritime security and freedom of navigation to the Arctic. Specifically, National Security Presidential Directive 41 (Maritime Security Policy), Presidential Decision Directive 32 (Freedom of Navigation), and the National Strategy for Maritime Security are referenced, collectively delineating security and economic interests in the oceans as a spatial domain for movement.

Russia and Canada are consulting with each other in developing restrictive rules governing the Northern Sea Route and the Northwest Passage. At a meeting in Moscow in February 2009, for example, representatives from the two nations met to coordinate how each country manages its polar passage under article 234 of UNC-LOS. The goal of the meeting was for the two nations to leverage each other's maritime claim and assertion of coastal state authority to generate broader international support for their own positions. Both sides stated that there was a high degree of similarity in their position on the issue of international shipping in the two transit routes. Ottawa and Moscow also agreed that the respective coastal state limitations imposed on each route are necessary to preserve the fragile Arctic maritime environment, and that each legal regime is consistent with the provisions on ice-covered areas set forth in article 234. Furthermore, the two states agreed to conduct detailed consultations on the issue. Part of future discussions will be the topic of the coastal state historic waters claims and each country's diplomatic disputes with the United States over the legal status of the transit routes.[43]

[41] The White House, National Security Presidential Directive-66/Homeland Security Presidential Directive-25, section III.B, paras. 1–5 (January 12, 2009).
[42] Ibid.
[43] Russia-Canada consultations on the legal status of the Arctic, February 20, 2009 (Moscow), (meeting between R. Kolodkin, legal adviser to the minister of foreign affairs of Russia, and A. Kessel, legal adviser to the minister of foreign affairs of Canada), http://byers.typepad.com/

Freedom of navigation throughout the prominent Arctic straits is an especially powerful U.S. interest. The Arctic Policy states, "The Northwest Passage is a strait used for international navigation, and the Northern Sea Route includes straits used for international navigation; the regime of transit passage applies to passage through those straits. Preserving the rights and duties relating to navigation and overflight in the Arctic region supports our ability to exercise these rights throughout the world, including through strategic straits."[44] Freedom of access in the Arctic affects the ability of the United States to support peacetime and wartime contingencies worldwide. To the extent that the melting ice opens the Northwest Passage, the Northern Sea Route, or even a transpolar route, strategic sealift in the Arctic may become connected to force surge and sustainment to virtually any corner of the globe. Forces responding to a crisis on the Korean Peninsula or heavy sealift to support forces in the Middle East and South Asia, for example, could arrive via Arctic transit.

The Northwest Passage extends 2,850 nautical miles and consists of five major routes, of which two are suitable as deep-draft channels of navigation by vessels up to twenty-six meters in draft, and several are suitable for navigation by submerged submarines. Looking from the west, the first of the two main routes passes through the Prince of Wales Strait, the Parry Channel, Lancaster Sound, and Baffin Bay, and emerges out of Davis Strait. The second route begins, also from the west, at McClure Strait into Parry Channel, north of Prince of Wales Strait. The Nares Strait between Greenland and Ellesmere Island, which is the most direct route; the Parry Channel south of the Queen Elizabeth Islands; and finally Jones Sound through the Cardigan Strait and the channels through the Sverdrup Islands are all navigable by submerged submarine transit. The eastern approaches to the Northwest Passage are dominated by icebergs, which calve from glaciers on the northwestern side of Greenland, Ellesmere Island, and Devon Island and are carried by the Labrador Current south to the waters off Newfoundland. In the Beaufort Sea along the western approaches to the passage, there is a zone of first-year ice extending between fifty and one hundred nautical miles between the pack ice and the coastal fast ice, or ice that has frozen along the shoreline and "fastened" to the land.

As the ice melts, Canada expects even more shipping to enter the area. In 2007, for example, three cruise ships appeared in the Northwest Passage without advance notice of arrival.[45] Two of the vessels stopped at Barrow, Alaska. The community was surprised by four hundred German-speaking tourists descending on the city.[46]

---

arctic/russiacanada-consultations-on-the-legal-status-of-the-arctic.html. See also Randy Boswell, "Thaw May Be Underway in Ottawa-Moscow Arctic Issues," *Canwest News Service*, May 12, 2009, http://www.vancouversun.com/Technology/Thaw+underway+Ottawa+Moscow+Arctic+issues/1589395/story.html.

[44] The White House, National Security Presidential Directive-66/Homeland Security Presidential Directive-25, section III.B, paras. 1–5 (January 12, 2009).

[45] Rear Admiral Gene Brooks, Arctic Journal, *US Fed News*, October 16, 2008.

[46] Ibid.

The prospect of even larger numbers of oil tankers and cargo vessels on intercontinental transits, cruise ships, and ecotourists threatens to accelerate warming even more.[47] These changes have rattled Canada, which prefers not to host increased shipping traffic throughout the North American Arctic, and the Northwest Passage in particular. Three-fourths of Canadians believe the Northwest Passage falls within Canadian internal waters, whereas citizens of other Arctic countries either do not know about the status of the waterway or believe that it is an international strait.[48] The belief that the legal status of the Northwest Passage is part of "Canadian waters" and now under assault represents a literary license that appeals to Canadian masses at the expense of accuracy. In fact, in those narrow portions of the waterway that are twenty-four nautical miles or less in width, the legal status of the water is Canadian sovereign territorial seas, but with the special navigation regime of transit passage applicable to international ships and aircraft.

The United States and the European Union have long held the Northwest Passage to be a strait used for international navigation, connecting one part of the high seas or exclusive economic zone with another part of the high seas or exclusive economic zone. As with all international straits, the Northwest Passage has dual status as territorial seas of the coastal state. In this case, those areas of the strait that are within twelve nautical miles of shoreline are Canadian territorial seas, although the international community has the right of unimpeded transit passage by surface vessels, submarines, and aircraft through the strait. This right of transit passage is more robust than the normal right of innocent passage through the territorial seas, and unlike innocent passage, transit passage cannot be suspended by Ottawa. In 1995, Defense Minister David Collenette was asked in the House of Commons whether there were foreign submarines transiting the Northwest Passage. Collenette responded, "Mr. Speaker, we have a number of bilateral agreements with the United States. One of them provides for the movement of U.S. vessels in Canadian waters upon agreement of such a maneuver. . . . When the United States requires such permission, they let us know that they intend to use our waters and we acquiesce."[49] Apparently mistaking a 1988 icebreaker agreement between the U.S. and Canada that covers Arctic marine scientific research only, the minister was compelled to retract his assurance months later, writing, "There is no formal agreement covering the passage of any nation's submarines through Canadian Arctic waters. However, as a country that operates submarines, Canada does receive information on submarine activities from our allies. This information is exchanged for operational and safety reasons with the emphasis on minimizing

[47] "As Arctic Warms, Increased Shipping Likely to Accelerate Climate Change," *Science Daily*, October 26, 2010, http://www.sciencedaily.com/releases/2010/10/101025161150.htm.

[48] *Rethinking the Top of the World*, at p. 45.

[49] Michael Byers, "Arctic Sovereignty: Another Threat Runs Silent and Deep," *Globe and Mail*, March 5, 2009, http://www.theglobeandmail.com/news/opinions/article974944.ece.

interference and the possibility of collisions between submerged submarines."[50] Although NATO states have provided information to ensure waterspace deconfliction, the purpose of the information is boat safety. There is no legal or political implication that can be drawn from the practice of sharing subsurface deconfliction.

Finally, under article 8(2) of UNCLOS, even if Canadian straight baselines were accepted as lawful, enclosing the entire archipelago as internal waters, the international community still would enjoy the right of nonsuspendable innocent passage throughout the Northwest Passage. These realities are unsettling in Canada because they expose a dimension of vulnerability never before experienced. While maintaining American rights and freedoms in the Northwest Passage, the United States and other NATO nations also have a solemn duty to integrate the region into alliance defense. Climate change cannot become a source of insecurity for Canada.

The United States has a fundamental interest not only in the defense of Alaska but also in protecting its northern neighbor. The area is replete with critical natural geography and industrial architecture that is important for both nations' economies. The world's largest coal deposit lies inland along the northwestern coast of Alaska. The world's largest zinc mine is located at Red Dog, Alaska, near the Chukchi Sea. Seventy miles into the Delong Mountains and inland from Kivalina above the Arctic Circle, Red Dog works throughout the year, pulling zinc and lead from an open pit mine. The ore is driven down a gravel road to the Delong Mountain Terminal, where it is stored until summer, when dozens of large ore carriers anchor offshore and load the ore from lighters.

More broadly, the United States shares with Canada an interest in securing the Northwest Passage, but Washington must not undermine its long-standing prerogative in preserving global freedom of the seas. Likewise, Canada shares the American interest in protecting freedom of the seas, on which North America's economic prosperity and military security depends, but it also possesses a practical and political imperative to control the shipping routes slicing through its northern islands. These two inseparable North American allies will have to find a way to manage the relationship so that the global interests and homeland security interests are maintained, with one not sacrificed to obtain the other.

ARCTIC NAVAL OPERATIONS

The U.S. surface fleet is unaccustomed to operating in extreme cold or navigating ice hazards. The harsh environment of the ocean surface makes conventional threats less likely.[51] Operations in extreme wind chill, darkness, low visibility, and on ice-covered decks while under way pose great challenges for people and equipment.

---

[50] Ibid.
[51] David Longshore, "American Naval Power and the Prevention of Terror," vol. 1 *Homeland Security Affairs* (Summer 2005).

Expanding naval operations in the Arctic will require new cold-weather gear and polar operations training for the armed forces. Tactics, techniques, and procedures to accomplish new polar operations will have to emerge. Accomplishing the range of new maritime missions in the Arctic, from constabulary presence to decisive joint force with complex strike packages, will require adaptation or development of new technical capabilities. The U.S. sea services should commit to designing ice-strengthened patrol ships, much as Canada has embarked on a program to build up to eight ice-strengthened Arctic offshore patrol vessels. Half of the Danish Navy's ships are ice-strengthened. The United States also should ensure that it deploys a robust icebreaker capability, something only the Russian Federation has done well. The former commandant of the U.S. Coast Guard has suggested that a fleet of six icebreakers would be ideal, providing each coast with a full-time presence and allowing enough hulls for training, workups, and postdeployment maintenance. So far, however, the United States has not found the political commitment to spend the funds necessary to ensure a maritime Arctic presence.

Real-time weather and dynamic environmental and ice prediction and oceano-graphic information is an especially important part of the intelligence prepara-tion of the battle space. Right now, polar operations are hampered by a lack of robust command, control, communications, computers, intelligences, surveillance, and reconnaissance (C4ISR) infrastructure for network-centric warfare capability. Existing platforms require weatherized upgrades to withstand the extreme north-ern conditions. New platforms and infrastructure would have to be developed for tasks that require greater tolerances than existing equipment, such as unmanned systems for surveillance or strike missions that can loiter in extreme cold and heavy wind. Synthetic-aperture radar (SAR) is particularly useful in the Arctic, as it can collect imagery in inclement weather and conduct broad area imag-ing at high resolution. But there is a shortfall in command and control, GPS, and automated navigation system availability at high latitudes. The effect of polar magnetic variation on inertial navigation disrupts navigational systems. The armed forces face a shortfall in surveillance and reconnaissance and appropriate sensors and weapons for the Arctic. All of these technological requirements are tied to a robust and dedicated polar-orbit space capability. And the required systems are very expensive.

Surface warships face unique problems of damage from topside icing when oper-ating at high latitudes. Rime ice (freezing fog) on the windward side and ice buildup coating the topside of surface vessels has to be monitored and manually removed to maintain the vessel's reserve buoyancy. This involves the unglamorous task of break-ing the ice free from vessel surfaces with baseball bats. In building patrol vessels for the Arctic, the navy could adapt existing naval architecture for operating in ice conditions, which have been developed by the major classification societies. Rules developed by the American Bureau of Shipping for design and construction of ships for ice-infested waters, for example, would be a useful starting point for developing maritime constabulary vessels to operate in the Arctic.

The presence of either floating ice or pack ice potentially affects all aspects of surface ship operations, endangering bow-mounted sonar domes and interfering with towed arrays. Expeditionary operations in Arctic littoral areas may have to contend not only with navigating among other users of the ocean but also with remote operating areas, ice hazards, high surf zones, and ice-encrusted shorelines.[52] Propellers, rudders, fin stabilizers, and sea chests are also affected by operations in ice-infested waters.[53] It is likely that most surface vessels will operate in areas covered by first-year ice, which is less than one meter thick. First-year ice can be reliably cut with vessels constructed with strengthened bows and sterns. The extreme cold, high atmospheric moisture, and icy conditions can affect more mundane systems as well, weakening steel hulls, changing hydraulic system temperatures, and cracking or shedding protective coatings and insulators. If the navy expects to operate in the Arctic in the coming decades, polar naval architecture will have to be addressed because vessels are acquired on multidecade procurement cycles.

In addition to strategic deterrence patrols by Trident-capable submarines, naval forces may be engaged in any of the missions set forth in the Naval Operations Concept, the navy's principle operational guidance, which was signed by the chief of naval operations and the commandant of the Marine Corps.[54] Most of the tasks contained in the mission set portfolio of the sea services may be applied to the Arctic Ocean, including freedom of navigation assertions, global strike, sea control, and antiaccess and sea denial strategies. Forward presence promotes conventional deterrence. The full range of maritime security (constabulary) operations include counterterrorism and counterproliferation, as well as maritime interception operations and visit, board, search, and seizure (VBSS), and can be applied against irregular maritime threats.[55] Naval forces also may conduct disaster relief and humanitarian assistance operations. These latter missions are particularly reliant on aviation and small boat operations, which are particularly challenging in the harsh environment.

ARCTIC AIR AND GROUND OPERATIONS

The United States maintains four major force elements in Alaska – Alaska Command, a subunified command under U.S. Pacific Command that prepares forces

---

[52] Roughead, Conway, and Allen, *Naval Operations Concept*, 91. Littoral areas are both those areas seaward of the open ocean to the shore that must be controlled to conduct effectively operations ashore and those areas inland and adjacent to the shore that can be supported from the sea. Ibid., 98. For analysis of the Naval Operations Concept, see Andrew Scutro, "Navy and Marine Corps Plan Together for Future," *Navy Times*, September p. 18, 2006, 18.

[53] A sea chest is a recess in the hull of a vessel that serves as an intake reservoir from which piping systems draw raw water from the ocean. Typically, sea chests are protected by steel gratings covered with baffle plates to dampen the effects of vessel speed or sea state.

[54] Roughead, Conway, and Allen, *Naval Operations Concept*, pp. 13–34.

[55] See, e.g., James Kraska, "Broken Taillight at Sea: The Peacetime Law of Visit, Board, Search and Seizure," vol. 16 *Ocean & Coastal Law Journal* (2010), pp. 1–46.

for deployment and conducts Alaskan defense; Joint Task Force Alaska, a standing joint task force under U.S. Northern Command created to provide civil support; the U.S.-Canadian Alaska NORAD region (ANR); and 11th Air Force, which operates F-15C/D and F-22 high-performance fighter jets as well as C-17 heavy fixed-wing airlift. Currently, the U.S. Air Force is the most active service component in the Arctic, followed by the U.S. Coast Guard. The U.S. Army is third, with its operation of the Cold Weather Training Center, which readies eight hundred soldiers each year. Ironically enough for this maritime region, the navy and marine corps currently have the least operational activity among all of the five armed forces in the Arctic.

The full range of aerospace missions also may be conducted in the Arctic, including strike operations, anti–air warfare, anti–surface warfare, support for amphibious and special operations, airborne command and control (including intelligence, surveillance, and reconnaissance and targeting), and in-flight refueling operations. Aircraft-carrier operations may be limited by rapidly changing ice and extreme weather conditions and by the restricted crosswind operating envelopes for both fixed-wing and rotary aircraft. The difficulty of aircraft handling and maintenance on carrier decks during the movement of rolling seas is further exacerbated by icy conditions. Deicing and anti-icing capabilities should be integrated into the force. Satellites in polar orbit and ground stations in the north provide intelligence and secure military telecommunications worldwide. Peacetime aviation may be directed toward enforcement of the exclusive economic zone, support for scientific missions, and search and rescue.

The use of air-delivered weapons may be affected by the availability and fidelity of sensor prediction models in conditions of extreme cold and ice, as well as obscurity from fog and snow. Tactical land-attack missile (TLAM) cruise-missile performance, for example, may be limited by gaps in GPS, and terminal guidance sensors can be hampered by low-visibility conditions. One of the primary roles for naval aviation in the Arctic is antisubmarine warfare, but aircraft have limited ability to prosecute the mission without sensors and weapons capable of being delivered through the ice. Whereas the deficiency in forward aviation logistics and operating infrastructure limits extended polar air operations for the air force, naval aviation has to overcome the challenges inherent in deck launch and recovery while under way.

While the United States enjoys an unparalleled submarine capability for operating in ice-covered waters, the nation has fairly minimal capability to operate above the ice in the extreme Arctic climate. There is little redundancy to ground and aviation units, and virtually no surface ship or aviation presence in the Arctic Ocean. The most capable tactical platforms in the region are the F-22 Raptor, which is based with the U.S. Pacific Air Forces Third Wing at Elemendorf Air Force Base, Alaska. But the United States decided in 2009 to build only 187 of the fifth generation fighter aircraft.[56]

---

[56] Adam Levine Mike Mount and Alan Silverleib, "Gates Announces Major Pentagon Priority Shifts," CNN, April 9, 2009

To what purpose is the United States likely to put its Arctic military assets? Deterrence and regional stability are the key goals of U.S. Arctic policy.

CONCLUSION

The United States and Russia are separated by several political differences, including the expansion of NATO and Russian failure to comply with its Istanbul commitments under the Conventional Forces Europe treaty and withdraw its forces from Moldova and Georgia. In the Arctic, however, there is reason to be quite optimistic about the superpower bilateral relationship and Arctic stability more generally. Certainly, Russia has embarked on a program to maximize its influence in the Arctic, and in doing so, it takes pride in dispensing a large dose of bellicose language and conducting military operations that raise concern among its neighbors. But such a posture diminishes Russia's stature as a responsible stakeholder. Despite the sometimes unnecessary rhetoric and calculated military exercises, however, Moscow has been surprisingly moderate in its actual conduct in the region. Russia is dutifully going through the process with the Commission on the Limits of the Continental Shelf to collect marine survey data that would support its claim for a vast extended continental shelf jutting out from Siberia. Russia also resolved its long-standing disagreement with Norway over rights to oil, gas, and fisheries in the Barents Sea, adopting an equitable and balanced approach to settling the issues by splitting the balance of disputed area with its Arctic neighbor. Russia also signed an agreement with Denmark in early February 2011 to initiate greater cooperation in areas of shared interest, including Afghanistan, the Baltic Sea, and the Arctic.[57] Moscow's resolution of the matter with Oslo and opening to Copenhagen is an apt lesson for China, which has frightened nearly every state in Southeast Asia over its bold and insensitive claims to 80 percent of the South China Sea. China is capable of doing the impossible, which is uniting the A5 against Beijing's embryonic efforts to establish "rights" in the Arctic.

[57] "Denmark and Russia Agree to Military Cooperation: Two Countries Will Collaborate on Maneuvers in Baltic and Arctic," *Copenhagen Post Online*, February 9, 2011, http://www.cphpost.dk/news/international/89-international/50933-denmark-and-russia-agree-to-military-cooperation.html.

15

Arctic Security Considerations and the U.S. Navy's "Arctic Roadmap"

David W. Titley and Courtney C. St. John

INTRODUCTION

Arctic sea-ice melting associated with global climate change has caused leaders from the United States and the international community to reconsider the national security implications of the region. Taking into account nearly a century of experience in the Arctic, new national policy, existing strategy, and geopolitical implications of the changing environment, the U.S. Navy has developed the Arctic Roadmap, which will guide policy, investment, and action regarding the region. With key themes of improved environmental understanding, informed investments, increased experience, cooperative partnerships, and support for the UN Convention on the Law of the Sea, the Arctic Roadmap is meant to ensure navy readiness and capability and result in recognition of the navy as a valued partner by the joint, interagency, and international communities.

THE CHANGING ARCTIC ENVIRONMENT

The Arctic has long been a dynamic and harsh environment in which virtually all maritime operations have been hazardous, if not impossible. Yet traditional views of the Arctic as a nonnavigable region are beginning to shift. Relative to the 1970s, the Earth's temperature has increased sufficiently to cause significant melting of glaciers and diminishment in Arctic sea ice. The prevailing and well-established scientific view attributes this temperature change to anthropogenic emissions of "greenhouse" gases.[1]

---

[1] S. Solomon, D. Qin, M. Manning, Z. Chen, M. Marquis, K. B. Averyt, M. Tignor, and H. L. Miller, eds., *Climate Change 2007: The Physical Science Basis – Contribution of Working Group I to the Fourth Assessment Report of the Intergovernmental Panel on Climate Change*, Intergovernmental Panel on Climate Change AR4 (Cambridge: Cambridge University Press, 2007), available at http://www.ipcc.ch/publications_and_data/publications_and_data_reports.shtml.

The greenhouse effect is the well-known process that keeps the Earth's temperature above the $-18°$ Celsius average temperature it would have were greenhouse gases in the atmosphere not to absorb the sun's heat and reradiate it back to the surface. However, the anthropogenic loading of additional greenhouse gases into the atmosphere since the Industrial Revolution has altered the natural climate change processes.[2] Since the 1880s, temperatures have risen $0.8°$ Celsius – a significant increase in a relatively short period.[3] Greenhouse gases trap more heat in the lower atmosphere, thereby increasing the average global temperature of the ocean and atmosphere.[4] The Arctic is especially vulnerable to global warming, because as snow and ice melt, darker land and ocean surfaces absorb more solar energy. As warming reduces the extent of sea ice, the solar heat absorbed by the oceans in the summer is more easily transferred to the atmosphere in the winter, which makes the air temperature warmer.[5]

As a result, the Arctic is warming twice as fast as the rest of the globe. Specifically, scientists are observing retreating sea ice, melting glaciers, and shrinking snow and permafrost areas.[6] The summer ice cap is estimated to be only half the size it was fifty years ago.[7] Sea-ice extent in the Arctic has decreased steadily since the 1950s and in September 2007 reached a record low that was 39 percent below the 1979–2000 mean. September 2008 experienced the second-lowest Arctic ice extent on record, at 34 percent below the 1970–2000 mean. When the Arctic reached its minimum ice extent for the year in September 2010, it was recorded at the third-lowest extent since 1979 satellite measurements began, further demonstrating the declining trend in summer sea ice over the past thirty years. Current sea-ice extent observations show that ice has fluctuated below and above the 2007 levels and has remained below the 1979–2000 average (see Figure 15.1).[8]

Although estimates for when the Arctic will experience ice-free conditions in the summer range from 2013 to 2060, the consensus of most models and researchers is that the Arctic will experience ice-free conditions for a portion of the summer by the 2030s.[9] It is important to point out that no research or model simulations indicate

[2] Ralph Cicerone, "Climate-Change Science and NAS Activities," presentation at the Consortium for Ocean Leadership, Washington, D.C., 15 October 2009.

[3] G. Marland, T. A. Boden, and R. J. Andres, "Global, Regional, and National CO_2 Emissions," in *Trends: A Compendium of Data on Global Change* (Oak Ridge, TN: Carbon Dioxide Information Analysis Center, Oak Ridge National Laboratory, U.S. Department of Energy, 2007).

[4] Cicerone, "Climate-Change Science and NAS Activities."

[5] Susan Joy Hassel, *Impacts of a Warming Arctic: Arctic Climate Impact Assessment* (Cambridge: Cambridge University Press, 2004), executive summary, p. 25.

[6] Erland Kallen, *The Vertical Structure of Arctic Warming* (Stockholm: Stockholm University, Department of Meteorology, 2009).

[7] U.S. Navy Department, "Task Force Climate Change and the Arctic Roadmap," *Rhumb Lines*, 30 November 2009.

[8] National Snow and Ice Data Center, "Arctic Sea Ice Reaches Annual Minimum Extent," *Arctic Sea Ice News and Analysis*, 17 September 2009, http://nsidc.org/arcticseaicenews/2009/091709.html.

[9] Navy Task Force Climate Change, *Navy Arctic Talking Points*, September 2009.

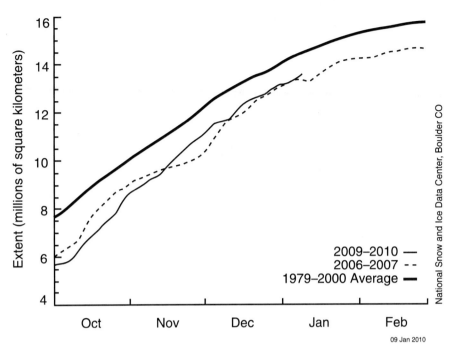

FIGURE 15.1. Daily Arctic Sea-Ice Extent, 1979–2010 (U.S. Naval War College).

that winter sea-ice cover of the Arctic Ocean will disappear during this century. This reinforces the point that the Arctic will still be a very challenging and harsh environment in which to operate.

Regardless of the exact year that the Arctic becomes ice-free in the summer, the widespread warming trend will continue. Multiyear sea ice has also declined rapidly in the central Arctic Ocean; one study based on satellite data for winters during 1978–98 showed that multiyear sea ice declined at a rate of 7 percent per decade.[10] A second study examined twenty-five years of summer ice minima (from 1978 to 2003) and demonstrated a decline of multiyear sea ice as high as 9.2 percent per decade.[11] The multiyear ice is being replaced by first-year sea ice that is considerably weaker and thinner. Because ice cover naturally cools air and water masses and plays a significant role in ocean circulation and the reflection of solar radiation back into space, weaker and thinner sea ice has the potential to change the global climate system significantly.[12] The well-observed decline in multiyear and summer sea ice

[10] Arctic Council, *Arctic Marine Shipping Assessment 2009 Report* (Tromsø, Norway: Arctic Council, 2009), p. 31.

[11] Ibid., p. 32.

[12] C. P. McMullen and J. Jabbour, *Climate Change Science Compendium 2009* (Nairobi, Kenya: UN Environment Programme, 2009), p. 17.

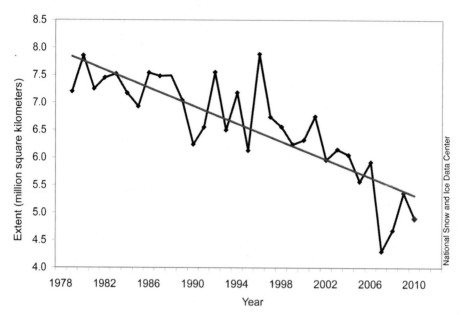

FIGURE 15.2. Average Monthly Arctic Sea-Ice Extent September, 1979–2010.

is a clear indicator that some of the most rapid climate change on Earth is occurring in the Arctic.[13]

The effects of climate change in the Arctic are observed in the sea, in the air, and on land. Indigenous Arctic people are facing relocation and loss of communities as sea-ice melt causes increased shoreline erosion and melting of permafrost. Impacts on Arctic species include the well-publicized decline of the polar bear population and a decline in the algae that attach to the bottom of the ice. The algae form the base of the food chain linking microscopic animals and fish to other animals.[14] In other cases, flora and fauna are experiencing extended growing seasons, and the Arctic is playing host to new species migrating northward with shifting climate patterns; changes in fish migrations coupled with intensified sea-ice melt will yield greater access to fish stocks. These trends demonstrate the need to better understand the complex processes occurring in the Arctic.[15]

Changes in sea ice, sea-level rise, and ocean acidity and their impacts on ecosystems are not well modeled. Most numerical modeling to date has focused on global change predictions, which have greater confidence than regional change

[13] Arctic Council, *Arctic Marine Shipping Assessment 2009 Report*, p. 26.
[14] Thomas R. Karl, Jerry M. Melillo, and Thomas C. Peterson, eds., *Global Climate Change Impacts in the United States* (Cambridge: Cambridge University Press, 2009), p. 85.
[15] J. Richter-Menge and J. E. Overland, eds., *Arctic Report Card 2009*, available at http://www.arctic .noaa.gov/reportcard.

predictions, where weather patterns and ecosystem impacts vary considerably.[16] Present climate projections based on the Intergovernmental Panel on Climate Change Assessment Report (2007) show substantial uncertainty in regional and decadal scales, especially with respect to ice-sheet dynamics and sea-level rise. Data-gathering methods used for climate data are typically designed for other purposes (like agricultural services, weather prediction, or water-resources management) and therefore may not contain the fidelity needed to detect gradual climate trends.[17] Because the Arctic is such a hostile environment, collecting in situ observations is extremely challenging. If we are to understand near- and long-term trends better, the international Arctic science community will need to deploy its resources in the most effective manner.

Natural Resources

One future change in the Arctic region is greater accessibility to, and availability of, natural resources, including offshore oil and gas, minerals, and fisheries. The Arctic contains 10 percent of the world's known petroleum reserves and approximately 25 percent of its undiscovered reserves.[18] The U.S. exclusive economic zone has a potential 30 billion barrels of oil reserves and 221 billion cubic feet in natural gas reserves.[19] Minerals available for extraction in the Arctic include manganese, copper, cobalt, zinc, and gold. Coupled with a rise in global demand for natural oil and gas resources and improved accessibility, the Arctic has become a new focus for oil companies looking for untapped resources. Already $2.6 billion has been spent on active oil and gas leases in the Chukchi Sea.[20] Yet the extraction of these minerals and petroleum reserves depends heavily on development and deployment of resilient technology that can function in conditions characterized by environmental extremes, lack of infrastructure, and long distances to markets.

The warming experienced recently in the Arctic region may improve the availability of certain resources, but it will redistribute others. In the United States alone, redistribution of fish stocks will cause changes for indigenous Alaskans who depend

---

[16] National Research Council, *Understanding and Responding to Climate Change: Highlights of National Academies Reports* (Washington, D.C.: National Research Council, 2008), p. 9.

[17] Ibid., p. 11.

[18] Kenneth J. Bird, Ronald R. Charpentier, Donald L. Gautier, David W. Houseknect, Timothy R. Klett, Janet K. Pitman, Thomas E. Moore, Christopher J. Schenk, Marilyn E. Tennyson, and Craig J. Wandrey, *Circum-Arctic Resource Appraisal: Estimates of Undiscovered Oil and Gas North of the Arctic Circle*, U.S. Geological Survey Fact Sheet 2008-3049 (Denver, CO: U.S. Geological Survey Information Services, 2008).

[19] As defined by the UN Convention on the Law of the Sea, a nation's exclusive economic zone is "an area beyond and adjacent to the territorial sea" that is not to extend "beyond 200 nautical miles from the baselines from which the breadth of the territorial sea is measured." United Nations, "United Nations Convention on Law of the Sea," Dec. 10, 1982, 1833 U.N.T.S. 397. Article 55, 57.

[20] Tim Holder, "Arctic Science: Alaska Outer Continental Shelf Focus for IWG Workshop," presentation at the Consortium for Ocean Leadership, Washington, D.C., 4 December 2009.

on the stocks for subsistence. In August 2009, the National Oceanic and Atmospheric Administration (NOAA) released a fishery management plan for the Arctic waters of the United States, including the Chukchi and Beaufort seas, which prohibits commercial fishing in the region until enough information is available to manage the fisheries sustainably.[21] Fisheries managers require an understanding of how to maintain sustainable fisheries while taking into account likely intensification in commercial fishing operations. Resource planners and policy makers will need to examine closely the best ways to manage newly opened areas of the Arctic, balancing multiple and competing uses.

Transportation Access and Operational Challenges

As for natural-resource availability, shipping and transportation will benefit from a more open Arctic. The fabled Northwest Passage and Northern Sea Route will both be navigable for greater periods of time during the summer, and may be utilized more often for commercial shipping. Indeed, the Northern Sea Route offers a 35–60 percent savings in distance for shipping between Northern Europe and the Far East in comparison to the Suez or Panama canals.[22] Surface-vessel access to open-water areas in the Arctic will gradually increase from the current few weeks a year to a few months a year, centered around mid-September (the minimum ice extent), although better access will be tempered by the challenges that operation in the Arctic environment poses for the shipping industry.[23] For example, marine insurers are currently offering insurance only on a case-by-case basis, and marine operations are impeded by lack of ice-navigator training programs, most of which are ad hoc in any case.[24] Sea-ice forecasts are limited by a lack of understanding of the exact interrelationships among ice, polar oceans, and the atmosphere, and inability to model variables like sea ice at a fully coupled, regional scale, taking account of complexities that arise from the interactions of global, regional, and local processes.[25] National standards that regulate ship-source pollution vary among Arctic states; shipping companies will also need to invest substantial amounts of money to develop new ice-strengthened vessels and ensure that they operate within environmental compliance guidelines.

[21] National Marine Fisheries Service, Alaska Regional Office, "Arctic Fisheries," National Oceanic and Atmospheric Adminstration Fisheries, http://www.fakr.noaa.gov/sustainablefisheries/arctic/.
[22] Arctic Council, *Arctic Marine Shipping Assessment 2009 Report*, p. 43.
[23] The term *open water*, nomenclature of the World Meteorological Organization (WMO), is defined as water that has a total ice concentration of less than one-tenth sea ice at any stage of development.
[24] Arctic Council, *Arctic Marine Shipping Assessment 2009 Report*, pp. 68–69.
[25] *Coupled modeling* can be defined as the combination of energy and interfaces between two different fluids, such as the atmosphere and the ocean. U.S. Navy Department, Task Force Climate Change, *Prioritized Climate Science and Technology Requirements* (Washington, D.C.: U.S. Navy Department, 2009).

Boundary Disputes, Security Concerns

Despite present good relations among Arctic nations, recent media attention paints the area as a source of potential international conflict as countries flex their muscles and seek to identify portions of the region to which they can lay claim. After a team of scientists planted a Russian flag on the seabed of the North Pole, a well-publicized article in *Time* magazine in October 2007 posed the question, "Who owns the Arctic?" Over the past few years, in the wake of Russia's actions, the recent years of decreased summer ice extent, and a swell of scientific reports published on climate change, the Arctic has experienced a rise in media attention. Media speculation has spoken of the Arctic as the site of a new Cold War, suggesting that the question of who "owns" the Arctic will cause international conflict. In reality, the "new" Arctic will be one with multiple competing uses by many countries. Indeed, the likelihood of large-scale international conflict is small, and the Arctic environment will continue to be harsh and challenging for much of the year, making operations difficult and dangerous for the remainder of the twenty-first century.

The legal regime applicable in the Arctic is the customary international law as reflected in the UN Convention on the Law of the Sea (UNCLOS). Although the United States has not ratified UNCLOS, it considers the convention's navigation and jurisdiction provisions binding international law. The convention advances and protects the national security, environmental, and economic interests of all nations, including the United States, codifying the navigational rights and freedoms that are critical to American military and commercial vessels. It also secures economic rights to offshore natural resources.[26] Article 76 of the convention allows nations to claim jurisdiction past their exclusive economic zones on the basis of undersea features that are considered extensions of the continental shelf, if a structure is geologically similar to a nation's continental landmass.[27] In May 2008, five of the Arctic nations adopted the Ilulissat Declaration, which acknowledges that "the Law of the Sea is the relevant legal framework in the Arctic" and that there is "no need to develop a new comprehensive international legal regime to govern the Arctic," committing the signatories to an "orderly settlement of any possible overlapping claims."[28]

Currently, there are overlapping, unresolved maritime boundary claims between the United States and Canada, Canada and Denmark, and Denmark and Norway. At this time, none of the disputed boundary claims poses a threat to global stability.

---

[26] Honorable Hillary Rodham Clinton, letter endorsing U.S. accession to the Convention on the Law of the Sea, 16 October 2009.

[27] Rear Admiral David Gove, U.S. Navy (Ret.), "Arctic Melt: Reopening a Naval Frontier," *U.S. Naval Institute Proceedings* (February 2009), http://www.usni.org/magazines/proceedings/2009-02/arctic-melt-reopening-naval-frontier.

[28] U.S. Navy Office of the Judge Advocate General, "Arctic Legal Issues," informational working PowerPoint document, July 2009.

Although the United States and Canada disagree on the location of the maritime boundary in and northward of the Beaufort Sea, the United States considers Canada a close ally, and the dispute does not jeopardize the relationship.[29] Unfortunately, the United States is the only Arctic nation that has not joined UNCLOS, despite support from President Barack Obama and the Bush and Clinton administrations. Because the Ilulissat Declaration recognizes the law of the sea as the framework for deciding issues of Arctic territoriality, the United States may find itself at a disadvantage when critical Arctic conversations occur.[30]

The U.S. Navy is mindful of other international challenges and opportunities in the Arctic. There is some concern in Japan that a renewed Arctic emphasis by the U.S. Navy may lead to a corresponding decrease in western Pacific presence and security. Conversely, there are unique opportunities for the U.S. Navy to develop "soft" partnerships with other nations, such as Russia and China, on research like hydrographic surveys. Although present boundary disputes and security concerns pose no major risk to international stability and security, the long-term potential for significant change in the Arctic must be recognized and thoroughly assessed.

THE U.S. NAVY'S ROLE IN A CHANGING ARCTIC

The U.S. Navy understands that a wide range of security considerations in the Arctic region and the effects of climate change in the Arctic will together influence the geostrategic landscape. Future maritime activity in the region will encompass many non-Arctic stakeholders; the potential exists for the overlap of new operations with indigenous uses and for the occurrence of multiple uses in Arctic waters.[31] The navy must carefully assess the effects of more severe weather and the rise of sea level on existing installations while concurrently determining future installation needs. Security, stability, and safety have been, and continue to be, the overarching objectives of the navy's Arctic activities.

The U.S. Navy has been operating in the Arctic for more than a century, beginning with the *Jeannette* expedition that attempted to reach the North Pole in 1879 and Admiral Richard E. Byrd's historic flight over the North Pole in 1926. The navy sustained its presence in the Arctic during and immediately after World War II, a presence that peaked in 1958, when the USS *Nautilus* (SSN 571) performed the first submerged transit of the North Pole. Navy submarines have remained active in the region ever since and continue to operate as required. Surface assets routinely operate in subarctic conditions. In the 1990s, a program known as Science Ice Expedition (SCICEX) used *Sturgeon*-class (SSN 637) nuclear-powered attack

[29] Ibid.
[30] Gove, "Arctic Melt."
[31] Arctic Council, *Arctic Marine Shipping Assessment 2009 Report*, p. 5.

submarines to conduct collaborative scientific cruises carrying civilian specialists to the Arctic basin. Six SCICEX missions took place from 1993 to 2000, and they were reinitiated in 2011. The missions allow scientists to gather data on the biological and physical properties of the northern waters with emphasis on understanding the dynamics of sea-ice cover, circulation patterns in the water, and the structure of the Arctic Ocean's bathymetry.[32]

Navy surface, aviation, and special warfare forces have participated in joint and combined exercises, such as Northern Edge, and will continue to do so. Although navy surface vessels are able to conduct some operations up to the marginal ice zone, they would require ice-strengthening to be fully mission capable in any ice conditions; navy aircraft are capable of operating in the Arctic, but the lack of divert fields limits their duration and range. The submarine force frequently uses the Arctic to move submarines between the Atlantic and Pacific fleets and has a long-standing research and development program, Ice Exercises (ICEX), to improve Arctic operability and tactics. The Arctic Submarine Lab leads the ICEX series, whose activities include temporary Arctic ice camps on the edge of the perennial ice.[33] The most recent camp was established in the spring of 2011 on a piece of Arctic pack ice approximately two hundred nautical miles north of Prudhoe Bay, Alaska.[34] Great Britain's Royal Navy shares the use of these camps, and cooperative operations involve both U.S. and British submarines. After military operations are concluded, ice camps have on occasion been turned over to civilian researchers, allowing them to take advantage of facilities that would otherwise be beyond their budgets.

Although the U.S. Navy has a rich history in the Arctic, several challenges must be met to ensure successful operations in the future. These include the lack of logistics support, environmental hazards such as drifting sea ice and icing on exposed surfaces, and communications difficulties. Antiquated nautical charts, low visibility, and the paucity of electronic and visual navigation aids hinder safety of navigation. A lack of coastal installations also contributes to the difficulty of search-and-rescue (SAR) operations. The only American-owned deepwater port near the Arctic basin is Dutch Harbor, in the Aleutian Islands.[35]

The navy and other federal government agencies are taking steps to address some of these challenges. Arctic Council nations are nearing completion of a memorandum of understanding for SAR in the Arctic. Senators Mark Begich and Lisa Murkowski of Alaska recently supported bills that would study the feasibility of a deepwater port in the Arctic. And the U.S. Navy has developed a roadmap to ensure its own readiness and capability in the region.

---

[32] Gove, "Arctic Melt."

[33] Ibid.

[34] U.S. Navy Department, "Ice Exercise 2009," *Rhumb Lines*, March 9, 2009 and U.S. Arctic Submarine Laboratory.

[35] Arctic Council, *Arctic Marine Shipping Assessment 2009 Report*, p. 177.

THE U.S. NAVY'S "ARCTIC ROADMAP"

Drivers

The time line for change in the Arctic represents a strategic challenge for the U.S. Navy. In October 2007, the U.S. Navy, Coast Guard, and Marine Corps released "A Cooperative Strategy for 21st Century Seapower" – commonly referred to as the "Maritime Strategy" – which states: "Climate change is gradually opening up the waters of the Arctic, not only to new resource development, but also to new shipping routes that may reshape the global transport system. While these opportunities offer potential for growth, they are potential sources of competition and conflict for access and natural resources." The Maritime Strategy clearly identifies freedom of navigation as a top national priority. Preserving the rights of navigation and overflight in the Arctic region supports the navy's ability to exercise those rights throughout the world, including transit rights in strategic straits.

The Maritime Strategy applies fully in the Arctic as it does in other regions of the globe; it sufficiently addresses the opening Arctic and the potential challenges and opportunities that phenomenon represents. The core capabilities of the Maritime Strategy that are most applicable to the Arctic are forward presence, deterrence, maritime security, and humanitarian assistance and disaster relief (HA/DR), through the formation and sustainment of cooperative relationships with international partners. As in every other region, the naval services must be prepared to prevent or limit regional conflict when required.

In January 2009, President George W. Bush signed National Security Presidential Directive-66/Homeland Security Presidential Directive-25 (NSPD-66/HSPD-25), which established Arctic-region policy priorities for the nation. The policy declares that the "United States is an Arctic nation, with varied and compelling interests in that region."[36] The directive takes into account altered policies on homeland security and defense, the effects of climate change and increasing human activity in the Arctic, the work of the Arctic Council, and the increasing awareness that the Arctic region is fragile but rich in resources.[37] The Arctic Region Policy directs the Departments of State, Homeland Security, and Defense to develop greater capabilities and capacity as necessary to protect U.S. borders; increase Arctic maritime domain awareness (MDA); preserve global mobility; project a sovereign American maritime presence; encourage peaceful resolution of disputes; cooperate with other Arctic nations to address likely issues arising from greater shipping activity; establish a risk-based capability to address hazards in the region, including cooperative SAR, basing, and logistical support; and evaluate the feasibility

---

[36] White House, *Arctic Region Policy*, National Security Presidential Directive/NSPD-66, Homeland Security Presidential Directive/HSPD-25 (Washington, D.C.: Office of the Press Secretary, 12 January 2009).

[37] Ibid.

of using the Arctic for strategic sealifts. These requirements do not promulgate new navy missions but imply that the service must be prepared to increase Arctic engagement.

In May 2009, the chief of naval operations (CNO), Admiral Gary Roughead, convened the CNO Executive Board to answer questions about the Arctic centering on the changing environment, past and present navy activity in the Arctic region, future navy investments, security requirements, fleet capabilities and limitations, and activities of other Arctic nations. The result was the establishment of the U.S. Navy's Task Force Climate Change (TFCC) to address navy implications of climate change, with a near-term focus on the Arctic.

The TFCC is directed by the lead coauthor of this article – the oceanographer of the navy, Rear Admiral David Titley – and is composed of representatives from offices within the CNO's staff, the fleet, the NOAA, and the U.S. Coast Guard. The TFCC also includes representatives from the Joint Chiefs of Staff and various interagency, international, scientific, and academic organizations, acting in advisory capacities; the task force consists of a flag-level steering committee, the Navy Climate Change Coordination Office, and several action-oriented working groups. More than five hundred individuals, representing more than 125 organizations and agencies, actively contribute to TFCC's mission. The TFCC was initially tasked with developing a document to guide navy policy, investment, and public discussion regarding the Arctic.

The vice chief of naval operations approved the resulting Arctic Roadmap in November 2009. The document is synchronized with a science-based time line; provides a framework for navy discussion of the Arctic; and lists appropriate objectives and actions, tempered by fiscal realities.[38] The need for a science-based time line is clear: if the navy acts too early, it will waste resources, but acting too late will result in mission failure. Understanding the complex changes occurring in the Arctic region requires sound scientific information, on which policy, strategy, and operations are based. Greater understanding leads to sound decision making that utilizes assets in the safest and most efficient manner.

The road map features a five-year action plan that implements both the national Arctic Region Policy and the navy's Maritime Strategy and lays out initiatives, such as science and technology and combined exercises, to carry out its goals. The road map seeks to answer several questions:

- What is the time line for naval Arctic access?
- What, if any, is the national security threat?
- Will the U.S. Navy be required to increase engagement in the Arctic?
- In what does the U.S. Navy need to invest to meet expected Arctic requirements?

---

[38] Admiral J. W. Greenert, USN, Task Force Climate Change Charter (Washington, D.C.: U.S. Navy Department, Vice Chief of Naval Operations, 30 October 2009).

Objectives

The main objective of the Arctic Roadmap is the execution of a series of actions that together will increase readiness, capability, and security. Specifically, the U.S. Navy seeks to gain improved understanding regarding the current and predicted environment, gain greater experience through established exercises, and make informed investments that will provide the right capability at the right time. The road map recognizes that key to its success is cooperative partnerships with interagency and international stakeholders that will improve the navy's capability to assess and predict climate changes in the Arctic. To achieve these objectives, the road map focuses on five areas: strategy, policy, missions, and plans; operations and training; investments; communications and outreach; and environmental assessment and prediction.

Strategy, Policy, Missions, and Plans

Actions in the focus area of strategy, policy, missions, and plans include the identification of navy strategic objectives in the Arctic region and the development of guidance to achieve those objectives so as to preserve a safe, stable, and secure Arctic region. Policy and recommendations to operational staffs will be developed to strengthen existing and foster new cooperative relationships.

Operations and Training

Actions in the operations and training focus area were identified by the navy headquarters staff, U.S. Fleet Forces Command, and the geographic combatant command staffs with the intent of providing a navy enterprisewide approach for action regarding the Arctic. Participation in Arctic exercises, operations, and supporting activities is identified, with the intent of increasing navy experience in the region.

Investments

The investments focus area seeks to ensure that Arctic requirements are assessed and included in the development of the program objective memorandum or navy budget. Investment areas that are addressed include weapons platforms and sensors; command, control, communications, computers, intelligence, surveillance, and reconnaissance (C4ISR); and installations and facilities.

Communications and Outreach

The communications and outreach focus area addresses the facts that the navy can benefit from exchanging information with the wide array of Arctic stakeholders and that media attention will grow as the Arctic endures further rapid and severe change.

Partnering with organizations in the media, government, Department of Defense, as well as international, scientific, academic, and indigenous communities will help to ensure that the navy is recognized as contributing to a safe, secure, and stable Arctic region.

Environmental Assessment and Prediction

Actions in the environmental assessment and prediction focus area will foster a comprehensive and improved understanding of the current and predicted Arctic physical environment on the tactical, operational, and strategic scales. Because of limited resources and the potential for significant requirements, reducing uncertainty in predictions of the magnitude, timing, and regional location of Arctic environmental change is essential to efficient and responsible navy action and investment.

Phasing

The road map specifies U.S. Navy action over three phases, allowing for necessary background studies and assessments to be completed, partnerships formed, and knowledge cultivated. The TFCC will be responsible for execution of the Arctic Roadmap and will provide quarterly progress reports to the chief of naval operations.

Phase 1 – Fiscal Year (FY) 2010

The first phase of the Arctic Roadmap included an assessment of strategic objectives and mission requirements in the Arctic region. External studies regarding Arctic security were reviewed. The navy continued work with NOAA and the U.S. Air force to develop a next-generation, coupled, air-ocean-ice modeling system to predict accurately Arctic environmental change; the navy also performed a joint hydrographic survey in the Bering Strait with NOAA. The navy participated in Arctic tabletop exercises with the Office of the Secretary of Defense and interagency partners and participated in a "Limited Objective experiment" with U.S. Northern Command and National Defense University in February 2010."

Phase 2 – FYs 2011 and 2012

Significant actions in phase 2 include initiation of capabilities-based assessments regarding required navy Arctic capabilities, completion of environmental assessments, and support for implementation of the national ocean policy and coastal and marine spatial planning framework in the Arctic.[39] Recommendations will also be developed to address Arctic requirements in "sponsor program proposals" for the

---

[39] In June 2009, the Ocean Policy Task Force was formed by President Obama to develop the National Ocean Policy and Framework for Marine and Coastal Planning. Recommendations from the task force are expected to be approved by the president in Spring 2010.

navy's program objective memorandum for FY 2014 (POM 14). Biennial participation in Arctic exercises such as ICEX-11 will continue, and the navy will formalize new cooperative relationships that increase experience and competence in search and rescue, maritime domain awareness, humanitarian assistance and disaster relief in the Arctic, and defense support of civil authorities in Alaska.

Phase 3 – FYs 2013 and 2014

During phase 3, the U.S. Navy will oversee execution of POM 14 budget initiatives while implementing and expanding new cooperative partnerships. The navy will commence Arctic environmental survey operations using unmanned undersea vehicles. In FY 2014, the Arctic Roadmap will be updated in coordination with the 2014 Quadrennial Defense Review, to ensure that the navy presence in the Arctic is aligned with the strategic objectives of the Department of Defense.

Conclusion

The scope and magnitude of changes to the Arctic region as a result of a changing climate are great, and they cannot all be identified within the scope of this chapter. Overall, continued sea-ice melting will cause shifts in species populations and distribution, more navigable transportation passages, and increased shipping activity and resource extraction. It also has the potential to modify significantly global circulation patterns around the world, the consequences of which scientists are just beginning to model and comprehend. Each of these changes will shape safety and security in the Arctic.

The U.S. Navy's Task Force Climate Change is addressing security considerations in the Arctic by implementing a science-based road map for action. Emphasizing the key themes of improved environmental understanding, informed investments, increased experience, cooperative partnerships, and support for the UN Convention on the Law of the Sea, the Arctic Roadmap will ensure the navy's readiness and capability to operate successfully and safely in the changing Arctic environment in the twenty-first century.

Afterword

A UNITED KINGDOM PERSPECTIVE ON THE ROLE OF NAVIES IN DELIVERING ARCTIC SECURITY

Lee Willett

INTRODUCTION

The United Kingdom is not an Arctic state. However, it retains prominent interests in the region. These interests include energy, other resources and access, as well as the political desire to support its commitment to major international organizations whose member states have interests in the region. More widely, the UK remains committed to supporting measures designed to maintain global stability through a robust, rules-based international system. In terms of the Arctic, perhaps the most notable aspect of the UK's interest in the region is its physical position in the North Atlantic. This position, when coupled with the UK's significant military – in particular, naval – power, gives the UK significant politico-strategic leverage in matters relating to Arctic security.

Two aspects of the UK's geostrategic position are worth noting. First, as a major power in the North Atlantic, the UK sits only 100 nautical miles from the Faeroe Islands – islands regarded by the Arctic Council (of which the UK holds the position of an observer nation) as the southerly limit of the Arctic region.[1] Second, alongside the political bridge the UK provides between North American states – particularly the United States – and Europe, in geostrategic terms it sits at the top of Northern Europe above the Dover Strait and English Channel and at the eastern end of the Greenland-Iceland-UK (GIUK) gap.

With the risks to global energy supplies and regional access posed by, for example, Somali piracy in the Horn of Africa region, by enduring concerns about security

[1] See Arctic Council map, available on-line at: <http://arctic-council.org/filearchive/AHDRmap_gen.ai. >. Accessed 15 March 2011. Established as a primary forum within which to discuss issues relating to the Arctic region, membership of the Arctic Council consists of the Canada, Denmark, Finland, Iceland, Norway, Russia, Sweden and the United States. Because of enduring national interests, there remains no desire for the Arctic Council or other multinational organizations to address governance issues relating to the Arctic (see: Parliamentary Office of Science and Technology, 'Arctic Changes.' *Post Note*, June 2009, no. 334, London: Parliamentary Office of Science and Technology. p. 2).

relations with Iran or by more current concerns about a domino effect of insecurity in the Middle East and North Africa region, today's international security literature is rich in discussion of the strategic importance of Sea Lines of Communication (SLOCs) and maritime choke points.[2] In the Cold War, the GIUK gap was a fundamental factor in the NATO's evolving strategic postures, such as the Maritime Strategy of the 1980s. Notwithstanding reports that the Russian Navy is now sending nuclear powered attack submarines (SSNs) south into the North Atlantic with greater frequency than at any time since 1987 and the end of the Cold War, the opening up of Arctic seaways would return the GIUK gap to a place of significant strategic prominence in global security affairs.[3] The UK's potential influence, supported by a Royal Navy which will continue to make a robust contribution to global affairs despite the drastic cuts suffered in the UK's Strategic Defence and Security Review (SDSR) of October 2010, is thus clear.

Precisely which Arctic waters will become more open – and to what degree, and by when – remains the subject of both much uncertainty and debate. All the same, the prospective implications of climate change in the Arctic are wide-ranging and critical to both regional and international security. Climate change should be a unifying issue in global politics. Yet the continuing predominance of the nation state means that the protection of national interest will remain the primary stimulus for national policy. The global defense and security debate borne out of climate change issues in the Arctic focuses largely on the implications for commercial shipping of the opening up of Arctic sea routes and on the risks of insecurity and conflict posed by potential disputes over resources, territory, access and other interests. Particularly, in the context of such potential for disputes, the presence of five NATO nations and Russia around the Arctic Rim raises the risk, however remote, of conflict with high consequences.[4] Much of today's strategic security debate focuses on the extent to which nations may co-operate with or confront each other. The Arctic region is a prime example of the uncertainty in attempting to answer this question.

In London, aside from the climate change question, there appears to be only limited discussion about the security consequences of the opening up of Arctic sea routes and the resultant possibility of disputes among the six states directly bordering the Arctic – two of whom are nuclear powers and five of whom are NATO members – over territory and resource access. The UK itself, while not of course bordering directly on the Arctic, is both a NATO and European Union (EU) member and, perhaps most importantly, remains a major maritime power in the North Atlantic. If

---

[2] There are 11 major maritime choke points in the world: the straits of Bab Al Mendeb, Bering, Bosporus, Dover, Gibraltar, Hormuz, Lombok and Malacca; the Panama and Suez canals; and the GIUK gap.

[3] For reference on the increasing Russian submarine activity, see Thomas Harding, 'Russian Subs Stalk Trident in Echo of Cold War,' *The Daily Telegraph*, 27 August 2010. Available online at: <http://www.telegraph.co.uk/news/uknews/defence/7969017/Russian-subs-stalk-Trident-in-echo-of-Cold-War.html >. Accessed 27 August 2010.

[4] Using the Arctic Council definition (*note 1*), Canada, Denmark, Iceland, Norway and the United States are regarded as the five NATO states with direct access to the Arctic region.

Arctic sea routes were to become open, the UK would have significant and new interests in the expanding maritime shipping activity – both commercial and military – which would move through the North Atlantic region as the gateway to the Arctic.

THE UK AND THE ARCTIC: HIGH STRATEGIC IMPORTANCE, BUT LOW POLITICAL PROFILE?

The UK's potential strategic interest in the Arctic region can be summarised under several key headings.

First, for the dual purposes of strengthening strategic relations with individual states and of assisting in the maintenance of a robust and stable rules-based international system, the UK is and will remain committed to its alliance contributions. In the context of Arctic security debates, its commitment to NATO and the EU remain strategically crucial.

Second, beyond its commitment to alliances, the UK also has significant national economic, political and wider strategic interests in the Arctic and its surrounding regions. The UK will retain a national desire to contribute to the environmental stability and security of the region. The UK's geostrategic position and its traditional maritime and wider military strength also will enable it to make a unique contribution as a major non-North American western power to regional stability and security.

Third, in economic terms, the UK will remain reliant upon oil and gas as its primary energy resource until the middle of this century. A significant proportion of this supply is sourced currently from the Middle East, but already the UK has a growing reliance on resources transiting indirectly through the Arctic region or emanating directly from it. This reliance may well become more significant as more traditional supplies dry up or, more presciently, as sourcing supply from more unstable regions becomes more difficult.

For these reasons, the UK should be considered as a major power with significant interest in and influence over the Arctic region. However, an overview of superficial coverage of the Arctic region in the UK security debate may make the Arctic appear peripheral at best to UK national interests.

THE NSS, THE SDSR AND THE UK GEOSTRATEGIC PERSPECTIVE ON THE ARCTIC REGION

When Secretary of State for Defence the Rt Hon Dr Liam Fox MP took office in May 2010, the High North question sat right at the top of his strategic agenda. However, the Conservative-led Coalition Government's SDSR took some decisions on the UK's strategic perspective and force structure which lead to the conclusion that the UK's current primary areas of interest lie elsewhere. In sum, the UK continues to look east of Suez towards the Persian Gulf and the Indian Ocean.

Moreover, recent events show that the UK's ability to protect its current primary interests is already, in naval capability terms, stretched to the limit. The 2011 Libya crisis has provided several examples of how decisions taken on naval capabilities under SDSR are already seriously restricting UK policy choices. First, with SDSR's decision to withdraw from service the UK's two aircraft carriers, HM Ships *Ark Royal* and *Illustrious*, in the initial phases of the crisis the UK found the options for evacuating its nationals to be more limited.[5] Second, following the United Nations (UN) Security Council decision to establish a no-fly zone, the UK's contribution from the air was limited to Royal Air Force Tornado GR4 aircraft conducting return flights from their base at RAF Marham in the UK in the longest round-trip air sorties flown by the RAF since the 1982 Falklands War.[6] The flexibility in operational tasking and timing of response would have been improved by the presence of an aircraft carrier in the Mediterranean. Indeed, both the United States and France moved aircraft carriers into the region to contribute to the operation. Third, and arguably as a direct result of the lack of aircraft carriers, in the context also of a reduced overall size of the Royal Navy under SDSR the UK was required to divert ships from other tasks to carry out the initial evacuation operation: the Type 22 frigate HMS *Cumberland* was re-tasked from counter-piracy operations in the Horn of Africa, and the Type 42 destroyer HMS *York* was diverted en route to its second deployment to the South Atlantic in a year. With strategic choice and policy flexibility severely limited by decreasing naval force levels, the UK was forced to make a policy choice to support only one of three tasks which, arguably, are all of equal significance in the context of national interest and security. With its focus on the Gulf, the Indian Ocean and now – for what seems likely to be a significant period of time – the Mediterranean Sea, how would the UK address any requirement to deploy forces, either in pursuit of national or alliance interests, more regularly to the North Atlantic?

As a result of the contribution that defense is required to make to the government's current austerity measures, the UK has been forced to define a defense policy, in SDSR, which will see the UK being 'more selective' in if, how and where it uses the military instrument. As stated in the Review:

> ... [The UK's] future forces, although smaller than now, will retain their geo-graphical reach and their ability to operate across the spectrum from high-intensity intervention to enduring stabilisation activity. But [the UK] will be more selective in [its] use of the Armed Forces, deploying them decisively at the right time but only

---

[5] It should be noted that, on the last three occasions, prior to the SDSR, in which the UK was required to conduct a major operation to evacuate its citizens from overseas, it used aircraft carriers: *Illustrious* was deployed to Sierra Leone in 2000 and the Lebanon in 2006; and ARK ROYAL, along with the Landing Platform Helicopter (LPH) HMS *Ocean* and the Landing Platform Dock (LPD) HMS *Albion*, were part of the relief operation when the Icelandic volcano Eyjafjallajökull closed European airspace in April 2010.

[6] See, for example, BBC, 'RAF Tornados Join Military Action in Libya.' 20 March 2011.

where key UK national interests are at stake; where [the UK has] a clear strategic aim; where the likely political, economic and human costs are in proportion to the likely benefits; where [the UK has] a viable exit strategy; and where justifiable under international law.[7]

While the SDSR discusses the issue of climate change, it makes no specific mention of the Arctic. Indeed, given the capability choices it makes – limiting in particular the number of assets the UK has – it seems that the term "more selective" applies more as a matter of policy choice, as the UK has less capability options to become involved in certain circumstances.

In the wake of the Afghanistan and Iraq campaigns, there seems to be an emerging, but more sustained, strategic shift away from an appetite for enduring embroilment on the ground. This is exemplified not only in the language of the SDSR (noted above), but also in U.S. Secretary of Defense Robert Gates' recent statement that the U.S. Army "must confront the reality that the most plausible, high-end scenarios for the U.S. military are primarily naval and air engagements."[8] Yet, in the wake of the SDSR's capability choices, the UK has a force structure which, according to Professor Michael Clarke, is now somewhat "eccentric" given its 65 per cent weighting in favour of the land component in the overall force balance: Professor Clarke argues that, by 2015, the UK "will look like a continental ground power in the make-up of [its] forces, when [it is] claiming to be an expeditionary capable power."[9] This strategic choice appears to be remarkably incongruent with the broad strategic principles set out by the National Security Strategy (NSS), the capstone strategic policy document under which the SDSR is intended to select capability options designed to enable the UK's Armed Forces to support the broad policy principles. While listing Afghanistan still as the main effort for UK defense policy, both the NSS and SDSR promote in principle an adaptable defense posture to enable the UK to respond to a range of circumstances in an unpredictable world. Yet the cuts set out in the SDSR seem to restrict this very adaptability, and this is particularly notable when considering the Royal Navy's ability to support UK national interests.

As part of a drive to set defense policy, quite correctly, within the context of the UK's overall security requirements and policy, the UK government published the third iteration of the NSS in October 2010 – one day prior to the publication of the SDSR. The history of the maritime security debate within the three iterations of the NSS is itself a story. Under the previous Labour Government, the UK published its first NSS in the summer of 2008. Other than an oblique reference to the *Maritime*

7 Ministry of Defence (MoD). *Securing Britain in an Age of Uncertainty: the Strategic Defence and Security Review*. Command 7948. Presented to Parliament by the Prime Minister by Command of Her Majesty, October 2010. Norwich: The Stationery Office (TSO). p. 17, para. 2.10.

8 Robert Gates. *Speech to United States Military Academy, West Point*, 25 February 2011. Available on-line at: http://www.defense.gov/speeches/speech.aspx?speechid=1539. Accessed 14 March 2011.

9 Michael Clarke, opening remarks to RUSI Conference on 'The Strategic Defence and Security Review: the Unfinished Business,' 10 January 2011.

Analysis and Operations Centre (MAOC) multinational counter-narcotics agency, no mention was made either of the concept or even the word *maritime*. By the summer of 2009, alongside mounting concerns regarding the risk of maritime-borne terrorist attacks (as borne out by the November 2008 Mumbai attacks), concerns about maritime security precipitated by the sudden rise of piracy in the Horn of Africa region, and principally because of both the rapidly-increasing number of hijackings and the risk to energy supplies, meant that the second iteration of NSS saw an entire section devoted to maritime security. This reflected also the emergence of a debate in London about cross-government and wider inter-agency and international maritime security structures, a debate which has seen the high-level participation of the UK in the international Contact Group on Piracy off the Coast of Somalia and the establishment, at the UK's Permanent Joint Headquarters in Northwood, of a National Maritime Information Centre (NMIC). By the summer of 2010 and the arrival of a new government, new priorities and a new version of the NSS, once again there was no mention of the term *maritime* in the document. Other than several references to "overseas," the word "sea" is mentioned only in relation to the threat of flood to the UK. This stark absence of reference to the use of the sea to protect UK interests is even more notable when the NSS makes significant and regular reference to concepts such as "strategic presence wherever we need it" and applying all instruments of power and influence "to shape the global environment and tackle potential risks at source."[10] Sea power-supported by a coherent maritime strategy and a robust, capable naval force structure – seems fundamental in supporting such principles.

In the context of the Arctic in particular as a matter for UK security interest, again its absence is notable from text of both the NSS and the SDSR. The NSS itself argues that the "physical effects of climate change are likely to become increasingly significant as a 'risk multiplier,' exacerbating existing tensions around the world."[11] In an unprecedented development, the NSS also published a list of 'Priority Risks' – effectively a National Security risk register. The list prioritizes a range of perceived potential circumstances into three tiers, based on a combination of likelihood of occurrence and severity of impact. Each circumstance is regarded as being possible, but those outcomes in Tier One are perceived at the present time as being far more likely to occur than those in Tier Three.

In the context of any security risk to UK interests in the Arctic, the NSS risk register seems to present a contradiction. A "conventional attack by a state on another NATO or EU member to which the UK would have to respond" is listed as a Tier Three risk only: however, Tier One identifies one of top four risk categories affecting the UK today as "an international military crisis between states, drawing in the UK, and

---

[10] For reference, see for example: Her Majesty's Government. *A Strong Britain in an Age of Uncertainty: the National Security Strategy*. Command 7953. Presented to Parliament by the Prime Minister by Command of Her Majesty, October 2010. Norwich: TSO. pp. 4 & 22 (para. 2.16).

[11] Ibid., p. 17, para. 1.29.

its allies as well as other states and non-state actors."[12] While it seems unlikely that, for example, Russia might attack U.S. mainland territory directly as the result of any crisis or clash in the Arctic, perhaps the grey area that links the Tier One and Tier Three contexts in terms of the Arctic will be the persisting issue Arctic Ocean sea-bed territory claims and, additionally, Arctic resource and access issues. For the UK, commitment to its international partners and alliances remains a critical national interest. Notwithstanding the traditionally difficult relations between Russia and NATO and also the fact that the UK does not have any formal alliance or treaty relationship with either Russia or China (an emerging state which is both a potential nuclear and energy superpower and which has significant Arctic resource and access claims which it will risk to both protect and promote), the existence of disputes over resources, territory and polar access suggests that the Arctic Ocean could be an area of dispute between states. These issues could drive political unrest amongst states and within multinational organizations whose member states have direct and indirect interests in the region.

The Arctic Ocean remains the most obvious current physical manifestation of the global security consequences of climate change. Such risks *should* be a unifying factor in global affairs. However, with international relations still dominated by the nation state and its interests, nations will continue to look after national interests as what the NSS terms as "the first duty" of government.[13] Moreover, in the case of the Arctic, even if the risk of conflict is low, the consequences could be very high, given the resource and access issues, the presence of NATO and EU states with interests in the region, and the interest of as many as five nuclear powers (Russia, the United States, China, France and the UK).

MILITARY PRESENCE IN THE ARCTIC REGION

The distinct national interests of several nations in the region, and the desire to support those interests at a national level, suggests there is little desire to create an Antarctic-style demilitarized zone in the Arctic region. In naval terms, the open nature of the high seas has been something which navies have often found to be a fundamental reason to co-operate, operating in the same maritime space and especially in circumstances of shared interest. A good, current example of this approach is the contribution of many nations to the various counter-piracy operations in the Horn of Africa. However, the geophysical nature of the Arctic, a region which is vast in size yet lacks extensive shore infrastructure (an issue compounded by the difficulty of developing shore infrastructure due to the thawing of the permafrost), suggests that any significant and regular opening up of Arctic waters as a result of climate change would see the persistent presence of ships from several major navies

---

[12] For reference, see ibid., p. 27.
[13] See ibid., p. 3.

as nations seek to secure their interests in the region. In the wake of the interventions in Afghanistan and Iraq, there is much discussion in the UK of the importance of deterrence and conflict prevention in reducing future security threats. Certainly, naval forces can play a significant role in generating low intensity global presence to support efforts to prevent conflict. Yet, in the case of the Arctic region, the presence of such naval forces in an ocean and in circumstances in which national interests are not necessarily shared – even if such navies are deployed there ostensibly to deter threats and to prevent conflict – presents a source of risk to Arctic security. This raises the issue of whether Arctic security challenges to the UK should be discussed in London more often than it is at the moment.

Indeed, it seems likely that navies will provide a significant presence in the Arctic to support taskings across the spectrum of military operations, at sea, in the air and perhaps even ashore. At the lower end of the scale, navies will be required to support search and rescue and environmental safety operations. In the middle, states will need a constabulary presence to deter terrorists and wider organized criminal trafficking threats in a region with particularly porous borders. At the higher end, nations will see navies as vital in protecting resource and territorial claims. At the highest of the high end of the spectrum, nations will continue to use the Arctic icepack to hide their submarines – both the nuclear-powered ballistic missile submarines (SSBNs) carrying nuclear weapons and SSNs which are used to hunt SSBNs. In terms of submarine operations, anti-submarine warfare (ASW) tasks will become increasingly more important as the thinning ice may allow SSBNs to launch their weapons from closer to target – a particular problem for the United States, as it would be more exposed to the risk of close-in, depressed trajectory ballistic missile launches from Russian and Chinese SSBNs. For its part, Russia is likely to feel very uncomfortable with the possibility of a sustained presence of Chinese SSBNs in the region.

From the UK's perspective, some of the capability decisions taken in recent years raise questions about its ability in the medium to longer term to support sustained operational commitments to the Arctic, and to deter threats to Arctic stability. As well as sending SSNs south again, Russia is investing heavily in an Arctic submarine presence by augmenting SSN and SSBN operations in the region, with both types of boat resuming permanent patrols of the region and expanding their operational boundaries.[14] In December 2007, the UK announced that it would be reducing its SSN force level to just seven boats.[15] New design, construction and logistical support

---

[14] See: Charles Strathdee, 'Russia's Growing Naval Might,' in *Warships International Fleet Review*, October 2008, p. 41; Adrian Blomfield, 'Russia Plans Military Build-Up in the Arctic,' *The Daily Telegraph*, 12th June 2008, p. 17; RIA Novosti. 'Russia Prioritizes Nuclear Triad, Hi-tech Weaponry in Future Wars,' 1st August 2008. Available on-line at <http://en.rian.ru/russia/20080801/115445726.html >. Accessed 3rd October 2008; Lee Willett, 'The Navy in Russia's Resurgence,' in *RUSI Journal*, February 2009, vol. 154, no. 1. London: Royal united Services Institute (RUSI).

[15] See Rt Hon Bob Ainsworth MP (then Minister for Armed Forces, UK Ministry of Defence), Response to a Parliamentary Question, in *House of Commons Hansard Written Answers*, Column 820W, 3

approaches may improve the ability to maintain a larger proportion of the fleet at sea at any one time. The UK will continue to send SSNs to train in the Arctic to maintain the skills sets required to conduct under-ice operations. However, with a strategic requirement to maintain one boat permanently East of Suez, and with the SSN's Tomahawk land attack role having strategic importance as one of the Royal Navy's four primary contributions to UK defense policy – for example, as demonstrated by the contribution of a *Trafalgar*-class SSN to operations in support of the No Fly Zone in Libya in 2011 -it is difficult to see how the UK would have enough SSNs available to consider a sustained ASW presence in the Arctic.[16] In terms of the security of SLoCs and maritime choke points, offensive and defensive submarine capabilities and operations have the potential to alter significantly the strategic balance. Andrew Davies has noted that a submarine capability offers navies and nations a quick way of jumping the queue in terms of national political influence.[17] Iran's opening in 2008 of the Jask naval base at the mouth of the Straits of Hormuz, for example, provides Tehran with a greater strategic access to and influence over regional waters than provided previously by its main naval base at Bandar Abbas. The opening of the Jask base is a clear demonstration of the potential role of submarines in holding at risk access to key choke points and sea lines.[18]

SDSR's own cancellation of the Nimrod maritime patrol aircraft (MPA) program will in the short term deny to the UK the ability to provide a long-range, air-based surveillance capability, which is clearly critical to a range of operations, including ASW, maritime situational awareness and search and rescue. Indeed, the UK is now the only NATO nation with a coastline *not* to have an MPA capability.[19] The challenge in providing surface forces to deploy to the region has already been revealed by the Libyan crisis and will be exacerbated in the future by a surface force level dropping to just 19 destroyers and frigates. The number of hulls could even dip below 19, if some reports surrounding the UK Ministry of Defence (MoD)'s annual planning rounds are to be believed.[20]

One of the major naval service concerns in the build-up to the SDSR was the potential loss of the Royal Marines and their amphibious capability. These concerns

December 2007. See also: Ainsworth, *House of Commons Hansard Written Answers*, Column 55W, 10 December 2007.

[16] For reference, the other three core roles are: providing the UK's independent strategic nuclear deterrent; support to Carrier Strike operations; and support to amphibious operations.

[17] Andrew Davies, 'Up Periscope: The Expansion of Submarine Capabilities in the Asia-Pacific Region,' *RUSI Journal*, vol. 152, no. 5, October 2007. London: Royal United Services Institute (RUSI).

[18] For reference, see: Julian Borger, 'Iran Opens a New Naval Base at the Mouth of the Gulf,' *The Guardian*, 29 October 2008. Available on-line at: <http://www.guardian.co.uk/world/2008/oct/29/iran>. Accessed 29 October 2008.

[19] Vice Admiral John McAnally, 'Piracy Could Put Out the UK's Lights.' Letter to *The Times*, 21 February 2011.

[20] James Blitz and Alex Barker, 'MoD Faces Fresh Crisis over Funding', in *The Financial Times*, 19 January 2011. Available on-line at: <http://www.ft.com/cms/s/0/7388b002-241e-11e0-a89a-00144feab49a.html#axzz1H9IYMzT8>. Accessed 19 January 2011.

were that the Royal Marines would be subsumed into the British Army, or that the amphibious capability would be cancelled altogether. Delivering ground troops ashore from the sea, and especially in extreme circumstances such as the High North, remains a highly-specialized military discipline which few nations can conduct. The Royal Marines have been performing high level combat operations in Afghanistan, but have been deployed to the region by air and not from the sea. Recent years have seen the Royal Navy conduct several high profile amphibious training operations, namely Operations:

- TAURUS 09 (led by the Landing Platform Dock, or LPD, HMS *Bulwark*, and 40 Commando Royal Marines) in the Mediterranean;
- COLD RESPONSE 10 (with the LPD HMS *Albion*, Landing Platform Helicopter, or LPH, ship HMS *Ocean*, and 3 Commando Brigade Royal Marines) in Northern Norway;
- and AURIGA 10 (with *Albion*, *Ocean*, and 42 Commando Royal Marines supporting the UK's Carrier Strike Task Group) off the U.S. Eastern seaboard.

Given the intensity of operations in Afghanistan and with the Royal Marines conducting a one-in-four rotation, such exercises have been vital in maintaining the capability to deploy forces ashore from the sea. Under the SDSR, even though the ability to deploy a high-readiness Commando group from the sea has remained intact within the naval service, one of the two LPDs is to be put in extended readiness and the Royal Marines will absorb a share of the 7,000 naval personnel to be cut.

Much of the discussion relating to the use of force in the Arctic region centres on the need to develop military capabilities which can withstand extreme environmental conditions, including different wave patterns, severe cold, condensation and electromagnetic pressures. There is no public evidence that the UK has designed or is designing its six new Type 45 *Daring*-class destroyers, two new *Queen Elizabeth*-class aircraft carriers and its next generation ASW frigate (the Type 26 Global Combat Ship) specifically with such capability parameters in mind. Yet – assuming it has assets available in sufficient numbers – this does not mean that the Royal Navy will not have the ability to affect matters relating to the Arctic region. Should the Arctic seaways become open at any point and to any degree, the flow of military and commercial maritime traffic through the waters of the North Atlantic will require a significant and sustained Royal Navy presence in the North Atlantic.

THE ARCTIC: UK PERSPECTIVES ON PARTNERSHIPS AND ALLIANCES

The UK is of course an original member of NATO and the EU, and has always placed particular political primacy on it perception of its special relationship with the United States. In the wake of the current government's wider austerity measures and the specific capability cuts made in the SDSR, the importance of partnering has become ever more acute to the UK.

The United States

The Arctic is an area onto which the United States borders directly, of course, and it will wish to ensure that its borders are not porous in defense and security terms. Yet there is little doubt that the United States is focused elsewhere, with particular concerns today – amongst broader focus on the Middle East, Indian Ocean and Asian subcontinent – including Afghanistan, Iran, Iraq and North Korea, and with a longer-term focus on China and the Pacific. As defined quite clearly in both the NSS and SDSR, from the UK's perspective its enduring relationship with the United States remains its primary partnering priority, over and above multinational relations with NATO and the EU and bilateral partnerships with France.[21]

For the UK, this U.S. geostrategic perspective raises a couple of key questions. First, will the United States expect its partners to stand alongside directly, wherever it goes, or instead to hold the fort in more traditional regions of interest while the United States addresses issues in new parts of the world, such as the Pacific? Second, in terms of the Arctic, will the United States focus on the Arctic increase, for what reason and – if so – what will this mean for the UK strategic need to pay greater attention to the region?

NATO

NATO remains the primary multinational security organization for western states. As well as representing the interests of its individual members, NATO also will see the Arctic region as important to its overall security interests, especially in the context of deterring the threat of any Russian aggression. The Alliance Maritime Strategy, as defined in NATO's new Strategic Concept, pays significant attention to Arctic security. While recent commitments to Afghanistan and Somali piracy operations have been out of area operations, the Arctic region remains very much in NATO's backyard.

In the context of NATO's Arctic interests, the relationship between Norway and Russia remains particularly crucial. Russia and Norway have been disputing territorial claims in the Barents Sea (although a compromise was reached on one dispute, over sea-bed oil and gas rights, in 2010).[22] Russian planes infamously conducted a mock bombing run on the Norwegian northern defense command headquarters

---

[21] See, for example: NSS, p. 4; SDSR, p. 12 point 8.

[22] References on this matter are numerous, but for brief coverage of the matter including comment on the compromise, see for example: Andrew E. Kramer, 'Russia and Norway Agree on Boundary,' in *The New York Times*, 15 September 2010. Available on-line at:<http://www.nytimes.com/2010/09/16/world/europe/16russia.html >. Accessed 20 March 2011; Alister Doyle and GwladysFouche, 'Russia, Norway, Ease Borders, Seek Oil Co-operation.' *Reuters*. Available on-line at: <http://www.reuters.com/article/2010/11/02/russia-norway-idUSLDE6A11LB20101102 >. Accessed 20 March 2011.

at Bodo.[23] Yet Russia recognises the degree to which it relies on co-operation with Norway for the secure movement of it resources.

A robust NATO, with member nations providing credible capability to support a clear policy and posture, will remain key to deterring threats to the interests of its member states – especially in a region like the Arctic where two major non-NATO powers, namely Russia and China, have significant interests. From the UK's perspective, its political commitment to NATO remains clear, and its military contribution to deterring threats to Alliance interests will remain central to the Alliance's overall military capability in relative terms – even if the UK's own absolute capability is somewhat reduced.

The European Union

The UK sits on the EU's north western border with the Arctic region. The EU is likely to have an increasing interest in the Arctic region, as it responds to and represents the interests of its member states. Such interests include, primarily, the need to secure access to energy resources and the ability for military and commercial assets to transit the region. The EU continues to seek opportunities to increase its global strategic influence and, whilst it has no presence on the Arctic Council and while it does not yet have a member state bordering directly on the Arctic, several members – such as Sweden, France and the UK – have close interest in the region and the potential membership of Iceland, an independent Greenland and Norway would give the EU direct geographical interest and influence. The EU also has close relations with each of the Baltic States.

THE ARCTIC: A PRIMARY SOURCE OF STATE-ON-STATE CONFRONTATION?

The Cold War, as it was understood in the last century, is over. However, this does not mean that great power rivalry (at best) and conflict (at worst) is impossible. While there may be a reduced risk of direct military confrontation on land between great powers in the immediate future, this does not mean that great powers will have neither need nor opportunity to improve their influence at the expense of other such powers. Indeed, in what Professor Eric Grove refers to as an 'inter war period,' in today's world great powers may simply be using other policy tools as a way of improving their influence. For example, the presence of all the great naval powers in the Horn of Africa region, ostensibly as part of the international counter-piracy campaign, could be attributed at least in part to separate national grand strategic power politics campaigns intended to fill a vacuum in the regional security structure and to increase national power and influence as a result.

[23] For reference on the latter point, see: 'The Arctic Contest Heats Up,' *The Economist*, 9 October 2008.

In the UK, contemporary defense and security debates pay limited attention to the risk of direct state-on-state confrontation. While there may be no immediate, apparent direct military threats to UK territory, this does not mean that threats to wider interests do not exist. Moreover, the UK debate perhaps should pay greater attention to the risks and responsibilities inherent in the country's alliance commitments and also to the NSS's prioritization of the risk of becoming embroiled as a third party in a confrontation between two other states. Indeed, alongside the Persian Gulf, the Arctic is perhaps the prime example of a region where primary state interests may see states confronting each other directly. The U.S. 2010 Quadrennial Defense Review (QDR) and the French 2008 *Livre Blanc* both appear to give a higher priority in the medium term to the risk of state-on-state conflict than the UK does in the NSS and the SDSR.

One matter to consider is the extent to which conflicts of interest may emerge not only between regional states, for example over territorial and resources disputes, but also between regional and non-regional players. The regional players may not be welcoming of overt external influence, whereas the non-regional players may fear being frozen out of key strategic debates relating to the region. For example, both China and the EU applied for observer nation status of the Arctic Council – and both have been refused.

Russia and the Arctic: Feeding the Bear's Re-Emergence from Strategic Hibernation?

In 2010, Vladimir Putin dismissed claims that the Arctic is a 'new strategic battleground,' stating instead that peace and co-operation in the Arctic, especially through developing regional ties, 'is of the utmost importance'.[24] The United States is of course no longer focused predominantly on relations with Moscow. On 21 March 2011, in a speech to Russian naval officers at the Kuznetsov Naval Academy in St Petersburg, U.S. Defense Secretary Bob Gates stated broadly that:

> [U.S.-Russian] co-operation to address common security challenges is real.... [With] leadership and far-sighted thinking from both nations, we can expand that co-operation.... [There] is an increasing recognition that by sharing knowledge, we can resolve common problems.... Discussing our intentions as well as our

24 See: The Arctic Governance Project. 'Prime Minister Vladimir Putin Addresses the Forum "The Arctic: Territory of Dialogue."' 23 September 2010. Available on-line at:<http://www.arcticgovernance.org/prime-minister-vladimir-putin-addresses-the-international-forum-the-arctic-territory-of-dialogue.4823958-142902.html >. Accessed 20 March 2011; 'Vladimir Putin Calls for Arctic Claims to be Resolved under UN Law,' *The Guardian*, 23 September 2011. Cited by Arctic Governance Project, and available on-line at: <http://www.arcticgovernance.org/vladimir-putin-calls-for-arctic-claims-to-be-resolved-under-un-law.4822186-147478.html >. Accessed 20 March 2011; RIA-Novosti. 'Putin Defends Russia's Arctic Rights, Calls for Dialogue.' 15 March 2010. Available on-line at: <http://en.rian.ru/russia/20100315/158203547.html >. Accessed 20 March 2010.

capabilities is a critical move forward. It is a given that on some issues and in some
arenas U.S. and Russian interests and goals will differ – no matter how much we talk
to one another. However, one critical lesson we [have] learned from the mistakes
of the past is to avoid dangerous circumstances that can emerge from mistrust and
a lack of transparency about each other's intentions.[25]

Secretary Gates did not mention the Arctic in his remarks. He even added how
the United States and Russia will continue to exchange best practices and strategies
for maritime co-operation as part of the broad effort to maintain the freedom of the
seas.

Yet, despite clear evidence of a thaw in relations, Russia remains the dominant
political and military power in the Arctic region, and it will wish to retain this
dominance for good reason. A significant percentage of its national resources and
gross domestic product are generated in the region, and it has a range of other
primary national interests it will wish to support – even before any potential opening
up of Arctic seaways means that the region becomes a strategic stage on which
several major nations and international organizations will have reason to appear. In
the Arctic geostrategic balance, the role of Russia – as a nuclear power, a potential
energy superpower and still the region's dominant conventional military power –
will remain significant.

Along with counter-terrorism and China, Russia continues to see NATO as its
principal adversary. From the UK's perspective, while it no longer poses a direct
threat to UK territory and west European alliance commitments in the way that it did
in the Cold War, Russia still retains the ability to threaten UK interests, for example
in terms of Russia's ability to control energy supplies in the Eurasian continent and in
terms of Russia's desire to offset NATO influence. In the latter instance, the Russian
invasion of Georgia in the summer of 2008 highlighted the argument that a growing
western and NATO presence around Russia's borders on its central, southern and
northern flanks may see Russia act, even in flagrant violation of international law, to
release some of the political pressure that western and NATO power may be creating
within Russian geostrategic perspectives. In this context, it is worth considering that
perceptions of such pressure can create a balloon effect: pressing down on one area
may generate directly a bulge, or even a rupture, in another. Military strength will
remain fundamental to Russia's ability to exert influence in support of its interests
in the Arctic region, and ongoing territory discussions and a lack of international
governance and oversight of regional issues arguably gives Russia more elbow room
in pursuit of these interests.

Given the enduring Russian concerns about NATO, its military predominance
in the Arctic region and the region's geostrategic significance to Russia, this raises
the question of whether NATO navies deployed to the Arctic region to bolster

---

[25] Robert Gates. Remarks as delivered by to the Kuznetsov Naval Academy, St Petersburg, Russia. 21
March 2011.

deterrence and deter conflict may, in certain circumstances, generate the opposite effect. Russia's ability to hold at risk the interests of other nations is of course bolstered by the simple fact that it remains the second largest nuclear power in the world. The UK recognises this fact implicitly in that, as demonstrated in its 2006 White Paper on its nuclear deterrent capability, its reference to the potential re-emergence of threats from an existing but unnamed nuclear weapon state is widely interpreted as referring to, of course, Russia.[26]

The China Factor

In terms of the potential for state-on-state confrontation in the Arctic, for Western states Russia may not be the only source of concern. With its strategic requirement to strengthen its import and export markets, China has an ever-growing maritime presence. In 2010, retired People's Liberation Army (Navy) Rear Admiral Yin Zhuo advised the Chinese government that the Arctic region is part of the "common wealth of the world's people and [does] not belong to any one country. . . . China must play an indispensable role in Arctic exploration as [it has] one-fifth of the world's population."[27]

The 'string of pearls' concept highlights China's increasing investments in particular South Asian which sit in significant geostrategic positions, particularly with regard to maritime access (such as Burma, Sri Lanka and Pakistan). What may not be quite so well understood, however, is what Alexander Neill argues may well be a similar approach to Northern waters, in that China may be seeking to improve access and influence opportunities in these waters as part of preparing a new strategic sea lane, should the Arctic Ocean become more open. Indeed, the collapse of Iceland's economy as a result of its banking crisis has presented China with a strategic investment opportunity that it is actively exploiting.[28] Yet, given Iceland's key strategic position, the growing influence of a major power that lies outside of established western alliances is a cause for discussion, if not concern. As with most areas of growing Chinese focus outside of the Pacific and the South China Sea in

[26] For reference, see MoD. *The Future of the United Kingdom's Nuclear Deterrent*. Command 6994. Presented to Parliament by the Secretary of State for Defence and the Secretary of State for Foreign and Commonwealth Affairs, by Command of Her Majesty. Norwich: TSO. December 2006. pp. 18 (para. 3.5) & 19 (para. 3.8).

[27] See *China News Service*, 5 March 2010. Cited in Joseph Spears (The Jamestown Foundation) 'China's *Snow Dragon* Sweeps into the Arctic Ocean.' 28 January 2011. Available on-line at: <http://www.arcticprogress.com/2011/02/chinas-snow-dragon-sweeps-into-arctic-ocean/ >. Accessed 20 March 2011. Rear Admiral Yin Xhuo is reported to be an analyst at the Institute of Strategic Studies, National Defense University (see Peter J. Brown, 'China's PLA Raises its Voice,' in *Asia Times*, 8 March 2010. Cited on-line at Center for New American Security: < http://www.cnas.org/node/4195 >. Accessed 20 March 2011.

[28] See, for example: William Underhill. 'China Eyes Investment in Iceland,' *Newsweek*, 8 March 2010. Available on-line at: <http://www.newsweek.com/blogs/wealth-of-nations/2010/03/18/china-eyes-investment-in-iceland.html>. Accessed 14 March 2011.

particular, the potential threat from China in the Arctic is uncertain. China is clearly not shy in moving to protect its current interests while simultaneously putting in place a strategic framework to enable it to project influence and protect interests in the future. For example, the strategic impact of the purchase by the Chinese state-owned shipping company Cosco of deep water pier access in the port of Piraeus in Greece, a NATO member, has not received the attention and analysis that it warrants.[29]

Given its resource requirements, unconfirmed reports of Chinese SSBNs operating in the Arctic and evidence of Chinese plans to build new ice-breaking ships could be seen as further pieces of a puzzle whose picture might show long-term Chinese intent to be a major player in the Arctic region.[30] In 2010, China conducted its fourth Arctic research expedition in recent years. In 2010, the *Xue Long* (or *Snow Dragon*) – the world's largest non-nuclear research icebreaker – reached a point only 120 nautical miles from the North Pole, with its research scientists transiting the remaining distance to the North Pole via helicopter.[31] Russia will not feel comfortable with an increasing Chinese Arctic presence. What perhaps is the crucial factor from the UK's perspective is whether this presence will engage U.S. interest.

COMMERCIAL SHIPPING

The sheer size of the waters of the Arctic region and the fundamental challenges in establishing and sustaining a comprehensive resource infrastructure on land suggests that undersea pipelines, maritime terminals and commercial ships using sea routes will remain a primary method of delivering resources both from and across the region. The question of the extent to which commercial ships will use Arctic waters is one which highlights again the uncertain balance between confrontation and co-operation. With some arguing that SLoCs are a demonstrable, physical manifestation of the World Wide Web, secure and unhindered shipping access to these sea lines is something upon which each nation relies and indeed it remains in the interests of the international community as a whole to ensure that such sea lines stay open. In critically-strategic regions such as the Arctic, there remains the issue that nations

[29] See: Harriet Alexander, 'China's New Silk Road into Europe,' in *The Sunday Telegraph*, 4 July 2010. Available on-line at: <http://www.telegraph.co.uk/news/worldnews/europe/greece/7869999/Chinas-new-Silk-Road-into-Europe.html >. Accessed 4 July 2010. In a £2.8 billion deal, Cosco will lease Pier Two for the next 35 years, investing £470 million in upgrading the port facilities, building a new Pier Three and almost tripling the volume of cargo the port can handle.

[30] In terms of an ice-breaking capability, China has ice-capable research ships which operate in the Antarctic Ocean. At least one of these ships is to be replaced in the future. It is not clear if such a ship will be designed purely for the Antarctic, or if it will have an ice-breaking capability more suited to the Arctic Ocean.

[31] See *China Daily*, 21 August 2010. Cited in Joseph Spears (The Jamestown Foundation) 'China's *Snow Dragon* Sweeps into the Arctic Ocean.' 28 January 2011. Available on-line at: <http://www.arcticprogress.com/2011/02/chinas-snow-dragon-sweeps-into-arctic-ocean >. Accessed 20 March 2011.

will use any necessary tool of government to ensure that access to such lines remains unhindered.

It is clear that uninterrupted access through the Arctic would cut the transit distance – if not time – between Rotterdam and Shanghai by around half.[32] In recent times, however, the major shipping lines have seemed content with the sustainability of both existing routes and business models. Indeed, uncertainty over what Arctic waters might be available, when and for how long may explain what appears to be a lack of appetite to try the shorter route. This lack of appetite is coupled with uncertainty about Russian policy towards international shipping operating within its Arctic national waters, or offshore areas under Russian economic jurisdiction. However, perhaps the ongoing challenge of Somali piracy, especially when coupled with the wider instability in the Middle East, might begin to make some energy companies think again about trans-Arctic shipping. Notably, the political and succession crisis in Egypt in early 2011 precipitated robust statements from government and military figures alike on the enduring need for access by all nations to the Suez Canal.[33] Whatever the reason for any potential shift in shipping to the polar route, any such shipping would pass through or immediately adjacent to UK waters.

CONCLUSIONS

There remains an argument that the UK, as a major maritime power with a desire to be involved in regions across the globe to promote stability in the international strategic balance, should be demonstrating greater interest in the Arctic region. Clearly, the UK has significant and sustained strategic interests in the Arctic and North Atlantic regions. Its current political and fiscal priorities tend to indicate, however, that the UK would struggle to sustain commitment to any such interests at this stage.

[32] The physical distance between one point in Europe and another in Asia would be cut in half using polar routes. For example, the distance between Rotterdam and Yokohama would be reduced from 11,250 nautical miles (nm) to 7,350 nm (see Des Upcraft, Lloyd's Register, *Arctic Shipping – Legislation and Governance*. Lecture to Greenwich Maritime Institute Research Seminar Series, University of Greenwich, 16 March 2011). However, challenges in using such routes (such as ice, more shallow water, or rights to transit through territorial waters) may mean that transit speeds would be slower.

[33] The Governor Port Said, Mustafa Abdelatif, needed to inform Egyptian state television that the Suez Canal remained open and under control (see BBC News Channel, 1 February 2011. Available online at: <http://news.bbc.co.uk/1/hi/world/middle_east/9384085.stm >. Accessed 1 February 2011).The Commander of United States Central Command (CENTCOM), General James Mattis United States Marine Corps, stated that however inconceivable such an eventuality might seem, the United States would respond "diplomatically, economically, militarily" to any closure of the Canal (see Mattis, speech to Policy Exchange, London, 1 February 2011. Available on-line at: <http://www.policyexchange.org.uk/news/news.cgi?id=1788 >. Accessed 21 March 2011).

The reality of the SDSR may be that it has prescribed the geophysical limit of the interests the UK can continue to afford to support. Perhaps, by the time the geophysical future of the Arctic is better understood, the UK's fiscal future may also be clear enough to allow it to consider properly how it might consider contributing to the security of a region which is only going to become ever more important in future international affairs.

Index